WINSTON CHURCHILL
and MACKENZIE KING

King and Churchill in the Speaker's Chamber on December 30, 1941, by Yousuf Karsh. King was annoyed when this photograph was published in Saturday Night, *as he is shown smiling — in wartime this was not appropriate.*

WINSTON CHURCHILL
and MACKENZIE KING

So Similar, So Different

TERRY REARDON

FOREWORD BY THE RIGHT HONOURABLE JOHN N. TURNER

DUNDURN
A J. PATRICK BOYER BOOK
TORONTO

Project Editor: Michael Carroll
Editor: Dominic Farrell
Design: Jennifer Scott
Printer: Webcom

Library and Archives Canada Cataloguing in Publication

Reardon, Terry
Winston Churchill and Mackenzie King : so similar, so different / Terry Reardon ; forward by John N. Turner.

Includes index.
Issued also in electronic format.
ISBN 978-1-4597-0589-0 (bound). – 978-1-4597-2427-3 (pbk.)

1. Churchill, Winston, 1874-1965. 2. King, William Lyon Mackenzie, 1874-1950. 3. World War, 1939-1945--Great Britain. 4. World War, 1939-1945--Canada. 5. Great Britain--Politics and government--1936-. 6. Canada--Politics and government--20th century. 7. Great Britain--Relations--Canada. 8. Canada--Relations--Great Britain. 9. Prime ministers--Great Britain--Biography. 10. Prime ministers--Canada--Biography. I. Title.

DA566.9.C5R43 2012   941.084092   C2012-903220-4

1   2   3   4   5   18   17   16   15   14

We acknowledge the support of the Canada Council for the Arts and the Ontario Arts Council for our publishing program. We also acknowledge the financial support of the Government of Canada through the Canada Book Fund and Livres Canada Books, and the Government of Ontario through the Ontario Book Publishing Tax Credit and the Ontario Media Development Corporation.

Care has been taken to trace the ownership of copyright material used in this book. The author and the publisher welcome any information enabling them to rectify any references or credits in subsequent editions.

J. Kirk Howard, President

The publisher is not responsible for websites or their content unless they are owned by the publisher.

Printed and bound in Canada.

Visit us at
Dundurn.com
@dundurnpress
Facebook.com/dundurnpress
Pinterest.com/dundurnpress

Dundurn
3 Church Street, Suite 500
Toronto, Ontario, Canada
M5E 1M2

Gazelle Book Services Limited
White Cross Mills
High Town, Lancaster, England
LA1 4XS

Dundurn
2250 Military Road
Tonawanda, NY
U.S.A. 14150

For my wife, Fran

CONTENTS

FOREWORD

BY THE RIGHT HONOURABLE JOHN N. TURNER, P.C., C.C., Q.C

W hile there have been many books written on the life and times of Winston Churchill, with more appearing every year, surprising to me are the few on William Lyon Mackenzie King, who was prime minister of Canada for twenty-one years, longer than any person in that office in any country in the British Commonwealth. Thus, I am delighted that Terry Reardon has undertaken this important work on the intertwining of their political careers.

Even though it was seven decades ago, I still vividly remember meeting Churchill. It was on December 30, 1941, when the British prime minister was in the House of Commons in Ottawa, delivering one of his most famous speeches. That was the one in which he referred to the fall of France in 1940 and his attempt to have the French government go to North Africa to continue the fight. Then he said, "But their generals misled them. When I warned them that Britain would fight on alone whatever they did, their generals told their prime minister and his divided cabinet, 'In three weeks England will have her neck wrung like a chicken.' Some chicken!" And when the laughter from the members had died down, "Some neck!" Well, the place broke up again![1]

The speech is best remembered for that one line, but it was also a great speech, mobilizing Canadian public opinion and bringing us up to date on the war and the nature of the unity of the Commonwealth. Now, I didn't recognize all that because at the time I was just twelve years old. I was with my mother and my sister Brenda outside the House of Commons, listening to the speech relayed by loudspeakers. Churchill was already a hero in Canada and there was a tremendous crowd. Unlike many politicians, he came out after his speech and mingled with the crowd, a gesture that was deeply moving. As Churchill came down the driveway, my mother introduced herself, then introduced Brenda and me. The great man looked me straight in the eye and said, "Good of you to be here, good luck!" That meeting, with the greatest person I ever met, became indelible in my memory.

That was also the occasion when the memorable Karsh photograph was taken in the Speaker's chambers. Yousuf Karsh was a good friend of our family, and I used to see him over the years. He displayed a touch of genius when he yanked that signature cigar from Churchill's mouth just before taking that photograph. The upset Winston Churchill scowled. The resulting photograph showed his defiance. It became the most famous one ever taken of Churchill, and has been used repeatedly ever since.

I didn't have the opportunity of meeting Churchill when I was in England as a Rhodes Scholar at Oxford, but my impression of him at that time, which I still hold, is that he was the greatest man of the twentieth century. It is clear in my mind that he rescued Britain and the free world. He turned the tide: one man's courage; one man's voice, coupled with his leadership, and later his close relationship with Roosevelt, were all crucial to turning near defeat into the allied victory.

Of course, the person who acted as the intermediary between Churchill and Roosevelt, before the United States entered the war, was King.

It is strange now, with all the security that surrounds major political figures, that I used to meet King when walking my dog, Blue, a springer spaniel, in Strathcona Park in Ottawa. We lived in Sandy Hill from 1934 to 1945, and Mr. King's official residence was Laurier House, also in Sandy Hill. King was a great dog lover, and he had his terrier, Pat, with him; he took a liking to Blue, and we had a number of chats while sitting on a bench overlooking the Rideau River.

My mother was vice-chair of the Wartime Prices and Trade Board. She knew Mr. King very well, and admired his gift of compromise and also his gift of intuition. On one occasion in late 1939, she went to see the Canadian prime minister on behalf of a number of senior female civil servants, who objected to being paid so much less than their male counterparts, even though they were doing identical work. She told Mr. King that they were ready to go on strike. King responded, "Phyllis, you can't go on strike; we're now at war." My mother responded, "Prime Minister, you'll survive the war. I hope to survive the war, and then we'll have another chat."

Well, after the war they didn't return to that subject, but in view of her war record, King, who was quite sparse in handing out honours, recommended my mother for a CBE (Commander of the Order of the British Empire).

King had a remarkable career, which, unfairly, has been overshadowed by his interest in spiritualism, which was dabbled in by many prominent people during the era after the First World War. He was a superb manager of Parliament and the government, but maybe his greatest talent was his ability to select ideal people to bring into his government. Even more remarkable was the lack of any challenge to his leadership in the almost thirty years he spent as the leader of the Liberal Party of Canada. He took the country into the Second World War united, and he even managed to handle the major conscription crisis with the resignation of only one Quebec minister. He left the Liberal Party and the country in great shape when he handed over power to his successor, Louis St. Laurent.

A great friend of Churchill's was Lord Beaverbrook, although in the early days this remarkable Canadian was not a political supporter. Beaverbrook was born William Maxwell Aitken in Maple, Ontario, in 1879, with his family moving the following year to Newcastle, New Brunswick. Max Aitken became a successful businessman and moved to England in 1910, where he entered Parliament and also started a newspaper chain, which included the *Daily Express*. He was also close to King, even though he wrote a biography of Conservative leader R.B. Bennett, who had defeated King in the 1930 election, a turn of events that in retrospect was fortunate for King as Bennett had to handle the crisis of the Great Depression.

Beaverbrook was a giant. Though not well known in most of Canada, he was much better known in Britain, where he did an outstanding job as minister of aircraft production, and later minister of supply during the Second World War. He was a good friend of my stepfather, Frank Ross, and we had him over to dinner at our house in St. Andrews, New Brunswick, on several occasions. Through that relationship, I did a little work for Beaverbrook, as a young lawyer. Beaverbrook gave the people of New Brunswick a magnificent gift: the Beaverbrook Art Gallery in Fredericton — the collection contains Graham Sutherland's preparatory sketches for his famous portrait of Churchill, given to Churchill by both Houses of the British Parliament on the occasion of Churchill's eightieth birthday in 1954. Churchill, in thanking the members, referred to the portrait as a remarkable example of modern art; privately, he hated it, as did his wife, who later had it destroyed. The last time I saw Beaverbrook was at the Ritz Hotel in Montreal, where we downed a Scotch together.

In my early years in the House of Commons, the prime ministers were John Diefenbaker and Lester Pearson, both great admirers of Churchill. Although I was from a different party than Diefenbaker, the members who enjoyed the House of Commons, like myself, had his affection. I was very fortunate in 1965 to be on a beach in Barbados with my wife, when she said that there was someone in trouble in the water. I rushed in and grabbed him by his trunks and swum him back to safety. It was John Diefenbaker. I am still the only non-Tory on the Diefenbaker Foundation.

Diefenbaker was a tea-totaller, unlike Churchill, and I like the story of the two meeting and Diefenbaker refusing a drink, but stating that he was not a prohibitionist, and Churchill responding, "Ah, I see you only hurt yourself."[2]

There was no mutual affection between Diefenbaker and King, but Diefenbaker certainly admired King's astuteness. As he stated in his autobiography, "Mackenzie King was prime minister for my first eight years in the House. There are some who will tell you that he was not an able parliamentarian. I do not accede to that view. Although he had the reputation of not paying sufficient attention to Parliament, he certainly far exceeded anything under his Liberal successors as prime minister. He had a basic respect for Parliament. On occasion he exaggerated the extent of his devotion, but he was a House of Commons man nonetheless."[3]

King prided himself on keeping control of his emotions, but Diefenbaker recorded one occasion when he lost his temper, in May 1942.

Diefenbaker had entered King's office in the East Block, and King said, "What business have you to be here? You strike me to the heart every time you speak. In your last speech, who did you mention? Did you say what I've done for this country? You spoke of Churchill. Churchill! Did he ever bleed for Canada?" There were tears in his eyes. There was rage on his face. Suddenly the storm blew over and he said with impressive calm, "I regret this, but something awful has happened. The great British battleship the *Hood* has been sunk. Where will we go from here?"[4]

Lester Pearson had a small part in a famous Churchill speech. That was the one delivered at Westminster College in Fulton, Missouri, in March 1946, where Churchill warned of Soviet expansionism. Churchill stated, "From Stettin in the Baltic to Trieste in the Adriatic, an Iron Curtain has descended across the Continent. Behind that line lie all the capitals of the ancient states of Central and Eastern Europe." Churchill had asked Mackenzie King to look over the speech he was intending to make. King hedged, as he did not want to take responsibility for anything Churchill might say, and he suggested his "dear friend" may wish to consult the Canadian ambassador in Washington, who knew his views on these matters and had his confidence.

Pearson recorded in his autobiography that he was ushered into Churchill's bedroom and there he was in bed with a big cigar in his mouth, and a glass on a tray that evidently did not contain water. Churchill then suggested that he might read the speech. Pearson stated, "This would have been a memorable experience for me, I know, but of course I would have heard him out without daring to interrupt the performance, which may have been what he had in mind. Hence I suggested that he let me take the script into a nearby room where I could read it with the care it deserved."

Pearson stated that after reading a page or two, it was evident that it was to be an important speech. He made two recommendations — one a factual one concerning the position of Missouri in the American Civil War, the other doubting the wisdom of naming the recent conflict as "The Unnecessary War." Churchill thought that this was an appropriate term, as he felt that the war could have been stopped by the right policy and actions in the 1920s and 1930s; however, it could also be interpreted, especially in the American Midwest, where the speech was to be delivered, as a justification for United States isolation and avoidance of foreign entanglements for the future.

Pearson stated that, "Mr. Churchill was courteous enough to agree with my two small suggestions and to thank me for them. That was my contribution to the famous Iron Curtain speech; a tiny footnote to contemporary history."[5]

Later, in 1951, when Pearson was the minister for external affairs, he visited Churchill at the British prime minister's official residence, known as Chequers. Churchill was initially in a grumpy mood, but the "the pre-lunch drinks arrived and things looked up; our host came to life. He got even livelier as the lunch went on, with its accompanying wines. Over coffee and brandy, Churchill continued to get brighter and brighter as I got droopier and droopier."[6]

In his autobiography, Pearson referred to King's "enigmatic and contradictory personality, with that combination of charming friendliness and self-centred calculation, of kindness and ruthlessness, of political vision and personal pettiness, which so many who worked for him found disconcerting."[7]

The 1926 constitutional crisis in Canada known as the "Byng-King affair" is covered in detail in this fine book. It is interesting to assess the circumstances at that time, as background to the Harper Government's request to Governor General Michaëlle Jean in late 2008 to prorogue Parliament. Both situations raised important constitutional issues on the role of the governor general. Lord Byng, in denying King's request for a dissolution of Parliament, established that his duty was to Parliament and not to the prime minister, and I agree with his decision.

Winston Churchill and Mackenzie King, born just seven years after Canadian Confederation, connected in vital ways at a critical time in history. Terry Reardon now gives us a fascinating account of their interaction during the rise of Canada from being a small part of the British Empire to its emergence as an independent country, while still retaining ties to Britain as a senior member of the British Commonwealth of Nations.

INTRODUCTION

May 8, 1945, VE Day, was a triumphant day for two seventy-year-olds: Winston Leonard Spencer Churchill, the most recognized septuagenarian in the world; and William Lyon Mackenzie King, the most recognized septuagenarian in Canada.

In assessing the legacy of the two men, we have to be conscious that they were very much influenced by the thinking and behaviour of the latter part of the nineteenth century. They were both born in 1874, five years before Edison produced the electric light bulb and two years before Bell invented the telephone. They were both progressive in their thinking, however, and as will be brought out in this book, they were clearly ahead of their time in their concerns for the plight of the "common man."

Their lengthy parliamentary careers encompass a period of radical change in the British Empire and the British Commonwealth, and this book will examine the major part played by King in this transition, notwithstanding the opposition of many senior British parliamentarians, including Winston Churchill.

Despite the many similarities in the careers and backgrounds of the two men, the personalities of Churchill and King were completely different, a contradiction alluded to in this book's subtitle: *So Similar, So Different.* Churchill was fiery, impetuous, and charismatic: an extrovert. King was cool, calculating, and bland: an introvert. When matters had to be confronted, Churchill charged forward; King, on the other hand, considered all aspects of a situation before cautiously proceeding. Churchill was a man of action, not afraid to make mistakes, whereas King, to quote J.W. Pickersgill in *The Mackenzie King Record*, "genuinely believed and frequently said that the real secret of political leadership was more in what was prevented than in what was accomplished."[1]

Besides the fact that they shared their year of birth and their zodiac sign (Sagittarius), there were other similarities between the two men. Some of these were not of their choosing: their height, five feet, six inches; and the colour of their eyes, blue. They were also given nicknames — Churchill's Winston was shortened to Winnie, and King's William became Willie to his family, and Rex, the Latin word for King, to his close friends. However, what they did both develop themselves was a high degree of self-confidence and dedication to the service of their countries.

Both had large egos, and the essential attribute for all politicians: the talent for acting. Churchill took every opportunity for self-aggrandisement, especially in his younger days. He was brought up in a privileged family, with a brilliant but self-destroying father, and Winston was fixated on obtaining the approval of this parent. King, on the other hand, had to sublimate his desire for self-promotion, as such a tendency was not one that would appeal to the Canadian public. Neither would it appeal to God, and King, who was convinced that he was the deity's chosen instrument to govern Canada, believed that the Supreme Being would not condone displays of pride. So, King consciously portrayed himself in public as a serious, non-threatening statesman — on one occasion, when he was photographed laughing, he instructed the cameraman not to publish the photograph, as that was not the image he wished to portray to the public. In modern parlance, King was his own "spin doctor."

Churchill was a renaissance man, of many interests and achievements; he was especially noted for his writings, which, besides being his major source of income, resulted in his winning the Nobel Prize for Literature in 1953. He looked on historical events as matters relevant to current times. As he stated, "The longer you can look back, the farther you can look forward."[2] Or, as he said on May 27, 1953, "Study history, study history. In history lie all the secrets of statecraft."[3]

King had no hobbies, and except for compilations of his speeches, only wrote one full-length book, *Industry and Humanity,* but he was one of the greatest diarists in history, and this book will quote extensively from it. He kept a diary for fifty-seven years, from the age of eighteen to his death, aged seventy-five, with only a few days missing. The diary texts comprise nearly thirty thousand pages, and more than seven and a half million words. Not only did he record major matters, but also the most intimate personal details — many people have questioned why this very private man, who would have been expected to have gone to great lengths to protect his public image, did not ensure that parts of the diary dealing with delicate aspects were destroyed. The answer is that he did make it abundantly clear that he intended to use the diaries to assist with his autobiography, and personal or confidential parts were not for the eyes of others.

His will, which was completed shortly before his death, named four literary executors. He gave them specific instructions to "destroy all of my diaries except those parts which I have indicated are and shall be available for publication or use." However, he did not indicate which parts were to be kept.

The clearest evidence of King's wishes is to be found in diary notations from near the end of his life. On March 4, 1950, less than five months before his death, he wrote in the diary: "It has been intended as a guide to myself.... I cannot, however, deny that it contains material about proceedings at the Cabinet Table, and as I have taken an oath not to disclose anything to anyone ... would make it impossible for me to leave the diary open to anyone save someone of the Cabinet ... a distinct understanding was ... that the diaries should be destroyed." He goes on to justify dictating the diary to a confidential secretary. Then he expands on his concern: "It is to be remembered, too, that some of the information I have had as, for example, given me by Roosevelt, given me by Churchill, would never have been given but for their trust in my not discussing some aspects of it. The information would never have been made known to me if it was believed it would be shown to a third party, other than under my immediate direction."

Three days later, on March 7, 1950, he wrote, "I intended to destroy the whole diary if I did not have a chance to go through it myself."

It is evident that the literary executors had not read all of the diary. On the March 4, 1950, diary page is a handwritten notation: "First seen by J.W.P. November 13, 1960." That was J.W. Pickersgill, who was a long-time member of King's staff and one of the four literary executors.

Even if they were not aware of every specific instruction, the literary executors knew the intentions of the late prime minister. They were in a quandary. To respect his wishes, they should destroy most of the diary, as it contained confidential information, which could have caused embarrassment. But this information gave a unique insight into high-level developments, especially prior to and during World War II. A further complication arose, in 1955, when a civil servant in what was then known as the Public Archives of Canada microfilmed and sold parts of the diary.

Accordingly, in true Canadian fashion, the literary executors decided that a compromise was appropriate. The diary would be made available in stages. The diaries up to 1931 would be released to the public in 1971; those dating from 1931 to 1943 would be made available in 1974; and the diaries from 1943 to the end of King's life would be released in 1981. The executors believed that, with the staggered release, few of the central people mentioned in the diary would still be alive when they were made public.

The literary executors may not have followed King's wishes, but many, including this writer, would like to commend them on their decision.

Winston Churchill was a prolific author, and his *Memoirs of the Second World War* is a standard reference work. However, there is a major difference between Churchill's *Memoirs* and King's diary. Although the *Memoirs* were written some years after the war, Churchill still felt the need to sanitize his descriptions; he could not include his true opinion on certain events and people, as many were still alive and in senior positions (Stalin, Eisenhower, et cetera).

Many have written on Churchill, as his swashbuckling and dramatic life is attractive to writers and makes engaging reading. On the other hand, the outwardly dull King is a difficult subject for writers and readers alike, even when they may admire him as a person and appreciate his achievements. Thus, there have been few books on his life. Those who have written on the man have all struggled to capture his complexity.

With Churchill, there was no ambiguity about the true nature of the man; however, with King, the public saw just what King wanted to be seen.

Understandably, due to the importance of the British-American connection, the personal relationship between Churchill and King did not develop the intensity of that between Churchill and Franklin Delano Roosevelt. Still, the relationship that did exist between Churchill and King was an important one, and one that has gone largely unexplored by historians writing on World War II. Among those that have written on the subject, there are varied opinions regarding the nature of their feelings towards each other. In her introduction to Professor David Dilks's book *The Great Dominion: Winston Churchill in Canada, 1900–1954,* Churchill's daughter Lady Mary Soames wrote, "Despite various disagreements under the flail of war, [they] would become true friends, if not soul mates."[4] Lady Soames repeated this opinion at a Churchill Centre conference in Quebec City in 2005. When asked by this writer about the relationship, she replied: "While they were not best buddies, they were certainly very good friends." However, a different opinion is expressed by one of Churchill's private secretaries, John Colville: "He could never quite bring himself to enjoy the company of Mr. Mackenzie King, though he sometimes tried quite hard to do so and he did value the unflinching support of the Canadian prime minister during the worst months of the war."[5]

As will be evident in this book, the facts support the opinion of Lady Soames.

While the main participants in World War II were Germany, Japan, and, to a lesser extent, Italy, on the Axis side, and the United States, the Soviet Union, and Great Britain on the Allied side, what will also be brought out in this book is the major contribution to the Allied victory by the "second division" participants. At the head of these was Canada, without which Great Britain may well not have survived prior to the point when the might of the United States and Soviet Russia entered the conflict. Churchill was at fault for his many comments on Britain being "alone," although at other times he did change the reference to "the tiger and her tiger cubs."

In assessing the two men, their separate leadership roles in World War II will be examined, along with the effect of their relationship, which contributed to the successful outcome of the war. For example, while King had been an enthusiastic supporter of the Baldwin-Chamberlain policy of appeasement with Hitler, when war was declared he became totally committed to effecting all measures to defeat the totalitarian regimes. The main achievement of his career was bringing Canada united into the war. Churchill, of course, saw clearly the danger of Hitler and Nazi Germany, long before any other prominent politician, but was denied the authority to effect measures to stop the menace before it became, almost, too late.

Churchill was renowned for his sense of humour, which he used to great effect in the House of Commons. On one occasion during World War II, he was questioned about problems with a tank bearing his name; he responded: "It had many defects and teething troubles, and when these became apparent, the tank was appropriately rechristened the 'Churchill.' These defects have now been largely overcome. I am sure that this tank will prove, in the end, a powerful, massive, and serviceable weapon of war."[6]

On the other hand, humour played almost no role in King's public life. However, he did change from his usually serious tone on one occasion, in 1928, when, during a debate in the House of Commons, he made a quip at the expense of the leader of the opposition, the Conservative R.B. Bennett, who was a bachelor and a noted ladies' man. The matter being debated was an expected protest by a group from the Doukhobor sect, whose members used to call attention to their protests by shedding their clothes. An indignant member from British Columbia asked what the prime minister would do if faced with a parade of naked women. King looked over at Bennett and said, "I'd send for the Leader of the Opposition."[7]

Churchill was the more appealing person, devoid of pomposity and blessed with an impish sense of humour. Although King projected few attractive qualities and was widely regarded as being pompous, he was a shrewd practitioner of the parliamentary process. Churchill was unable to be devious, and when in the position of prime minister, he even held the grudging respect and admiration of his opponents On the other hand, King made no attempt to cultivate a spirit of comradeship with the parliamentary opposition, and his feelings for R.B. Bennett and — especially — Arthur Meighen bordered on hatred. His mode of handling his parliamentary duties was well-capsulated in Henry Ferns's and Bernard Ostry's study of the man, *The Age of Mackenzie King*: "He never invited men to love him, and very few did. Nor did he invite them to hate him, and very few did. But he knew how to manipulate them, and he did."[8]

Given the character of the two men, it is somewhat ironic that in the general elections held in 1945, after the end of the war in Europe, Great Britain saw the Conservative Party, led by the charismatic Churchill, defeated, while in Canada, the Liberal Party, led by the bland King, was victorious.

Despite their skill and character, it must be said that luck and timing, which are often overlooked by historians, also played a major role in both men's lives, as will be evident in this book. Although both men ended up having stellar careers, it is also possible that both men could have faded early from the political stage. However, each man benefitted from what might be considered good luck. For example, King was fortunate to lose the 1930 federal election, since that meant the Conservative Party had to deal with the Great Depression. And Churchill, it must be admitted, owes his later reputation to the fact that Hitler was not killed in the trenches during World War I. Had Hitler not survived to lead Germany into World War II, it is unlikely that Churchill would have recovered from the negative reputation he acquired as a result of his strenuous opposition to Indian independence in the 1930s, and his support for King Edward VIII in the abdication crisis of 1936.

While this book is concerned with the two men, in their fifty-year acquaintance, it will also show the change in the relationship between Britain and Canada during that same period. In the first half of the twentieth century, Canada grew steadily in confidence and maturity. This development was accompanied by an inevitable movement away from the mother country, and a corresponding movement towards the new major power in the world, its immediate neighbour, the United States of America.

1

THE EARLY YEARS

Winston Leonard Spencer Churchill was born on November 30, 1874. His father, Randolph, was the second son of the future seventh duke of Marlborough, and his ancestor, the renowned first duke, achieved fame and riches in his military exploits, the most prominent of which was the Battle of Blenheim, fought in 1704, during the War of the Spanish Succession, against the forces of King Louis XIV of France.

William Lyon Mackenzie King was born seventeen days after Churchill on December 17, 1874. His maternal grandfather was William Lyon Mackenzie, elected the first mayor of Toronto in 1834; in the eighteenth century, two of William Lyon Mackenzie's great-grandfathers fought with Bonnie Prince Charlie at the Battle of Culloden.

Their illustrious pedigrees were a key part of their makeup. Churchill was proud of his family's history; he even wrote a biography of his brilliant, egotistical father, and defended his record, which had been denigrated after his resignation from the senior cabinet position of chancellor of the exchequer in 1886, in an apparent effort to improve his status, or even take over as prime minister. King worshipped the memory of his grandfather, who led the 1837 Rebellion in Upper Canada against the upper-class "Family Compact," and with its failure went into exile in the United States, until amnesty was granted him in 1849. King wrote in his diary in 1895: "Reading the life of my dear grandfather, I have become a greater admirer of his than ever.... Many of his principles I pray that I have inherited."

If the two men were similar in both having remarkable ancestors, their upbringing was decidedly different. Winston's parents were involved in the social scene and paid little attention to him. As was usual for upper-class boys, he was shipped off to boarding schools commencing at eight years of age. With his stubborn attitude to discipline, he proved to be a challenge to his teachers. His granddaughter Celia Sandys stated at a Churchill Centre conference in Calgary, Alberta, in 1994, "If Winston had been my son, I would have adored him, but if he had been my son's best friend, I would have been fairly hesitant about asking him to come and stay for the holidays."

Even by the standards of the late nineteenth century, the off-hand attitude of his parents was unusual, but Churchill later propounded a positive result for their lack of attention. In 1898, in *The River War,* he wrote of the Mahdi, the Sudanese leader: "Solitary trees, if they grow at all, grow strong; and a boy deprived of a father's care often develops, if he escapes the perils of youth, an independence and vigour of thought which may restore in after life the heavy loss of early days."[1] And in his *Marlborough: His Life and Times,* written in 1933, he stated, "It is said that famous men are usually the product of an unhappy childhood. The stern compression of circumstances, the twinges of adversity, the spur of slights and taunts in early years, are needed to evoke that ruthless fixity of purpose and tenacious mother-wit without which great actions are seldom accomplished."[2]

King's father, John, was a lawyer in Berlin, Ontario (renamed Kitchener in 1916) before moving to Toronto. He lectured in the law school at Osgoode Hall and was well-regarded, but despite his status, he was unable to make a success of his law practice. As a result, there was continuing family cash flow pressure. However, despite the family's financial distress, the Kings were a very close knit, happy family, with William's mother, Isabel Grace, providing a much loved family life to the eldest child, William (referred to as Willie or Billie) and his three siblings.

One matter that should be clarified is William's surname. The indexes in many books show it as Mackenzie King. A search of the files of the Ontario Government Archives confirms that it is, in fact, King.

William's interest in politics commenced when he heard Canada's first prime minister, Sir John A. Macdonald, speak in Berlin (Kitchener) during the 1882 election campaign. As he later recollected: "I remember best not the political argument but that Sir John was presented with some flowers by a pretty young lady whom he thanked with an embrace. I could do nothing but envy him, and decided then that politics had its rewards."[3]

Although he went to the prestigious Harrow School, Winston did not apply himself to anything that did not interest him, with English being a notable exception. William, on the other hand, was a brilliant student, entering the University of Toronto in 1891, although he was not quite seventeen. After graduation from there, he later went on to take degrees at the University of Chicago and Harvard.

After graduating from the Royal Military College, Churchill joined the military and served in India. There he fought with the Malakand Field Force, and supplemented his income by writing a book on the expedition, which was well-received and opened up a new sideline for him. He later served in Egypt and in the Boer War in South Africa, where he was captured, escaped, and became a national hero.

In the spring of 1899, King had his fellowship at Harvard renewed for a further year, with the privilege of using it to study abroad. He sailed for England, and in London he gave a number of lectures on industrial matters to working-class people.

King returned from his travels, expecting an offer to join the faculty of Harvard; however, the offer, when received, was only for work as a part-time instructor. After much deliberation he accepted instead an offer from the Canadian government to become the editor of a new publication, the *Labour Gazette*, which he commenced on September 15, 1900. Soon afterwards his title was changed to the more prestigious position of deputy minister of labour.

The two men were different in their religious beliefs. Churchill was a non-believer, although he brought God into many of his speeches. King was a believer, and although he belonged to the Presbyterian Church and like to attend services, he also believed that there existed a direct relationship between God and himself, and that God spoke to him. The major decisions in life, however, both personal and political, were made in the belief that God either instigated them or would approve.

King's interest in spiritualism, which had been known to only a few loyal people before his death, and shocked and titillated the public when his diaries were made available, was not a feature of his youth. While it was certainly a part of his adult life, it did not affect his political decisions, although King was comforted when his nocturnal visitors confirmed the correctness of his actions.

In matters of the heart, the two men also differed. Churchill experienced a fairly typical romantic life, eventually marrying Clementine Hozier, whom he had met in 1908, and having children. He later stated: "My ability to persuade my wife to marry me was quite my most brilliant achievement."[4]

Although King never married, he certainly was attracted to the opposite sex. In reading his diary, it is difficult to come to any conclusion other than that King employed the services of prostitutes during his university days. His most serious relationship was with Mathilde Grossert, a nurse twelve years older than him, whom he had met while in hospital in Chicago in March 1897. He proposed marriage to her, and after some hesitation on her part, she accepted. However, when William advised his family of the good news, their reaction was just the opposite of what he had expected. Letters from one of his sisters and his father pointedly objected, and finally his mother wrote, "The struggles have been long and hard at home and I hope you will not think me selfish when I say I had counted on you to help lift the cloud…. I am not grasping for myself, but I do feel for your sisters and I know you, who have such a big heart, will not forsake me."[5]

King's diary of that day concludes with a clear indication of his anguish: "What storm is this; what sea. Oh God, bring peace and understanding soon. Let thy purpose be revealed. Bless us all." The diary over the next few weeks was full of his torment, and his jottings would bring a blush to the face of a Harlequin Romance editor. The affair eventually ended, and Mathilde married a George Barchet. Surprisingly, King kept in touch with her. Even in the last year of his life, his diary of December 21, 1949, recorded him sending her a biography of himself by H.R. Hardy and a twenty-dollar cheque.

There were later attempts by others to set King up with a wife, with matchmakers including Sir Wilfrid Laurier, who was most insistent that

Mathilde Barchet (née Grossert), the love of William Lyon Mackenzie King's early life, taken on August 21, 1907, nine years after her relationship with King ended.

his protégé marry a Canadian girl; however, nothing came of the prime minister's efforts. It is evident that King compared every potential bride to his mother. All, in the end, were considered lacking, something his diary emphasizes. For example, on July 29, 1899, he wrote: "If only I can win such a wife as I have such a mother, how infinitely happy!" But the underlying theme of his life — that he was an instrument of God's will — made him unsure if God agreed whether any potential bride would be suitable for him to achieve the divine destiny.

2

THE EDWARDIAN DECADE: 1900–1910

Churchill took advantage of his international reputation after his Boer War escape to stand for election to Parliament, and he was successful. He increased his prestige and finances by embarking on a lecture tour of the United States and Canada in late 1900.

His reception in the United States was not too friendly, as the majority of Americans were on the side of the Boers, but all that changed when he crossed the Canadian border. "Here again," he wrote, "were the enthusiastic throngs to which I had so easily accustomed myself at home. Alas, I could only spend ten days in these inspiring scenes."[1]

He spoke in Toronto on December 22, 1900, and the vote of thanks was moved by William Mulock, the postmaster general, who six months before had appointed King as the editor of the *Labour Gazette*.

The first meeting between Churchill and King occurred at that time, in Ottawa. King was less than impressed with Churchill. His opinion is recorded in *Churchill: Taken from the Diaries of Lord Moran*. Charles Wilson (the future Lord Moran) remarked to King years later that he (King) must have known Churchill for a long time:

"King: 'Yes: I have. I first met him when he was going around Canada on a lecture tour.'

"Wilson: 'That can't have been long after the Boer War.'

"King: 'No. I found him at his hotel drinking champagne at eleven o'clock in the morning.'"[2]

Churchill had been elected to Parliament as a Conservative but he "crossed the floor" in 1904, taking a stance against the Tory Party's support of tariffs. This was fortuitous, as the Liberals were triumphant in the general election of December 1905, and Churchill was appointed undersecretary of state for the colonies. His achievements in that post led to his appointment to cabinet as president of the Board of Trade in April 1908. There, with David Lloyd George, the chancellor of the exchequer, he threw himself into measures to improve the lives of the mass of the people. These two men have justifiably been called the founders of the welfare state, as they were the instigators of the Old Age Pension and Unemployment Insurance.

King also had a genuine interest in the welfare of the working class. During a summer break in his university days, he had been given an assignment to investigate the abuses in the treatment of workers making clothing for the Canadian government. He recommended standard hours of labour, fair wages, and sanitary conditions. King's recommendations were accepted and Prime Minister Wilfrid Laurier also announced that similar regulations would be enacted throughout the government service.

In his position as deputy minister of labour, King became involved with immigration problems, in particular the false description of employment prospects. Accordingly, he was instructed to travel to England, with the object of having the British government pass legislation, similar to that enacted by the Government of Canada, which would curtail false representations to induce or deter immigration.[3]

When he arrived in England in September 1906, King was told he must meet the under-secretary of state for the colonies, Winston Churchill. The negative opinion that King had formed of the man in 1900 was evident in his response to this instruction: "I've met him and he's the last person in England I want to see." However, when he received a handwritten luncheon invitation, he felt that he would have to attend.

Churchill disarmed King by greeting him with the question: "We met in Canada four [*sic*] years ago, I think. I did make a frightful ass of myself on that trip, didn't I?"

King responded, "Well, Mr. Churchill, there were many Canadians who thought so. I was one of them."[4]

The luncheon was also attended by Sir Evelyn Wrench, the editor of *The Spectator* and the founder of the English-Speaking Union. In *Churchill By His Contemporaries*, Wrench recounted the event in his diary. Writing about it on November 1, 1906, he stated that the luncheon was held in Churchill's rooms at 12 Bolton Street: "There were five of us at lunch, Marsh, his [Churchill's] secretary, W. Mackenzie King (Churchill's first [*sic*] meeting with the young Canadian, then Deputy Minister of Labour in Laurier's Government and later Prime Minister of Canada for so many years), John Burns, President of the Local Government Board, and myself."[5]

Wrench stated that at the meeting he expressed support to the encouragement of British emigration to the colonies, with John Burns responding, "Why do you wish to establish under the British flag replicas of Tooting around the seven seas." According to Wrench, Churchill just "smiled benignly."[6]

King's visit was successful, and an amendment was made to the Merchant Shipping Act that offenders could be prosecuted in Britain.

In January 1908 King received a surprising invitation to meet with U.S. President Theodore (Teddy) Roosevelt to discuss "matters of common interest." He wondered if it would be appropriate for a young civil servant to represent the country, but after receiving approval from Sir Wilfrid Laurier, he journeyed to Washington.

King had lunch with the president and Elihu Root, the secretary of state. Roosevelt outlined that he wished King to be a channel of communication between the American and British governments, with the objective of achieving a settlement of the Japanese immigration problem. Roosevelt expressed concern at British indifference in this matter and his lack of confidence in the British ambassador. He even talked of sending the U.S. fleet into the Pacific to focus the attention of the Japanese government on the requirement for a definite arrangement on the matter.

King returned to Ottawa and reported back to Laurier and Earl Grey, the governor general. Laurier had formed a highly negative opinion of Roosevelt, based on past dealings, and he did not take seriously the threat of war. Grey had the same opinion, and he reported to James Bryce, the British ambassador in Washington, that Roosevelt's speech was "all flam."[7]

However, Laurier acceded to Roosevelt's request and King set out to Britain again. The Canadian government didn't wish the visit to be construed as a request from the president of the United States. Accordingly, the official reason given for King's journey was that since he was very familiar with the problem of Asiatic immigration, and as this problem involved relations with both foreign powers and fellow British subjects in India, he was being sent to England to discuss various aspects of the matter with the Government of England.[8]

King was somewhat overwhelmed at being given this important assignment, but it was certainly a measure of the confidence that Prime Minister Laurier placed in him.

King sailed eastward and arrived in England in mid-March 1908. He met with senior politicians there, including the Canadian-born future British prime minister Arthur Bonar Law. Law introduced King to the former prime minister Arthur Balfour, with the comment, "You will welcome Mr. King some day as the Prime Minister of Canada."[9]

King also met Winston Churchill again. Writing of their meeting, he recorded in his diary, "One cannot talk with him without being impressed at the nibbleness [nimbleness] of his mind, his quickness of perception, and his undoubted ability. He seems to have lost a good deal of the egotism, at least so far as his manner is concerned, though one feels that even yet it is Churchill rather than the movement with which he is identified that is the mainspring of his conduct." One remark of Churchill's that King recorded as "rather characteristic and perhaps no less true" occurred in a discussion of the movement of peoples and the possibilities of war. "On large questions of this kind I have a true instinct and seldom err."[10]

King outlined the immigration concerns of the Canadian government and of President Roosevelt to British Foreign Minister Sir Edward Grey, who assured him that the British government would see that Japan observed the undertakings that she had previously given to Canada, and that he (Grey) would also seek the same assurance regarding Japan's obligations under her "gentleman's agreement" with the United States.[11]

The result of King's efforts and the pressure put on Japan by the United States was a much-reduced flow of Japanese immigrants, and improved relations between the two countries.

King had become the government's expert on labour relations. During the period 1900 to 1907, he was involved in forty-one separate labour disputes, and settlements were achieved in thirty-nine of them. However, his ambition was to be elected to Parliament, and this was realized in 1908. The following year he became the first minister of labour, as well as a privy councillor. He had taken longer than Churchill to achieve ministerial rank but a decade later he would surpass him.

3

MIXED FORTUNES: 1911–1921

After attaining cabinet positions at relatively young ages in the first decade of the century, Churchill and King struggled during the following decade to live up to their early promise. After initial successes, both men experienced serious disappointment in the next decade, but each finally overcame the obstacles that appeared in their respective paths, and re-emerged successful.

Churchill's political career continued to blossom in the early years of the decade. He was promoted to the position of first lord of the Admiralty in October 1911. He soon recognized the looming danger of Germany, which had embarked on a rapid expansion of its naval strength, and with his usual drive and gusto he reorganized the navy, including making the change of fuel from coal to oil. He was also involved with the development of the Royal Naval Air Service, which his foresight had identified as a future vital part of the country's defence.

Soon after Churchill's appointment came World War I, which saw immense armies inflict enormous destruction on each other on the Western Front. The tragic loss of life prompted Churchill to write to Prime Minister Asquith on December 29, 1914: "Are there not other alternatives than sending our armies to chew barbed wire in Flanders?"[1]

One alternative that the British cabinet accepted was a naval assault on the Dardanelles against Germany's ally, Turkey. The intent was to take Constantinople, relieve pressure off the Russians, and encourage other

Churchill when First Lord of the Admiralty with Canadian Prime Minister Sir Robert Borden, leaving the Admiralty, London, 1912.

Balkan states to join the Allies; however, the ability of the Turks to resist was underestimated, and the result was a disaster. While Churchill had been a late convert to the undertaking, he was the head of the Admiralty, and became the scapegoat for the failure of the operation. As a result, he was fired in May 1915.

Churchill was devastated at his dismissal. As a sop, he was given the sinecure cabinet position of chancellor of the Duchy of Lancaster, which, as Lloyd George said, was "generally reserved either for beginners to the cabinet or for distinguished politicians who had reached the final stages of unmistakable decrepitude."[2]

Of course, his new position was no real compensation for the loss of his job with the navy, and Churchill sank into deep depression. Clementine later recalled, "I thought he would never get over the Dardanelles. I thought he would die of grief."[3] Churchill's mood was somewhat alleviated by "the muse of painting," which he took up; however, his frustration at being on the sidelines of the war led him to resign from the junior cabinet position in November 1915 and join the army, where he was given the rank of major.

On November 18, 1915, he arrived in France, and on New Year's Day, 1916, he was promoted to the position of lieutenant colonel, serving with the Sixth Royal Scots Fusiliers. In May 1916 his battalion, which was under-strength, was amalgamated with another battalion. Churchill was the junior of the two commanding officers and was told that he had to forfeit his command. While he could probably have secured another position at the same level, he was being pressured to return to political life. Since he had retained his seat in the House of Commons during his sojourn in the army, he was able to simply return to Parliament.

After Churchill's return to Parliament, the commission established to investigate the Dardanelles disaster issued its report. It accused the War Council of usurping its authority and the cabinet for permitting it. No one was exonerated, including Winston Churchill.

He was left to languish on the back benches for a year before an old colleague came to his rescue. David Lloyd George was now the prime minister of a coalition government, and, in spite of opposition from the Conservatives in his cabinet, he appointed Churchill as minister of munitions. *The Sunday Times* responded to this decision thus: "We say with all deliberation and with the utmost emphasis that nothing would tend more effectively to damn Mr. Lloyd George's Government in the eyes of the whole country than the co-option of Mr. Churchill."[4]

Churchill presents the Daily Mail *aviation prize of 10,000 pounds for the first crossing of the Atlantic to Alcock and Brown in 1919.*

Lloyd George stood firm and the cabinet outrage died down. After the signing of the armistice on November 11, 1918, which ended the war, and a general election, Churchill was appointed secretary of state for war and air in the coalition government on January 9, 1919.

With various departments overlapping, Lloyd George reorganized the Colonial Office, and gave it additional responsibilities. He appointed Churchill as secretary of state for the colonies on January 8, 1921. In that position Churchill had to assess Britain's role in the Middle East, which was proving a drain on the exchequer. This he did by setting up Arab princes on the thrones of Iraq and Transjordan. Some recent books have criticized his decisions on Iraq, but the fact that relative stability was achieved for some thirty-seven years is to his credit.

King's initial tenure as a Member of Parliament and minister of labour came to an end in the general election of September 21, 1911. The Laurier government was defeated, primarily due to its support of reciprocity with the United States, and King lost his seat. He became head of the Federal Liberal Information Office, and although he was given the Liberal nomination for the riding of North York in March 1913, an election was not in the near future.

King kept a close watch on the darkening scene in Europe. On July 31, 1914, he was furious with an article in the *Montreal Star,* "suggesting England should throw down the gauntlet to Germany." He had a high opinion of the British Liberal government leaders Asquith, Grey, and Haldane, and was satisfied that they would not be drawn into a war. However, he still retained a suspicion of the first lord of the Admiralty: "Winston Churchill is the one dangerous factor. If he saw his way to being head of the Admiralty at a moment that meant the crushing of German power, he might try the step, but he will be restrained by the other three."

On August 4, 1914, Britain was forced to declare war on Germany, Austria-Hungary, and Italy. Those three nations were part of a mutual self-defence alliance known as the Triple Alliance. Britain was part of another alliance, called the Triple Entente, but it also had a treaty with Belgium, committing it to come to the aid of the latter if it was attacked. When Germany invaded Belgium, en route to France, Britain declared war on Germany and its allies. Since Britain still had control of Canada's foreign policy at the time — Canada did not win full control of its foreign policy until the passage of the Statute of Westminster in 1931 — Britain's declaration of war automatically meant that Canada was also at war.

King was almost forty years of age and an unlikely prospect for the military. Another prospect soon presented itself, however. His impressive record in solving industrial disputes had come to the attention of the Rockefeller Foundation, which was involved in a serious and bloody labour dispute in Colorado, and he was invited to join the Foundation as director of research. He did so on October 1, 1914, with the salary of twelve thousand dollars a year — a substantial remuneration that solved King's and his family's financial worries. The position had the added benefit of allowing him to retain his Canadian citizenship and continue to live in Ottawa, and thus be able to engage in Canadian politics when the opportunity arose. His personal relationship with the Rockefeller family is illustrated by John D. Rockefeller's biographer stating that King was "the closest friend John D., Jr. ever had."[5]

King with John D. Rockefeller and a miner in Colorado, 1915.

King achieved notable success in the Foundation's labour problems, with John D. Rockefeller Jr. telling his biographer years later: "I was merely King's mouthpiece. I needed education. No other man did so much for me. He had vast experience in industrial relations and I had none. I needed guidance. He had an intuitive sense of the right thing to do — whether it was a man who ought to be talked with or a situation that ought to be met."[6]

In November 1918 King published *Industry and Humanity*; in it, he laid out his experiences and ideas gleaned from his years dealing with labour disputes and as a politician. This is a weighty and ponderous tome, with the first edition containing ten charts and diagrams "Illustrative of Industrial Relations." The book does not see management and labour as having conflicting interests, but as partners in industry, with each benefiting from this partnership, and each suffering when industrial disputes occur. In it, both sides are encouraged to take the high road when disputes arise, especially where the general public is affected. Such behaviour would, of course, be ideal, but it is difficult to understand how King could have believed that this would occur. As David Jay Bercuson stated in his introduction to a 1973 edition of the book, "When King became Prime Minister he discovered that society was indeed dominated by carnivorous beasts who would not bow to the simple application of reason."

Although King found his work for Rockefeller stimulating, his political ambitions were paramount, and while working for the Foundation he kept in touch with his North York constituency, albeit at arm's length. He also maintained contact with the Liberal Party leader, Sir Wilfrid Laurier, and supported him, in 1917, when a major challenge to the unity of the Liberal Party arose.

The ruling Conservative Party and its leader, Sir Robert Borden, had proposed bringing in conscription to solve the serious manpower shortage in the armed forces. Laurier, conscious of the strong objection of his Quebec supporters, was adamantly opposed, although the majority of the population in the rest of the country was in favour of compulsory national service.

A general election was announced for December 17, 1917, in order to resolve the dispute. King was concerned that the overwhelming support for conscription in all of Canada except Quebec would be fatal to the Liberal Party. In a letter to Laurier on October 17, he exhorted him to "imply that you are willing to allow the Conscription Act to remain, to sanction what had been done under it, and that if the needed number of men cannot be secured voluntarily, they will nevertheless be secured, which means that conscription in such an emergency would be a necessary resort?"[7]

It is an interesting position, and shows King's consistency, since he was to return to this position in World War II with his famous, ambiguous

Library and Archives Canada C 031020

King with Sir Wilfrid Laurier at Sydney Fisher's (former minister of agriculture) home on August 12, 1915.

remark at the time of the 1942 plebiscite on compulsory overseas service: "Conscription if necessary; but not necessarily conscription."

King's recommendation, however, was not accepted by Laurier. What became known as the "Khaki Election" was a disaster for the Laurier Liberals, resulting in them winning only twenty seats outside Quebec and King being defeated in North York by 1,078 votes.

King had the choice of going back to the Rockefeller Foundation, or accepting a very large salary to be the director of the Carnegie Corporation. King decided to rejoin the Rockefeller Foundation, but he stayed only a short time, leaving in February 1918. At the suggestion of John D. Rockefeller, King set himself up as an industrial relations advisor, working for a number of major American firms, including Bethlehem Steel, General Electric, and Standard Oil. But he kept in close touch with major figures in the Liberal Party, and when Sir Wilfrid Laurier died on February 17, 1919, King stood for the leadership at the Liberal Party convention on August 7, 1919.

His main opponent, William Stevens Fielding, a former finance minister, was seventy years of age and had deserted Laurier at the general election two years before. King was elected leader after three ballots. His diary written that evening stated: "It is the call of duty. I have sought nothing, it has come. It has come from God.... It is to His work I am called, and to do it I dedicate my life." In a by-election on October 20, 1919, in Prince Edward Island, King was elected and returned to Parliament to face the new Unionist prime minister, Arthur Meighen.

King's early leadership of the opposition in the House of Commons was unimpressive and Meighen treated him with contempt. However, in the years ahead, Meighen would find that he had underestimated his opponent.

King toured the country to make himself known, and he was well-placed when Meighen called a general election for December 6, 1921, at which time the Unionist Party reverted back to the Conservative name.

King's mode of political leadership was to avoid making promises that could come back to haunt him later. As we will see, this was exactly contrary to Churchill's attitude. Nevertheless, it was a practice that served King and the Liberals well. The Liberals turned the tables in the election, although they failed by two seats to gain an overall majority.

King had now achieved his ambition: prime minister of Canada. His main challenge was to heal wounds from the conscription crisis in 1917, and make the Liberal Party a truly national one. However, only nine months into his administration, just as he was getting to work on this goal, he was faced with an international crisis.

4

CHANAK

In World War I, the Ottoman Empire was an ally of Germany; following the war and the signing of the Treaty of Sèvres on August 10, 1920, the Ottoman Empire was abolished. It was replaced by a new entity, Turkey, which was given a substantially reduced territory, and which had imposed on it numerous restrictions — military and otherwise — by the Allies. However, a charismatic and brilliant military leader, Mustafa Kemal Atatürk, led Turkish resistance to the treaty, formed a provisional government, and routed the occupying Greek forces in 1921, clearing them from Turkish soil.

The Treaty of Sèvres had established a neutral zone, which included the Straits of the Dardanelles, the shores of the Sea of Marmora, the capital of Constantinople, and the southern shore of the Black Sea. On September 11, 1922, Atatürk was notified by the high commissioners of the three victorious powers (Britain, France, and Italy) that he must not transgress the neutral zone; however, the victorious Turkish forces were in a confident, aggressive mood, and a large army marched on the small British contingent in the town of Chanak, on the Asiatic shore of the Dardanelles.

Colonial Minister Winston Churchill drafted a telegram, which was approved by Prime Minister Lloyd George, to the Dominions, advising them of the serious situation and requesting their military assistance. The telegram to Canada was headed "Secret":

London, September 15th, 1922

Following from Prime Minister for your Prime Minister, begins:

Cabinet today decided to resist Turkish aggression upon Europe and to make exertions to prevent Allies being driven out of Constantinople by Mustafa Kemal and in particular and above all to maintain freedom of Straits by securing firmly the Gallipoli Peninsula.... I should be glad to know whether Dominion Government wish to associate themselves with the action we are taking and whether they would desire to be represented by a contingent.... The announcement that all or any of the Dominions were prepared to send contingents even of a moderate size would undoubtedly in itself exercise a most favourable influence on situation and might conceivably be a potent factor in preventing actual hostilities.

Signed Churchill.[1]

On September 16 Churchill provided a communiqué to the press, which stated that the Dominions had been invited to be represented in the defence of the peninsula. King, as he recorded in his diary of September 16, was taken by surprise. "I was about to go into the Temple of Peace at Sharon [north of Toronto], when the *Toronto Star* reporter, about 2:45, handed me a despatch to the effect that Britain had invited Canada to participate in an attack against the Turks, and in the maintenance of the Dardanelles. I replied that I had nothing to say, other than that there was a meeting of the Cabinet on Monday [September 18] when the representations of the kind would be considered by my colleagues & myself in Council."

In the diary for the next day, Sunday, King recorded: "On reaching Ottawa, McGregor [his secretary] brought to my state room in the car about 7:30 the cable from Churchill to the G.G. [governor general] suggesting intervention by Canada & sending of a contingent. I confess it annoyed me. It is drafted designedly to play the imperial game, to test out centralization vs. autonomy as regards European wars. I went from the train to the office & sent a cable at once to Churchill."

This cypher telegram had to be routed through the governor general, the established procedure. "Following from my Prime Minister for your Prime Minister. Before it was possible to have contents of your cable sent through Governor General communicated to myself or other members of the Canadian Government, our press carried cable despatches from England announcing invitation by British Government to Canada to participate in resistance of Turkish forces by sending contingent. A most embarrassing situation has arisen in consequence.... Signed Byng."[2]

Actually, Churchill's cable had been received, but as it was marked "Secret," it was not opened until King returned.

King's position was that no contingent would go without Parliament approving. Although he was aware that Australia and New Zealand, which looked to Britain for protection, would probably comply.

King sent another cable to Churchill, again via the governor general. "The Cabinet has had under consideration the representations contained in your telegram of the fifteenth instant. It is the view of the Government that public opinion in Canada would demand authorization on the part of Parliament as a necessary preliminary to the despatch of a contingent to participate in the conflict of the Near East. We will welcome the fullest possible information in order to decide upon the advisability of summoning Parliament."[3]

The next day Lloyd George cabled: "The attitude of Canada is most important. We do not ask for any immediate decision to send troops.... A definite statement, however, that Canada will stand by the Empire in the event of terms of Armistice being broken will do much to ensure maintenance of peace."

King responded through the governor general: "We have not thought it necessary to reassert the loyalty of Canada to the British Empire." The British government, he continued, could "rest assured that should it become necessary to summon Parliament, Canada, by decision of its Parliament, will so act as to carry out the full duty of the Canadian people."[4] However, King was determined that Canada would not be drawn into the matter and he had no intention of an early recall of Parliament.

The main opposition party in the Canadian House of Commons was the Conservative Party, and its leader, Arthur Meighen, clearly laid out his party's stance in a speech on September 21: "Britain ... sends a message to the Dominions, not a mere indifferent enquiry as to what is in the mind of Canada, but a message to see if the Dominions were solid behind the Motherland.... Let there be no dispute as to where I stand. When Britain's message came then Canada should have said: Ready, aye ready; we stand behind you."[5]

King had the opposite view, as he recorded in his diary: "I shall do the right as I see & leave the rest to God. God give me vision & strength, for all that lies ahead, to lead the country aright — in the path that is best for the people and ultimate peace."

King's desire for a peaceful settlement seemed to be fulfilled when Atatürk agreed to withdraw after the offer of a conference to address the Turks' demands. Despite the optimistic indications, the situation was still a dangerous one — something that was confirmed in a note King received on October 4, which he recorded in his diary: "Winston Churchill sent a very startling message, to effect he did not think Conference w[oul]d come to anything & feared a worst situation w[oul]d develop in Constantinople in a week." However, he goes on to state, "The evening papers report peace certain — It is a serious business having matters in hand of a man like Churchill — the fate of an empire! — I am sure we had done right & aided the cause of peace by holding back."

In the end a convention was signed on October 11, with the formal Treaty of Lausanne executed on July 24, 1923, giving international recognition of the sovereignty of the new Republic of Turkey.

It is interesting that Churchill, in his description of the events, does acknowledge the protests of Canada and Australia to the fact that the newspapers reported the request to the Dominions prior to the official communiqué being received, which he excused as due to the growing seriousness of the situation; but he also does give a false interpretation of

Canada's attitude by stating: "Nevertheless, all the Dominions responded to the call and declared their readiness if a great emergency arose to bear their part, subject of course to the consent of their Parliaments."[6]

After a by-election in Britain on October 19, in which the Conservative candidate defeated a Coalition opponent, the Conservatives formally withdrew their support, and Lloyd George tendered his resignation. As Churchill later wrote, "At the crucial moment, I was prostrated by a severe operation for appendicitis, and … the [following] morning when I recovered consciousness I learned that the Lloyd George Government had resigned, and that I had lost not only my appendix, but my office as Secretary of State for the Dominions and Colonies."[7]

King's diary of October 19 noted the resignation: "It w[oul]d be a good thing for England if she could get rid of L[loyd]G[eorge], Churchill, Birkenhead, [and] Beaverbrook." King later added, with a high degree of venom: "Churchill is said to have had an operation for appendicitis. I w[oul]d not be surprised if he were on a spree."

The new British government called for an election, which was held on November 15. Churchill stood as a "Liberal and Free Trader" and lost. After twenty-two years in the House of Commons, he was out. Across the Atlantic Ocean, on the other hand, a fellow Liberal, King, had enhanced his position by asserting Canada's independence.

The Turkish crisis not only had opposite effects on the careers of the two men, it also served to drive them further apart politically. Writing a few months after the end of the crisis, on January 26, 1923, King made clear his suspicion of the motives of the prior British government in the Chanak affair: "The more one goes into the matter, the clearer it becomes that Lloyd George, Churchill & others were out to try an Imperialist game to help the Coalition politically. They were ready 'to go it alone' with Turkey in the Near East, to bluff the Allies — France & Italy alike, as well as the rest of the world. One cannot be sure, but there seems good reason to believe that our action prevented actual war, of what a character one can scarcely contemplate."

This was obviously an unfair and inaccurate opinion, but it reinforced King's determination to create a new policy for Canada to undertake in dealing with the mother country.

5

THE DECLINE OF THE EMPIRE
AND THE BIRTH OF THE COMMONWEALTH

The 1920s saw Canada, through the efforts or stubbornness — depending on your point of view — of King, move from being a child of Britain to being an independent country, albeit one with a strong attachment to the motherland.

This transition had been a steady journey, beginning in 1848 with the granting of responsible government in Nova Scotia, and progressing to 1867, when, with the passage of the British North America Act, Canada became responsible for its internal affairs, although Great Britain retained responsibility for external relations.

In the four Colonial Conferences held between 1897 and 1911, Prime Minister Wilfrid Laurier emphasized that Canada was a "nation that voluntarily accepted to be a part of the British Empire. There would be no more reference to Canada as a colony: it was a self-governing Dominion."[1]

Another conference was scheduled for October–November 1923 — they were renamed Imperial Conferences after 1911 — and beforehand King was sworn in as a member of the British privy council. He was also given the "Freedom of the City of London." In expressing thanks he showed his anglophile feelings: "Enjoying and bestowing freedom, may the community of British Nations forever flourish and expand, conferring upon countless millions the benefits of its social and political civilization! Such is my sincere wish as a Canadian, and my first wish as a Freeman of the City of London."[2]

Foreign Minister Curzon opened the conference, and reiterated his and his government's attitude to the relationship between Britain and the Dominions: In international matters, when the foreign minister of Britain spoke, he spoke not just for Britain but also for the whole of the Empire. While the majority of the Dominion delegates were agreeable to this arrangement —Australia was especially enthusiastic, since it was concerned with the rising military attitude of Japan, and was looking to Britain for protection — King was part of the minority that opposed this position. Canada was steadily loosening its economic ties with Britain, and moving steadily towards the United States, which had become its major trading partner. King was also conscious of the fact that in the future Canada's political policy, especially in foreign affairs, would not necessarily coincide with that of Great Britain.

Curzon, trying to muster support for his position, compared the gathering to an Imperial cabinet, with King arguing that it was a conference of governments, each responsible to its own Parliament. Soon the delegates were in opposite camps, with the Irish Free State supporting King; Australia and New Zealand supporting Curzon; and the most experienced Dominion leader, General Jan Smuts of South Africa, treading a middle path.

King had been prime minister for less than two years, and he now faced the challenge of articulating his vision of Canada's status: it was a proud member of the British Empire and Commonwealth, but one that did not bow down to the decisions of Britain, and one that required that any matters directly affecting Canada be debated and decided upon by its Parliament. This King did in a remarkable performance, parrying the proposals of the highly articulate Lord Curzon and standing his ground, much to the frustration of Curzon and the prime ministers of Australia and New Zealand.

King, using the low-key method he had utilized when negotiating labour disputes as deputy minister of labour in the early 1900s, quietly but firmly set out his position. In spite of the efforts of fellow Dominion delegates, as well as those of Curzon and Leo Amery, the first lord of the Admiralty, he did not deviate

King's position irritated Curzon, who, on November 8, wrote to his wife: "The obstacle has been Mackenzie King, the Canadian, who is both obstinate, tiresome and stupid, and is nervously afraid of being turned out of his own Parliament when he gets back."[3]

Despite the considerable opposition King faced, he won the day. The section of the published "Summary of Proceedings of the Conference" relating to foreign relations states, "This Conference is a conference of representatives of the several Governments of the Empire; its views and conclusions on Foreign Policy, as recorded above, are necessarily subject to the action of the Governments and Parliaments of the various portions of the Empire." That clause was insisted upon by King.

At the final session of the conference, Jan Smuts remarked to King, "You ought to be satisfied. Canada has had her way in everything."[4]

J.W. Dafoe, the influential editor of the *Manitoba Free Press* (which became the *Winnipeg Free Press* in 1931), accompanied King to the conference. Commenting on the proceedings there, he wrote: "As for King, my regard for him has perceptibly increased by what I saw of him in London. He is an abler man than I thought: he has more courage than I gave him credit for."[5]

Churchill had no involvement in the Imperial Conference, as he was still out of Parliament, but he certainly would have agreed with the stance taken by Curzon. Churchill would not return to Parliament until the general election of October 29, 1924, when he won the riding of Epping as a "Constitutionalist," although supported by the Conservative Party. Much to his surprise, on November 5 Prime Minister Stanley Baldwin appointed him to the position of chancellor of the exchequer, the post that had once been held by his father. He was elated — he was back in a major position in the government.

King was baffled by the appointment, as he wrote: "The appointment of Churchill — as Chancellor of the Exchequer, was a surprise & Birkenhead for India. Baldwin spoke strongly against the two to many, including Lloyd George. He said they were 'the three most dangerous men in the Empire,' now he has taken them to his breast."

Baldwin's reason for what *The Times* called, "the most daring appointment, from the public point of view,"[6] was that he genuinely thought that

Churchill would be an asset to the government. However, that was a turnaround from his earlier attitude, as is illustrated in a letter from Lord Beaverbrook, the Canadian-born newspaper baron, to King on February 9, 1926. Beaverbrook wrote, "[As] recently as 1923, when Baldwin formed his first administration, he would not hear of Churchill's inclusion in any capacity. He told people that Churchill would do far less harm outside than inside, and that he feared his support more than his opposition."[7]

Churchill threw himself into his new duties with gusto, and one intervention in Parliament resulted in Stanley Baldwin writing to King George V on December 18, 1924: "The whole [H]ouse was enthralled by his speech. It was Mr. Churchill at his best, full of confidence and fight, crushing yet good humoured in the scorn which he heaped upon his opponents, never at a loss for a word and full of eloquence and power which cannot be surpassed by any Member sitting in the House of Commons."[8]

Churchill now had the opportunity of furthering the social problems that he and Lloyd George had pioneered. In his first budget, in 1925, he introduced pensions for widows and orphans from the moment of their bereavement, and he reduced the age for old age pensions from seventy years to sixty-five years.

There was also a major undertaking — from the prior chancellor — on which a decision had to be made. Churchill was guided by experts, including Montague Norman, the governor of the Bank of England, and despite misgivings Churchill took their advice and in the budget he announced that Britain would return to the gold standard. This resulted in an increase in the cost of British exports, with a corresponding reduction in their volume. The result was increased unemployment. Labour issues would soon be a major source of problems for Churchill.

Despite King's success in London, he soon had domestic problems to contend with. Initially, all seemed well. After his success at the Imperial Conference, he came back to Canada and its Parliament with an improved stature and increased self-confidence, although he still needed to tread carefully with his cabinet colleagues, since only two of them were younger than he was.

In early September of 1925, he announced that a general election would be held on October 29, 1925. The campaign promised to be a fraught one, as he was plagued by a scandal in the Department of Customs and Excise, regarding smuggling from the United States, with senior department officials involved. King, with the intent of diffusing a situation that could affect the election, appointed a nine-man committee to examine the matter. This achieved his short-term objective of deferring the matter until after the election.

The election was a disappointment for the Liberals, and resulted in the Conservatives holding 116 seats, the Liberals holding 101 seats, with the balance of power being held by the Progressives, with 24 seats. It would have been expected that King's Liberals would step down in favour of Meighen's Conservatives; however, that was not what happened. King wooed the Progressives, who gave him a degree of comfort, but it was evident that he would have to tailor his policies to suit that party.

King also made overtures to two Labour MPs: J.S. Woodsworth and A.A. Heaps. On January 7, 1926, they responded by enquiring if he was intending to introduce legislation to provide insurance for the unemployed, and pensions for the elderly.

Even though these measures had not been included in the Throne Speech, he answered in the affirmative. True to his word, the legislation was introduced in March 1926, and was promptly passed by the House of Commons two months later. The bill, however, was defeated by the Senate. Although the senators earned a sizable pension themselves, they reasoned that it was the job of each family to look after the elderly. Legislation was reintroduced in 1927, and this time was passed by both the Commons and the Senate.

The committee reported on the Customs Department, and it showed that there was widespread corruption. A vote of censure on the government was put forward. King tried all he could to delay and then defeat the motion, but he eventually had to admit that he could not continue. He had a number of choices, and decided that, rather than face certain defeat in the vote of censure, he would approach the governor general with a request that Parliament be dissolved. This led to a major confrontation that has found its place in the history books. To this day there are different opinions as to the role of the governor general, Lord Byng, and the decision he made in this matter.

Byng was a pleasant and affable gentleman, and King got on well with him. However, Byng was astonished that, only some eight months since the election — at which the Conservatives had won more seats — and five months since the commencement of the parliamentary session, King would approach him to dissolve Parliament and call for another election. It seemed that an unbridgeable difference of opinion was developing.

There are twelve pages of King's diary devoted to the events of June 26, 1926. After meeting with his cabinet, which agreed with his approach, King visited Byng and advised him that it "was the constitutional duty of the Governor General to give a dissolution on the advice of the Prime Minister; [that] this had not been refused in 100 years in British history nor since Confederation in Canadian history; that it was not advisable to ask him to call on Mr. Meighen as [King] did not think that Mr. Meighen could carry on."

King recounted Byng's response: "He hoped I would not ask for a dissolution as he did not see how he would be able to grant it.... I had had my chance; that to allow me to use the powerful machinery of Government control for another election would not be fair to my political opponents; without using the words, he intimated that it was for him to see that each side got its proper chance."

Using his well-honed negotiating ability, King endeavoured to change Byng's mind, but he failed. On June 28 King resigned as prime minister and Meighen took over. As correctly predicted by King in his meetings with Byng, the Meighen-led Conservative government failed, lasting only from June 28 until July 1. However, this was after a bizarre incident where a dozing Progressive MP, paired with a Liberal, suddenly woke up and voted the wrong way in favour of King's motion of non-confidence. If he had not done so, the vote would have been tied and the Speaker would have had to cast the deciding vote.

Meighen approached Lord Byng for a dissolution of Parliament, which put Byng in the difficult situation of having to grant Meighen a dissolution that he had refused to King. In his diary of July 2, King recorded that the "Governor General's constitutional duty was to send for me," but after failing in his endeavour to persuade Meighen to resign, Byng reluctantly granted the dissolution.

In his diary of July 2, King tells of being advised of Byng's decision, "No words can express the relief I feel at the turn things have taken. I was dreading the task of returning to office having to complete business of [Parliament] and then go to the country." Nevertheless, he continued, "I felt it was the constitutional duty of Lord Byng to send for me — I could not believe he [would] deliver himself so completely into my hands.... It must have been the spirit of my grandfather working through me which caused me to press on & on."

King took full advantage of the constitutional question by presenting himself to the electorate as the defender of Canadian interests against an antiquated colonial mentality. The general election was held on September 14, 1926, and the result was a turnaround, with the Liberals winning 116 seats, the Conservatives 91, and the other parties 38; there was a minority Parliament again.

So the King-Byng affair was over. History has, in most peoples' opinion, shown Byng to be right about the first decision not to grant King a dissolution. On the second decision, not to go back to King, but to grant the dissolution to Meighen, there has been a mixed reaction. This writer's opinion is that Byng was wrong.

While King was embroiled in a political maelstrom in Canada, Churchill had a major problem of his own to contend with. The coal industry had been granted a subsidy from the government, but the mine owners claimed that this was not enough for an adequate level of profitability. They stated that they required the miners' union to accept a reduction in wages. This demand was rejected by the union; the owners responded by stating that the miners would be locked out on May 1, 1926.

The Trades Union Congress (TUC) called for a general strike of all industries, which occurred on May 3. Although Churchill had sympathy with the workers, the threat of anarchy, coupled with the absence of newspapers to keep the public informed, resulted in him taking an active stance against the strike in the government newspaper, the *British Gazette*. The strike lasted only a few days, and on May 13, TUC called off the strike. Eventually, the coal miners had to accept a reduction in wages, but the bitter feelings lasted.

On July 7, 1926, Churchill defended a claim by the Labour Party that the government's newspaper should have been impartial. Stanley Baldwin reported to King George V that there was uproar in the House.

> But the climax to it all came in the last sentence of Mr. Churchill's speech ... shaking his finger in a threatening manner at the Members of the Opposition, Mr. Churchill, in a House that was tense with anticipation, delivered this solemn pronouncement. "One last word ... when another trial of strength will occur and something like this will be tried again upon the country or the community. I have no wish to make threats or to use language which may disturb the House and cause bad blood. But this I must say; make your minds perfectly clear that if ever you let loose upon us again a general strike, we will loose upon you — another *British Gazette*." The anticlimax was perfect. The shouts of defiance which were waiting on the lips of the Labour Party gave way to an outburst of unrestrained laughter in which the House was convulsed.[9]

King decided that Churchill was the cause of the whole problem, although he did not explain how he came to that conclusion. His diary of May 3 makes astonishing reading: "Baldwin did splendidly till the last moment; he has been influenced by Winston Churchill against his better judgement, for his Tory instincts have asserted themselves in spite of himself. I learn at midnight tonight that the general strike has been declared. No [government] can long cope with that [—] with troops out, aeroplanes employed, etc. some fool will make a mistake. Churchill may be shot.... I feel sorry for Baldwin, for the King & many others — for Churchill I feel a scorn too great for words. He has been the evil genius in this."

Why King came to the conclusion that Churchill was responsible is not known. But King's opinion of Churchill at that time was coloured by the fact that Churchill's way of handling a confrontation, through actions and not just words, was almost the opposite of how King handled a serious situation.

With the situation in Parliament more stable, King felt confident enough to depart for England to attend an Imperial Conference. Ironically, one of his first engagements on arriving in London was a Canada Club dinner, held on October 18, 1926, in honour of Lord Byng at the Savoy Hotel. There he was seated with the Prince of Wales (the future King Edward VIII) on one side and Winston Churchill on the other. His diary recorded the event: "I had pleasant conversations with the Prince and Churchill.... Churchill and I talked of the Byng episode, and I found his attitude was that Meighen should have advised the Governor General to send for me; that he thought he was much to blame in not having done so after Meighen had been unable to carry on. He said that he was glad that I had not attacked Byng or brought the British Government into it."

King's diary goes on, recording a further conversation at the dinner, concerning the matter that had caused King to explode in a vitriolic outburst in his diary just six months prior. Churchill, referring to the coal strike, said: "Speaking confidentially and very privately, the employers had been a damn selfish lot; that there was a stage when, if they had been at all decent, all parties could have been brought together; this was when the general strike began."

King recorded giving advice to Churchill that the government should not have let the issue become one between the government and labour. Churchill responded that they were faced with a revolution, and that if the general strike had succeeded, the government itself could not have stood. But he was very proud of the fact that not a shot had been fired and that no one had been injured.

Churchill spoke at the dinner, and King's attitude to him showed a remarkable improvement, no doubt due to Churchill's comments on the Byng confrontation, as he recorded: "Churchill's was a great effort and very suitable; it gave evidence of real oratorical power."

After his endeavours at the 1923 conference, King found himself, three years later, in the unusual position of defending the Empire and Commonwealth against the hard line of James Hertzog, the South

African prime minister, who put forward a resolution arguing for "the fundamental facts of the Dominions' independent status and mak[ing] these facts known to the world."[10]

Lengthy deliberations and meetings ensued, with the end result being the Balfour Declaration, which stated that the United Kingdom and the Dominions: "are autonomous Communities within the British Empire, equal in status, in no way subordinate one to another in any aspect of their domestic or external affairs, though united by a common allegiance to the Crown, and freely associated as members of the British Commonwealth of Nations."

King had played a significant part in this successful conclusion, and now he could put forward his own resolution regarding the role of the governor general. He did not want a repeat of the Chanak embarrassment, due to communications between Britain and Canada having to be routed via the governor general. His proposal was accepted, with the final report declaring that the governor general was the representative of the Crown and not an agent of the British government. The report also stated that the official line of communications should be directly between governments in future, and promised that the existing procedure would be changed in any Dominion that desired it.

King's position, that Canada was an independent nation, as well as a proud member of the British Commonwealth, was by no means shared by many Canadians. Churchill was also concerned with the change in the relationship of the Dominions to the motherland.

His attitude is illustrated in King's diary of January 25, 1928, where he recalls a conversation with Leo Amery, the colonial secretary, who was involved with the negotiations which led to the declaration. "I had a good talk with Amery of the last conference. He said Balfour & he were the only ones at the outset who favoured 'equality' of status. That Winston Churchill was furious.... He liked to rule over people.... Churchill & others did not like His Majesty['s] Br[itish]. Gov[ernmen]t & H[is]M[ajesty's] other Governments; they wanted only H[is] M[ajesty's] Gov[ernmen]t in England."

6

OPPOSITION AND THE RUMBLINGS OF WAR

The final years of the 1920s in Canada were placid, with a stable Liberal government and budget surpluses. A memorable event occurred on July 1, 1927. On that day, marking the sixtieth anniversary of Confederation, elaborate ceremonies were held on Parliament Hill as well as in most towns and villages across the country. For the first time in the country's history, a national radio hookup was created, which allowed King's remarks, spoken at the Ottawa ceremony, to be broadcast across Canada. In his remarks King traced the history of the country, speaking of its development from a time when it "was a primeval forest, unknown to the civilized world," to more recent times, when, because of its sharing "in the sacrifices of the world's war," it had been able to take an active part in shaping "the terms of the world's peace." He concluded by saying that "in the larger Councils of Empire her position has been increasingly acknowledged," and that "it has been accorded the highest recognition in the League of Nations as well."[1]

Canada had been elected to the Council of the League of Nations, and the following year King headed across the Atlantic Ocean to address the assembly. Many of the themes and subjects that he had touched on in his Dominion Day speech found their way into the talk he gave in Geneva on September 7, 1928. His diary relates that he was a little nervous, but his speech on the importance of the League and the lessons that Europe could learn from Canada's example was well-received.

The next day King went for a few days to the French spa town of Aix-les-Bains. He met the former (and future) British prime minister Stanley Baldwin, who was taking the waters. They discussed the British electoral scene and its people, with Baldwin telling King that he thought highly of Churchill. The following day the diary recorded a further conversation with Baldwin: "He speaks of [Churchill] as most companionable, coming to his room at 10 Downing Street, each day walking up & down with cigar and water. He read me part of a letter from him [in which Churchill relates his time spent] re-laying bricks and writing a book."

King took the opportunity of his stay in Europe, where he had few official engagements, to take an extended holiday. On September 25 he arrived in Rome and decided to call on the Italian Fascist leader and dictator, Benito Mussolini. His diary recorded the meeting, with Mussolini expressing interest in Canada's governance, although it was clear that the Italian leader knew little of the country — he was surprised that Canada was not still tied to Britain, and that Canada had a legation in the United States. King also noted that Mussolini was surprised that the population was not mainly of French extraction.

King was not distracted by Mussolini's lack of knowledge of his country. In his diary he stated: "The impression he made upon me was a very real and vivid one. He was more sparse in appearance — eyes very dark.... There was evidence of sadness & tenderness as well as great decision in his countenance.... I would not have missed this conference for anything."

With the benefit of hindsight, King's lack of concern about the nature of Mussolini's Fascist dictatorship can be criticized, but in the 1920s, after the bloodbath of World War I in the previous decade, the idea of a benevolent dictatorship was widely popular. Winston Churchill had met with Mussolini twenty months before King, in January 1927, and, while his subsequent press statement was couched in diplomatic niceties, there is no doubt that Churchill was also impressed. He mentioned Mussolini's charm and his dedication to the well-being of the Italian people, and, "his triumphant struggle against the bestial appetites and passions of Leninism."[2]

The British ambassador to Italy, Sir Ronald Graham, wrote to the foreign minister, Austen Chamberlain, on the press release of Churchill's statement on January 21: "Mussolini was delighted with it, but I cannot say the same as regards the Russian press representative!"[3]

As expected Churchill's statement was vehemently criticized by the Labour press in Britain, and also by a former Liberal MP, the influential editor of the *Manchester Guardian*, C.P. Scott. While Churchill's hatred of Communism was the primary reason for his enthusiasm, it is difficult to understand how he could have been blind to the dangers inherent in a system where all power is held by one person.

Churchill was not the only one in Britain who was unconcerned, however. In July 1928 the British Committee of Imperial Defence proposed what was known as the "Ten Year Rule," whereby defence spending for the coming year was based on the assumption that there would be no European war expected for a decade. This was to be reviewed annually.

The review the following year gave an inkling of what was to come, with reports that Germany had developed a new battle cruiser, with better manoeuvrability and more fire power than conventional ships at the time. Even this news did not generate disquiet, though — the more immediate matter in Britain was Baldwin's announcement of a general election for May 30, 1929.

The election resulted in a victory for Ramsay MacDonald's Labour Party, although it was forty-two seats short of a majority. Churchill was returned at Epping, but now he was out of office, after four years in the public eye as chancellor of the exchequer.

Churchill took advantage of what he hoped was just a hiatus from government by embarking on a journey to Canada and the United States, with his son, Randolph, his brother, Jack, and Jack's son, Johnny. Before leaving he had written to Beaverbrook: "What fun it is to get away from England and feel no responsibility for her exceedingly tiresome and embarrassing affairs."[4]

The four crossed the Atlantic Ocean on the *Empress of Australia*. Churchill, writing to Clementine on August 12 of his arrival in Quebec City, described the Château Frontenac as "a tremendous hotel on the most modern lines." He visited the tourist sites of the Citadel, Wolfe's Cove, and the Plains of Abraham, "where the battle which decided the fate of Canada was fought," and then went by car into the countryside, as he "wanted to see the country at close quarters and nibble the grass and champ the branches." After leaving the confines of England, he wrote of the "immense size of this country which goes on for thousands of miles of good fertile land, well watered, well wooded, unlimited in possibilities. How silly for people to live crowded up in particular parts of the Empire, when there is so much larger and better a life open here for millions."[5]

Randolph kept a diary, recording his impressions of the trip: "From our window we can see at night the Rothermere Paper Mills all lit up. Papa said apropos of them, 'Fancy cutting down those beautiful trees we saw this afternoon to make pulp for those bloody newspapers, and calling it civilization.'"[6]

They proceeded across the country in a special rail car, which the CPR had made available for them. Churchill spoke in Montreal and Ottawa, and wrote to Clementine of the overflowing, enthusiastic audiences. He noted that "the Prime Minister, Mackenzie King, has been most kind and cordial. We all went out and lunched at his small country place about fifteen miles from Ottawa." Churchill toured the House of Commons, and was impressed. "It seems to be much more sumptuously looked after than ours. Mackenzie King took us around everywhere, we climbed the towers, rang the carillon, which is one of the finest in the world, etc."[7]

King's diary recorded Churchill's visit to Kingsmere and his keen interest in the construction of the dams. The next day, August 15, the diary stated, of Churchill's luncheon address to the Canadian Club: "Churchill made a very good speech, touching just the two themes, Naval parity [between the] U.S. & [Great Britain] & Inter-Empire trade, closing with a very fine and very true peroration re 'united we stand, divided we fall' re British Empire." King also wrote of Churchill's method of carefully preparing speeches, noting how he dictated his books, then revised them, often six times. "Says his books [on World War I] *The [World] Crisis* have paid well; 40,000 pounds thus far."

The diary then covered Churchill's visit to the Parliament buildings, with King adding, "He took pleasure being seated in my chair at the council table and in the [House of Commons]." The diary goes on to show the further improvement in King's opinion of Churchill: "Throughout the

Library and Archives Canada PA 126203

Churchill and King at Moorside, August 14, 1929.

visit yesterday and today he was exceedingly pleasant and companionable. A fine mind, nice nature.... Have really much enjoyed his visit and society."

The following day's *Ottawa Journal* reported that Churchill was greeted with loud applause. The paper reported that in an address to the governor general, Churchill stated, "And I am glad to sit next to my old friend, Mr. Mackenzie King, your Prime Minister, with whom I have, ever since the year 1907, been brought repeatedly in contact in matters of national or Imperial importance." He referred to the World War I battle of Vimy Ridge, at which the Canadian army had gained an important victory, which drew loud applause. Then he acknowledged the change in the relationship between Britain and Canada: "The ties which join this great country to the Mother Country are more flexible than elastic, stronger than steel and tenser than any material known to science." He finished with a theme which would be further emphasized in World War II. "Canada bridges the gap between the old world and the new, and unites the world with a new bond of comradeship."

The *Ottawa Journal* also included King's comments at the luncheon: "We welcome him for his great personality and remarkable ability. But above all for his great services to the Empire and the world at the time of the world's great crisis. His career is one that fills the minds of men, communities, and of nations with admiration. It is a source of pride to us that he should, with his first free moments, come to Canada to give us the benefit of his great experience."[8]

Following his visit to Ottawa, Churchill continued to Toronto, where he spoke to a combined luncheon of the Empire Club, the Canadian Club, and the Toronto Board of Trade. His speech was heard by three thousand people by way of loudspeakers placed outside the Royal York Hotel, which advertised itself as "the largest Hotel in the British Empire." Present were both the premier and lieutenant-governor of Ontario, as well as the mayor of Toronto. The *Toronto Star* newspaper reported, "He roused his vast audience to applause as he spoke of the ties of love that bind the overseas dominions to the motherland ... long before the hour set long queues formed outside the banquet hall ... it was to be the biggest event of the kind in Toronto."

One prediction made by Churchill in that speech was sadly not to come true: "I believe that President Hoover was right when he said that peace was assured for fifty years."

Afterwards Churchill wrote to Clementine: "I have just come back from the Toronto Meeting — A tremendous affair. I made my best speech so far. Tonight we go to Niagara, see the falls tomorrow at 7 a.m., then back here for a large luncheon — then off for 36 hours run to Winnipeg. More speeches — too much!"[9]

In Calgary Randolph's diary recorded visiting the oilfields. He decried the actions of the oil magnates, which he felt were "pigging up a beautiful valley," and criticized the oilmen for their lack of culture. "Instantly Papa flared up, 'Cultured people are merely the glittering scum which floats upon the deep river of production.' Damn good!"[10]

The Churchills stayed at the Banff Springs Hotel, and Winston wrote to Clementine: "I have been wonderfully received in Canada. Never in my whole life have I been welcomed with so much genuine interest & admiration as throughout this vast country.... I am profoundly touched; & I intend to devote my strength to interpreting Canada to our people & vice versa; & to bringing about an even closer association between us."

Library and Archives Canada C 077605

Churchill with son Randolph, brother Jack, and nephew Johnnie in Calgary, Alberta, August 24, 1929.

Then he wrote of his great attraction to the country and of the opportunities it offered: "I have made up my mind that if [Neville Chamberlain] is made leader of the [Conservative Party] or anyone else of that kind, I [will] clear out of politics & see if I can make you and the kittens a little more comfortable before I die." He spoke of his remaining ambition, which was to become prime minister of Britain, stating that, "if that were barred, [he would] quit the dreary field for pastures new. As Daniel Peggotty says, 'There's mighty lands beyond the seas.' However, the time to take decision is not yet."[11]

Was Churchill serious? Probably not — he never acted on this statement, despite his upcoming lonely decade in the House of Commons that would have given him every reason to move to Canada. Civilization can be grateful that he stayed in Britain and was the dynamic presence called on to rally the country and its Dominion allies to withstand the German onslaught.

—»—

The relatively placid period enjoyed by King, Churchill, and the rest of the world was given a sudden jolt on October 29, 1929, with the stock market crash on Wall Street. King was not personally affected — his careful management of his finances caused him to eschew the risk of stocks, and so he had all his savings in government bonds, which continued to pay a dividend. Churchill, however, had placed much of his savings into stocks, and he suffered a major loss.

The suffering of Churchill paled, though, in comparison to most in the world. The aftermath of the crash was devastating for the many who saw their life savings disappear. A great many also lost their jobs, when thousands of businesses went bankrupt. To make matters worse, a major drought occurred in North America. The drought resulted in the failure of many farms. Even those farms that were able to grow something suffered, since the widespread poverty lessened demand, causing the price of produce to fall. As a result, even the little that was grown often spoiled since it could not be sold.

Unemployment in Canada, which was 116,000 in 1929, rose to 371,000 in 1930. King took the view of the bankers and industrialists, who felt that the situation was a temporary one. When people pressed the government to take some action, he countered that it was not the federal government's role to assist the unemployed; that was the responsibility of the provincial governments, King claimed.

There was no central bank to help manage the economy in 1930, and Keynes's concept of deficit spending was unknown at the time (Keynes would not publish his theory until 1936). The federal government's sole responsibility, according to general thinking (and King certainly concurred with this), was to prudently manage the country's finances. This approach was illustrated by the finance minister's announcement on May 1, 1930, of a budgetary surplus of forty-seven million dollars.

In the midst of all of this economic turmoil, King had to face the people. A general election was held on July 28, 1930. King's campaign centred on the government's record over nine years, and he was confident that he would be rewarded by the electorate. The Conservative opposition, led by R.B. Bennett, concentrated on unemployment and their plan to generate jobs.

The vote resulted in a major turnaround in Canadian politics, with the Conservatives obtaining 137 seats, the Liberals 88, and the minor parties and independents 20. There was a clear Conservative majority.

Both Churchill and King were now on the sidelines, politically speaking, with King serving as leader of the opposition, while Churchill held the post of the Conservative shadow chancellor of the exchequer. Thus, both were relieved of the responsibility of reacting to the Great Depression.

However, King was disappointed that he could not attend the Imperial Conference in the fall of 1930. This meeting was to finalize the work of the previous conferences in 1923 and 1926, at which King had been a primary force in establishing the independence of the Dominions. King was concerned that Bennett would undo his work; his fears proved groundless, however, and the Statute of Westminster, passed in 1931 as a result of the conference, clearly laid out that the Dominions were self-governing countries. While King was gratified at the outcome, he resented Bennett taking the glory for the work that he, King, had done.

King has been credited by some with a mystic power in ensuring his own defeat, but it really was just a matter of luck. Interestingly, despite the loss, there was little pressure for a change in the leadership of the Liberal Party, which is indicative of the hold that King had established after eleven years in that position, almost all as prime minister. In opposition, King was satisfied to limit himself to criticizing Bennett on his inability to meet his pre-election promises; King had no alternative policy to meet the growing problems caused by the Depression.

Across the Atlantic Ocean, Churchill was confronted by a problem of a different sort: independence for India. A national government had been formed in Britain in August 1931, which united most of the members of the Labour Party and the Conservative Party. Among other positions formulated by the united group was a policy that cleared the way for India to work towards Dominion status for itself. Churchill was opposed to this, and he made seven speeches on the matter, which were published in a book *India*. The speeches outline his objections to the granting of Dominion status to India. One of his main objections was his fear that the antagonism between the two major religions — at the time India had a population of 350 million, which was divided between 280 million

Hindus and 70 million Moslems — would result in an unstable country. This instability was exacerbated, Churchill felt, by the caste system used by the Hindus, whose population included sixty million "untouchables," the treatment of whom Churchill strongly criticized.

Even staunch Churchillians generally agree that he was wrong in his attitude to Indian aspirations. While the terrible bloodletting that he predicted did occur, he should have accepted that people have a right to govern themselves. Certainly, his attitude was at odds with his future reputation as a defender of freedom.

As a result of leading a faction of Conservatives in defiance of its leader, Stanley Baldwin, and the mainstream of the party, Churchill was asked to resign his position on the Conservative Party Finance Committee, as well as his post of shadow chancellor of the exchequer, which he did on April 2, 1931.

Relieved of responsibility Churchill threw himself into his writings, producing a very well-received autobiography of his formative years, *My Early Life*. He sent a copy to King, who recorded in his diary, "an exceedingly nice letter."

Later that year Churchill sailed to the United States to give a series of lectures, with the intent of recouping his stock exchange losses; however, on December 13, 1931, he was struck by a taxi in New York City, and experienced a long and painful period of recovery, which put back his speaking tour.

He recommenced the tour on January 28, 1932, with a stop in Toronto on March 3, where he spoke at Maple Leaf Gardens in an event sponsored by the Simpson's department store. The fee to the speaker was the princely sum of $2,500. The arena had been built the year before, and Churchill was the first person of international renown to speak there. Despite newspaper hype and ticket prices of less than a dollar, the audience totalled only six thousand, which was a disappointment. Churchill had used lapel microphones during his U.S. tour, but the hockey broadcaster Foster Hewitt warned him that using such a device with the Gardens sound system would cause an echo. "Churchill turned to Hewitt and said, 'Young man, if I want your advice I will ask for it.'"[12] Hewitt was right and Churchill discarded the lapel microphone, but he also refused to use the stand-up microphone, and, thus, many could not hear him.

Shortly after his speech in Toronto, Churchill lunched with King at Rideau Hall. King's diary recorded that he was dreading the affair, although he did not give his reason. However, King noted, "It turned out to be quite the most pleasant and profitable visit to Government House, since His Excellency's arrival.... Churchill talked in an agreeable & interesting way at the table re his seat in [House of Commons]. He had thought of sitting with [the Liberal] Opposition on front bench; as a Privy Councillor he had a right to a front bench. His present arrangement was a 'landlord & tenant' one ... he got the seat when no one was there & when he wanted to speak!"

The diary goes on to record their conversation regarding two subjects that King was touchy about: the Byng incident, and Chanak. Churchill repeated his opinion that after Meighen's government had been defeated, Byng should have called on King. This was a subject on which the two could agree. On Chanak, which obviously was a matter of some embarrassment to the then colonial secretary, King wrote that Churchill admitted that he (King) was right. According to King: "He could see I could not have done otherwise."

The two discussed the upcoming Imperial Economic Conference in Ottawa, set for July 1932. King was still suspicious of Britain's intentions, even though the Statute of Westminster had clearly established Canada's independence. His diary stated, "We talked re the forthcoming conference. I told him all centralized efforts [would] be a failure, that a decentralized Empire was the only form it could take ... we would never agree to any central council regulating tariff or other affairs."

In late 1934 King went on a two-month holiday to Europe to relax and fortify himself prior to the upcoming election — one would have to be held in 1935, the end of the Conservative government's five-year term. He met with prominent people, including the prime minister of the national government, Ramsay MacDonald, and the lord president of the council, Stanley Baldwin, and on October 26 he travelled to Chartwell in Kent, Churchill's home.

WINSTON CHURCHILL *and* MACKENZIE KING

When King arrived Churchill was in an ebullient mood, as he had just been informed that the national government candidate had been defeated at a by-election. Churchill stated that he was opposed to coalition governments, and was sure that the present government would soon have to go. He, of course, would inherit a coalition government in 1940, and this worked well for the country. On the other hand, in Canada, King strongly resisted this form of government, as he felt that allowing one would bring people of a different persuasion into his highly regulated administration.

Churchill was still actively opposed to Indian self-government, and King's diary recorded him stating, "The Conservative Party will not stand for what they [the Indians] want in India. He clearly hopes to divide the forces in the coming [Parliament]."

The diary also included an accurate Churchill prediction, which showed his change of opinion from that of five years previous. "He thinks Germany is heading for war; a certainty & may come in 2 to 5 years. Says army in control in Germany, they get all the food they need, all they want etc. & certain to be a powerful tyranny."

King included his own side opinion on the certainty of war: "Of this I am not quite sure."

While Churchill was apprehensive of the Germans, he was not so worried about the Italians. He accurately predicted that "Italy [was] not likely to be so formidable." His estimation of Mussolini, which had been so positive in 1928, had now changed. According to King: "Mussolini he regards as a dictator."

Churchill reciprocated the tour that King had given him of Kingsmere in 1929, and took him around Chartwell. King's diary recorded that he was most impressed with the house and gardens, including the wall that Churchill had built, which had been modelled after the wall around General Wolfe's property in the nearby village of Westerham.

King went on to visit France and Italy, and although he did not meet Mussolini this time, he was not persuaded by Churchill's opinion of the dictator. He recorded on November 5: "I find myself admiring him increasingly — a man of ideals for the people — with labour on his side — giving it dignity & much of its own rights. I feel he has helped to inspire me to noble effort & given me what I need in going back to take up reform of Industry and Humanity!"

Less than a year later King would have a much different opinion.

Interestingly, King's diary at this time does not touch on the possibility of war, and any concerns he might have had about a threat from Germany is not evident. This contrasts with Churchill, who was increasingly anxious about Hitler and his intentions, and the lack of a positive response from the British government. Churchill's influence with the Conservative Party hierarchy continued to be adversely affected by his vehement speeches against the India bill, which continued until July 1935, when the bill became law. After ceding that battle, he was able to concentrate on his warnings, which accelerated as the country and the world moved inexorably to war.

7

THE COMING OF WAR

With a federal election due in 1935, the Bennett government was still endeavouring to find some way of leading the country out of the Great Depression. Despite its efforts the situation remained bleak. Unemployment had climbed from 371,000 in 1930 to 826,000 in 1933, the peak of the slump. Even then things had improved only slightly, and Bennett had no real plan for how to solve the country's economic crisis.

King had a strong belief in fiscal prudence; he certainly did not subscribe to the theory of deficit spending. He adopted a policy of wait and see: not criticizing any of the remedial attempts put forward by the Conservatives, while not promising any other measures. When the election was announced to be held on October 14, 1935, he counted on the unpopularity of the Bennett government to assist him in ensuring the return to power of the Liberal Party. The Liberals ran a campaign with the slogan "King or Chaos," and this was enough to convince the voters that anything was better than the Bennett administration. It was a stunning success: the Liberals achieved an overwhelming victory, winning 171 of the 245 seats, with the Conservatives reduced to just 39 seats.

Just as Canada focused on its domestic problems and the election, the world outside was similarly focused on the economic havoc that gripped the globe — most seemingly unaware or unconcerned with the rising militarism of Japan, Italy, and Germany. Churchill was alone in the ranks of senior British politicians in warning about the danger posed by this development. On November 23, 1932, he spoke on the subject in the House of Commons, saying that the members should not be deluded into thinking that all Germany wanted was equal status. "Here is my general principal. The removal of the just grievances of the vanquished ought to precede the disarmament of the victors. To bring about anything like equality of armaments ... while those grievances remain un-redressed, would be almost to appoint the day for another European war — to fix it as if it were a prize-fight."[1]

Adolf Hitler had become chancellor of Germany on January 30, 1933, and in the following year, on the death of President Hindenburg, he abolished that office and ordained himself führer, or "leader." He renounced the restrictions on German rearmament and industrialization that had been imposed by the Treaty of Versailles, and, dissatisfied with the progress of the Disarmament Treaty, he withdrew Germany from the talks on that issue. Going further, he withdrew Germany from the League of Nations in October 1933.

Germany accelerated its military production, especially in air power, while Britain was making modest expenditures on defence. Churchill continued his warnings, and on March 8, 1934, he spoke in the House of Commons: "I dread the day when the means of threatening the heart of the British Empire should pass into the hands of the present rulers of Germany.... I dread that day, but it is not, perhaps, far distant."[2]

The previous chapter included the initial gushing comments made by both Churchill and King on the "benevolent" dictatorship of Benito Mussolini. Churchill changed his opinion relatively quickly; King was to join him in his re-evaluation of the man when Mussolini set his sights on Ethiopia.

Churchill's thoughts on the subject are captured perfectly in remarks made while he was on holiday in the south of France in September 1935. When confronted by a French woman on the hypocrisy of Britain, which had built up an empire on conquests, objecting to the Italian intent, he smiled benevolently and retorted, "Ah, but you see that belongs to the unregenerate past, is locked away in the limbo of the old, the wicked days." He then changed to a serious tone when outlining his grave concerns: "With Germany arming at breakneck speed, England lost in a pacifist dream, France corrupt and torn by dissension, America remote and indifferent — Madame, my dear lady, do you not tremble for your children?"[3]

Churchill continued to warn of the dangers of Germany rearming, while the Britain government was focused on disarmament. On June 12, 1936, writing in a fortnightly letter he published that dealt mainly with issues of foreign policy and defence, he correctly predicted the puzzlement of subsequent generations regarding the world's inaction in the face of the growing threat from Germany, Italy, and Japan. "'How was it,' the historians of the future will ask, 'that these vast, fairly intelligent, educated and, on the whole, virtuous communities were so helpless and futile as to allow themselves to become the victims of their own processes, and of what they most abhorred?'"[4] He concluded that what was required was a "Grand Alliance" of all the nations who wish for peace against a potential aggressor.

In September 1936 King led a Canadian delegation to the League of Nations in Geneva. He stated that all Canadians favoured international co-operation to preserve peace, but noted that it was against sanctions, which had failed in the past. Although he had favoured the collective security offered by the League when addressing a specific incident, such as Italy's invasion of Ethiopia, he was against this being generally applied, as this could require Canada to become involved in a situation against its own interests. He stated that any decision on Canada participating in a war would be made in Ottawa and not in Geneva.

Back in London on October 21, King attended a dinner for the U.S. ambassador to Britain, Robert Bingham. King sat next to Winston Churchill, who, he wrote, "talked to me at considerable length, and quite earnestly. He said that England was never ... in greater danger, and that inside of five years, it was possible that she would be a vassal state of Germany."

Churchill spoke of the production in Germany of armaments at a prodigious rate, and that she had built up a powerful war machine. He continued, according to King, saying that Britain, on the other hand, was "all drift, drift, drift." King was obviously impressed by Churchill's rhetorical gifts and by his efforts: "It might not matter so much to him; he had done the best he could to save the situation but he believed it was coming.... He has a great intellect."

Concerns with the rearming of Germany and its intentions took a back seat in the media in October 1936. King Edward VIII had announced that he planned to marry Mrs. Wallis Simpson, an American divorcee. Baldwin handled the matter well by firmly telling the king that to remain as monarch he would have to give up Mrs. Simpson. Baldwin asked King to advise King Edward of the concerns in Canada on the liaison. They met on October 27, but the subject was not touched on. King recorded in his diary: "He ... said to me that he meant to keep England out of war at all costs. I said: 'Your Majesty, I am pleased to hear you say that' ... I said that nothing could be worse than war; that to avoid it one should be prepared to incur almost all sacrifice.'"

While Baldwin correctly judged the mood of the country relative to the matter, Churchill completely misread it. He urged patience in the House of Commons and was received with shouts of derision from all sides. He thought that, with time, King Edward would give up Mrs. Simpson, but that was not evident, and the king eventually abdicated on December 10.

Churchill's reputation in the House of Commons, already affected by his India policy, was further damaged by his attempted intervention in the abdication crisis. Thus, with his loss of credibility, his warnings of the dangers of Germany fell on deaf ears.

Britain continued to fall further behind Germany in the development of its air strength. In a debate in the House of Commons, on November 12, 1936, Churchill said, "This Government simply cannot make up their minds, or they cannot get the Prime Minister to make up his mind. So they go on in strange paradox, decided only to be undecided, resolved to be irresolute, adamant for drift, solid for fluidity, all-powerful to be impotent."[5]

A further warning of a future conflict occurred on November 25, with the signing of the Anti-Comintern Pact between Germany and Japan, which Italy later joined. Churchill referred to this as "another formidable step upon the downward road along which mankind is allowing itself to be led or forced."[6]

Despite the clear danger this new alliance presented, the British government continued to avoid confronting Germany. King had built his reputation from his early years in the Ministry of Labour as a conciliator, and so this policy of appeasement seemed the natural course.

In this, he was in line with the attitude of King George VI, and both were enthusiastic supporters of the arch-appeaser, the new prime minister, Neville Chamberlain.

Churchill was obviously very much in the minority in his desire to actively oppose German militarism, but he did have some influence, as is shown in a comment made by future Canadian prime minister Lester Pearson after hearing Churchill speak at Claridge's Hotel. At the time, Churchill had almost no support in the House of Commons, or for action on his pleadings of the perils which lay ahead. However, as Pearson remarked, "That night ... he had a captive and enthralled audience, however small. For the first time, I was exposed to the force of his personality, to the magic of his words, and to the conviction of his argument."[7]

While King was also impressed with the magic of Churchill's words, he was decidedly unconvinced by his arguments. In fact, he remained opposed to the policies that Churchill proposed. King had the opportunity of further pursuing what he thought was the better option — appeasement — when he returned to England in May 1937 for the coronation of King George VI. At a state dinner at Buckingham Palace on May 10, King was introduced to the German ambassador, Joachim von Ribbentrop, who was soon to move up in the Nazi hierarchy, when he was appointed foreign minister on February 4, 1938.

There was a common link between the two. Von Ribbentrop had travelled to Canada in 1910 at the age of seventeen, where he worked at Molson's Bank (later merged with the Bank of Montreal) in Montreal, and at other jobs across the country. He opened a small business in Ottawa in 1914, importing German wines, and he became a well-known figure in social circles. He was a frequent guest at Government House, as the governor general, the duke of Connaught, was of German heritage — in fact, he was the uncle of Kaiser Wilhelm II. However, the Canadian connection was concluded when war was declared on August 4, 1914, and Von Ribbentrop fled the city and sailed from New York back to Germany.

King's diary stated, "I found him exceedingly friendly, and pleasant both in appearance and manner. We got into the pleasantest sort of conversation together, he telling me of his life in Canada.... He asked me if I could not go to Germany, and said he would like to arrange for me to

King with King George VI in a highly informal moment during the Imperial Conference, May 11, 1937.

meet Hitler." Von Ribbentrop had stressed the seriousness of the situation to King and the necessity of appeasement; however, when Churchill joined the conversation, Von Ribbentrop's friendly attitude changed.

On May 26 King went to the German Embassy to have lunch with Von Ribbentrop, and the record of the event took seven pages in King's diary. After the niceties Von Ribbentrop explained that the aggressive steps that Germany had taken had only been from a sense of humiliation after the war. He stated that if war came, it would be "better for all of us that we had not been born; that it did not matter who won … what it would probably mean would be the destruction of all Europe, a complete destruction of civilization."

Von Ribbentrop brought up again his suggestion that King visit Hitler, and also suggested that King talk to other leading public men, such as Hess or Göring, and visit some industrial plants. King agreed.

King went on his mission on June 29. He was greeted by a guard of honour at the Hindenburg Palace before being ushered in to meet Hitler. His diary recorded King opening the conversation by telling Hitler of his birth in Berlin, Ontario. He went on to express his main desire, which was to erase the suspicions that nations had of each other, which had resulted in the increase in expenditures for military purposes. Hitler responded that in Germany they had had to do some things which they, themselves, did not like, as they had to defend themselves.

The diary continued with Hitler going to great lengths to show that he was a man of peace. In the light of his actions just two years later, Hitler's comments seem astounding, but it might be possible that from Hitler's point of view he was being truthful — as long as he got what he wanted without having to go to war, he would be a man of peace.

As King noted, "Hitler went on to say, as far as war is concerned, you need have no fear of war at the instance of Germany. We have no desire for war; our people don't want war, and we don't want war. Remember that I, myself, have been through a war, and all the members of the Government. We know what a terrible thing war is, and not one of us wants to see another war."

Still, it was clear from his conversation with King that Hitler could certainly contemplate a war breaking out. After making the same contention as had Von Ribbentrop that war would obliterate civilization, Hitler's tone changed, King observed: "While he was speaking of the possibility of war, he warned of the dangers from Russia and Communism, and there were legitimate aspirations which a nation like Germany, in her position, should have, and be permitted to develop. That if they were not permitted to develop them in a natural way, then there might be trouble."

King took the opportunity of stating Canada's position in the international sphere, and specifically as a member of the British Commonwealth, which he said greatly strengthened the peace and security for all. He emphasized that "if that peace were threatened by an aggressive act of any kind on the part of any country, there was little doubt that all parts would resent it. We value our freedom above everything else, and anything which would destroy the security of that freedom by destroying any part of the Empire would be certain to cause all carefully to view the whole."

King noted that Hitler said he could understand how that would be. King stated in his diary that he continued to impress on Hitler that "there was no thought of aggression on the part of the Empire; and we would not countenance anything of an aggressive nature on our part any more than we would wish to countenance it on the part of others." King made it clear that if Germany attacked Britain, Canada would come to Britain's aid — whether this made an impression on Hitler is not evident, but certainly it made no impact on his future decisions.

The interview concluded with Hitler giving King a mounted, silver picture of himself, personally inscribed. King wrote: "I let him see that I was most appreciat[ive] of it, shook him by the hand, and thanked him warmly for it, saying that I greatly appreciated all that it expressed of his friendship, and would always deeply value this gift."

The diary of the same day continued with King's impressions. "My sizing up of the man as I sat and talked with him was that he is really one who truly loves his fellow-man, and his country, and would make any sacrifice for their good. That he feels himself to be a deliverer of his people from tyranny.... To understand Hitler, one has to remember his limited opportunities in his early life, his imprisonment, etc. It is truly marvellous what he has attained unto himself through his self-education ... one could see how [his people], particularly humble folk, would come to have a profound love for the man.... As I talked with him, I could not but think of Joan of Arc. He is distinctly a mystic."

King's thoughts were written soon after the meeting, and he can be forgiven for his enthusiastic assessment; however, it is baffling that he could have written in that vein when he knew that the Nazis were operating concentration camps for political prisoners, and that laws had been placed on the books since 1933 to deny Jews the freedoms which the rest of the citizens enjoyed.

Winston Churchill was to have met Hitler in 1932, but he made a statement on Hitler's anti-Semitic views. "Anti-Semitism may be a good starter, but it is a bad sticker. Why should you be against a man because of his birth? How can any man help how he is born?' When this was reported back, Hitler decided not to meet his future adversary."[8]

In his book *Great Contemporaries*, published in 1937, Churchill included a chapter headed "Hitler and His Choice," written in 1935. After stating that it was too soon to form a just judgment until his life-work was complete, Churchill wrote: "We cannot tell whether Hitler will be the man who will once again let loose upon the world another war in which civilization will irretrievably succumb, or whether he will go down in history as the man who restored honour and peace of mind to the great Germanic nation and brought it back serene, helpful and strong, to the forefront of the European family circle ... the world hopes that the worst is over, and that we may yet live to see Hitler a gentler figure in a happier age."[9]

Such was not to be, of course. Adolph Hitler's plan from the outset was to bring all German speaking people into a German Reich, and this included the land of his birth, Austria. The country had experienced a civil war, which ended in February 1934, and the government was no match for the country's pro-Hitler sympathizers. Chancellor Schuschnigg attempted to avert annexation by Germany by announcing on March 9, 1938, that a plebiscite would be held on March 13. The response from Hitler was that the voting would be subject to fraud, and on March 12, German troops crossed the border, to "liberate" the country in a bloodless invasion.

The news of the invasion reaching Chamberlain was recounted by Philip Guedalla: "The grossness of his [Hitler's] crime was aggravated ...

by the indelicacy of his ambassador, Von Ribbentrop, in lunching with the British cabinet on that very day; and Mr. Churchill, who was a slightly unexpected guest, remarked to somebody that evening, 'Well, I suppose they asked me to show him that, if they couldn't bite themselves, they kept a dog who could bark, and might bite.'"[10]

At the same function, Von Ribbentrop is reported to have said to Churchill: "Don't forget, Mr. Churchill, if there is a war, we will have the Italians on our side."

This elicited Churchill's response, recollecting World War I: "My dear Ambassador, it's only fair. We had them the last time."[11]

Neville Chamberlain spoke in the House of Commons on March 14, and his comments must have been music to Hitler's ears. Rather than taking a tough stance, he advised that the British ambassador in Berlin had registered a protest in the strongest possible terms with the German government against such use of coercion, backed by force, against an independent state. Then he diffused any thought that other measures would be forthcoming by stating that the situation called not for hasty decisions or for careless words, but for cool judgment.

Hitler got away with it, and it would not be for the last time.

On March 24 Churchill stated in the House of Commons that peace could only be preserved by an "accumulation of deterrents against the aggressor." He pressed for a formal military alliance with France, as "the present rulers of Germany will hesitate long before they attack the British Empire and the French Republic if those are woven together for defence purposes into one powerful unit."

He ended the speech by reminding the MPs of his warnings in the past, and his correct prediction that future generations would be baffled at how Britain had descended into this lamentable position:

> For five years I have talked to the House on these matters — not with very great success. I have watched this famous island descending incontinently, fecklessly, the stairway which leads to a dark gulf … if mortal catastrophe should overtake the British Nation and the British Empire, historians a thousand years hence will still be

baffled by the mystery of our affairs. They will never understand how it was that a victorious nation, with everything in hand, suffered themselves to be brought low, and to cast away all that they had gained by measureless sacrifice and absolute victory — gone with the wind. Now the victors are vanquished, and those who threw down their arms in the field and sued for an armistice are striding on to world mastery.[12]

Collective security had been opposed by King, as it could take Canada's foreign policy decisions into the hands of others. His reaction is recorded in his diary entry of March 12: "I felt all along that sooner or later the annexation of Austria was inevitable.... Much depends upon whether it is possible to avoid bloodshed in Austria, and the moderation shown by the Nazi Government in dealing with those formerly in office. The danger, of course, lies in Czechoslovakia's position."

The German position on Czechoslovakia was that the three and a half million Sudeten Germans were being ill-treated by the government of that country and needed to be protected from their Czech rulers. Hitler demanded the return to the Reich of the land occupied by these people, even though this territory had never been a part of Germany. Negotiations between Germany and Czechoslovakia broke down in late May, and tension steadily increased, with German troops massing on the Czech border. Churchill called at 10 Downing Street and strongly proposed to Neville Chamberlain that an ultimatum be given to Hitler, based on the responsibility that both France and Russia had given to Czechoslovakia to come to its aid if it was attacked.

On June 18 Hitler issued a final directive for the attack on Czechoslovakia. He wrote: "I will decide to take action against Czechoslovakia only if I am firmly convinced, as in the case of the demilitarized zone and the entry into Austria, that France will not march, and that therefore England will not intervene."[13]

The message clearly showed that, even at that late stage, the war could have been prevented if Churchill's proposal had been accepted. However, based on Chamberlain's lack of action in the past, Hitler was almost sure that he would soon be able to take the next stage in his plan for German pre-eminence in Europe.

Chamberlain formulated a plan to diffuse the situation by meeting face to face with the German dictator. Hitler had little choice but to agree to meet the prime minister. On September 15, 1938, Chamberlain flew to Hitler's mountain retreat of Berchtesgaden in the Bavarian Alps. He conceded to Hitler that he had no problem with the Sudetenland being separated from Czechoslovakia; France concurred, even though it had given a solemn pledge to that country. The result of the meeting was that pressure was made on the Czech president, by the British and French ambassadors in Prague, to accede to Hitler's demands.

King wholeheartedly supported Chamberlain, as he stated in his diary entry of September 14. He issued a press release stating that he regarded Chamberlain's decision as a truly noble act and the right one. His diary

The villains of the piece — Hitler and Mussolini before the start of the Munich Conference. With Hermann Göring on the left, Rudolf Hess behind Hitler's right shoulder, Heinrich Himmler in between Hitler and Italian Foreign Minister Galeazzo Ciano.

Library and Archives Canada PA 114781

that day stated: "It is well for Chamberlain that he was born into this world, and for the world he was born into it. His name will go down in history as one of the greatest men that ever lived — a great conciliator."

A further meeting with Hitler was held in Munich. Chamberlain returned to England on September 30, and after alighting from his aircraft, he waved a piece of paper to the relieved and grateful crowd, remarking that it contained the signatures of Hitler and himself, and was a commitment from both to never go to war with each other again. He stated it was "peace with honour," and "peace in our time."

The front page of the *Toronto Star* of September 30 caught the mood of the people as the news was received: "Men and women, mostly young, stood in mid-street, frozen in their tracks until news of the agreement had been digested. Their eyes alight, faces gleaming, arms around each other, they danced happily off to celebrate the lifting of the curtain of death which hung like a black heart-stopping pall over their lives during the last week and more."

A debate on the Munich agreement opened in the House of Commons on October 3. Two days later Churchill gave one of the most intense, passionate, and significant speeches he had ever made to the House of Commons. It also was one his longest. In reading it now, one is struck by how clearly Churchill predicted the chain of events that Hitler was about to unleash, and what the British people would soon have to undergo.

Churchill commenced by paying tribute to the prime minister, then admitting that what he would be saying would be a most unpopular and unwelcome thing:

> I will begin by saying what everybody would like to ignore or forget, but which must nevertheless be stated, namely, that we have sustained a total and unmitigated defeat, and that France has suffered even more than we have. The utmost my Right Hon. Friend the Prime Minister has been able to secure by all his immense exertions, by all the great efforts and mobilization which took place in this country, and by all the anguish and strain through which we have passed in this country,

the utmost he has been able to gain for Czechoslovakia
in the matters which were in dispute has been that the
German dictator, instead of snatching the victuals from
the table, has been content to have [them] served to him
course by course.

Churchill talked of the negotiating policy of Hitler. "They can be
very simply epitomized if the House will permit me to vary the metaphor.
One pound was demanded at the pistol's point. When it was given, two
pounds were demanded at the pistol's point. Finally, the dictator con-
sented to take one pound seventeen shillings and six pence and the rest
in promises of goodwill for the future."

Churchill went on to criticize the government's initial refusal to
guarantee Czechoslovakia protection against an unprovoked aggression,
and denigrated its subsequent offer, noting that it now had not the slightest power to make it good. Then he added: "All is over. Silent, mournful,
abandoned, broken, Czechoslovakia recedes into the darkness. She has
suffered in every respect by her association with the Western democracies and with the League of Nations."

Churchill referred to the almost unanimous outbreak of relief from
the public, saying that he did not begrudge them this reaction, but
warned: "They should know that there has been gross neglect and defi-
ciency in our defences; they should know that we have sustained a defeat
without a war, the consequences of which will travel far with us along
our road." He followed with his prediction of the future: "Do not suppose that this is the end.... This is only the first sip, the first foretaste of a
bitter cup which will be proffered to us year by year unless by a supreme
recovery of moral health and martial vigour, we arise again and take our
stand for freedom as in the olden time."[14]

When a vote was taken, thirty Conservative MPs abstained, including Churchill, who remained seated.

Chamberlain continued to enjoy widespread support, but Churchill
knew that the prime minister was living in a fool's paradise. Subsequently,
during a debate on Palestine in the House of Commons, Malcolm
MacDonald, the secretary of state for the colonies, and the soon-to-be high

commissioner to Canada, "had come to a passage of which he was particularly pleased, 'Bethlehem, where the prince of Peace was born,' when Churchill's voice was heard from his seat below the gangway: 'Bethlehem? I thought Neville was born in Birmingham.'"[15]

On March 15, 1939, Churchill's prediction came true: German troops marched into Prague and occupied the rest of Czechoslovakia. Neville Chamberlain denounced the invasion, finally coming face to face with the realization that his policy of appeasement had failed.

He should have passed the prime minister's torch on to another at that time, but he did not. Surprisingly, he faced no pressure to resign; the mainstream of the party had fully backed his appeasement policy, so it was difficult to now turn against him. Also, there was no other person who could have generated an adequate level of support. Churchill, in spite of the accuracy of his predictions, remained *persona non grata,* and even Eden, who had resigned as foreign secretary in February 1938, over Chamberlain's appeasement of Mussolini, would not have garnered sufficient support.

Chamberlain knew that he had to act, and so he decided to draw a line in the sand. He released an announcement on March 31, which declared that the British government would intervene militarily if Poland's independence were to be endangered.

The action of Chamberlain shows that he accepted that his appeasement policies had failed. However, Britain's threat carried little real weight, since it was logistically impossible for it to protect Poland. Hitler apparently did not believe that Britain and France would back up their position, that is unless Germany took direct action against them. After all, Hitler had been given the Sudetenland, and he faced no military opposition when he completed the takeover of the rest of the country.

Chamberlain was being pressured by the newspapers to bring Churchill into the cabinet. An article in the *Sunday Pictorial* on April 23, which consumed all of the front and second pages, ran with the headline, "The Great Churchill Scandal," and included the question, "Why Isn't Winston Churchill in the Cabinet?" The article then proceeded to provide the answer: "The personal suspicions and fear and jealousies of others are crushing him out, and the desire of the nation is disregarded with contempt."[16]

The writer of the article, Hugh Cudlipp, wrote to Churchill on April 26, and informed him, "I have received 2,400 letters from readers. They are overwhelmingly in your favour, and I have never known such an unqualified response.... 'No more boot-licking to Hitler' is the general line of comment."[17]

Despite the unfolding events in Europe, King still considered appeasement the preferred option. In his diary of April 27, he wrote of the danger of taking Churchill and Eden in the government, stating that this could be taken by the Germans as a sign that they would be attacked, which would thus provoke them to attack first.

The European situation may have been front and centre in King's mind, but this briefly took second place to a happier event. King had proposed a royal tour in order to improve British-Canadian relations, and in May, King George VI and Queen Elizabeth arrived in Canada.

They travelled across the country, and were met by large and admiring crowds. In 1985 Queen Elizabeth, on a trip to Canada as the queen mother, stated of the tour: "I shall always look back upon that visit with feelings of affection and happiness. I think I lost my heart to Canada and Canadians, and my feelings have not changed with the passage of time."[18]

As the cliché goes, "Timing is everything," and King could not have wished for a better outcome from the royal visit. It accomplished admirably his objective of unifying the country, serving also to underline the connection between Canadians and Britain — a connection that would be crucial in considering a decision on taking the country into war on behalf of Britain.

While the visit may have helped to solidify the links between Canadians and the Crown, making it easier for King when war was finally unavoidable, King still believed that no such thing was necessary. He felt it was crucial to do everything possible to avoid war — foremost of which was keeping Churchill out of the British government. There had been an improvement in the personal relationship between Churchill and King in the 1930s, but it is clear that the Canadian prime minister was apoplectic at the thought of Churchill having high office, as this would, in his opinion, immediately result in Germany declaring war. In his diary of July 1, 1939, King stated that the radio had announced that

Chamberlain was reorganizing the government and taking in Churchill and Eden, adding that if that was true, "there will be war without doubt, & London will be bombed [within] 24 hours." He added, "I felt greatly concerned; to that moment I had never feared actual war — but if that report be true, war is inevitable."

He continued his train of thought, stating that this would be interpreted by Hitler and Göring of the intent of Britain to encircle them: "Goering hates & fears Churchill and if he and Eden are not taken into cabinet, we shall be saved a war — perhaps much and long continued discord & uncertainty — but civilization saved. If they go in — war seems to me inevitable."

We may well be puzzled by King's desire to treat Hitler with kid gloves, but he certainly cannot be accused of inconsistency — once he embraced appeasement, he stuck with it, in spite of the changing situation.

The steadily worsening climate in Europe was discussed by the Canadian cabinet on August 24. King recorded the subsequent press statement in his diary: "We regard it of supreme importance at this critical hour that the country should remain united and this can best be met by proceeding with caution with respect to every step to be taken as the situation may develop."

Germany invaded Poland on September 1, and Chamberlain issued a statement that if the troops were not withdrawn, a state of war would exist. With the invasion continuing, he gave a broadcast statement on September 3 that Britain and France were at war with Germany.

King also broadcast on that day to the people of Canada. He said that "the forces of evil have been loosed in the world.... There is no home in Canada, no family, and no individual whose fortunes and freedom are not bound up in the present struggle. I appeal to my fellow-Canadians to unite in a national effort to save from destruction all that makes life worth living, and to preserve for future generations those liberties and institutions which others have bequeathed to us."[19]

While Canada could have shielded itself behind the might and power of the United States, it is to the credit of King and his government that they saw the obligation to become involved again, for the betterment, in the long run, of mankind. Further credit must also go to King for manoeuvring the factions in his government, including ministers

Library and Archives C 016770

King, with C.G. Power, Ernest Lapointe, and Norman Rogers, broadcasts to the nation with the announcement of Britain's declaration of war, September 3, 1939.

from Quebec, into a united group, fully committed to Canada coming to Britain's side.

Canada's Parliament met on September 7, and King spoke in the House of Commons the following day, with Churchill-like phrases:

> I never dreamed that the day would come when, after spending a lifetime in a continuous effort to promote and preserve peace and good-will, in international as well as in industrial relations, it should fall to my lot to lead this Dominion of Canada into a great war. But that responsibility I assume with a sense of being true to the very blood that is in my veins. I assume it in the defence of freedom — the freedom of my fellow-countrymen, the freedom of those whose lives are unprotected in other countries, the freedom of mankind itself.... When

it comes to a fight between good and evil, when the evil forces of the world are let loose upon mankind, are those of us who believe in the tenets of Christianity, and all that Christianity means and has meant to the homes and lives of men, in the present and through generations in the past — are those of us who have reflected with reverence upon the Supreme Sacrifice that was made for the well-being of mankind, going to allow evil forces to triumph without, if necessary, opposing them by our very lives.[20]

The following day, September 9, with almost unanimous support in the House, the Canadian Parliament passed legislation declaring war. This received royal assent by King George VI on September 10.

Thus, twenty years after the end of World War I, civilization was plunged into a second conflict, more universal and destructive than the first.

8

AT WAR

On the morning of September 3, 1939, while still a backbench MP, Winston Churchill spoke in the House of Commons: "In this solemn hour, it is a consolation to recall and to dwell upon our repeated efforts for peace. All have been ill-starred, but all have been faithful and sincere.... This is not a question of fighting for Danzig or fighting for Poland. We are fighting to save the whole world from the pestilence of Nazi tyranny and in defence of all that is sacred to man."[1]

Later that day Churchill was summoned to 10 Downing Street, where Neville Chamberlain offered him his old Great War position of first lord of the Admiralty. It would have been completely understandable if Churchill had responded to Chamberlain's offer by reminding the prime minister of the warnings and pleadings that he had given over the years — warnings that may have prevented Hitler from pursuing his expansionist ambitions. But instead of declining the invitation and allowing Chamberlain to "stew in his own juice," Churchill accepted the position, which he advised his wife was better than he had expected, and he threw himself with enthusiasm into his new challenge.

The advent of war also helped to reinvigorate King. Although he was an unlikely war prime minister, especially in view of his support for the appeasement policies of Chamberlain, King seemed to find a new lease of life once the decision was finally made to go to war. He seemed full of purpose, and he recorded that when he went for a physical examination to determine if he was fit enough for the task ahead, his doctor pronounced that he was in excellent condition.

Ensuring that the country was fit for war was another thing, though. As always, there was the problem of maintaining national unity, given Quebec's traditional resistance to participating in what it thought of as England's wars. A key part of King's strategy to overcome this problem and bring Canada into the war united was his decision there would be no conscription for overseas service, and this satisfied the members of Parliament from Quebec. That province, naturally, did not have the same attachment to Great Britain as did the other provinces; but neither did Quebec have an emotional attachment to France. Whatever connection there had once been had long since dwindled away, since its association with France had ceased with the Treaty of Paris of 1763, which transferred all French possessions in Canada (except for the small islands of St. Pierre and Miquelon) to Great Britain. Nevertheless, many Quebeckers did volunteer for overseas service.

In September 1939 the Canadian army was totally unprepared for war. The government's defence expenditures had been rising in the years leading up to the war — in 1935–36, they totalled seventeen million dollars; in 1936–37, twenty-three million dollars; in 1937–38, thirty-three million dollars; and in 1938–39, sixty-four million dollars — but even the larger amounts were wholly inadequate to fund a major war.

With the declaration of war, expenditures soared. The deficiencies were quickly remedied, and training of the flood of volunteers was efficiently commenced. This resulted in the army being in a position to commit to sending an expeditionary force to Britain, with an infantry division comprising twenty thousand men to be despatched as soon as possible, and a second to be trained and sent over, if necessary.

King recorded on September 26 that Canada was to be a training ground for airmen from Australia and New Zealand, as well as from Canada and Britain. The British Commonwealth Air Training Plan (BCATP) was a major contribution from Canada to the war effort, with 131,000 pilots and aircrew trained, and the country assuming three-quarters of the total cost, amounting to $1.6 billion.[2]

Library and Archives Canada C 024696

*King signs the British Commonwealth Air Training Plan Agreement,
December 16, 1939.*

The navy was not neglected in the war effort. When war broke out, the fleet consisted of seven old destroyers and a few other vessels. By the end of the war, it consisted of almost one thousand merchant ships and naval vessels.

King's diary of October 1 referred to a "magnificent broadcast by Winston Churchill, on the first month of the war. At its close I cabled him: 'Your speech magnificent — as perfect in its appeal to the New World as to the old.'"

This was the speech in which Churchill had begun with an assessment of the Soviet Union: "I cannot forecast to you the action of Russia. It is a riddle wrapped in a mystery inside an enigma; but perhaps there is a key. That key is Russian national interest."

Commenting on the U-boat attacks on Allied shipping, Churchill went on to say that the Royal Navy was "hunting them day and night — I will not say without mercy, because God forbid we should ever part company with that — but at any rate with zeal, and not altogether without relish." He emphasized the British command of the high seas, which "will enable us to bring the immense resources of Canada and the New World into play as a decisive ultimate air factor, a factor beyond the reach of what we have to give and take from here."

On the duration of war, he said, "It was for Hitler to say when the war would begin; but it is not for him or for his successors to say when it will end. It began when he wanted it, and it will end only when we are convinced that he has had enough."[3]

On October 27 King made his first broadcast to the nation following Canada's declaration of war. He spoke of the rise of Hitler, and stated that only by overcoming the ruthless aggression of the Nazis could the world be "spared a descent into a new and terrible age of barbarism."[4] While his government colleagues were complimentary on his broadcast speeches, King was not fully satisfied, especially when comparing his talks to the oratory of Winston Churchill.

On December 17 the First Division of the Canadian Permanent Expeditionary Force began arriving in Britain (the force would not be officially named the "Canadian Army" until November 1940). "The welcoming party was led by Anthony Eden [secretary of state for Dominion affairs] and Vincent Massey [the Canadian high commissioner]. With wartime security precautions in force, the local population had no idea who were arriving until enlightened by a chorus of 'O Canada' from the ships."[5]

An arrangement had been made with the British Admiralty that no announcement would be made of the arrival until forty-eight hours later, and that the announcement of their arrival would be made first in Canada. However, the head of the British navy, Winston Churchill, made the announcement on December 18. King was furious. He contended that Churchill's motive was to "monopolize the stage for the Admiralty."

There was no time for petty annoyances, however. Germany continued to entrench itself on the Continent, and Russia was on the move too, invading Finland. In his fourth radio broadcast, delivered on January 20, 1940, Churchill began by congratulating Finland on its staunch defence against the invading Russian army, then he dwelt on the neutral nations of Europe, urging them to stand together with Britain and France. He described their current situation: "Each one hopes that if he feeds the crocodile enough, the crocodile will eat him last. All of them hope that the storm will pass before their turn comes to be devoured. But I fear — I fear greatly — the storm will not pass. It will rage and it will roar, ever more loudly, ever more widely. It will spread to the South; it will spread to the North."

Churchill ended his broadcast as he usually did on an uplifting note: "Let the great cities of Warsaw, of Prague, of Vienna banish despair even in the midst of their agony. Their liberation is sure. The day will come when the joy bells will ring again throughout Europe, and when victorious nations, masters not only of their foes but of themselves, will plan and build in justice, in tradition, and in freedom a house of many mansions where there will be room for all."[6]

Millions listened to Churchill's speech, not only in Britain and France, but also on clandestine radios in German-occupied countries. But the neutral nations continued to act just as Churchill had said. This was illustrated by Belgium, which refused to allow Allied troops to enter its country to protect the northern end of the French line of defence known as the Maginot Line.

King had now forgiven Churchill for upstaging him on the arrival of the Canadian troops a month before, as evidenced by the cable he sent him: "A magnificent interpretation of the present conflict, and its significance should deeply stir the conscience of mankind."

Churchill responded the next day: "Most grateful for your telegram of appreciation and greatly encouraged by it."[7]

Churchill was able to reciprocate the kind words several months later, when King won re-election in a landslide vote following a campaign that focused on his handling of the war effort. Following King's victory Churchill cabled King: "Sincere personal congratulations on your victory. I am very glad we shall be able to continue our work for the common cause. Fondest regards from us both. Winston."[8]

King was in need of a vacation, after the rigours of the election campaign, and he decided to combine this with a working holiday in the United States. He was well aware that the participation of the United States, in one form or another, would be essential for the Allies to win the war. It was important, therefore, to keep in close touch with President Roosevelt, and his administration.

King left by train on April 12, and in New York the next day he received an invitation from President Roosevelt to meet him at the "Little White House," in Warm Springs, Georgia. King accepted, and so as not to offend the Neutrality Act, the visit was referred to as a holiday. However, serious discussions were held over the next two days. Roosevelt was anxious to offer assistance to the Allies, but was constrained by the Neutrality Act, and by the upcoming presidential election, although at the time he was not a committed candidate. He did moot the possibility of sending "some destroyers across the Atlantic to assist Britain," according to King's diary. This would come to fruition later, after months of negotiation.

He met again with Roosevelt, this time in Washington, with Secretary of State Cordell Hull also in attendance. King's diary of April 29 recorded Roosevelt as saying, "Chamberlain and Churchill were the only two in the Government who really saw the magnitude of the problems ahead; and ... Churchill was tight most of the time."

On the matter of Churchill's drinking, Under-Secretary of State Sumner Welles, who had recently visited Britain, reported finding Churchill much the same. King added his own opinion that it was, "shameful that he should have been in this condition when Sumner Welles went to see him."

Churchill's alcohol intake has been the subject of much assessment, with Richard Langworth, in *Churchill by Himself,* referring to Churchill's "assiduous fanning of his reputation for his capacity — though only once [after a bout of Russian toasts at Tehran] did anyone testify to seeing him the worse for drink."[9]

Churchill himself commented: "All I can say is ... I have taken more out of alcohol than alcohol has taken out of me."[10] Churchill also wrote in *My Early Life*, "I had been brought up and trained to have the utmost contempt for people who get drunk."[11]

While Churchill's alcohol consumption has been a popular subject, there is no evidence that Churchill's alcohol consumption affected the performance of his duties; in fact, Churchill remained focused and productive.

He saw his problems as stemming mostly from his colleagues, not his habits. In the fall of 1939, for example, Churchill was frustrated by the Chamberlain-led cabinet in his efforts to ignore Norwegian neutrality by taking action against German ships bringing iron ore from Sweden, via the port of Narvik, in northern Norway. A landing at Narvik was eventually approved, but before the action could be successfully completed, the German invasion of Norway occurred, and the whole country was soon overrun.

In the spring of 1940, the British government was faced with criticism from the opposition parties and the press because of their handling of the war effort, and especially the Norway campaign. Churchill, who should have been the main target in his position as first lord of the Admiralty, actually became the beneficiary of the outcry.

The opposition in the House of Commons asked for a debate on the war situation and this commenced on May 7. The debate over the next two days was one of the most dramatic and momentous in the long history of the British Parliament. While Chamberlain had received strong support from the members at the outbreak of the war, it was soon clear that the mood had changed and there was widespread dissatisfaction with his leadership, including the incautious statement he had made on April 5, that Hitler had "missed the bus."[12]

The speakers included Leopold Amery, a former schoolmate of Churchill at Harrow School. He had been a colleague of Chamberlain when Amery was colonial secretary in the Baldwin Conservative government. Amery bitterly attacked Chamberlain, and quoted Oliver Cromwell's words to the Rump Parliament in 1653: "You have sat too long here for any good you have been doing. Depart I say, and let us have done with you. In the name of God, go."[13]

The former prime minister Lloyd George directed his fire and fury on Chamberlain: "He has appealed for sacrifice.... I say solemnly that the Prime Minister should give an example of sacrifice, because there is nothing which can contribute more to victory than that he should sacrifice the seals of office."[14]

Churchill had the duty of replying for the government. The future prime minister Harold Macmillan, who had been one of Churchill's few supporters in his "Wilderness Years," stated in his autobiography: "During the evening I saw Churchill in the smoking-room. He beckoned to me, and I moved to speak to him. I wished him luck, but added that I hoped his speech would not be too convincing. 'Why not?' he asked. 'Because,' I replied, 'we must have a new Prime Minister, and it must be you.' He answered gruffly that he had signed on for the voyage and would stick to the ship. But I don't think he was angry with me."[15]

Sir Henry Channon, MP, was a strong Chamberlain supporter. He was a great diarist, and he wrote that Churchill's speech was a magnificent piece of oratory but he doubted that he was fully sincere in his defence of Chamberlain and the government.[16]

The Conservatives held 387 seats in the House of Commons, which compared to Labour's 166. When the vote was tallied, there were 281 in favour of the government and 200 against; many Conservatives had voted against their party, and many others had abstained.

King was busy making appointments to his new administration, but he kept in touch with the debate in London. His diary of May 7 shows that he was still fully supportive of Chamberlain, whom he contended had done his utmost to prepare Britain for war. He also stuck to his contention that if Chamberlain had not made the agreement at Munich, it would have been disastrous to France and Britain, as they were not ready for war.

King's consistency and support of Chamberlain is commendable, but the facts do not support his belief that the period after Munich offered any advantage to the Allies. Churchill wrote on March 9, 1939, that British military expenditures were estimated to be 405 million pounds for the financial year ending on March 31, 1939, with 580 million pounds budgeted for the following year. Churchill compared these figures to those from three years earlier, in 1936, when German expenditures were the equivalent of eight hundred million pounds, and noted in the following three years the annual cost did not go below one billion pounds.[17]

On May 9 King reported in his diary the result of the non-confidence motion and added that he believed that Chamberlain would resign. He expressed tremendous sympathy for Chamberlain, whom he contended had been most unfairly treated. There was also a strange comment, stating that Chamberlain had had to bear the consequences of the failures of his predecessors to appreciate the situation in Germany. The fact was, prior to becoming prime minister, Chamberlain had, from November 1931 to May 1937, been the chancellor of the exchequer, and was undoubtedly the strong man of the government in comparison to the weak Stanley Baldwin. Chamberlain had a responsibility to ensure that Britain would, for its own security, not allow itself to be vulnerable to another country. He had been given clear information about the dangers from Germany, which had been reinforced by the warnings and pleadings from Winston Churchill, but he chose to ignore them on the basis that Britain could not afford to compete with a dictatorship.

Interestingly, and somewhat surprisingly, Churchill retained a positive opinion of Chamberlain. On the other hand, he nurtured a bitterness against Baldwin, as illustrated in a quote in Sir Martin Gilbert's book *In Search of Churchill*: "Shortly after the war, when he was asked to send Baldwin, then aged eighty, a birthday letter, he declined to do so, writing to an intermediary: 'I wish Stanley Baldwin no ill will, but it would have been much better if he had never lived.'"[18] Churchill never forgot that Baldwin had basically admitted that he had not taken the necessary action to build up Britain's defences, in light of pacifism in the country.

After the non-confidence outcome, Chamberlain decided that a national government was required, and he had not given up hope that he could continue as prime minister. However, he was clearly told by the Labour Party leaders that they would not serve under him.[19]

Chamberlain agreed to resign. The only two realistic choices for his successor were the foreign secretary, Lord Halifax, and Winston Churchill. Lord Halifax, a fellow appeaser, was the choice of King George VI and Chamberlain, but he knew his limitations. Not only was he a member of the House of Lords, but as he stated in his diary of a meeting on May 9 with Chamberlain and Churchill: "Winston would be running Defence, and ... I should speedily become a more or less honorary Prime Minister, living in a kind of twilight just outside the things that really mattered. Winston, with suitable expression of regard and humility, said that he could not but feel the force of what I had said, and the P.M. reluctantly, and Winston evidently with much less reluctance, finished by accepting my view."[20]

The following morning, May 10, the Germans invaded Holland and Belgium. Chamberlain initially thought he should stay on, but he was quickly disabused of this idea after speaking with Sir Kingsley Wood, the secretary of state for air. Thereupon, Churchill met with King George and was appointed prime minister.

King's diary of May 10 recorded his dictation of a wire to Chamberlain, expressing pride at being at his side when he assumed the office of prime minister and being at his side as he laid down the burdens of office. King also telegraphed Churchill, assuring him of the wholehearted co-operation and support of himself and his government colleagues, and wishing him vision and endurance in guiding public affairs at this most critical of all hours.

Churchill went to bed that night, and he later wrote of the challenge that he now faced: feeling greatly relieved at the change of circumstance:

> I was conscious of a profound sense of relief. At last I had the authority to give directions over the whole scene. I felt as if I were walking with Destiny, and that all my past life had been but a preparation for this hour and for this trial. Eleven years in the political wilderness had freed me from ordinary party antagonisms. My warnings over the last six years had been so numerous, so detailed, and were now so terribly vindicated, that no one could gainsay me. I could not be reproached either for making the war or with want of preparation for it. I thought I knew a good deal about it all, and I was sure I should not fail. Therefore, although impatient for the morning, I slept soundly and had no need for cheering dreams. Facts are better than dreams.[21]

9

FIGHTING FOR THEIR LIVES

King had the luxury of sufficient time to ensure that the right incumbents were given posts in his cabinet after the 1940 election. Churchill did not have that luxury when he commenced this process on May 11 of that year. His choices were also limited: he could not just pick the most suitable candidates, as the government was a coalition of three parties, and positions had to be allocated proportionately. He said, "I well appreciate the necessity of preserving the piebald complexion of my pony."[1]

Churchill was more than usually circumspect in his actions at that time, since he was acutely aware that he was "on probation," and he needed the support of the former government's cabinet ministers — in particular, he needed the support of Neville Chamberlain, who although he had resigned as prime minister, was still the leader of the Conservative Party.

King still retained his admiration of Chamberlain and his suspicions of Churchill. In his diary of May 11, he commented on how very wise Chamberlain was and how reckless the nation had been in their condemnation of him. Although King was full of admiration for Churchill's powers of oratory, he noted in his diary that he had more confidence in the judgment and guidance of Chamberlain.

On May 13 Churchill faced the House of Commons for the first time as prime minister. While he could have expected to receive an enthusiastic welcome, this did not occur. Instead, it was given to his predecessor, Neville Chamberlain — as with King, those who had supported

Chamberlain in his appeasement policy were not going to quickly change their spots.

Churchill gave a short speech:

> I would say to the House as I have said to those who have joined the Government: I have nothing to offer but blood, toil, tears and sweat.... You ask what is our policy? I can say: It is to wage war, by sea, land and air, with all our might and with all the strength that God can give us; to wage war against a monstrous tyranny, never surpassed in the dark lamentable catalogue of human crime. That is our policy. You ask what is our aim? I can answer in one word: Victory — It is victory, victory at all costs, victory in spite of all terror, victory however long and hard the road may be; for without victory, there is no survival.... But I take up my task with buoyancy and hope. I feel sure that our cause will not be suffered to fail among men. At this time I feel entitled to claim the aid of all, and I say, Come then, let us go forward together with our united strength.[2]

While these words have now become immortal, at the time they did not have a major impact on the House. The diarist Harold Nicholson just commented that it was a short speech but to the point.[3] Another diarist, Chips Channon, wrote that Churchill spoke well, even dramatically, but added that he was not well-received.[4]

Churchill was immediately faced with the German mechanized army steamrolling through Holland and Belgium. On May 16 it had broken through the Maginot Line. He flew to Paris to meet with Premier Reynaud and his cabinet, and was faced with a dejected group, who admitted that they had no plans for a counterattack.

Churchill spoke to the nation on May 19, his first public address since assuming office. There was no attempt to sugar-coat the desperate situation facing the Allies, and his final words were more of desperation than conviction: "Conquer we must and conquer we shall."[5]

Churchill knew that the "we" had to include the United States if victory was to be achieved.

The previous day, May 18, his son Randolph recounted talking with his father, who was shaving: "He half turned and said: 'I think I see my way through.' He resumed his shaving.

"I was astounded, and said: 'Do you mean that we can avoid defeat? (which seemed credible) or beat the bastards' (which seemed incredible).

"He flung his Valet razor in to the basin, swung around and said: 'Of course I mean we can beat them.'

"Me: 'Well I'm all for it, but I don't see how you can do it.'

"By this time he had dried and sponged his face, and turning round to me, said with great intensity: 'I shall drag the United States in.'"[6]

King congratulated Churchill on his speech saying that he had heard it "with feelings deeply stirred and with profound admiration and pride."[7]

The need to bring in the United States was also apparent to King, who became an ardent wooer of President Roosevelt and his secretary of state, Cordell Hull. He had already spent some time working on the issue during the working vacation he took in the United States in April 1940. This trip had resulted in criticism from some in Canada, who objected to his leaving the country at a critical time, but hindsight shows he was right to neglect domestic problems in order to improve relations between the Canadian and American governments.

On May 23 Britain requested all available destroyers be sent from Canada to protect Britain. To his credit King immediately complied, although it would leave Canada vulnerable. But he saw the big picture, and knew that the only hope for freedom at that time was that Britain should survive.

King's attitude and action shows not only his deep anglophile feelings, but also his strong sense of decency and loyalty. It could be argued that Canada was secure in the knowledge that the United States would, for its own interests, repel any attack on Canada. However, the United States did not have the fighting power then that it would have when it entered the war. Due to its isolationist position — it had refused to join the League of Nations and had adopted an attitude of no further involvement in European wars — it had allowed its defences to weaken and was woefully deficient in armaments, so relying on it for defence was not as sure a bet as one would think.

On May 24 King was telephoned by Cordell Hull, who expressed concern at the gravity of the present situation and requested that someone be sent from Ottawa to Washington for a discussion with him and someone higher up. Obviously, that person higher up was Roosevelt.

Hugh Keenleyside, of the Department of External Affairs, was sent. He reported back on May 26. King recorded in his diary his abhorrence at the position put forward by the Americans. They had decided that the French would not be able to hold out, and that Britain would not be able to bear up against the stronger German air force. Their information was that Hitler might make an offer of settlement, which would be based on Britain turning over of the whole of its empire and fleet to the Germans. The Germany navy, combined with the British navy and the French fleet, would then be much superior to the U.S. navy.

The Americans requested that King line up the Dominions to bring concerted pressure to bear on Britain to not make a soft peace with Germany, even though it might mean destruction of the country.

The American proposal, which they wished King to claim as coming from Canada, and not the United States, was that if it seemed likely that Britain was going to be defeated, then its fleet should retreat, so that it could still operate from a base away from Britain, and King George should go to Bermuda. The United States would open her ports to repairs for the British fleet, and in this way, a cordon, from Greenland to Africa, could be thrown around Germany. Though it might take a couple of years, Germany would be defeated in the end.

King was critical of the United States for seeking to save itself at the expense of Britain. He was also unhappy with the fact that, for the second time in his life, he was being asked by a President Roosevelt to put forward a proposal to Britain and act as if it was his idea. As outlined in Chapter 2, President Teddy Roosevelt had made a similar request. Now that president's fifth cousin was asking the Canadian government, through its prime minister, to again make a presentation to Britain on its behalf — while pretending that it was a Canadian proposal. Canada's role, it seemed, was only to serve as a conduit, or a linchpin, between the United States and Britain.

King spent some time deciding on the format of the communication he would send to Churchill, which, after he made up his mind, was finally sent on May 30. The message of almost two thousand words was marked "Most Secret," and sent by cipher.

King gave the beleaguered British prime minister no doubt of Canada's support, despite the serious reversals in France, and he reiterated that the government and people of Canada were more determined than ever to lend every assistance in their power to the Allied cause.

Then he turned to the all-important matter of what if anything could be expected from the United States. King referred to his visit to Warm Springs and Washington, and the intimate personal conversations with Roosevelt and Hull. He stressed that he had told them how essential it was that they give every assistance they could to the Allied cause. However, he outlined the reality of their being handicapped by public opinion and Congress. Then he raised the distasteful matter of the United States' self-interest. King had no intention of disguising the input of Roosevelt and Hull, or of sugar-coating their stance. Although King had to again state that the United States could not give immediate aid, he put forward Roosevelt's proposal that if Britain and France could hold out for some months, aid could probably then be given. But if further resistance by the fleet in British waters became impossible before such aid could be given, for ultimate victory of the Allies and the final defeat of the enemy, it was essential that it should be sent to South Africa, Singapore, Australia, the Caribbean, and Canada.

As a further encouragement to Churchill to remove the fleet out of Germany's control, King had to also convey the message that if this resulted in Germany punishing Britain with any unusual or vicious action for allowing the fleet to escape when further resistance had become useless, public opinion in the United States would demand active intervention.

It is hardly likely that Churchill would have believed that the United States was likely to change from an isolationist country to a belligerent one — particularly when faced by a Germany in control of most of Europe, including Britain. He was doubtless little comforted either by a further statement in the same telegram, that the president and Hull were quite certain that Hitlerism could not last long if even remote pressure was steadily applied. Then, again emphasizing that the fleet must not be surrendered, they expressed confidence in ultimate victory, so long as the United States was not faced with a hostile German fleet [that also included the British and French fleets] in the Atlantic, and a hostile Japanese fleet in the Pacific.

Churchill now knew, beyond doubt, that Britain could expect no military assistance from the Americans.

With only minimal support, Britain now faced the German juggernaut as it continued across France, with only paper-thin resistance. The Allied troops in eastern France retreated into a small pocket around the port city of Dunkirk. Then occurred one of the most dissected decisions in the war.

In his book *Adolf Hitler,* John Toland states that German tanks were halted below Dunkirk, as Reichsmarschall Herman Göring convinced Hitler to let his Luftwaffe finish off the Allied troops on the beach.[8] The announced intent being to preserve the Fourth Army for the final operations against the remainder of the French army, which had retreated westward.

Aided by the Royal Air Force, and with fog hampering the German bombers, a flotilla of some nine hundred ships — including some sailboats — evacuated 338,000 Allied troops, in the period from May 27 to June 4. Thus occurred the "Miracle of Dunkirk."

Toland questioned Hitler's "strange behaviour":

> Why had he given Göring the license to bomb the encircled army "to teach them a lesson," then apparently assisted in [the army's] escape by not acting forcefully? His own words only confused matters. He told his naval adjutant that he had expected the BEF [British Expeditionary Force] would fight to the last man as they had done in *his* war, and hoped to contain them until they ran out of ammunition, thus gaining for himself a mass of prisoners for use in peace negotiations.... He also told Bormann [a senior Nazi] that he had purposely spared the English. "Churchill," he complained, "was

quite unable to appreciate the sporting spirit of which I had given proof by refraining from creating an irreparable breach between the British and ourselves."[9]

To accept that Hitler could have acted as he did through tender feelings for Churchill and Britain stretches the bounds of credulity. However, his decision to allow Britain and France to evacuate almost all the army at Dunkirk to fight again was one of Hitler's biggest mistakes, and it profoundly affected the outcome of the war.

Churchill spoke in the House of Commons on June 4 and conceded that a week before he had feared that he would be faced with announcing "the greatest military disaster in our long history." After recounting the unexpected surrender of the five hundred thousand-strong Belgian army, which had exposed the flanks of the British Army, he spoke of the deliverance of the army at Dunkirk by the Royal Navy, aided by the small ships and the Royal Air Force. He balanced the uplifting news by a sobering comment: "We must be very careful not to assign to this deliverance the attributes of a victory. Wars are not won by evacuation."

The final part of the speech contained one of his most famous exhortations: "We shall go on to the end. We shall fight in France, we shall fight on the seas and the oceans, we shall fight with growing confidence and growing strength in the air, we shall defend our Island, whatever the cost may be, we shall fight on the beaches, we shall fight on the landing grounds, we shall fight in the fields and in the streets, we shall fight in the hills; we shall never surrender."

Churchill ended his speech with words that were music to King's ears: "And even if, which I do not for a moment believe, this Island or a large part of it were subjugated and starving, then our Empire beyond the seas, armed and guarded by the British Fleet, would carry on the struggle, until in God's good time, the New World, with all its power and might, steps forth to the rescue and the liberation of the Old."[10]

King rightly attributed the concluding words to the despatch he had sent. However, Churchill also rightly interpreted the American concerns as being primarily interested in saving her own skin. He was less than pleased with the attitude of the Americans to a possible collapse of

Britain, i.e., their interest in taking control of the British fleet, and the guardianship of the British Empire, minus Great Britain.

Churchill sent a message to King the following day, expressing his frustration at the attitude and actions of the United States: "If United States were in the war and England [were] conquered locally, it would be natural that events should follow the above course. But if America continued neutral and we were overpowered, I cannot tell what policy might be adopted by a pro-German administration, such as would undoubtedly be set up."

While accepting that the president was Britain's best friend, he pointed out that no practical help had been provided. He stated that he had not expected them to send military aid, but noted that they had not even sent any worthy contribution in destroyers or planes. The message requested that King continue his "linchpin" activities, and added, "Any pressure which you can apply in this direction would be invaluable." Churchill concluded by thanking King for Canada's actions in meeting his recent request: "We are most deeply grateful to you for all the help and for the [four Canadian] destroyers, which have already gone into action against a U-boat. Kindest Regards."[11]

The reference to "best friend" should really have been amended to "potential best friend," in view of the lack of practical assistance, which was desperately required. While Roosevelt has been criticized for his lack of help to Britain at that time, he had to tread carefully, as his Democratic Party had been rocked by the losses in the 1938 mid-term election. This had seen the Democrats lose 6 Senate seats, support in the House of Representatives being reduced from 334 seats to 262, and the Republican Party having an increase in representatives from 88 to 169.

Roosevelt was also constrained by the provisions of the Neutrality Act, enacted by Congress on November 4, 1939. Its aim was "to preserve the neutrality and peace of the United States and to secure the safety of its citizens and their interests." There were provisions in the act, however, that reserved the right to modify the resolution "in the interests of the peace, security or welfare of the United States and its people."

On June 6 Keenleyside was sent again to Washington — this time to pass on Churchill's message. He took with him a memorandum from King, explaining Churchill's reference to a "pro-German administration."

King stated that it should not be interpreted as meaning that Churchill was considering the surrender of Britain to the enemy, but, rather, a recognition that if circumstances made it necessary, he might be forced to go to the king, tender his resignation, and ask the king to call on someone else to form a government to negotiate terms of surrender. King continued that this was neither a bluff nor a threat made for the purpose of bargaining, but a statement made solely to make the position absolutely clear to Mr. R. [Roosevelt].[12]

In the midst of trying to negotiate between the British and the Americans, King was also kept busy organizing the Canadian war effort. Part of that effort included mustering public support, which he did through his regular radio broadcasts. On June 7 he delivered a talk, "New Situations and Responsibilities." This addressed the vast amounts of money being expended on the army, navy, and air force, the current tense situation, and new challenges, which King said Canada was proud to accept.

While King did not have the same ability as Churchill to rouse an audience, the content of his speeches and broadcasts, which he wrote himself, was not unequal. He finished the broadcast by talking of the formation of Canada from the chivalry of France and the gallantry of Britain, saying, "I speak the heart and mind of our country when I say that every fort in Canada will be another Calais, and every harbour will be another Dunkirk, before the men and women of our land allow the light and the life of their Christian faith to be extinguished by the powers of evil, or yield their liberties to the tyranny of Nazi brutality."[13]

King, who was often critical of his own broadcasts, stated in his diary that this time he was "well-pleased." As well he should have been.

On June 10 Italy declared war on Britain and France, in order to enjoy the spoils of victory, which Mussolini was convinced would soon occur. President Roosevelt spoke at Virginia University that same day and stated, "The hand that held the dagger has struck it into the back of its neighbour." He promised "to extend to the opponents of force the material resources of this nation."[14]

Churchill had still not given up hope that the United States would become militarily involved, in spite of the recent correspondence with King. He picked up on the promised material resources and asked specifically for thirty or forty old destroyers, which had been reconditioned. He added a promise, which he knew he could not fulfill: We will "return them or their equivalents to you, without fail, at six months' notice if at any time you need them." He emphasized that "the next six months are vital.... Not a day should be lost. I send you my heartfelt thanks and those of my colleagues for all you are doing and seeking to do for what we may now, indeed, call the Common Cause."[15]

At Churchill's request, Roosevelt sent a message to Premier Reynaud of France, to encourage the French to stay in the war. He stated that the United States was doing everything in its power to provide urgently needed material to the Allied governments and its efforts would be redoubled. But France needed to be assured that the United States would join the Allies in the war, and thus the message fell on deaf ears.

The United States did send some surplus military equipment, including half a million rifles, circumventing the Neutrality Act by selling them first to a steel company, which then sold the items to Britain for thirty-seven million dollars. But the destroyers would not be despatched for some time. This happened via a different route, as will be covered later.

Churchill was desperate to keep the French in the war; to ensure that they did so, he flew five times to France to meet and encourage the French cabinet. The penultimate trip was on June 11, when he met with the members of the French government near Orleans. He put to them the necessity of them continuing their resistance until the United States came into the war. However, almost all were in a defeatist frame and his persuasion came to naught.

On June 12 Churchill flew again, this time to Tours, the new seat of the French government. He was confronted with their declaration that they had no option other than to ask for an armistice, and were requesting that Britain release them from their previous solemn vow not to make a separate peace. Churchill expressed sympathy with them, but pointed out that they could continue the fight from their North African possessions. This suggestion did not bear fruit, but they did agree to send a further telegram to President Roosevelt, and ask for immediate help.

After Churchill had returned to London from Tours, he received a copy of the reply from Roosevelt to a previous request from the French.

The reply stated: "Your message of June 10 has moved me very deeply." After restating the commitment of the United States to send all the material it could, he wrote: "The magnificent resistance of the French and British Armies has profoundly impressed the American people. I am, personally, particularly impressed by your declaration, even if it means slow withdrawal, even to North Africa and the Atlantic."[16] But there was no assurance in Roosevelt's message that the United States could be expected to enter the war as a belligerent, at least in the near term — and at that time it was not a sure thing that there would be a long term.

Churchill sent a telegram to Roosevelt asking that his communication to the French be published, to attempt to steel their resolve. However, this request was denied, with the reply emphasizing that the previous message should not be construed as a commitment of the Government of the United States to military participation.

Churchill requested that King also appeal to Premier Reynaud to urge the French to continue in the war. This King did, and on that same day, June 14, he read out the message he had sent in the House of Commons: "If I know the heart of the American people as I believe I do, and as I am certain I know the heart of the Canadian people, I believe I can say to Premier Reynaud in this hour of the agony of France, that the resources of the whole of the North American continent will be thrown into the struggle for liberty at the side of the European democracies ere this continent will see itself trodden under the iron heel of Nazism."[17]

The claim by King that he was speaking not only for Canada but for the United States was out of character for him, but in his diary he justified his decision: "It was received with strong applause from all parts of the House. The part referring to the Continent, which S. [Oscar Skelton, under-secretary of state for external affairs] had wished me to leave out, was, as I had seen from the start, the part that made the strongest appeal of all. It was a bold stroke but that is what is needed at this time, and will be justified historically by the sequence of events."

The defeatist faction of the French government was now in the ascendancy, and Marshal Pétain, the soon-to-be president, rejected the British offer of an Anglo-French union as "fusion with a corpse."[18]

On June 18 Winston Churchill spoke in the House of Commons. Even accepting his mastery of the English language and his high level of production, it is awe-inspiring that he could compose a masterly presentation at such short notice, and conjure up a phrase which has gone down as one of the highlights of his many dramatic utterances.

He commenced with detailing how the collapse of France occurred. Then he addressed the state of Britain's military forces, both men and equipment. Churchill reminded the House of the strength of the Royal Navy, and stated that while the Royal Air Force was not as powerful as the German air force, it had proven itself so far to be superior. The main part of the speech focused on the ability of Britain to successfully defend itself against an invasion, and here he referred to the Dominions, reminding the House of their devotion to the mother country, and of how they felt themselves inspired by the same emotions, which would lead them to stake all upon duty and honour. He continued, admitting that Hitler would gain when he had harnessed the industries of the countries he had conquered, but stating that this would be offset by the promised assistance from the United States.

He then rallied the nation for the upcoming struggle:

> The Battle of Britain is about to begin. Upon this battle depends the survival of Christian civilization. Upon it depends our own British way of life, and the long continuity of our institutions and our Empire. The whole fury and might of the enemy must very soon be turned on us. Hitler knows that he will have to break us in this Island or lose the war. If we can stand up to him, all Europe will be free and the life of the world may move forward into broad, sunlit uplands. But if we fail, the whole world, including the United States, including all that we have known and cared for, will sink into the abyss of a new Dark Age made more sinister, and perhaps more protracted, by the lights of perverted science. Let us therefore brace ourselves to our duties, and so bear ourselves that, if the British Empire and

Commonwealth last for a thousand years, men will still say, "This was their finest hour."[19]

The reference to the United States was a further wake-up call that they could not avoid the repercussions of a Britain controlled by Germany.

On June 22 France surrendered. The terms of the armistice specified the territory that Germany would control — 60 percent of the country, including all the Channel and Atlantic Ocean ports. The signing of the agreement was, to further humiliate the French, executed in the railway carriage in Compiegne where the 1918 Armistice that ended World War I had been signed. While the locale was the same, the conditions imposed by the Nazis were much harsher.

Although France was no longer in the war, she still possessed an impressive fleet. Under the terms of the armistice, the fleet was to be demobilized and laid up under German and/or Italian control; however, the German government solemnly declared that it would not use the fleet for war purposes.

Churchill referred to the Germans' "solemn declaration," asking, "who in his senses would trust the work of Hitler after his shameful record?"[20]

Churchill and his war cabinet decided that under no circumstances would they permit the French fleet to become vulnerable to takeover by Germany. Accordingly, a decision was made, which Churchill referred to as "the most unnatural and painful in which I have ever been concerned … the French had been only yesterday our dear allies, and our sympathy for the misery of France was sincere. On the other hand, the life of the State and the salvation of our cause were at stake. It was Greek tragedy. But no act was ever more necessary for the life of Britain and for all that depended upon it."[21]

On July 3 all French vessels at Plymouth and Portsmouth were taken under British control, with minor resistance. However, the major part of the French fleet sat in ports in North Africa, and the captains of the vessels were given an ultimatum by the British navy to either join it and continue the war against Germany, sail to British ports, sail to French possessions, such as Martinique, to be demilitarized, or to scuttle their ships. If the French fleet did not comply, then the British navy would open fire and sink the ships. Compliance did not occur, and the British navy commenced the operation.

The following day, July 4, Churchill spoke in the House of Commons. He stated his sincere sorrow at the measures taken in order to prevent the French fleet from falling into German hands. But he criticized the French government for inflicting needless injury upon a faithful comrade, in whose final victory the sole chance of French freedom lay. He pointed out that France had committed itself not to make a separate peace, but, in spite of that, it had signed an armistice with Germany, which was bound to place the French fleet effectively in the power of Germany.

Churchill gave details of the action: "A large proportion of the French Fleet has, therefore, passed into our hands or has been put out of action or otherwise withheld from Germany by yesterday's events.... I leave the judgement of our action, with confidence to Parliament. I leave it to the nation, and I leave it to the United States. I leave it to the world and history."[22]

The reaction to his speech by the members was astonishing. The socialite MP "Chips" Channon, one of Neville Chamberlain's supporters, wrote: "The House rose, cheered, waved order papers — as I have so often seen them do for Neville. Only it was not little Neville's turn now. Winston suddenly wept."[23]

On July 4, 1940, the Members of Parliament, many of whom had previously had a negative opinion of Churchill, now realized that they had a leader to handle the tremendous challenge facing the country and its allies. From that day forward Churchill's position as the wartime prime minister was secure.

On that same day, King recorded in his diary his support of the action: "This is a terribly serious matter. I really think, however, that Britain is justified in seeing that the French fleet was destroyed, before it got into the hands of Germany. The condition of a separate treaty was certainly that the French fleet was not to be handed over to the enemy."

Later that day King was visited by the French ambassador, René Ristelhueber. The ambassador quoted from a memorandum he had received from the Bordeaux government, which advised of the solemn promise given by Hitler regarding the fleet; mentioning also the fact that the French themselves had adopted methods that would ensure the fleet would not be used by the Germans.

King stated in his diary: "I asked Mr. Ristelhueber if he thought any value could be attached to any promise by Hitler. He smiled at this and shook his head, but he stressed anew the methods the Bordeaux Government itself had taken. I said to him that I questioned if any methods taken by a government under the control of another government could affect anything. That I felt that the right step had been taken by the British in seeing that there could be no chance of the French fleet falling into German hands."

General de Gaulle, whom the British government had recognized as the leader of the Free French, the force committed to carrying on the fight against Germany and Italy, broadcast on July 8 on the BBC. He had thought hard before deciding on his response; but he backed Churchill's decision: "By an agreement contrary to all honour, the Government then established at Bordeaux agreed to place our ships at the mercy of the enemy. There cannot be the slightest doubt that, on principle and of necessity, the enemy would have used them either against Britain or against our own empire. I therefore have no hesitation that they are better destroyed."[24]

A side benefit of the British action, but an important one, was that President Roosevelt amended his negative opinion on the odds of Britain holding out. He now believed that Churchill's fighting words and defiance might actually have substance behind them.

10

THE TIGER AND HER CUBS

King continued to be frustrated by Roosevelt's lack of action in the desperate struggle against the might of Germany. However, while he had strong personal sympathy with Britain in its plight, Roosevelt could do little to help, since the American people were decidedly against involvement — a public opinion poll "indicated that only 7.7 percent of the population was in favour of entering the war at once and only 19 percent believed that the country should intervene if the defeat of the Allies became certain, as against 40 percent that opposed American participation under any circumstances."[1]

Further complicating matters was the fact that a presidential election was to be held on November 5, 1940, and Roosevelt had decided to take the unprecedented step of standing for a third term. To give any statement that could be construed as committing the United States to joining the war would, at that time, have been fatal to his chances of re-election. His Republican opponent, Wendell Willkie, clearly stated his position throughout the election campaign, and this was published by the *New York Times* on September 14, 1940: "Let me say to you, if you elect me President of the United States, no American boys will ever be sent to the shambles of the European trenches."[2]

In spite of the obvious concerns of the effect any action to aid the Allies might have on Roosevelt's re-election prospects, senior members of the president's staff, including Treasury Secretary Henry Morgenthau, were pressing Roosevelt to do more, as they were not optimistic of Britain's chance of surviving. However, the president had no intention of presenting Willkie with the keys to the White House and he was unmoved by the pleas. Even a letter from King George VI, who had spent a memorable day at Roosevelt's home, Hyde Park, in June 1939, had no effect.

On July 19 Roosevelt gave his acceptance speech at the Democratic convention in Chicago. He was careful not to give any indication that the United States would enter the war, but he justified his standing for a third term by referring to the crisis in the world, which threatened the kind of society the United States had become.

Hitler took comfort in the mood prevailing in the United States, as he was used to easy victories, and at that time he was in no position to challenge that major power. He also knew that he would have his hands full in fighting Britain, which still had substantial resources, and the benefit of the English Channel for protection – a formidable challenge for an invader. On July 19 Hitler spoke in the Reichstag: "From Britain I now hear only a single cry — not of the people but of the politicians — that the war must go on.... They do, it is true, declare that they will carry on with the war and that, even if Great Britain should perish, they would carry on from Canada. I can hardly believe that they mean by this that the people of Britain are to go to Canada. Presumably only those gentlemen interested in the continuation of their war will go there. The people, I am afraid, will have to remain in Britain and … will certainly regard the war with other eyes than their so-called leaders in Canada."

Hitler then came to the point of his speech — an alternative; a peace offering: "In this hour I feel it to be my duty before my own conscience to appeal once more to reason and common sense in Great Britain as much as elsewhere. I consider myself in a position to make this appeal, since I am not a vanquished foe begging favours, but the victor, speaking in the name of reason. I can see no reason why the war needs to go on."[3]

Churchill was asked by one of his staff if he intended to reply. He responded that he had no intention of doing so as he was not on speaking terms with Hitler.[4]

King had built his reputation on conciliation. But there is no evidence in King's diary of July 19 that he now, for one moment, considered that an armistice should be considered. He dismissed the notion that Hitler had a conscience: "Words cannot describe my feelings as I read Hitler's speech, particularly with its threats of extermination of the peoples of Britain. There is something terribly diabolical about a nature that could express its determination to destroy human life regardless of its innocence or extent. A man who had sold himself to the lower depths of hell could not have expressed himself more damnably."

So, King was convinced of the necessity of continuing the war, but wars, of course, are expensive, and require money and arms. The commitment of Canada to assisting in the defeat of Germany came with a substantial financial cost. Considering King's tight management of the country's purse strings prior to the war, it is perhaps surprising how easily he ignored his former frugality during the war. But the enormous expenditures had to be paid for. This was done by the issuance of War Savings Certificates and war bonds known as "Victory Bonds." There was a limit of six hundred dollars per person for the former, and, as a result, sales of those only raised $318 million. The latter had no restrictions on the amount that could be purchased, and sales of those raised the astonishing amount of $12.5 billion, with purchases almost equally divided between corporations and individuals.

Canada had denuded its own defences by sending almost all its war material and ships, as well as two divisions of its army, to Britain, where the need obviously was greatest, and it now had to rearm itself. King expected that the United States would, for its own interests, not allow Canada to be successfully invaded, but there was no agreement to that effect — something that would change.

On August 16 King recorded receiving a telephone call from Roosevelt, with an invitation to meet with him in Ogdensburg, New York. In their meeting Roosevelt stated that he had been in communication with Churchill, and was arranging to let Britain have destroyers. In return Britain was to let the United States use its bases on some of its Atlantic colonial possessions for American naval and air forces. The importance of this decision can be gauged from Churchill's attitude: During the Ogdensburg meeting, Roosevelt told King that Churchill had said that the destroyers would be as precious to the British as rubies.

The president's actions — his promise of substantial aid, even if it had to be disguised as a quid pro quo — showed that there had been a major change in his attitude from the pessimistic one of just a few weeks before. His change of heart was no doubt affected by improved feelings in the population in favour of providing the destroyers to Britain. This was confirmed by a public opinion poll showing 62 percent approval. [5]

Following the discussion of the transfer of the destroyers to Britain, the conversation moved to the matter of the defence of North America. King and Roosevelt agreed in principle on the establishment of a joint board, comprised of an equal number of representatives from each country, to study common problems of defence, and to make recommendations to their respective governments. The purpose of the board was to devise strategies for ensuring the protection of the northern half of the Western Hemisphere. By agreeing to the creation of such a board, Roosevelt was, in effect, guaranteeing that the United States would help to protect Canadian territory. The board was given the formal title of the Permanent Joint Board of Defence; the finalized negotiations that led to its creation became known as the Ogdensburg Agreement.

CBC Radio news commented on the agreement reached between the United States and Canada, describing it as "marking a new epoch ... [an] event of something more than Empire significance." It concluded that the agreement made "a real contribution to the cause of freedom."

King received many tributes for the Ogdensburg Agreement, including one from his under-secretary of external affairs, O.D. Skelton, "who said if I did nothing for the next five years for the country, I should be satisfied with what was now done." Defence Minister Ralston also praised King. He "said it had given new life to them all at the Defence Department."

The Toronto *Globe & Mail* of July 19 noted the importance of the agreement: "Good Neighbours Make History at Ogdensburg." The commentary pointed out that, "It was not one sided. Canada must assist in the defense of the United States."

One who did not appreciate the agreement was Winston Churchill, who responded to King's message by countering: "Supposing Mr. Hitler cannot invade us ... all these transactions will be judged in a mood different to that prevailing while the issue still hangs in the balance."[6]

Not only Churchill was dismayed. Arthur Meighen was furious and wrote to a friend: "Really, I lost my breakfast when I read the account this morning ... and gazed at the disgusting picture of these potentates posing like monkeys in the middle of the very blackest crisis of this Empire."[7] Meighen was living in the past. The most powerful country in the world had supplanted Britain as Canada's major trading partner. The implication of the Ogdensburg Agreement was that the United States was also supplanting the mother country as the guarantor of the security of Canada's territory. While Canada had no intention of giving up its Dominion status, the ties that bound Canada to Britain and the Empire had been loosened, and the country had moved closer to its North American neighbour.

While King and Roosevelt were accomplishing much in slowly moving the United States towards greater involvement in the war, in Europe Hitler was implementing his strategy for the necessary defeat of Britain, which was essential if Germany was to win the war. The first requirement was to defeat the Allied air force. The Battle of Britain, which had commenced on July 10, was well underway when Churchill gave a report to the House of Commons on the war situation on August 20. He was in an upbeat mood when he spoke of the success of the RAF in the battles with the Luftwaffe, and he thrilled the House with this memorable utterance: "The gratitude of every home in our Island, in our Empire, and indeed throughout the world, except in the abodes of the guilty, goes out to the British airmen who, undaunted by odds, unwearied in their constant challenge and mortal danger, are turning the tide of the World War by their prowess and by their devotion. Never in the field of human conflict was so much owed by so many to so few."

The final part of the speech dealt with the interest of the United States in having suitable facilities for the naval and air defence of the Western Hemisphere, and stated that Britain had placed "suitable sites in our Transatlantic possessions for their greater security against the unmeasured dangers of the future.... In all this we found ourselves in very close harmony with the Government of Canada."[8]

On September 1, one year to the day from when Germany invaded Poland, King gave a broadcast on the CBC, entitled "Labour and the War."

The signing of the Atlantic bases agreement by U.S. Ambassador John G. Winant, Churchill, and Canadian High Commissioner Vincent Massey in London on March 27, 1941.

He stated the tragic situation: "Millions of innocent, peace-loving, plain, ordinary, simple men and women, who have asked nothing more than to live their lives in the quiet of their own homes, and the shelter of their native valleys, have been dispossessed, robbed, and enslaved." He spoke of Canada: "a land in which men and women, regardless of race, creed, or class, can live their lives without fear." Then harkening back to his book *Industry and Humanity* of some twenty years before, he expounded its ideals in more down-to-earth language: "We have cherished the realities of freedom, which are also its ideals; the right to think, the right to speak, the right to organize, the right to work, the right to worship. We believe in the rights of man to enjoy the fruits of their honest labour."[9]

On September 11 Churchill broadcast to the nation. Comparing Britain's situation with another time in its history when it had faced the danger of invasion — with the Spanish Armada threatening and Drake finishing his game of bowls — Churchill said, "What is happening now is on a far greater scale and of far more consequence to the life and future of the world and its civilization than these brave old days of the past."[10]

King was moved by the broadcast, and he wrote to Churchill assuring him of Canada's continuing support to the utmost of its strength.[11]

Churchill responded and was quoted by King in the House of Commons, on November 12, 1940, during the debate on the Ogdensburg Agreement. "I am very glad to have this opportunity of thanking you personally for all you have done for the common cause and especially in promoting a harmony of sentiment throughout the new world. This deep understanding will be a dominant factor in the rescue of Europe from a relapse into the dark ages."[12]

King had now changed his opinion of Winston Churchill, and his admiration increased, almost to the point of hero worship, in the following years.

Despite the agreements and positive words that were being exchanged, the reality for Britain was bleak at this time. The aerial bombardment of London, popularly called "the Blitz," continued for sixty-seven nights without a break, and the devastation and loss of life was horrendous. Although the success of the Allied air force in defending the country from the efforts of the German Luftwaffe had resulted in the end of the Battle of Britain, this was not the end of the suffering for the people of London. Their world would become even more frightening when Germany began to launch the V1 and then V2 rockets.

While the civilian population was being subjected to increasing danger due to the Luftwaffe's relentless attacks on British cities, the ability to defend the country was improved due to a secret source. Before the war the Poles had secured an Enigma machine, which Germany used to transmit information by secret code to its military. Brilliant minds at Britain's Bletchley Park had broken the codes, and of the many messages that Churchill received, one, on September 17, which related to the German operation to invade Britain, code-named Sea Lion, was especially welcomed. This incident is recounted in *"C": The Secret Life of Sir Stewart Graham Menzies, Spymaster to Winston Churchill* by Anthony Cave Brown.

A message came from the headquarters of the German supreme command to the officer commanding the troop-carrying squadrons in Holland. He was authorized to dismantle the air-loading equipment on the Dutch airfields. It followed that if the troop carriers were being withdrawn, then Sea Lion had been cancelled. "'C' sent the signal to Churchill.... According to Squadron Leader Winterbotham, who claimed to have been present at the meeting, 'there was a very broad smile on Churchill's face now as he lit up his massive cigar.'"[13]

There was also sad news on that same day, however. The liner *City of Benares,* sailing from Liverpool to Canada, was sunk by a German U-boat. There were one hundred children on board, who were being evacuated for safety reasons, and only thirteen survived. Churchill had been against the evacuation of schoolchildren, and just two months before, on July 18, he had written to the home secretary concerning another group of evacuees sailing on the *Duchess of Bedford.* "I certainly do not propose to send a letter by the senior child to Mr. Mackenzie King, or by the junior child either. If I sent any message by anyone, it would be that I entirely deprecate any stampede from this country at the present time."[14]

The evacuation scheme was abandoned, after the *Benares* tragedy.

Churchill also turned down a recommendation from the director of the National Gallery to send important paintings to Canada: "No, bury them in caves and cellars. None must go. We are going to beat them."[15]

Churchill's determination can also be seen in a speech he broadcast on October 21 to the people of France. While he could have been critical of the French government's decision to ignore the solemn treaty it had made with Britain to not make a separate peace, or of their refusal to continue the fight from North Africa, he did no such thing. He stated that Britain would "never stop, never weary, and never give in, and that our whole people and Empire have vowed themselves to the task of cleansing Europe from the Nazi pestilence and saving the world from the new Dark Age.... We seek to beat the life and soul out of Hitler and Hitlerism. That alone, that all the time, that to the end."

As usual Churchill finished on an upbeat note: "Good night, then: sleep to gather strength for the morning. For the morning will come.... Vive La France. Long live the forward march of the common people in all the lands towards their just and true inheritance, and towards the broader and fuller age."[16]

King liked the speech but thought that Churchill had gone too far when he referred in it to Hitler: "This evil man, this monstrous abortion of hatred and defeat." To King it seemed that Churchill was just venting his anger, but Churchill did have an objective in mind: to ensure that there was no question as to Britain's resolve never to make peace with Germany. In his book *Churchill and De Gaulle,* François Kersaudy, referring to the speech, said: "'The many Frenchmen who heard this broadcast never forgot it, as they were to make abundantly clear four years later.' This referred to the part played by the Free French forces and many of the civilian population when D-Day occurred."[17]

While there was now no threat of an immediate invasion, since the Royal Air Force was holding its own against the Luftwaffe, Britain was still hanging on by the skin of its teeth. In October 1940 the sinking of the five hundredth British merchant ship occurred, with the loss of over two million tons of shipping.

One bright spot at the time was the re-election of President Roosevelt on November 5. Churchill wrote to him the next day and said that while it was inappropriate for a foreigner to express an opinion, he had prayed for Roosevelt's success. Five thousand kilometres away, in Ottawa, King was also elated. He recorded his thoughts in his diary: "It means that we have the United States with us for the next four years; already committed to give all aid possible to Britain. This should mean, in the end, the certain defeat of Germany & Italy." He telephoned Roosevelt and congratulated him.

A few days later, on November 9, Neville Chamberlain died of cancer. King sent messages of sympathy to Churchill and Mrs. Chamberlain. He also gave instructions that the flags on Parliament Hill be at half-mast.

On November 11 Churchill spoke in the House of Commons, giving a remarkable and generous tribute to one who had been the main obstacle to his being brought into the government in the late 1930s: "History with its flickering lamp stumbles along the trail of the past, trying to reconstruct scenes, to revive its echoes, and kindle with pale gleams the passion of former days.... The only guide to a man is his conscience.... It fell to Neville Chamberlain in one of the supreme crises of the world to be contradicted by events, to be disappointed in his hopes, and to be deceived and cheated by a wicked man."[18]

While it was evident that Churchill appreciated the support he had been given by the former prime minister when he had taken over from him, and he had developed a genuine affection for him in the time since then, the depth and quality of his tribute went beyond what would have been expected. However, Mrs. Hill, Churchill's secretary, disclosed to Churchill's official biographer, Martin Gilbert, that his speech wasn't completely honest: "As Mrs. Hill, who took the dictation, later recalled: 'Then he showed it to Mrs. Churchill. She said, "It is very good." "Well," he replied with a twinkle in his eye, "of course I could have done it the other way round.""[19]

Churchill, of course, was famous for his oratory. His private secretary, John Colville, referred in his diary to, "The magnificence of his language and the balance of his phrases…. Tommy Lascelles [King George's private secretary] … said that only the P.M., of living orators, could make one realize what it must have been like to hear Burke or Chatham."[20]

On December 8 Churchill wrote to Roosevelt, with the text consuming ten pages of *Their Finest Hour,* the second volume of his war memoir, *The Second World War.* He outlined the status of the war and the prospects for 1941, and repeatedly pointed out that the interests of the United States were "bound up with the survival and independence of the British Commonwealth of Nations."[21] The intent of the letter was to make clear what Britain needed in the way of munitions from the United States, if it was to survive and beat the enemy. However, he plainly stated that Britain was broke and couldn't pay for the equipment and shipping.

Roosevelt was on the spot. He was secure in the presidential chair for another four years; however, he couldn't do another "destroyers for leases" manoeuvre again. The president gave much thought to the problem and he made a suggestion to the anglophile treasury secretary, Henry Morgenthau, on December 17. "We will say to England, 'We will give you the guns and the ships that you need, provided that when the war is over you will return to us in kind the guns and the ships that we have loaned to you, or you will return to us the ships repaired and pay us, always in kind, to make up for the depreciation.' … What do you think of it?"[22]

Morgenthau liked the idea, which Roosevelt then outlined at a press conference. The president was adept at outlining his message or request in simple terms that could be understood by all; here he gave a masterful illustration. He explained his intention by way of comparing Britain to a neighbour whose home had caught fire and who requests a garden hose. The neighbour, Roosevelt explained, has asked "if he can take my garden hose and connect it up with his hydrant [so that] I may help him to put out his fire.... I don't say to him before that operation, 'Neighbour, my garden hose cost me $15; you have got to pay me $15 for it.' ... I don't want $15 — I want my garden hose back after the fire is over."[23]

Public opinion supported the proposal, but Congress had to be convinced, and it would not meet until January. In the interim Roosevelt kept up the pressure. Speaking on a radio broadcast on December 29, he urged the adoption of his scheme with another inspired phrase: "We must be the great arsenal of democracy."[24]

As Roosevelt was using his rhetorical skills to rouse his country to the aid of the Allies, Churchill was using his to try to sway public opinion amongst the citizenry of Britain's enemies. On December 23, two months after the speech to the French, Churchill addressed the Italians. Churchill questioned why the two countries were at war, and he gave the answer: "One man and one man alone was resolved to plunge Italy … into the whirlpool of war."[25]

King listened to the broadcast. He concurred: "Most true and most effective. Never did a nation allow itself to be destroyed by an individual as Italy has by Mussolini." Then he repeated an accurate prediction from the past: "He, I believe, will come to a sad end before very long."

Despite his efforts Roosevelt was facing fierce opposition to his "Lend-Lease" scheme, as his plan came to be known, from the isolationist America First Committee, which "launched a massive campaign of opposition. The young John F. Kennedy was one of those who contributed to its funds."[26]

If Roosevelt's words had failed to inspire the support of those on the America First Committee, they still resonated with King. Two days after Roosevelt's speech, King made a New Year's Eve broadcast, in which he quoted Roosevelt's "arsenal of democracy" promise. King also commented on the vast increase in Canada's capacity to aid in the war effort and spoke of "the heroic endurance by the men, women and children of Britain in the midst of fire and death from the clouds."[27] Although there was perhaps little cause for optimism at that point, King tried his best to inspire hope in the hearts of the Canadian public.

The year 1940 came to an end. It had been a momentous year in the world's history. It had started with the so-called Phony War — the period following the declaration of war, before hostilities on land between Germany and the Allies actually commenced — and ended with Hitler having conquered most of Western Europe, with the notable exception of Great Britain. Winston Churchill, who had had to tread carefully after becoming prime minister, was now firmly in control, with Canada, under King, wholeheartedly supporting him. Churchill and King had also combined to nudge the United States slowly but significantly into joining them in the conflagration.

Winston Churchill was chosen by *Time Magazine* as its Man of the Year. The article on him quoted from one of Churchill's most famous speeches: "To the men of Britain in 1940, Winston Churchill spoke words that may live as long as Shakespeare's: 'Let us brace ourselves to our duty and so bear ourselves that if the British Commonwealth and Empire last for a thousand years, men will still say, This was their finest hour!'"[28]

THE EAGLE FLAPS ITS WINGS

In his diary for December 31, 1940, King made a New Year's resolution. He vowed to "be faithful to my task as the leader of the Canadian people, to keep the Country united, and to see that all is done that can possibly be done to cement the friendships between the English-speaking peoples; to render less difficult and more helpful relations with France, and to do all that in my power lies to help the U.K. in this time of its appalling need, and to develop and extend freedom."

King had a distinguished visitor on the first day of the new year: Sir Hugh Dowding, chief air marshal of the RAF, already legendary as the leader of the "Few" in the Battle of Britain, who was to speak to the Canadian Club the next day. Dowding admitted to King that, "but for Lord Beaverbrook [minister of aircraft production], we would have been defeated. That his work had been well-nigh miraculous in getting the aircraft production needed."

In Britain Winston Churchill was fully occupied with the war on the home front, which was a defensive one against the Luftwaffe; although with bad weather in January and February, the Blitz was thankfully somewhat frustrated. Welcome news came from North Africa, where the Desert Army was finding that the Italian army was providing little resistance, and eighty thousand prisoners had been taken by mid-January.

President Roosevelt, in power for another four years, was able to take his efforts to support the Allies further to the next level. This he did in his annual State of the Union address to Congress on January 6. He set the tone of his speech at the outset, when he referred to the external forces that threatened the United States; he stated that the future and safety of the country was overwhelmingly involved in events far beyond its borders.

Of course, making a statement is one thing; acting on it is another. Roosevelt was determined to do more to ensure that the United States was involved in the events that were taking place beyond its borders. To do that, he needed to be better connected to the Allied leadership, particularly Churchill. Although correspondence between Roosevelt and Churchill was voluminous, they had not met each other, except for a brief encounter in 1918. Churchill did not remember the occasion, which they both attended, but Roosevelt certainly did, stating that Churchill acted like a "stinker." So the president decided to send over his right-hand man, Harry Hopkins, to bring back a first-hand impression of the prime minister and the war situation.

Hopkins arrived at 10 Downing Street on January 10, 1941. He was given the royal treatment, as Churchill was anxious to impress him. Luckily, the two hit it off. Churchill recorded his impressions of the meeting: "From this hour began a friendship between us which sailed serenely over all earthquakes and convulsions.... He was the most faithful and perfect channel of communication between the President and me."[1]

Hopkins was equally impressed. He wrote to Roosevelt: "People here are amazing from Churchill down, and if courage alone can win — the result will be inevitable. But they need our help desperately, and I am sure you will permit nothing to stand in the way.... Churchill is the gov't in every sense of the word.... I cannot emphasize too strongly that he is the one and only person over here with whom you need to have a full meeting of minds."[2]

Churchill took Hopkins up to Scotland, ostensibly to say bon voyage to Lord Halifax, who was sailing to the United States to take up his duties as ambassador. Charles Wilson recounted in his diary a dinner in Glasgow at which he was present, with the American quoting from the Book of Ruth in the Bible. Hopkins turned to Churchill and said, "I suppose you wish to know what I am going to say to President Roosevelt on my return.

Well, I'm going to quote you one verse from that Book of Books.... 'Whither thou goest, I will go; and where thou lodgest, I will lodge: thy people shall be my people, and thy God my God.' Then he added very quietly, 'Even to the end.' I was surprised to find the P.M. in tears. He knew what it meant."[3]

Favourable reports of Churchill and his team were also sent back to King. At the same time that Hopkins was in Britain, Canadian cabinet ministers C.D. Howe and James Ralston were there, consulting with their British counterparts. They returned and reported to King and the war committee that they came back full of admiration for the people and for Churchill, who "ran everything."

Despite the kind words and good intentions that were accorded Churchill and the British, the situation was grim. It was expected that Hitler would launch a major onslaught in the spring and Britain would be stretched to the utmost to counter it.

King wrote in his diary entry for January 27, that Howe "Believes absolutely that without Canada, Britain could not [win]. Says government speaks in highest terms of Canada's war effort. The feeling generally is that it has been magnificent; that we are doing all that can possibly be expected of us. Said Churchill was most appreciative; and kindest messages to myself. Spoke of our army as being the best trained and equipped in England."

Howe may be considered to have exaggerated Canada's importance. However, British professor Richard Holmes, in his *In the Footsteps of Churchill*, wrote: "In 1940–41 Britain would not have survived as an independent nation had it not been for the agricultural, industrial and financial aid received from Canada."[4]

Canada did contribute significantly to Britain during the war, but at great cost to the country. King was constantly reminding Canadians of the importance of the struggle, and trying to encourage them to work harder and donate more. For example, on February 2, King gave another of his broadcasts on the subject, this one entitled "Total War and Total Effort." He spoke of the tremendous effort that had already been made and gave as an example the expansion of the Royal Canadian Navy. The navy complement at the outbreak of the war was 15 ships and 1,774 men. This had grown to 175 ships and 15,319 men. The plan for the next year was a further increase to 413 ships and 26,920 men.

King finished with an exhortation: "It is for each one to seek out for himself, in the circumstances in which he finds himself, how he can best play his part.... Neither let us be dismayed at the magnitude of the task, nor discouraged by the length of the road."[5]

Churchill, of course, was famous for similar such broadcasts. One week after King's broadcast, Churchill made a similar one. He had recently welcomed another visitor from the United States, Wendell Willkie, the losing candidate in the recent election. Willkie had brought with him a message from Roosevelt. It contained a verse from Longfellow, which Churchill recited in a broadcast on February 9:

Sail on, O Ship of State!
Sail on, O Union, strong and great!
Humanity with all its fears,
With all the hopes of future years,
Is hanging breathless on thy fate.

Churchill told the listeners the response he would give to Roosevelt: "Put your confidence in us. Give us your faith and your blessing, and under Providence all will be well. We shall not fail or falter; we shall not weaken or tire. Neither the sudden shock of battle, nor the long-drawn trials of vigilance and exertion will wear us down. Give us the tools, and we will finish the job."[6]

In that same broadcast, Churchill stated that Britain did not need manpower from the United States, but did need materials. This was a clear message to the United States Congress; he wanted to reassure them that Lend-Lease was not a further step to that country's involvement in the war.

Churchill was being less than truthful in the statement that its manpower was adequate, and that it did not need the United States to become militarily involved. In their confidential report to the Canadian war committee, Ralston and Howe stated that Britain needed more troops to defend the country and to meet the requirements of the North African campaign.

Speaking in the House of Commons on February 17, King gave a review of the war, which he titled "Brighter Skies and Gathering Storms." It was a balanced assessment. He spoke of the improvements in the defences of the British Isles and the unshaken morale of the people. He spoke also of the increasing involvement of the United States. But he acknowledged that German ambitions were unabated, and stated that it would be wrong to consider "that Hitler [was] abandoning his attack upon the British Isles.... Only by the defeat of Britain," King said, "can the combined totalitarian powers gain their world sway."[7]

Churchill was impressed with King's speech. He wrote to King on February 21 of how encouraged people in Britain were by his remarks. Churchill also stated that the Canadian ships and planes were doing great work, and the air-training scheme had becomes one of the major factors, and possibly the decisive factor, in the war. He finished by complimenting King on his efforts: "What a pleasure it is to see the whole Empire pulling as one man, and believe me, my friend, I understand the reasons for your success in marshalling the great war effort of Canada."[8]

Lieutenant-General A.G.L. McNaughton and Churchill study a map in Canadian Military Headquarters eighteen months before Churchill was disappointed with McNaughton and Canada, February 1941.

137

On March 11 Congress passed the Lend-Lease Act. Churchill responded to this development the next day in the House of Commons. He spoke of "our deep and respectful appreciation of this monument of generous and far-seeing statesmanship.... By so doing, the Government and people of the United States have in fact written a new Magna Carta."[9]

Churchill later referred to this again in a speech in the House of Commons on November 10, 1941. He said: "Never again let us hear the taunt that money is the ruling thought or power in the hearts of American democracy. The Lend and Lease Bill must be regarded without question as the most unsordid act in the whole of recorded history."[10]

King was equally relieved, and he spoke in the House of Commons of the significance of the passing of the Lend-Lease Act, which he said would, throughout time, be one of the milestones of freedom. The act, he proclaimed, pointed the way to ultimate and certain victory.

While King praised the Americans, he wasn't shy about extolling the importance of Canada's efforts and its linchpin contribution in the negotiations between Britain and the United States; nor was he shy in taking some credit for "arousing the people of the United Sates to their present realization that freedom itself was at stake in the war and it was in their interest that they help even further, which would ensure final victory."[11]

Despite his relief at the passage of the Lend-Lease Act, King was not without some misgivings about the significance of the agreement. In his diary, he wrote of the sad plight of Britain, especially as it now had an obligation to a country that was once a colony. He acknowledged that it was likely that the "garden hose" could not be returned, and that when that happened, the United States would wipe off a good part of the obligation — which did happen. Britain, which had borrowed thirty-one billion dollars by 1945, was given a substantial discount, but it still had to repay $4.34 billion, with the final payment not being made until December 2006.

King took some credit for the change in the attitude of the United States, but he was astounded to receive a message from Lord Beaverbrook who, referring to the Lend-Lease Act, said that grateful recognition must be given to King, whose initiative was responsible for such an immense improvement in Britain's fortunes. High praise, indeed, especially from someone who had been closer to King's opponent, R.B. Bennett. King obviously agreed with the comment, but while his early appreciation of the need to bridge the wide divide between Britain and the United States was certainly very important and timely, the actions taken by Roosevelt were from initiatives of his own. Once the president was assured that Britain and Churchill were worthy of his help, he found ways to stick-handle his way around the attitude of Congress, with the "Destroyers for Bases" transaction, and then through Congress, with the Lend-Lease Act.

Despite the passage of the Lend-Lease Act, Roosevelt felt that Britain's situation was still very precarious and that further action was needed. On April 16 King arrived in Washington to discuss matters. Roosevelt advised King that the United States would be extending its patrols further out in the Atlantic, as he was concerned with Britain's situation and considered the real battle at that time was in that ocean.

Roosevelt was right to be concerned about Britain. Back on February 3, King had received a depressing report from Arthur Purvis, the Montreal businessman who was acting as the British purchasing agent in the United States. Purvis had stated that Britain was basically bankrupt, and that the government was very much divided, with Churchill exercising the powers of a dictator.

After his talk with the president, King met with the American treasury secretary, Henry Morgenthau. King spoke of Britain's financial problems and he outlined his own agenda. There was a serious shortage of U.S. dollars in Canada, he said, and the country could not continue paying in cash for U.S. supplies. Unless a new arrangement could be made, Canada would have to reduce the manufacture of munitions for Britain.

King proposed a form of barter, with Canada manufacturing munitions for the United States in exchange for the purchase of American war material. Morgenthau was very supportive of the suggestion and he asked for a list of the things which Canada could manufacture for them.

On April 20 King was welcomed by Roosevelt to Hyde Park. The president was waiting for him at the front door and informed the prime minister that he would be sleeping in "the king's room." There was a double sense to the term — the room was where King George VI had slept two years before. King's ego was bolstered.

The proposal that King had made to Morgenthau had already been transmitted to Roosevelt. He was less than enthusiastic with the proposal; he thought it might be going too far to have something manufactured in Canada for the United States to lend-lease to Britain. King responded that there must be many items that the United States needed. After further discussions King drafted an agreement. "I confess," King wrote in his diary, "that I was never more surprised in my life than when he accepted the statement as a whole without a word."

The agreement resulted in the "Hyde Park Declaration":

> The President and the Prime Minister discussed measures by which the most prompt and effective utilization might be made of the productive facilities of North America for the purposes both of local and hemisphere defence and of the assistance which in addition to their own programs both Canada and the United States are rendering to Great Britain and the other democracies.... [E]ach country should provide the other with the defence articles which it is best able to produce ... it is hoped that during the next twelve months Canada can supply the United States with between $200 million and $300 million worth of such defence articles ... the payment by the United States for these supplies will materially assist Canada in meeting part of the cost of Canadian defence purchases in the United States.[12]

An initial assessment of the agreement seemed to suggest that it was a great win for Canada; in the long run, however, it benefitted both countries. Roosevelt realized this as he "scrawled his famous postscript: 'Done by Mackenzie King and F.D.R. on a grand Sunday in April.' It was a good Sabbath's work."[13]

On his return to Ottawa, King received accolades for the agreement. Professors J.L. Granatstein and Desmond Morton later wrote: "It was a triumph for King, one that ended his Country's financial difficulties for the duration of the war. And once freed of the problem posed by the shortage of American dollars, Canada was able to do far more for Britain."[14]

King advised Churchill of the agreement. Five days later he received a response from Churchill, which King quoted in his diary. He is "crediting me with initiative on a matter of international policy which he, himself, regards as of great importance." Along with Churchill's praise, King also had "the great pleasure of opening a box containing a photograph of Churchill which he had sent me and which he has inscribed, 'To my old and valued friend.'"

Churchill was genuinely happy with the agreement that King had forged with Roosevelt, as well as with the Lend-Lease Act that King had helped to push for. However, he knew that more was needed from the Americans if Britain was to win the fight. To achieve his goal, Churchill needed to help persuade the American people that helping Britain was in their best interests. Unfortunately, he had a few opportunities to address his comments to the American people directly, and so he frequently had to adopt a more oblique approach.

Like Roosevelt, who broadcast his fireside chats to the American people, Churchill gave regular radio broadcasts. These were not only directed to the British people but to a worldwide audience, not the least important being that in the United States. On April 27 Churchill gave a report on the war. As usual in Churchill's speeches, he pointed out that Britain was not just fighting for itself, but for the interests of the United States too, because they deemed the Allied cause was just, and because their own interests and safety would be endangered if Britain were to be destroyed. After predicting the eventual and total defeat of Hitler and Mussolini, he gave as the basis for that statement the fact that Germany had a population of seventy million, while "the peoples of the British Empire and of the United States number nearly two hundred million."[15]

Bringing in the population of the United States to justify his prediction went further than his previous "nudges." Churchill in reality was stating that they were fully in the war, which was obviously completely untrue at that time, but he was in a desperate position and knew, full well, that for the Allies to win the war that had to happen. While Roosevelt may have been prepared to take that step, he knew that at that time Congress would not give approval.

King listened to Churchill's broadcast. The reference to the United States did not escape his notice, although he thought he had gone a little too far in his statement.

While relations between King and Churchill were now on a strong footing, a hiccup occurred in May 1941. Churchill wished to hold a Commonwealth Prime Ministers' Conference. King, who had declined an invitation from Neville Chamberlain in May 1940, now gave the same response to Churchill. King emphasized to him that each prime minister could render an infinitely greater service by staying with his own people in his own country. "My place, until the war is over, is on this continent, not across the ocean."[16] His attitude was shared by Smuts of South Africa, who also declined the invitation. He was put out when Churchill laid the blame for the cancellation on the two of them, not mentioning the difficulty the overseas prime ministers faced in leaving their countries at the time.

King was also faced with a disagreement within his own cabinet. He opposed the unnecessary use of Canadian servicemen in military action. The first Canadian soldiers had arrived in Britain in December 1939. They underwent training, but were not called on to fight when the German army opened its Blitzkrieg in May 1940 against the Low Countries and France. After Dunkirk they formed one of the two fully armed divisions stationed in Britain to defend the island, which was their designated duty. A year later the Canadians had still not engaged in armed combat, while British, Australian, New Zealand, South African, and other Allied troops were fighting in North Africa.

On May 20 Ralston proposed that the British authorities be informed that Canada wished its troops to be put into combat. King was adamantly opposed, as he felt that they should not put the troops in needless danger for "spectacular" purposes, and that the Canadian troops were doing the highest service in protecting the heart of the Empire and making it possible for Churchill and his government to carry on with a sense of security.

Ralston's concerns would only increase as time went on, as subsequent chapters will relate.

During the month of June 1941, the Canadian people were asked to subscribe to the third of the war's Victory Loan programs. The symbol of the program was a Victory torch, which was flown across the country from the Pacific to the Atlantic. It was then borne across the sea and presented to Winston Churchill as a symbol of the "spirit of the Canadian people and their determination to share Britain's burdens till the hour of victory."[17]

King launched the appeal with a broadcast on June 1. He talked of the losses and sufferings of the British people, and, speaking on behalf of Canadians, he addressed the people of Britain: "Our minds have been stricken with horror at the brutal bombing of innocent babies and little children, of men and women at their daily tasks, of the sick, the aged and the infirm ... we have been inspired by your bravery, your undaunted courage, your determination to fight to the end, that the flag of a free people may never cease to fly over the citadel of the world's freedom."

In finishing the broadcast, King addressed Churchill directly. If there were any doubts of his changed feelings for the British prime minister, they were dispelled.

> In conclusion, may I send to you, Mr. Churchill, warmest greetings and remembrances of what to me has been a valued friendship of many years. It is a proud privilege, indeed, to share with you some of the responsibilities and burdens of a people's trust. To us you are the personification of Britain in this her greatest hour. Your noble words, your high courage, your inflexible resolve, have been an inspiration and a tower of strength. Our citizens, English-speaking and French-speaking alike, and all who have come to us from other lands, hail you as the captain of the great host of free men. Your gallant leadership is marshalling the forces of freedom throughout the world. May God continue to give to you, the strength, the vision and the wisdom so greatly needed in so great a task.[18]

As pre-arranged, Churchill broadcast the following day.

I am glad to have an opportunity of speaking again to the people of Canada. Your comradeship in this mortal struggle cheers and fortifies the people of these islands. To Nazi tyrants and gangsters, it must seem strange that Canada, free from all compulsion or pressure, so many thousands of miles away, should hasten forward into the van of the battle against the evil forces of the world. These wicked men cannot understand the deep currents of loyalty and tradition that flow between the different self-governing nations of the British Empire. The people of Great Britain are proud of the fact that the liberty of thought and action they have won in the course of their long, romantic history should have taken root throughout the length and breadth of a vast continent, from Halifax to Victoria.... I have heard from your Prime Minister, my friend — my old friend, Mr. Mackenzie King — of the remarkable organization which has been built up in Canada, to raise this, the greatest war loan in her history; and I am confident that this tremendous effort will be crowned by success.[19]

King took the opportunity on June 17 of addressing a wide American audience, when the Associated Canadian Organizations of New York City invited him to speak to them. This address was broadcast throughout the United States and Canada, and King took full advantage of the occasion. After emphasizing that Canada did not go to war just for its own stake and Britain's, but also for the freedom of humanity, he outlined the tremendous effort in financial and human terms being expended. He was careful not to imply that the United States should physically enter the war, but in finishing he did allude to eventual peace, and declared that "when that day comes, the peoples of the British Commonwealth and the peoples of the United States will be found at each other's side, united more closely than ever in one great endeavour to undo the wrongs that have been done mankind."[20]

A few days later, the mood of the Allies received a lift. On June 22 Germany declared war on Russia. If Hitler had made a grave error in allowing the British troops to escape from Dunkirk, he made a colossal error in launching the attack on Russia, especially before having subdued Britain.

So why did Hitler take this step? King recorded his thoughts on the subject in his diary: "Clearly he desires to outdo Napoleon and to have their names brought into comparison; the former suffering defeat in the end, and he himself as the victor."

Churchill gave his opinion in much more graphic words in a radio broadcast: "Hitler is a monster of wickedness in his lust for blood and plunder.... So now this bloodthirsty guttersnipe must launch his mechanized armies upon new fields of slaughter, pillage and devastation."

Churchill, ever one to appreciate the significance of events, had started his broadcast by referring to the invasion as the fourth "climacteric" of the war — following the other three: The fall of France, the RAF winning the Battle of Britain, and the Lend-Lease Agreement. Then he employed sarcasm: "At four o'clock this morning Hitler attacked and invaded Russia. All his usual formalities were observed with scrupulous technique. A non-aggression treaty had been solemnly signed and was in force between the two countries. No complaint had been made by Germany of its non-fulfilment."[21]

Churchill was in a quandary regarding his future attitude to Russia. He had long been an opponent of Communism. The question became now: How would he reconcile his stance with the fact that Britain and Russia were on the same side against Germany? He showed in the broadcast that he had no doubts about his position. "Any man or state who fights on against Nazidom will have our aid. Any man or state who marches with Hitler is our foe.... It follows, therefore, that we shall give whatever help we can to Russia and the Russian people."[22]

John Colville commented to him that it was ironic that he was expressing sympathy and support for Russia; Colville later wrote that the prime minister replied that, "if Hitler invaded Hell he would at least make a favourable reference to the Devil!"[23]

While King had a clear opinion on the reason behind Hitler's attack against Russia, it was, in fact, the product of more than just a lust for plunder and power, more than just an attack made with no concern for its possible consequences. In *Mein Kampf* Hitler had determined that

Germany needed to expand, and that it would be easiest for it to do so to the east. He also had a fierce ideological hatred of Communism; and Russia's expansion into Finland, the three Baltic States, and part of Romania was disturbing to him. Thus, Hitler decided that it was timely to fight Russia, before it became militarily stronger, and, he felt, it was important to overcome it within the next six months. By that point, in the führer's opinion, the British would realize that the war was lost and would accept his offer of peace. Although France had been defeated in a few months, Hitler knew that to successfully invade Britain the Germans needed to win the air war and control of the English Channel. Neither of these things had been achieved in 1940 and Hitler had no illusions that these would be achieved in 1941.

Hitler based his military decisions on his intuition. It had been shown to be right in 1936, when he sent his armies into the Rhineland and encountered no opposition. Hitler had also guessed correctly that Germany would be able to take over Austria and Czechoslovakia without a fight, and although his intuition was proved wrong in 1939, when it had told him that France and Britain would not enter the war to back up their undertaking to Poland, it was again correct when it led Hitler to believe that Germany would be able to gain easy victories in Belgium, Holland, Denmark, and Norway in 1940.

After early 1940, however, his intuition was to let him down more frequently — with increasingly disastrous results for Germany. It was wrong when he allowed the "miracle" of Dunkirk. It was also wrong when he underestimated the resistance of Russia. After that "Corporal" Hitler made one calamitous mistake after the other. He was the reason why Germany started World War II, and he was the reason why Germany lost World War II.

With the change in the war's direction, King now decided that a visit to Britain would be advantageous — despite his earlier protestations that it was not possible for him to contemplate leaving Canada. This thought was transmitted to Britain, and King recorded on July 27 receiving a telegram from Churchill, "worded in a very kindly way, stating he agreed with me that there was really no need for an Imperial Conference, but adding that he understood I was thinking of coming over myself, and that I would receive a great welcome ... as it would enable me to see the morale and the ordeal of the people." Thus, Churchill made it clear that the visit would be on King's terms, with no Imperial Conference where he could be pressured into a common policy in some matters, which he had successfully resisted in past conferences.

King's preparations to go to Britain were delayed by the news that Churchill and Roosevelt were to meet in Placentia Bay, Newfoundland. King's reaction was one of disappointment and concern: disappointment that Canada, as represented by himself, had not been invited; and concern about the risks involved in arranging such a meeting. As he noted in his diary: "Personally I feel that it is taking a gambler's risk, with large stakes, appalling losses, even to that of an Empire, should some disaster overtake the gamble. To me, it is the apotheosis of the craze for publicity and show. At the bottom, it is a matter of vanity. There is no need for any meeting of the kind."

King was right to be concerned with the welfare of Winston Churchill. But he was wrong to dismiss the meeting as of no real value.

The arrangements for the meeting were shrouded in a cloak of secrecy. But Churchill wished to have a public record made of this historic event. Accordingly, a well-known British travel writer, H.V. Morton, was approached. In his book *Atlantic Meeting*, Morton stated that he was called to London on August 2, 1941, to meet the minister of information, Brendan Bracken, who asked him if he would consent to taking on a special mission. "I regret to say I can't tell you where you are going or what you will see when you get there. I can only say that if you go you will see history in the making and be present at one of the great moments of the war."[24]

Morton shared the concerns King expressed as the *Prince of Wales* was taking its precious cargo to Newfoundland. "What a target we were — Winston Churchill and the Chiefs of Staff! We were undoubtedly the best target that Hitler had been offered. Could he sink us, could he send the loathed and detested Churchill to the bottom of the sea — the monster who alone among English statesmen had seen through him and had the courage to say so in days of our colossal inertia — what a shattering blow to the confidence of all nations still fighting to be free."[25] The *Prince of Wales* arrived safely in Newfoundland on August 8.

The next day was to see the promised history in the making. Churchill and Roosevelt had first met during World War I, and as was mentioned earlier, Roosevelt was not impressed with the Englishman at that time. For the success of the Allied war effort, it was essential that the two leaders establish a good working relationship now.

The meeting started well, and it was immediately evident that the two men now liked and respected one another. The end result was the drafting and adoption of the Atlantic Charter. This contained basic common principles that Roosevelt had included in his speech to Congress on January 6, 1941 — principles that would serve as a blueprint for the Charter of the United Nations, after the conclusion of the war.

While the Atlantic Charter was a significant milestone in the history of the world, as it laid out the basis for the United Nations charter, it was a disappointment to Churchill — it did not bring the United States any closer to becoming a belligerent. This fact was emphasized by Roosevelt in a press conference while still on board his ship, the *Potomac*, on August 16.

Churchill returned to Britain, and King finalized the plans for his trans-Atlantic flight. But beforehand he telephoned Roosevelt. In previous communications King had adopted a deferential attitude, addressing Roosevelt as "the President," even though he was addressed as Mackenzie. Now he wrote: "I greeted the President by his first name, and he did the same with me, saying he was delighted to hear my voice again. I told him I was delighted to hear his. I said I wished to congratulate him on the success of the conference.... The President then said that everything was very successful and that they were able to straighten out a lot of the tangles with respect to supplies from here."

In the conversation the president said that with regard to Article 4 of the Atlantic Charter, which dealt with the lowering of trade barriers, Winston went "up in the air," as this would interfere with the Ottawa agreement, relative to imperial preference.

King agreed that he would visit Roosevelt after his return from Britain. Now that he had touched base with one side of the Great Britain-United States partnership, he could fulfill his "linchpin" duty by going to see the other.

12

MR. KING GOES TO LONDON

In one respect King's trip to England resembled Neville Chamberlain's trip to see Hitler three years before — for both men it was their first flight. King, though, actually enjoyed the experience of air travel. When his Liberator bomber touched down in Glasgow, on August 20, 1941, he was met by Vincent Massey. There was also a telegram from Winston Churchill, extending a "thousand welcomes" and inviting him to a meeting of the cabinet the next day.

King recounted his arrival at 10 Downing Street and his welcome by Churchill: "He was glad that I came over. It really meant much to him for me to be here.... I expressed my amazement, which was very real, at his appearance of health. He looked as fresh as could be, and really more youthful than I have seen him on different occasions. He said the trip at sea had done him great good."

Churchill started the cabinet meeting by "extending a very warm welcome ... [to King] and saying some exceedingly kind things in the presence of his colleagues. Among other things he spoke of the great part Canada was taking. Very much greater than anything done in the last war." King noted Churchill's acknowledgement of Canada's military and financial help and of King's close relationship with the president, which had helped in bringing together the English-speaking peoples. King responded that the purpose of his visit was to find ways in which Canada could make its war effort more effective. He also declared Canada's

Library and Archives Canada C 047565

Churchill welcomes King to London in their first wartime meeting — outside 10 Downing Street on August 21, 1941.

"determination to be in the war at the side of Britain till the end, with all the resources, human and material, that we could effectively employ."

King outlined that his objective was also to visit the Canadian armed forces, see the situation in Britain, study the British war effort, and express the admiration of Canada to the British people for "their indomitable courage in the manner in which they were defending the citadel of freedom."

Just a few months before, the Australian prime minister, Robert Menzies, had complained to King of Churchill's tendency to dominate cabinet meetings, but King disagreed. "Throughout the morning I listened to the discussion, which I found carried on in an admirable manner. Each Minister seemed well up on the subject with which he was expected to deal."

One matter that King thought particularly interesting was Churchill's statement that it would be a great mistake to make any premature attempt at an invasion of Europe, since that might necessitate another Dunkirk-type evacuation. Churchill was later to outline the situation in his war memoirs, writing that even in the summer of 1941 the Russians were clamouring for British landings in Europe, regardless of risk and cost, to establish a second front. "The British Communists," Churchill continued, "who had hereto done their worst, which was not much, in our factories, and had denounced, 'the capitalist and imperialist war,' turned about again overnight and began to scrawl the slogan, 'Second Front Now,' upon the walls and hoardings."[1]

King described his admiration of Churchill's handling of the cabinet meeting. "He has a marvellous way of summing up situations in graphic phrases, a wonderful command of language and knowledge of history, which he uses freely, and an ability to keep looking ahead, making decisions in the light of the long run, rather than the short one."

At the conclusion of the cabinet meeting, it was time for lunch; King refused a glass of sherry because he had given up alcohol for the duration of the war. His answer to Churchill, who asked him if it was for health reasons, was to reply that he felt better without it. But not Churchill, who, much to King's surprise, imbibed "several kinds of wine." After, according to King: "His face got quite a different appearance — lost something of the intellectual look which it had had through the morning, though it was clear that his brain became very stimulated and he talked very freely and most interestingly."

During the luncheon Churchill brought up the matter of conscription in Canada, and stated that he saw no need for it to be implemented, as this war was one of machines and not the numbers of men. King was relieved by the comment, but he should have considered Churchill's speech of February 9, 1941 (Chapter 11), in which Churchill stated that American manpower was not required — something that was clearly not the case.

A favourite topic of Churchill was the Treaty of Versailles, which concluded World War I. He talked of it with King, stressing its injustice, which had led to the present conflict. King agreed, and responded that another mistake was the creation of a British national government, as it prevented one party from fighting for rearmament. Churchill concurred. According to King's diary, the conversation continued with Churchill blaming Baldwin "very strongly for having tried simply to pacify right and left, with a view to having a quiet, peaceful time. He used some expression like a 'toad basking in the sun,' while Neville Chamberlain had done all the hard work."

King continued Churchill's theme, and showed intestinal fortitude in bringing up a controversial subject: "I said I thought full justice was not being done Chamberlain. He was the one who had tried to get Britain to arm at the start. Churchill agreed that at the beginning that was so, but said that after he went to Munich, he came back with the idea that peace was practically assured and rather swung away from his previous view."

Canada's attitude was then stated by King. If Chamberlain had not gone to Munich, and there had been war at that time, he would not have been able to take Canada into the war united. "I said I had gone through my Gethsemane knowing that the country ought to go to war, and intending to make that my policy but that I would have lost a good portion of the Cabinet, which would have been divided.... That as a result of Chamberlain's visit and the deferring of the war for a year, nations had got a chance to really see the issue and to become convinced that aggression was the aim."

Churchill was not prepared to let Chamberlain off the hook, and he bounced King's ball back. "He said that to offset that, one had to realize that Hitler would have been much more easily stopped at that time. He said that war could have been saved at any time up to 2 or 3 years ago. That the people to blame for this war are the British themselves.... He felt that Chamberlain had gone too far on the pacifist side and appeasement side after Munich, and had really been deceived thereby. The country suffered accordingly."

They let the matter drop, then a concern that had been brought up by James Ralston in a cabinet meeting in Ottawa (see Chapter 11) was addressed by Churchill. He spoke of the Canadian soldiers possibly feeling restless at the lack of action, adding that he hoped that King would impress on them the importance of their continuing to guard the country. He said that they would certainly be fighting before the end of the war.

King showed Churchill the preparatory pages of his book *Canada at Britain's Side*. It included a photograph of him and Churchill, which King stated was symbolic of their unity. Then they had obligatory photographs taken by the press.

The following day, August 22, King, accompanied by Vincent Massey, was entertained for lunch by the cabinet at the Savoy Hotel. He sat between Churchill and the deputy prime minister, Clement Attlee. Among others present were the chancellor of the exchequer, Sir Kingsley Wood, and the foreign secretary, Anthony Eden.

Meals with Churchill, while including a plethora of alcoholic refreshments, were occasions for robust talk, although this often took the form of a monologue by the British prime minister. On this occasion Churchill covered a wide range of subjects.

He began by saying that he wished that King could have been at the conference with the president, but he wished it to be a one-on-one, to allow them to get to know each other. King diplomatically responded that he fully understood, and that it would have been an embarrassment to the other Dominions if only he was invited. That, of course, was not his attitude at the time, which was that Canada was being ignored.

Then the subject of Stalin came up. Churchill referred to him as a great man, but he also labelled him a medieval tyrant. He said that Russia should have come in with Britain and France in September 1939, and that if she had, Germany would have already been beaten. King questioned why Russia had not joined with the two allies. This gave Churchill the opportunity of renewing his opinion of the day before: "He replied that that all went back to Munich. That Russia got the idea at the time of Munich that Britain would not fight. Believing that she would not fight, she had been unwilling to sacrifice herself at that later stage. He said, 'I sent Stalin a word a month before, that I was perfectly sure Germany intended to attack Russia.'"

Churchill talked of Hitler and his group, saying that "when the war is over and we have won, I intend to take advantage of the Lend-Lease Act to ask the President to lend me an electric chair from Sing Sing [prison] where these gangsters' lives will end. That the ordinary gallows is too good for a fellow of that kind, and he and the others, along with him, will be put in these chairs and their lives ended in that way."

Any friction in the relationship between King and Churchill was clearly gone now, and they both spoke highly of each other, acknowledging the heavy responsibilities that each had undertaken. Churchill proposed a toast to King's health, and spoke of the years they had known each other and of the magnificent part played by Canada in the war, which he attributed to King's leadership. King responded in kind, declaring how proud he was to hear of the confidence placed in Canada and his government.

The following day King attended the track and field championship of Canadian forces in Britain, where he gave a short address to the troops. During his speech there occurred a much publicized incident — he was booed. The *Globe & Mail* reported the incident: "At the beginning there were some vocal interruptions rather in the nature of a lark and symptomatic of a certain impatience to get into action." According to the article, the reason for the outburst was the fact of King being late in arriving, which resulted in the men being kept waiting in the rain for over an hour, and also the frustration of the troops at not being called into action. Some had been in England for almost two years, and the passive role they had been forced to play was not what they had expected.

Later that day King set out for the prime minister's residence at Chequers, where Churchill met him at the door. The events at dinner that evening left a strong impression on King: "When it was time for dinner, Churchill appeared in the hall and called down to me and one or two others: 'Now children, dinner is ready.'" He remarked to King shortly after: "'I suppose it is a long time since you have been addressed that way.' It was characteristic of his whole outlook."

At dinner King sat between Winston and Clementine Churchill. He noticed that Winston "took a good deal of wine to drink at dinner. It did not seem to affect him beyond quickening his intellect and intensifying his facility of expression. It is really a great delight to hear him converse."

King wrote of Churchill's instinctive love of truth and right and justice, and his tremendous courage in asserting their claims. The conversation was not restricted to serious matters, though. King was a dog person, with his own Irish terrier, Pat, and he especially noticed how fond Churchill was of Mary Churchill's little dog, which was a curly, grey little creature. "Spoke to me about her personality. Picked her up and put him in his arms and around his neck like a little child."

According to King the conversation at dinner was altogether free from any restraint, and he noted that Churchill "was clearly enjoying relaxation from his work and entering completely into the spirit of the occasion with a real buoyancy. He really is a big boy at heart, untiring in energy and interest."

After dinner a movie was shown of the meeting between Churchill and Roosevelt. King was terribly shocked at the appearance of the president. "He looked to me like a man who was near the end of his life.... It was quite clear that in meeting the Prime Minister ... he was conscious in participating in a momentous event, and feeling, one might almost imagine, the kind of ... consciousness of what his critics might be saying regarding it. Over and over again, Churchill referred to his great courage, his bravery in meeting physical pain; his fine spirit."

Then Churchill brought up a matter that would become a subject of major disagreement when the United States entered the war — the timing of the invasion of the European mainland. He said it would be 1943 before it would be wise to attempt any invasion of Europe; until the people began to rise themselves, it would be to run far too great a risk. He said the Allies would have to build barges in large number, to carry tanks and for purposes of sending them across the Channel.

The conversation between Churchill and King moved to personal matters, confirming the close bond that had developed between them. "He then began to speak quite freely to me about himself at the present time, saying, 'I have no ambition beyond getting us through this mess. There is nothing that anyone could give me or that I could wish for. They cannot take away what I have done.' That as soon as the war was over, he would get out of public life." Churchill continued that he would not continue in office after the war. King recorded Churchill as saying: "'If I went on after the war what more could be added, what could I wish for.' I responded that there was a destiny about his life. He had been meant for these times. Speaking of it in a modest way, he said, 'It looks like it in a way, as though it was meant.'"

The next day, August 24, Churchill gave a radio broadcast on his meeting with President Roosevelt. He asked King to vet the draft, and King expressed strong reservations about commenting on the United States entering the war, a strange comment considering King's own speech a few days later.

Churchill began by referring to the Newfoundland meeting, saying, "I don't think I shall be indiscreet if I go so far as to say that it was 'somewhere in the Atlantic.'" He referred to the prime purpose of the meeting with Roosevelt, as symbolic of the deep underlying unities of the English-speaking peoples throughout the world. He spoke of the German invasion of Russia and the atrocities which were being conducted. "Since the Mongol invasions of Europe in the sixteenth century, there has never been methodical, merciless butchery on such a scale." He turned to Japan, declaring that he hoped that U.S.-Japanese negotiations would succeed. But he clearly stated, "If these hopes should fail, we shall of course range ourselves unhesitatingly at the side of the United States."

Churchill spoke of the Atlantic Charter, in which both the United States and Britain had jointly pledged to the destruction of Nazism. Then he asked a question: "How near is the United States to war?" In answering the question, he accurately predicted how such an event might occur. It would be brought about, not by an action of the United States, but by that of Hitler. "If Hitler has not yet declared war upon the United States; it is surely not out of his love for American institutions; it is certainly not because he could not find a pretext. He has murdered half a dozen countries for far less. [And he has done it] one by one: that is his plan; that is his guiding rule; that is the trick by which he has enslaved so large a portion of the world."[2]

King wrote in his diary that they all thought it the best broadcast he had made. He stated he was the first to congratulate Churchill, and mentioned that he felt the most moving part was his talk of the hymns sung during the service on the *Prince of Wales*. Churchill responded that during the service itself he felt overcome. "He pretended it was the cold he had, but really found it impossible to keep back the tears."

After dinner that evening, King took part in something that was certainly out of character for him, as he recounted: "Churchill turned on the radio for music, songs, and in the course of the evening, began to walk up and down and perform a sort of dance. He turned to me: 'Could I not do the same?' whereupon I joined him, and the two of us took each other by the arm and performed a dance together. All present were almost in hysterics with laughter.... It was really a delight to see him in his own home. I know he was very happy throughout the evening."

The next day, August 25, King was driven back to London. He met with the press, and reported on the visit to Chequers. He proceeded to a meeting of the war cabinet. The major part of the meeting was concerned with the ongoing necessity of bringing the United States into the war. Lord Beaverbrook — like Churchill, a man who espoused action — said that what was needed was some dramatic incident, and he recommended that Churchill go over and address Congress. Needless to say King "did not like that at all."

King then gave his recommendation regarding the United States: "I thought the best approach was the kind of speech that Churchill had made last night where he pictured the various nations of Europe being drawn into a pit and unable to get out, emphasizing the enlarging power of Hitler and his inability to meet him at every turn while he was getting stronger himself. In a way they would have to be frightened into participating."

Anthony Eden agreed with King, passing him a note on the U.S. attitude: "This is your war. We will help you all we can, but short of war."

King then recited the prime minister's attitude: "Churchill felt, and I think wisely, that the best way to have America come into the war was through an attack by Hitler on American ships convoying supplies to Britain. That once an attack came there, the President would be prepared to take action at once without waiting for Congress. That if he waited for Congress, debate might take a very long time."

The following day, King inspected twelve thousand Canadian soldiers in four locations, and he impressed on them that it was not the Canadian government's decision that they had not been involved in action, but the British government's desire that they would be confined to the vital responsibility of defending Britain.

In his diary of that day, King expressed his own feelings of inadequacy in a military setting, and this was the reason why, in spite of the significant part played by Canada, he was content to leave the decisions in the war to others, principally Churchill and, later, Roosevelt. He has been criticized for not being involved in the direction of the war, but his sensitive nature abhorred the sacrifices that had to be made: "Offering their lives is infinitely greater than anything I myself am called upon to do."

On August 30 King travelled by rail to Balmoral in Scotland, to stay with King George and Queen Elizabeth. King recorded a conversation with the queen regarding their tour of Canada in 1939. "Among the first words she said to me, after meeting her in the drawing room, was that 'that tour made us.' I interpreted [the words] as meaning it had helped to make the Empire one, but pointing to herself, she said 'I mean us, the King and myself.' She spoke of it coming just at the right time, particularly for them."

Back in London on September 1, King worked on the speech he was to give at the Mansion House, the official residence of the lord mayor of London, on September 4. While Churchill took great pains to prepare his speeches, he was very comfortable in addressing audiences. King also took great pains, too, but he knew that public speaking was not his forte and he envied Churchill's abilities in that regard. Thus, the occasion of the luncheon at the Mansion House was a major test in King's mind, especially as it was to be broadcast to Britain and to Canada. He was also nervous about the subject matter of his speech — he had decided to reverse his previous tentative position of subtly pushing the United States towards belligerency.

He commenced by speaking of the courage of the British people, and especially the Londoners. Their actions, King said, have "added to her story so illustrious that her historic glories pale by comparison.... Of London it will be written and spoken in proud memory, that when the skies rained destruction upon her she stood amidst the ruins of her ancient monuments, unbowed, unweeping, undespairing, but erect, resolute, unafraid."

King then went on to talk of his friendship with Churchill, which he claimed had existed for more than a third of a century. Addressing Churchill directly, King continued: "Perhaps you will permit me to express in the presence of your fellow-countrymen something of the feelings which Canadians, one and all, cherish towards yourself. In the hour of Britain's greatest need, we have seen you personify the unbending determination, the dogged courage, and the unyielding perseverance of the British people.... By the power of your eloquence, by the energy of your conduct, and by the genius of your leadership, you have galvanized a great people into heroic action, rarely equalled and never excelled in the history of warfare."

King is entertained at a luncheon by the Lord Mayor of London, with Churchill, at the Mansion House London, September 4, 1941.

King then moved to the other side of the war, referring to Hitler as a "man possessed by the evil of perverted power [who] seeks to crush all free peoples.... Nazi Germany," King continued, "has been maddened by the poison of the evil doctrines of race and force; that the lust and passion of her rulers could be satisfied only by the blood and soil and treasure of her neighbours."

He mentioned the Air Training Plan and then came the most important part of his speech. "Your declaration, Mr. Prime Minister, that, in the Far East, Britain would stand at the side of the United States, is a sure sign of the deepening interdependence of the free world. A similar declaration on the part of the United States, as respects Nazi Germany, would, I believe, serve to shorten this perilous conflict. Such a declaration would be full of meaning for the German people. At the same time, it would constitute a realistic recognition that Britain is the one obstacle in the way of a Nazi attack upon the New World."

King finished, referring to a new heaven and a new earth, "an earth no longer scarred by warfare and torn by greed, but where the lowly and humble of all races may work in ways of pleasantness and walk in paths of peace." Then he talked of the vision of Britain, Canada, other nations of the British Commonwealth, the United States, and allies in all parts of the world working together to bring about a brighter future: "No lesser vision will suffice to gain the victory. No lesser service to humanity will hold the faith and win the gratitude of mankind."[3]

Vincent Massey remarked favourably on King's speech: "My P.M. made an impressive speech with a direct message to the U.S.A. to the effect that to win the war we needed their full participation. He was the only man who could have said it and he said it well and at the right moment."[4]

King later wrote of his talk: "Once I was on my feet, I felt a real security in the manner of speaking, and knew that all was going well.... Without doubt, I was conscious, while speaking, that the message was getting across all right, and could see Churchill and others were appreciating sincerely what was being said. I was given a splendid ovation at the close."

Churchill was to respond and he asked Vincent Massey if he would like to see his notes, which were blank cards. Massey recalled: "I didn't engage him much in conversation so as to leave him free to collect his thoughts."[5]

Although, for once, Churchill talked extemporaneously, he found the right touch. He referred to the early years he and King spent together and to the long friendship they had enjoyed. The close relationship King enjoyed with President Roosevelt was mentioned, which led Churchill to pick up from King's reference to the need for the United States to become fully involved in the war: "I am grateful to Mr. Mackenzie King today for having put in terms perhaps more pointed than I, as a British Minister, would use, that overpowering sense we have that the time is short, that the struggle is dire, and that all free men of the world must stand together in one line if humanity is to be spared a deepening and darkening and widening tragedy."

Then a familiar phrase: "Canada is the linchpin of the English-speaking world. Canada, with those relations of friendly, affectionate intimacy with the United States on the one hand and with her unswerving fidelity to the British Commonwealth and the Motherland on the other, is the link which joins together these great branches of the human family."[6]

After the luncheon King recorded speaking with Churchill: "He told me he was delighted with what I had said, and particularly well pleased with the part that related to America. I said to him I had thought of going a bit further and, like him, had held back."

King may have thought he hadn't gone far enough. But that was not what the *New York Herald Tribune* thought. It referred to King's acknowledgement of the fact that in 1938 Roosevelt had stated that the United States would not stand idly by if Canada was threatened by another power. In his speech King had asked the United States to give the same protection to Britain. The *Herald Tribune* disagreed flatly with his proposal: "To the Canadian Prime Minister, whose nation is doing so much to maintain Britain intact for the furtherance of its own security, such an extension of Mr. Roosevelt's statement must seem quite logical. But the strategic necessities and military capabilities of the United States have their own logic and in that scheme of things the British Isles cannot assume the same position as Canada."

Not surprisingly, the British newspapers were enthusiastically positive. The *Daily Express* [owned by Lord Beaverbrook] concluded: "Mr. King's frank statement that the United States Government should make an open declaration of war against Nazi policy of aggression had caused a sensation among London politicians."

The next day, September 5, King went to Dover, on the south coast of England, to visit the castle fortress and was given a tour by General Montgomery, the future commander of the Desert Army, that included the small submarine in which Montgomery had escaped from Dunkirk. Churchill had intended to go to Dover as well, but when King later met him at 10 Downing Street, he was given the reason for his non-appearance. Churchill had received a communication from Sir Stafford Cripps, the British ambassador in Russia, containing a letter from Stalin, pointing out that they could not hold out much longer, and were requesting that Britain establish a new line in France or the Near East, to take German forces away from Russia; also stressing the need for additional planes and equipment. This letter was one of many from the Soviets that had

King with Vincent Massey examines bomb damage near St. Paul's Cathedral, September 4, 1941.

bombarded Churchill in the previous few days, many with unrealistic demands. This time Churchill responded to Stalin, including a reference to the availability of American Lend-Lease, and he copied Roosevelt.

King recorded Churchill's final comments before he left. "He came to the front door with me. On the way he said he was so glad we had been in touch with each other. He said he was sorry I had not been able to stay longer. He said if he sent any papers to me marked 'Winch,' to know that they were wholly personal, to have my private secretary decode them, and not to let them on to the files."

In the official biography of King, J.W. Pickersgill wrote: "There is no question that these many personal contacts with Churchill during the visit established a sympathy between him and Mackenzie King which had not existed before and which continued to the end of Mackenzie King's life."[7]

13

SO WE HAD WON AFTER ALL!

On September 17 King spoke to the Men's and Women's Canadian Clubs of Ottawa at the Château Laurier about his visit to Britain. In his diary he referred to the speech, which he entitled "Servitude or Freedom," as more important than the one he gave at the Mansion House in London. It certainly is one of his best "fighting" speeches, and illustrates his ability to compose speeches in a Churchillian mode, although he did not have the same ability to rouse an audience.

After detailing the suffering of the British people and the destruction of its cities, its national monuments and its homes, he outlined the role Canada was playing with over one hundred thousand fighting men, and stated that "every Canadian heart must have been thrilled by Mr. Churchill's words [at the Mansion House] when he said that our Canadian soldiers stood 'at the very point where they would be the first to be hurled into a counter-stroke against the invader.'"

His feelings for Churchill's contribution were clearly outlined: "History, I believe, will record that, by his example, and his leadership, he had helped to save the world, not his country only, but the freedom of the world." That was a far-sighted prediction, especially as the Allies, at that time, were just the "Tiger and her Tiger Cubs," but it certainly is now generally accepted as accurate.

However, important as the respective efforts of Britain and Canada were, from the outset of the war both Churchill and King knew that to achieve victory the United States had to become militarily involved. If President Roosevelt had not appreciated that earlier, he certainly knew by the summer of 1941 that that was necessary. The problem was, the mood of the population and of Congress was still not conducive to that major step. But on September 4 there occurred an incident of which he took full advantage.

The U.S. destroyer *Greer* was attacked by a German submarine, although the torpedoes missed their target. A week later Roosevelt, in one of his fireside chats, announced that he had given orders to the navy to shoot any German ships they encountered "on sight," and warned that Axis warships entering American waters did so at their own peril. After stating that it was the United States's intention to "protect the seas that are vital to American defence," he maintained, "we have sought no shooting war with Hitler. We do not seek it now.... But when you see a rattlesnake poised to strike, you do not wait until he has struck before you crush him."[1]

This was a clear challenge to Hitler and he was furious. As Von Ribbentrop recounted during the Nuremberg trials, Hitler "was greatly excited" by Roosevelt's threat, but then quietened down, as the time was not ripe to further antagonize the Americans. Accordingly, he gave the order to the German navy "that care be taken to avoid any incidents in the war on merchant shipping before about the middle of October."[2]

King was elated with Roosevelt's attitude, but knew that such a change was still insufficient. The next day, September 18, King met with the U.S. ambassador, Pierrepont Moffat, who was leaving that day to go to Washington. He gave the ambassador a clear message to deliver to President Roosevelt — the war could not be won without the active participation of the United States. To emphasize this he stated that Churchill had told him that he would rather lose several months of supplies and have that declaration of war.

Meanwhile, the German juggernaut continued to make progress in Russia, and in early October the invaders were only 140 kilometres from Moscow. On October 10 King recorded: "I have never felt more anxious since the war began about this situation than I do about the Russian at the present time. Germany's might is proving to be terrific. How England can hold out against her if she, as she probably will, conquers Russia, is difficult, short of some miracle."

With the war situation at a critical stage, it would have been expected that Churchill would have been under great stress, but his fighting spirit thrived in that atmosphere. On October 29 he visited his old school, Harrow, and he taught the boys there an important lesson: "Never give in, never, never, never, never — in nothing, great or small, large or petty — never give in, except to convictions of honour and good sense. Never yield to force; never yield to the apparently overwhelmingly might of the enemy." Then he finished: "Do not let us speak of darker days; let us speak of sterner days. These are not dark days; these are great days — the greatest our country has ever lived; and we must thank God that we have been allowed ... to play a part in making these days memorable in the history of our race."[3]

In America, there had been an improvement in public opinion regarding the desirability of direct intervention, and so Roosevelt felt able to approach Congress to modify the Neutrality Act. He followed his September 11 theme with a recommendation that merchant ships be armed, as they were "faced with modern pirates of the sea who were destroying defenceless ships." He followed by stating that U.S. ships should be allowed to transport Lend-Lease articles, rather than requiring these to continue to be taken by ships of the Allies. This amendment was passed by Congress on November 17, 1941.

King was "tremendously relieved" at the passing of the amendment to the act. Churchill stated it was "the virtual repeal of the Neutrality Act." However, the United States was still not a belligerent in the war.

While Roosevelt was trying to loosen the restrictive legislation that circumscribed the ability of the United States to aid the Allies, King was under heavy pressure to do more himself, by bringing in legislation to impose compulsory overseas service. The English-language media, which had been relentlessly urging the government to take this step since early in the war, was joined by the federal Conservative Party. Now there was support for overseas conscription from members of King's cabinet, too — principally Defence Minister Ralston. King was asked by the minister of national defence for naval services, Angus Macdonald, the basis for the French-Canadian objection. King recorded his answer: "That it meant in their minds, domination of conquered people, and minority, by an Orange protestant majority."

King received a major blow, both practical and emotional, on November 26, with the death of his Quebec lieutenant, Ernest Lapointe, the minister of justice. At this critical juncture, King needed a strong ally to help him deal with Quebec. In picking Lapointe's replacement, King made an inspired choice: Louis St. Laurent. Initially, St. Laurent committed to accepting the position on the understanding that he would serve for no more than two years — as with many other politicians, including the two in the title of this book, he did not stick to his original intention. He succeeded King as prime minster in 1948, and led the country until his resignation in 1957, at the age of seventy-five years.

King's political crisis would soon be forgotten, however, in the events surrounding the Japanese attack on Pearl Harbor. While King and Churchill were primarily concerned with the war in the West, they were also well aware of the expansionist ambitions of Japan. That country had signed the Tripartite Pact with Germany and Italy in September 1940, which designated their spheres of interest in a new world order. Germany and Italy were accorded control of Europe, and Japan was to have supremacy in East Asia.

The United States and Japan had been involved in a dispute from the early 1930s, after the Japanese invasion of China and its neighbouring countries. The United States banned exports of essential materials, including oil, and, with Britain and Canada, froze all Japanese assets. Negotiations between the two countries were not fruitful and tensions were high.

On November 30 Churchill had urged the president to send "a plain declaration, secret or public as may be thought best, that any further aggression by Japan will lead immediately to the gravest consequences."[4] By that time, however, Japan already had military preparations underway, and on December 7 Pearl Harbor was attacked.

Churchill wrote of receiving the news on the evening of that day, while he was at Chequers, entertaining the new United States ambassador, John G. Winant, and the U.S. special envoy, Averell Harriman.

Churchill turned on the radio for the nine o'clock news, which had just started. Harriman said there was something about the Japanese attacking the Americans. Churchill's butler came in and confirmed that that had indeed occurred.

Churchill later wrote: "There was a silence.... I asked for a call to the President.... In two or three minutes Mr. Roosevelt came through. 'Mr. President, what's this about Japan?' 'It's quite true,' he replied. 'They have attacked us at Pearl Harbor. We are all in the same boat now.'"[5]

How the United States got caught "napping" continues to be one of the incredible, baffling questions in the military history of the United States. A meeting of the cabinet was hurriedly arranged, and Secretary of Labour Frances Perkins later recalled that "Roosevelt, a former Assistant Secretary of the Navy, who took great pride in the service, said twice to Knox [secretary of the navy], 'Find out for God's sake why those ships were tied up in rows.' Knox said, 'That's the way they berth them.' It was obvious to me that Roosevelt was having a dreadful time just accepting the idea that the Navy could be caught unawares."[6]

Churchill in his memoirs of the war stated, "No American will think it wrong of me if I proclaim that to have the United States at our side was to me the greatest joy. I could not foretell the course of events. I do not pretend to have measured accurately the martial might of Japan, but now at this very moment I knew the United States was in the war, up to the neck and in to the death. So we had won after all!"[7]

On November 10, 1941, in a speech in the Mansion House, Churchill had referred to the efforts of the United States to preserve peace in the Pacific, "but should they fail and the United States became involved in a war with Japan, it is my duty to say that the British declaration will follow within the hour."[8]

Churchill's attitude was that if Japan and the United States were at war, the Axis Tripartite Pact bound Germany and Italy to also declare war on the United States. [9] However, that was not actually the case. The relevant section of the pact, Article 3, included: "They further undertake to assist one another with all political, economic and military means if one of the Contracting Powers is attacked by a power at present not involved in the European War or in the Japanese-Chinese Conflict."

As Japan had not been attacked, Germany and Italy were not obliged to declare war on the United States. However, Britain's position in giving that undertaking to the United States became something of mere academic interest, as on the same day, December 7, Japan also attacked a British possession, Malaya, and the following day, Hong Kong.

Churchill immediately recalled Parliament, and on December 8, speaking in the House of Commons, stated that the cabinet had authorized an immediate declaration of war upon Japan. He followed by saying: "It only remained for the two great democracies to face their task with whatever strength God may give them." Churchill finished with a dramatic statement: "In the past we have had a light which flickered, in the present we have a light which flames, and in the future there will be a light which shines over the land and sea."[10] (In keeping with Churchill's usual practice, he did not include in the "democracies" the other countries, including Canada, involved in the war.)

King may have expected to have been advised directly by the president of the Pearl Harbor attack, but he was informed, instead, by way of a telephone call from the British ambassador to the United States, Lord Halifax, who had been informed by Roosevelt. In any case King was relieved that the "opening shots were not between Great Britain and Japan."

King had firmly stated previously that in matters of war Canada's Parliament had to decide. But regarding Japan and its actions, not only against the United States, but also against British possessions, King did not consider it necessary for Parliament to be re-called to vote on the matter. An order-in-council was signed and submitted to King George. Canada was at war with Japan; Canada remained "At Britain's Side."

On December 8 Churchill sent a formal letter declaring the state of war to the Japanese ambassador. This made no reference to Pearl Harbor but referred instead to the attempted landings "on the coast of Malaya" and the bombing of "Singapore and Hong Kong." He finished the letter thus: "I have the honour to be, with high consideration, Sir, Your obedient servant, Winston S. Churchill." In his war memoirs, he wrote: "Some people did not like this ceremonial style. But after all when you have to kill a man it costs nothing to be polite."[11]

The following day, Roosevelt held one of his famous fireside chats. He spoke of the Japanese attack, and he listed the strategy of the Axis powers, including the steps Germany had taken in conquering the countries in Europe. If listeners were expecting a declaration of war against Germany, they were disappointed; what Roosevelt did say was: "Remember always that Germany and Italy, regardless of any declaration of war, consider themselves at war with the United States at this moment just as much as they consider themselves at war with Britain and Russia."[12]

That slight distinction, between the United States being almost at war with Germany, and actually at war with Germany, was done away with once and for all two days later. On December 11 Adolf Hitler addressed the Reichstag. After a long preamble, including the charge that the president had provoked the war "to cover up the failures of the New Deal.... As for the German nation ... it wants only its rights! It will secure for itself this right even if thousands of Churchills and Roosevelts conspire against it." Then came the crucial statement: "The Reich Government therefore breaks off all diplomatic relations with the United States and declares that under these circumstances, brought about by President Roosevelt, Germany too considers herself to be at war with the United States, as from today."[13]

President Roosevelt now had the problem of finding a way to justify declaring war on Germany solved, with no fear that he could be blamed by the still sizable isolationist sector of the public.

Hitler's decision to take on the most powerful country in the world has rightly been depicted as another stupid decision. However, with almost the whole world at war, it is impossible to accept that the United States could have kept out of the conflict for long.

Churchill had wished to sail to the United States to confer with Roosevelt when the Pearl Harbor news came through. This was initially considered premature by the Americans, but after December 11 the offer was accepted. They were now full partners. As previously recounted Churchill had carefully wooed the president when he met with Roosevelt in August 1941. Now, as Churchill explained to General Brooke, there was a different relationship, and he did not need to be as diplomatic. "Now she is in the harem we talk to her quite differently."[14]

King received a telephone call from Roosevelt asking him to attend the discussions after the formal ones had been concluded. Although King was happy to be invited, he was chagrined that Canada was not to be included in the formal talks. The Canadian cabinet had agreed to present Britain with a gift of one billion dollars to enable it to purchase food, materials, and military equipment from Canada, and King had firmly told them that he would ensure, before the gift was handed over, that Canada's significant participation in the war had to be acknowledged. He was determined to do this at the meeting.

Churchill arrived on the *Duke of York* battleship, and took a flight for the final leg to Washington. The president met him at the airport and they were driven in a limousine, which had once been owned by mobster Al Capone.[15] The talks commenced that same evening and Churchill brought up his main concern: Would Roosevelt keep to the agreement made at the Atlantic Conference, of "Europe first," in view of the Japanese action, from which the Americans were still smarting? Churchill was greatly relieved to receive the president's assurance in that regard.

The next matter discussed was the deployment of the American troops. Roosevelt was anxious to have them engaged in action, without delay. As the only campaign then being fought by the British was the one in North Africa, it was decided that that would be their destination.

Lengthy discussions ensued, with Churchill informing Roosevelt that they had broken the German military codes, by use of a stolen Enigma machine. Roosevelt was impressed; Churchill was similarly impressed when the president provided details of the American atomic energy research.

The following day, December 23, they held a press conference. When asked when he thought the Allies "may lick these boys," Churchill responded: "If we manage it well, it will only take half as long as if we manage it badly." This resulted in laughter. He followed up by saying that if the Allies pressed the war vigorously, they might, as in the last war, "wake up and find we had run short of Huns." It was a successful opener for the prime minister, with the *Washington Post* headline stating, "Churchill Conquers the Press."[16]

On Christmas Eve the president pushed a button for the lights on the National Community Christmas Tree outside the White House. The ceremony was broadcast, and Roosevelt spoke briefly, proclaiming January 1, 1942, as a day of prayer; as a day "asking forgiveness for our shortcomings of the past, of consecration to the tasks of the present, of asking God's help in days to come."[17]

Churchill also spoke. He talked of spending Christmas away from home, but said that in the United States he did not consider himself a stranger because of the friends he had developed over the years and the blood on his mother's side. He talked of the war raging over the lands and the seas. He finished: "Let the children have their night of fun and laughter ... before we turn again to the stern task and the formidable years that lie before us, resolved that by our sacrifice and daring, these same children shall not be robbed of their inheritance or denied their right to live in a free and decent world."[18]

In Ottawa on Christmas Eve, King informed Ralston where Canada would stand in the upcoming talks. Whereas the United States and Britain would be fully represented, the Canadian contingent to attend the Washington meeting would just consist of the prime minister and four ministers. King had backed off from his previous stance that Canada's contribution had to be clearly evident to all. Ralston objected, but King countered by stating that although Canada was parting with a billion dollars as a gift to Britain, it had to accept the situation.

King has been criticized by many historians, including Andrew Roberts, in his *Masters and Commanders:* "No one seems to have considered promoting a Canadian to an important international command, despite the numbers of their troops, the quality of their commanders, the size of their Navy, and the generosity of their exchequer. A more assertive prime minister than Mackenzie King could probably have secured a better deal for Canada in particular and the British Dominions in general."[19]

Mr. Roberts is correct. However, it is to the credit of King that while he required that Canada's contribution be fully recognized, he did not need "a better deal," unless that would help in his objective, which was the winning of the war.

An alternative opinion to Andrew Roberts's was given by another respected British historian, the late Richard Holmes: "As usual, only the squeaking wheels get the grease: the quietly competent Canadians and their low-key Prime Minister deserve more credit than they have received, or that I can give them here." In the same context, Mr. Holmes gave his decided opinion on the crucial role that Canada had played in 1940–41. This has been stated earlier in this book but deserves repeating: "Britain would not have survived as an independent nation had it not been for the agricultural, industrial and financial aid received from Canada."[20]

On Boxing Day morning, Churchill spoke to a joint session of Congress. He talked of this being a moving experience, and created laughter when referring to his parentage: "I cannot help reflecting that if my father had been American and my mother British, instead of the other way round, I might have got here on my own. In that case this would not have been the first time you would have heard my voice."

Churchill compared the superior strength of the Allies to the Axis powers, but recognized that many disappointments and unpleasant surprises would be experienced. When referring to what he would later call the "Unnecessary War," he stated: "If we had kept together after the last War, if we had taken common measures for our safety, this renewal of the curse need never have fallen upon us.... Five or six years ago it would have been easy, without shedding a drop of blood, for the United States and Great Britain to have insisted on fulfillment of the disarmament clauses of the treaties, which Germany signed after the Great War."

This did not go down well with the majority of Congress, who had urged that their country stay out of further European wars. However, he got them back on side with his final phrases when he passionately exhorted: "It is not given to us to peer into the mysteries of the future. Still, I avow my hope and faith, sure and inviolate, that in days to come the British and American peoples will for their own safety and for the good of all, walk together side by side in majesty, in justice, and in peace."[21]

King arrived in Washington on Boxing Day, accompanied by Ralston, Howe, Powers [the minister of national defence for air], and Macdonald [the minister of defence for naval affairs]. He met with Roosevelt, who "was most cordial and friendly in his greeting, as was Churchill. He immediately recalled our tiptoe dance together and spoke in a very friendly way."

The major part of the conversation concerned the islands of St. Pierre and Miquelon, which will be covered in the next chapter. Also discussed was the visit in a few days' time to Ottawa by Churchill and the speech which he would give.

During the conversation a report was received that the garrison in Hong Kong had been overrun by the Japanese. While the suffering of Canadian soldiers in this tragedy has not received the same attention as has that of the soldiers who participated in the Dieppe raid, it was as great, if not greater, and the loss was the result of equally stupid and disastrous decisions.

As early as January 1941, Churchill had written to his chief of staff, saying that there was not the slightest chance of holding Hong Kong, and that the garrison should be reduced to a symbolic number. However, this was not done, as the military thought that even a token show of strength at Hong Kong might help to deter the Japanese from going to war.

The Canadian government was not told of Churchill's very specific statement, however. The two battalions of 1,975 soldiers that arrived in Hong Kong on November 16, to supplement the 14,000 British defenders, were not fully trained. They were able to offer little resistance to the superior Japanese force. As a result, 290 were killed and 493 were wounded. The survivors were brutally treated, and after the Japanese surrender in 1945, just 1,418 returned to Canada, many never to fully recover.

The loss of Hong Kong weighed heavily on Churchill. Not only was he deep in negotiations with Roosevelt and King, he was also preparing two important speeches, for the legislatures of Britain's two greatest allies. Churchill had the ability to compose brilliant speeches on short notice, but even he was under an intense strain, giving two major speeches within four days of each other. He wrote: "Quite soon I realized that immediately after Christmas I must address the Congress of the United States, and a few days later the Canadian Parliament in Ottawa. These great occasions imposed heavy demands on my life and strength, and were additional to all the daily consultations and mass of current business. In fact, I do not know how I got through it all."[22]

It certainly was remarkable how he got through it, especially in view of his health. On the night of December 27, his doctor, Charles Wilson, received a telephone call at his hotel asking him to go and see his patient. He wrote in his diary that Churchill told him, "I was short of breath. I had a dull pain over my heart. It went down my left arm. It didn't last very long, but it has never happened before. What is it? Is my heart all right?" Wilson wrote that he examined Churchill's heart and diagnosed his symptoms as being those of coronary insufficiency. The textbook treatment for this is at least six weeks in bed.

Wilson had to decide between announcing to the world that the prime minister was an invalid with a crippled heart and a doubtful future, or playing the matter down. "And this at a moment when America had just come into the war, and there was no one but Winston to take her by the hand. I felt that the effect of announcing that the P.M. had had a heart attack could only be disastrous.... On the other hand, if I did nothing and he had another and severer attack — perhaps a fatal seizure — the world would undoubtedly say that I had killed him through not insisting on rest."[23]

Wilson decided to play the matter down and advise Churchill he had been overdoing things and must take it easier.

Churchill arrived in Ottawa on December 29, and, King recorded that there was a "splendid crowd at the station to welcome Churchill; batteries of cameras.... Walked with him through the station to his car. He thoroughly enjoyed meeting the crowds and adopting characteristic poses with cigar, hat on end of cane, making the sign 'V' with his two fingers, and generally stirring up enthusiasm like a ten year old."

The *Toronto Star* included a report by Gregory Clark, headed: "Churchill Is Mobbed By Thousands." Clark went on to say, "Never in the history of the capital has there been such an unstemmed outburst of enthusiasm."

Churchill met the cabinet and gave his assessment of the war situation. "He said that things were three times better with Japan fighting America, thereby bringing her into the war unanimously, than the situation would have been if Japan had kept out of the war altogether, and America not brought in."

At the subsequent luncheon at the Château Laurier, King, not knowing of the heart attack just two days before, proposed Churchill's health, and "spoke of Canada at the side of Britain; [told him] we would be there till the end.... [He] concluded by saying God had given him vision and courage and protected him. That the prayers of Canada would be that he might continue to be given vision, strength and endurance to share in the day of liberation of the oppressed nations, and we could all work together for the good of mankind."

That afternoon Churchill was sworn in as a member of the privy council of Canada.

The following day Churchill received great ovations from the large crowds along the route from the governor general's residence at Rideau Hall, where Churchill was staying, to Parliament Hill and the House of Commons, where he was greeted with tremendous applause.

Churchill began his speech by referring to Canada as the senior Dominion and by acknowledging "my old friend, Mr. Mackenzie King." He then talked of the country: "Canada occupies a unique position in the British Empire because of its unbreakable ties with Britain and its ever-growing friendship and intimate association with the United States. Canada is a potent magnet, drawing together those in the new world and in the old whose fortunes are now united in a deadly struggle for life and honour against the common foe. The contribution of Canada to the Imperial war effort in troops, in ships, in aircraft, in food, and in finance has been magnificent."

He went on with phrases later to be included in the many books of Churchill quotations. "We have not journeyed all this way across the centuries, across the oceans, across the mountains, across the prairies, because we are made of cotton candy.... Hitler and his Nazi gang have sown the wind; let them reap the whirlwind."

He described the horror experienced by countries that Germany had overrun, before proceeding to criticize the men of Vichy, in one of his most memorable illustrations: "When I warned them that Britain would fight on alone whatever they did, their generals told their Prime Minister

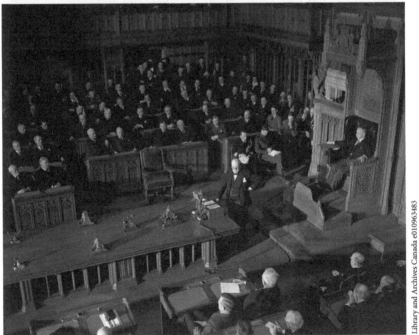

Churchill addresses the combined Houses of Parliament, Ottawa, December 30, 1941.

and his divided Cabinet, 'In three weeks England will have her neck wrung like a chicken.' Some chicken!" And after the laughter died down, he added: "Some neck!" which resulted in more laughter.

Churchill also spoke for a few minutes in French, something suggested by King. This was well-received by the Quebec members.

Churchill finished in typical fashion: "Let us then, sir, address ourselves to our task, not in any way underrating its tremendous difficulties and perils, but in good heart and sober confidence, resolved that, whatever the cost, whatever the suffering, we shall stand by one another, true and faithful comrades and do our duty. God helping us, to the end."[24]

Not only were Churchill's words able to stir the MPs present, they were heard by citizens across the country: "For the first time in history, microphones were installed in the House of Commons so that Churchill's speech could be broadcast via radio to the entire nation."[25]

It is unfortunate that Churchill's efforts to allow radio broadcasts from the British House of Commons came to nought, and the public there were denied the opportunity of hearing them first-hand. Thus an overworked prime minister had to repeat his speeches over the BBC, usually the same day, and not surprisingly some sound as if he was bored with the process, which he was.

After completing his speech, Churchill sat for a photograph. The result was not only the most famous photograph of Churchill, but one of the most famous in the annals of photography. In the Churchill Centre magazine, *Finest Hour,* of Spring 1997, in an article entitled "The Portraits That Changed My Life," Yousuf Karsh described how it came about. He had been called by King, who, over the years, had become his patron and friend. He was advised that Winston Churchill would be in Ottawa shortly to address the combined Houses of Parliament, and King wished Karsh to take his portrait.

Karsh was thrilled at the prospect, and on the big day, he nervously waited in the Speaker's chamber for Churchill to be brought to him.

> Soon I heard the approach of many feet and the mutter
> of voices. I switched on the floodlights. The group halted

179

outside; Mr. King, walking arm-in-arm with Churchill, ushered him into the room. Churchill stood there defiantly, his bulldog like face bristling with surprise.

"What's going on?" he demanded.

I bowed respectfully, quaking inside. "Sir I hope to be fortunate enough to make a worthy photograph of this historic occasion."

"Why wasn't I told?" he barked, chewing vigorously on his cigar.

Everyone looked at the floor; no one answered.

Churchill turned to me. "All right," he conceded, "you may take *one*."

He reluctantly followed me to where my lights and camera were set up. I offered him an ashtray for his cigar but he pointedly ignored it, his eyes boring into mine. At the camera, I made sure everything was in focus, closed the lens and stood up, my hand ready to squeeze the shutter release, when something made me hesitate. Then suddenly, with a strange boldness, almost as if it were an unconscious act, I stepped forward and said, "Forgive me, sir." Without premeditation, I reached up and removed the cigar from his mouth. His jaw tightened in belligerence; his eyes blazed. I clicked the shutter.

Churchill was obviously surprised at the nerve of Karsh, but afterwards he relaxed and told him that he could take another.

Actually five more were taken, four with King. The negatives of three of the photos are in the files of Library and Archives Canada and are reproduced, possibly for the first time, in this book.

Churchill shook Karsh's hand and said: "You can even make a roaring lion stand still to be photographed."

Back in his lab, Karsh waited, "as anxiously as a father expecting his first child. But I wasn't quite prepared for the words of the technician as she watched the image materialize: 'This is a triumph.'"[26]

Neither Churchill nor his wife, on the other hand, liked the picture. Later, King wrote in his diary of May 6, 1944, of learning this news from Clementine some years later: "She does not like the Karsh picture, neither does Churchill himself. She said: 'He really has a more playful expression about his mouth.'"

King, however, thought it was a wonderful photograph. He wrote in his diary that the one of Churchill "could not have been better." However, he added, "the ones of myself, where we were together, were unfortunately not as good. I was sorry to learn Karsh had given one of them [the picture on page 2 in this book] in which C. and I were laughing to *Saturday Night*. I do not like that kind of expression in relation to the war."

As they were leaving Parliament, future Conservative prime minister John Diefenbaker recorded a backbencher saying, "Isn't that wonderful. There is Mr. King making that sign that Churchill had made his."

Diefenbaker replied: "The V has different meanings. For Churchill it means Victory; for King it means Votes."[27]

That evening King hosted a dinner at his home, Laurier House, and went off the wagon. "I had earlier had the Country Club prepare me some cocktails.... Felt that because of Churchill's guests as well as the Ministers, I might make an exception for this dinner ... after proposing the King's health, I rose and proposed the health of our latest Privy Councillor; thanked him for the honour he had done myself and my colleagues in coming to dine with us."

After dinner King recorded: "We came to the library. C[hurchill] sat in the big chair, facing my mother's picture. When I showed it to him, he spoke of how very beautiful her face was, kept repeating: a lovely face: a lovely face."

King showed Churchill the proclamation putting a price of one thousand pounds on the head of his grandfather, William Lyon Mackenzie, in 1837. Churchill's reaction was the same as two decades before, "when the Irish Republican Army leader, Michael Collins, complained that Britain had put a price on his head of five thousand pounds. Churchill referred to this amount in relation to the price the Boers had placed on his head after his escape: "At any rate it was a good price. Look at me — twenty five pounds, dead or alive."[28]

Library and Archives Canada e010700994

Library and Archives Canada e010934574

Library and Archives Canada e010934573

Library and Archives Canada e010934572

A portfolio of Churchill portrait photographs by Yousuf Karsh: the definitive image of the British prime minister in the Speaker's Chamber, Ottawa, December 30, 1941; striking a less stern pose; with King, arms on hips; with King again, a little stiffer; and once more with King (facing page top left).

Facing page top right: Churchill is assisted with the lighting of his cigar possibly by Speaker James Glen. Almost certainly this picture was also taken by Karsh.

Churchill, with King, leaves the Parliament Building after the British prime minister's speech and the taking of the Karsh photos.

The painting of King's mother that so entranced Churchill, as King recorded.

Library and Archives Canada C114873

They discussed Churchill's years in opposition and then moved on to a subject in which they differed. Churchill, King wrote, stated "that he certainly would have been opposed to appeasement at Munich. He feels they would have been better to have fought at that time, largely because they had, in Britain, not made much additional headway in arming in the next year, whereas the Germans had gone much farther." King noted in his diary that he felt differently, but he diplomatically did not think it timely to bring it up.

Churchill returned to Washington on New Year's Eve, where, speaking at a press conference, he wished the Americans a glorious New Year, adding, "Here's to 1942. Here's to a year of toil — a year of struggle and peril, and a long step forward towards victory. May we all come through safe and with honour."[29]

14

THE THIRTY-MINUTE INVASION

W orld War II contained many significant events, which Churchill referred to as *climacterics*, such as Dunkirk, Germany's attack on Russia, the Japanese attack on Pearl Harbor, and Hitler's declaration of war on the United States. It also contained many other incidents, some of which are still examined in depth today, such as the Dieppe raid. Then there are others, of lesser importance, which have been more or less forgotten in the passage of time. One in that category concerns the invasion of the small islands of St. Pierre and Miquelon.

Christmas Eve, 1941, was a bitterly cold night on the island of St. Pierre. A solitary gendarme was on sentry duty at the Harbor. He ran out of coal for his stove and walked into the town to his home to fill his coal scuttle. In the warmth of his home, he convinced himself that it was pointless to go back to his sentry duty — nothing was happening — and so he went to bed.

Meanwhile, back at the Harbor, three corvettes and a submarine of the Free French navy, each proudly displaying the Cross of Lorraine — the symbol of the Free French forces — glided into the quay, and 360 sailors disembarked. This was the beginning of an action that would later be referred to as a "tempest in a teacup"; others described it as "trivial to the point of ridiculous."

The islands of St. Pierre and Miquelon, with an area of 242 square kilometres and a population of 6,500, are located thirty kilometres southwest of Newfoundland. They are the oldest French overseas possessions, and today receive the equivalent of some twenty-five million dollars annually, the highest per capita aid paid in the world.

In 1536 Jacques Cartier claimed the islands on behalf of France, but ownership of them bounced backed and forth between France and Britain until, in 1815, the Treaty of Paris finally established French sovereignty.

The islands were for a long time a major fishing centre, but the early years of the twentieth century saw an economic crisis. Fortunately for the islanders, the United States enacted Prohibition in 1920, and until its repeal in 1933, this French outpost became a major alcohol exporter, with rum runners operating a fleet of trawlers from St. Pierre. Taxpayer number one during that period was Al Capone, who visited his St. Pierre operation in 1927. The end of Prohibition brought about another economic crisis, and the islands languished through the remainder of the 1930s.

With the advent of World War II, the colony mobilized, and 550 citizens joined the armed forces. After the fall of France, the islands came under Vichy control. Britain did not recognize the Vichy government, but Canada and the United States did. Although Canada was at war with Germany, and Vichy France was essentially a creature of Nazi Germany, Canada maintained diplomatic relations with the Vichy regime. This was partly at the request of the British government, which wanted to keep open a channel of communications, but also to encourage Vichy to remain neutral — even if its neutrality was in many ways little more than a technical one. The United States was especially committed to avoiding actions which could give Vichy an excuse to declare war on the Allies, and transfer its fleet to the Axis powers.

The Vichy administrator over the islands was Baron Gilbert de Bournat, who was intensely loyal to the Pétain-led Vichy regime. With the support of the Catholic Church leadership on the islands, he resisted pressure to hold a plebiscite to decide the colony's loyalties.

The Canadian government was suspicious of de Bournat. There had been a number of merchant ship sinkings that took place far to the west of the previous ones, and the Canadian government surmised that de Bournat had ordered that the powerful St. Pierre radio transmitter be used to send coded messages to Germany about the location and nature of British-bound convoys. The British government shared this concern, and Churchill also wrote that the radio station was "spreading Vichy lies and poison throughout the world."[1]

General de Gaulle, the head of the Free French forces, was anxious to seize the islands. He considered it scandalous that there was a community kept in obedience to Vichy so close to Newfoundland. So, he instructed the commander-in-chief of the Free French navy, Vice Admiral Émile Henri Muselier, to take the islands. However, Muselier decided to ask the Canadian and American governments for their assent beforehand. De Gaulle later wrote in his war memoirs: "The secret was thus out. I found myself obliged to warn the British in order to avoid the appearance of concealment."

The British had no objection, but the American government was very much opposed. De Gaulle now felt that, barring some new fact, the operation would have to be postponed. However, he received a report from the British Foreign Office that the Canadian government, in agreement with the United States, if not at the instigation of the United States, had decided to land on St. Pierre the staff necessary to take over the radio station — with or without consent. "We at once protested in London and Washington. But as soon as foreign intervention on French territory was in question, no hesitation seemed to me permissible. I gave Admiral Muselier the order to win St. Pierre and Miquelon over at once."[2]

Unbeknownst to de Gaulle, Canada had decided not to land at St. Pierre. King's diary of December 19 recorded: "War Committee decided to do nothing re St. Pierre and Miquelon for the present, as both Great Britain and the U.S. have each taken different views at different times and are now taking opposite views.... I read out the British despatch asking that nothing be done at present." The Canadian decision was transmitted to the U.S. State Department by Hume Wrong, the counsellor at the Canadian legation in Washington.

Meanwhile, in Montreal, a Free French leader deliberately tipped off the *New York Times*, which assigned reporter Ira Wolfert to cover the story. Wolfert caught up with Muselier's party at the Lord Nelson Hotel in Halifax, Nova Scotia, and bluffed them into thinking he knew more than he actually did. He threatened to publish the story, in order to blackmail them to taking him along. His tactics were successful, and he was bundled into the naval dockyard on the floor of a taxi, and locked in a cabin on Muselier's ship.

On December 23 Muselier advised the senior Canadian naval officer in Halifax that he was commencing naval exercises at sea, and once at sea, went through the motion of carrying out manoeuvres.

Muselier's conscience began to trouble him, however. He signalled his change of course to London, in order, as he later said, to give the British the opportunity to intercede with de Gaulle to cancel the operation, if they so desired. This was an unnecessary precaution, as the British had already cracked the Free French codes; however, the Admiralty and the Foreign Office took no action.

The unopposed landing on St. Pierre took just thirty minutes. Not a gun was fired and not a drop of blood was spilled. De Bournat was taken into custody and detained on Muselier's flagship. The eleven gendarmes offered to round up "the usual suspects."

Muselier read a proclamation from the town hall advising that a plebiscite would be held, so that the islanders could decide between being governed by the Free French or the Vichy regime, "the collaborators with Germany, who starve, humiliate and martyr the people of France."

King wrote of his reaction on being informed of the invasion:

> Was shocked to hear that Muselier, of the Free French forces, had taken possession of St. Pierre and Miquelon and welcomed by the population there. It may prove to be a very critical business, and I am terribly annoyed as well as distressed about it. Fortunately, I have fought from the beginning against attempting anything against St. Pierre and Miquelon by force. I have kept up the fight at each meeting by the War Committee and the record is perfectly clear, even to the point of Norman Robertson [under-secretary of state for external affairs] advising Muselier not to interfere at St. Pierre and Miquelon at this time.

King then went on to write of the British and Americans, blowing hot and cold in the matter: "I have been holding back any action till they agreed upon a course. Only yesterday Robertson had talked with the French Minister and assured him there was no likelihood of any overt act there; that we would confer with him first. When he told me, Robertson said he thought he should go and see the Minister at once. I told him by all means to do so, and to tell him how annoyed I was."

Christmas Day saw high-ranking officials on both sides of the Atlantic transmitting urgent communications. The British war secretary, Anthony Eden, wrote to Lord Halifax, the British ambassador in Washington, of the previous assurance from de Gaulle that the operation would not be undertaken, concluding that "Muselier [seems to have] gone off on his own with or without de Gaulle's knowledge and assent." Then, after receiving more news, he wrote again:"[the] blame [falls] very squarely on de Gaulle, whom I see has issued a congratulatory telegram in London to Admiral Muselier." Lord Halifax responded that he would be seeing Secretary of State Cordell Hull.[3]

King recorded in his diary that Hull was very disturbed, asking Canada to order the Free French forces away and reinstate the governor. This request was followed by a report from the Canadian assistant under-secretary of state for external affairs, Lester Pearson, that Moffat, the U.S. ambassador in Ottawa, had come up with what amounted to an ultimatum that Canada should take action immediately. The situation was critical.

Lester Pearson recorded in his autobiography: "The Americans thought, wrongly, that this seizure had been made with the knowledge and approval of the Canadian Government. Cordell Hull, a courtly but explosive southern gentleman, was particularly angry and tried to browbeat us [into] forcing the 'so-called Free French' (a phrase which made us angry) from the islands [and] restoring them to Vichy. Mr. Hull was informed that the Canadian Government would do no such thing. We made it clear that we were no banana republic to be pushed around by Washington."[4]

In his diary King recorded that Pearson had stated that "we could not take action without thereby implying that we had been responsible for what the Free French had done. Also that until the President and Mr. Churchill agreed on the action to be taken, we could not take action without precipitating a new situation of which we would be wholly and solely responsible."

King saw this as a very touchy matter, which could be a no-win situation for Canada if it took action. He was concerned, as was Cordell Hull, that the incident might be made an excuse by François Darlan [the commander of the Vichy government's navy] to turn over what remained of the French fleet to the Germans, to protect their island possessions. But King had no intention of being involved militarily, and he responded that the Americans should order the Free French to leave. As was mentioned earlier, King was scheduled to travel to the United States to meet Roosevelt and Churchill on Boxing Day. The meeting would provide the perfect opportunity for him to discuss the situation with the British and the Americans.

The day King set forth, a plebiscite was conducted in St. Pierre and Miquelon concerning the question of who was to govern them. The result was 98 percent support for the Free French. Although it seemed that the citizens of the colony had decided the issue, King soon found that his allies were not willing to let the matter drop.

King arrived in New York at lunch time on Boxing Day, and was confronted by reporters. He stated, regarding St. Pierre, that Canada was co-operating with the United States and Great Britain in the matter. He arrived in Washington in mid-afternoon and discussed the St. Pierre matter with Lord Halifax, and the Canadian ambassador, Leighton McCarthy. Halifax warned King that Hull "might suggest some kind of a compromise to clean up the situation, and that Churchill would be favourable to such a course; that de Gaulle had gone much too far and that Churchill would be prepared to pull him up summarily."

King wrote of the subsequent meeting with Hull. The secretary of state said that he had been doing everything in his power to keep the French from turning over the fleet, and that the invasion of the islands might well unsettle the relations between Vichy and the United States. Hull proposed that a commission of four experts be established to look after the radio, but recommended that the Free French be expelled from the islands and that the old order be restored.

King disagreed with restoring the governor, as he was pro-Axis, and his wife was a German. Courageously, in view of Hull's high state of anxiety,

King stated that while Canada had nothing to do with the matter, the public was relieved by and pleased with the de Gaulle accomplishment. He also told Hull that he had been subject to criticism from some, who saw his decision to allow the French minister to remain in Ottawa as an indication that he leaned too much towards Vichy. Thus, it was important, he explained, that whatever was done should not be seen as sacrificing the Free French.

King and Hull then joined Roosevelt and Churchill. King recorded that all agreed on the need to ensure that the incident did not develop into a serious matter. Roosevelt agreed with Hull that a commission of some kind should be established, and that the governor should be restored and the Free French forces withdrawn. Churchill said he was prepared to take de Gaulle by the back of the neck and tell him he had gone too far and bring him to his senses.

King brought his negotiation skills into play, and stated that they needed to let de Gaulle feel that, although he had been precipitate, he had cleared up a problem with the radio transmitter, and that would now be handled by others, after the withdrawal of the Free French troops.

As the Allies were trying to find some way of placating Vichy without offending de Gaulle and the rest of the Free French, the Axis shortwave stations broadcast fictitious claims of a bloodbath on St. Pierre, claiming that one thousand refugees were forced to escape to safety in Canada and the United States, and that Muselier had ordered de Bournat and the seigneur of the Catholic clergy, Monsignor Poisson, to be shot.

The American press, on the other hand, continued to support the invasion. The *New York Times* praised Muselier's expedition, which it said was accomplished with a display of style and manners in the best tradition of Alexander Dumas. On the other hand, it accused Hull of treason for supporting Vichy in its collaboration with Hitler. That newspaper also published Ira Wolfert's report from St. Pierre, about the "nicest Christmas present the world got that year," which struck a State Department official as a "hell of a Christmas present."

On December 27 King met with Hull again. They finally agreed on a solution to the St. Pierre problem. After the meeting Hull mentioned that he was going in to face the press, and asked King if he would like to come along. Not surprisingly, King replied in the negative.

The Vichy ambassador to the United States, Gaston Henry-Haye, had been full of praise for the American disapproval of the action and demanded a return to the status quo, including the reinstallation of the governor. On St. Pierre Monsignor Poisson bluntly told Muselier that he had concluded that, "I cannot in all conscience recognize you as the legitimate governor of St. Pierre," and nailed this declaration on the door of the cathedral.[5]

The *Toronto Star* of December 29 quoted Muselier: "We will hold the Islands to the end."

An editorial in the *Globe & Mail* fully supported the attitude of the American press, making a perceptive observation: "The only proper course is to recognize the wishes of the islanders themselves. If not what is the provision of the Atlantic Charter conceding the rights of people to choose. The Dominion of Canada should do nothing to counteract their decision."

That same day de Gaulle wrote to Churchill. After stating that the attitude of the United States government was doing a great deal of harm to the French fighting spirit, he added: "It does not seem to me a good thing that, in war, the prize should be handed to the apostles of dishonour. I am saying this to you because I know that you feel it and that you are the only man capable of saying as it should be said."[6]

Although Churchill had agreed with the American policy of requiring the Free French forces to vacate the islands, he certainly did not back up his support in his speech to the Canadian Parliament on December 30.

He referred to the men of Vichy as powerless, saying that Hitler was playing a "cat and mouse game" with them, and that he would give them some concessions and then "shoot a hundred French hostages to give them a taste of the lash.... At any moment it may suit Hitler's plans to brush them away. Their only guarantee is Hitler's good faith, which, as everybody knows, biteth like the adder and stingeth like the asp."

Then Churchill went on: "But some Frenchmen there were who would not bow their knees and who under General de Gaulle have continued the fight on the side of the Allies. They have been condemned to death by the men of Vichy, but their names will be held and are being held in increasing respect by nine Frenchmen out of ten throughout the once, happy, smiling land of France."[7]

Cordell Hull listened to Churchill's speech on the radio and his anger reached "hurricane proportions."[8]

But one person was very happy. The following day de Gaulle broadcast to France: "We entirely concur with the statements made yesterday by the great Churchill." He also cabled the prime minister, stating, "What you said yesterday about France at the Canadian Parliament has touched the whole French nation."[9]

The *Toronto Star* of December 31 reported: "St. Pierre and Miquelon Re-Declare War on Nazis," adding in a sub-head:"Population of French Isles Flock to Join New Defence Forces."

On New Year's Eve, Churchill was asked at a press conference in Ottawa about the invasion. He responded: "I would not say anything about this now. No doubt things will be settled in a satisfactory way. I regard it as a very minor matter in comparison with the other things which were going on."[10]

Hull did not look on the invasion as a "minor matter," however, and on January 2 he admonished Churchill, in front of Roosevelt, saying that his comments were "highly incendiary." He pleaded with Churchill to send a statement supporting the United States policy towards Vichy, but Churchill "was not cordial to the suggestion."[11]

The issue of the radio transmitter continued to be a particular sticking point. The Canadian Press reported that on July 22, 1940, while the island was under Vichy control, a telegram was sent from Vichy to the governor. This concerned transmissions and instructed him that the transmitter was to be used "exceptionally only and only for very secret transmissions, use V.N. marine code as known to the German & Italian authorities."[12]

Ira Wolfert confirmed this when he reported from St. Pierre on January 4: "Proof has been discovered in the files of the radio station here that movements of Allied warships were signalled to Vichy in code by the preceding administration."[13]

Given all of this, it is hardly surprising that the U.S. newspapers continued to criticize the State Department, with the *Washington Post* sympathizing with those who were "bewildered by the psychology of men who wage war with their right hand and appease with their left."

On January 8 President Roosevelt telephoned King, who noted in his diary that Roosevelt was anxious to get the St. Pierre and Miquelon matter settled, as it was causing Cordell Hull great distress and he was threatening to resign.

Churchill, still in Washington on January 12, telegraphed Anthony Eden in London. Eden was to advise de Gaulle that he must agree to a joint communiqué that would declare that the islands were French and would remain French, that the radio station would be subject to the supervision and control by observers appointed by the American and Canadian governments, and that all armed forces would be withdrawn. Churchill added, "However you dish it up, he has got to take it. They are in a mood to use force.... It is intolerable that the great movement of events should be obstructed, and I shall certainly not intervene to save de Gaulle or other Free French from the consequencies."[14]

So Eden met with de Gaulle on January 14, and put to him the Allies demands. Eden stated that the United States was thinking of sending a cruiser and two destroyers to St. Pierre. De Gaulle responded that Muselier would be delighted to have them come to lunch on St. Pierre. Eden continued by pointedly asking what would they do if the American ships entered the island's territorial waters.

De Gaulle responded: "'Our people will summon her to stop in the usual way.'

"'If she holds on her course?' Eden asked

"'That would be most unfortunate, for then our people would have to open fire.'

"Mr. Eden threw up his arms.

"'I can understand your alarm,' I concluded with a smile, 'but I have confidence in the democracies.'"[15]

Later in the day, Eden noted Churchill's reaction: "The P.M. was very angry. He thought his original proposal eminently fair.... He thought I had failed lamentably with General de Gaulle."[16]

On January 22 Churchill, back in London, sent for de Gaulle. Churchill proposed, on behalf of Washington, London, and Ottawa, an arrangement, according to which everything on St. Pierre and Miquelon would remain as de Gaulle had ordered it. In exchange the Free French were to let the three governments publish a communiqué that would to some extent save the face of the State Department.

De Gaulle later wrote: "'After which,' the British Ministers told us, 'no one will meddle in the business.' We accepted the arrangement. In the end nothing was published. We kept St. Pierre and Miquelon, and none of the Allies bothered about it anymore."[17]

While this incident in the war is now all but forgotten, at the time it was a major, albeit short-lived, political and diplomatic incident. Historically, its greatest value may be that it throws light on the subsequent attitude of Roosevelt, who never warmed to de Gaulle.

"Remember, Winston," said Churchill's friend and crony Brendan Bracken at a low point in the de Gaulle relationship, "he thinks of himself as the reincarnation of St. Joan."

"Yes" Churchill replied, "but my bishops won't burn him."[18]

15

TRULY A WORLD WAR

With the United States joining Britain, Canada, and the rest of the Allies in fighting Japan, Germany, Italy, and the other Axis powers, the war extended into almost the whole world. Fighting a world war required a complete commitment from each nation. In Canada King addressed the House of Commons on that subject in a speech he gave on January 26, 1942, entitled "The Real Meaning of a Total War Effort."

In his diary entry of that day, King stated that he received "a prolonged ovation from our men on rising to speak and again on concluding." He spoke for two hours and twenty minutes, though this was broken up into two segments delivered on the same day. The full narrative was published in a collection of his speeches entitled *Canada and the Fight for Freedom*, where it consumes forty-eight pages.

The speech was not designed to stir the listener but to provide solid facts about the progress made by Canada since the war broke out. King first addressed the ongoing matter of conscription for overseas service, to which he was opposed. He continued to face opposition to his position from the English-language press and the Conservative opposition. For example the *Ottawa Journal,* in its editorial of January 14, pulled no punches, stating that "the simple truth is that in this country public opinion for conscription is becoming a full flood tide and no Government in any democracy can ignore such opinion. Not without peril!"

As previously stated, King also faced opposition in his own cabinet from the minister of national defence, James Ralston. However, King, in his speech, continued to emphasize that "a vital aspect of Canada's war effort is our contribution to the food supply of Great Britain ... the very lives of the British people and our own armed forces overseas depend upon the exertions of Canadian farmers and fishermen." Making the point that men had to be available for the manufacture of military munitions in Canada, King repeated Churchill's contention that "the cry we hear from every front is not so much for numbers of men as it is for tanks, for planes and for ships."

King then delivered an impressive statement about the increase in materials and personnel in the three services since the beginning of the war. The navy had grown from 20 ships and 2,000 men to 350 ships and 27,600 men. The regular army had grown from 4,500 men to 260,000 men. The air force had grown from 4,000 men to over 100,000 men.

The frugality displayed by King and the Canadian exchequer in the Depression years, when a balanced budget was gospel, were forgotten in the face of the staggering disbursements required to wage war, with the prime minister proudly announcing the vast sums expended. Supplies provided to Britain, totalled over one billion dollars. Direct war expenditures amounted to $1,721,000,000, with $2 billion raised from increased taxes.

In the final part of the speech, King returned to the subject of conscription. King's fertile mind producing a formula to cut the wind out of the sails of the supporters of conscription. He announced that a national plebiscite was to be held on the question: "Are you in favour of releasing the government from any obligation arising out of any past commitments restricting the methods of raising men for military service?"[1]

Churchill did not have to "go to the people," as did King, but he realized the importance of keeping his Parliament and citizens fully informed of the current situation, and what could be expected in the future. On January 27 he reported on the war to the British House of Commons. Similar to the one by King, his speech was a workmanlike recitation, without his usual brilliant phrases and exhortations. However, the two speeches differed in one important respect: Churchill's also included the requirement for a vote of confidence on himself. This, he contended, was a thoroughly normal, constitutional, democratic procedure — one that allowed him to ascertain the support and confidence of the House.

He talked of the overall progress that had been made, although he admitted that "in two and a half years of fighting we have only just managed to keep our heads above water. When I was called upon to be Prime Minister, now nearly two years ago, there were not many applicants for the job. Since then, perhaps, the market has improved." After acknowledging the many failures to date and the criticisms received, "from which chidings we endeavour to profit," he confidently stated that if all efforts are taken, "it looks more than it ever did before, as if we were going to win."

The entry of the Japanese into the war was then dealt with at length, with Churchill admitting that the British could expect "ill-usage" from them in 1942, although he predicted improvement in 1943. But any concerns arising from the threat offered by the Japanese were more than offset by the promise of support from the United States, now that it was in the conflict.

After stating his duty to "cross the Atlantic and establish the closest possible relationship with the President and Government of the United States," he said, "it was plainly my duty to visit the great Dominion of Canada. The House will have read with admiration and deep interest the speech made by the Prime Minister of Canada yesterday on Canada's great and growing contribution to the common cause in men, in money, and in materials." Then he mentioned the financial help that the Canadian government had made to this country. "The sum is one billion Canadian dollars, about 225 million pounds. I know the House will wish me to convey to the Government of Canada, our lively appreciation of their timely and most generous offer. It is unequalled in its scale in the whole history of the British Empire, and it is convincing proof of the determination of Canada to make her maximum contribution towards the successful prosecution of the war."[2]

The *Toronto Star* of January 27 stated that Churchill's announcement of the gift was cheered by the MPs.

While Churchill's speech was not designed to ignite emotions, it certainly impressed the Canadian diplomat and diarist Charles Ritchie. "Heard the Prime Minister defend the Government's conduct of the war in the House. It was the greatest speech I have ever heard. It was an orchestral performance; lesser motifs interspersed were all handled with the same easy strength. To read it would be to lose half of it — the implications in his slightest side-glance were significant."[3]

King was thrilled with Churchill's acknowledgement of Canada's contribution, which he thought was an effective answer to the opposition's contention of the inadequacy of the war effort.

At the conclusion of the debate in the House of Commons on January 29, the vote of confidence in Churchill was carried by 464 to 1. While Churchill was gratified by the level of support, with reversals in the war, such as the shock of the fall of Singapore, there was pressure for a reconstruction of the government. This was accomplished with a reduction in the war cabinet from nine members to seven. Retained were Churchill, Bevin, Attlee, Anderson, and Eden. The two new members were Oliver Lyttelton and Stafford Cripps.

There were changes afoot on the Canadian political scene also. In late 1941 Richard Hanson, the leader of the Conservative Party, announced that he would be stepping down because of his ill health. The likely successor was King's political nemesis: Arthur Meighen. Although King took great pride in his Christianity, his love for his fellow man certainly did not include Arthur Meighen. King's feelings, recorded in his diary of November 8, 1941, leave nothing to the imagination: "This has been one of the most trying days of my life." Writing of Meighen, King described him as "the meanest & most contemptible of all political adversaries, bitter, unscrupulous, sarcastic.... He will stop at nothing in seeking to bringing conscription into force, will misrepresent wilfully, and will have all Canada 'by the ears' in short time."

King actually feared Meighen, who was a skilled debater and orator, and this is clear from his further diary comments on the possibility of Meighen returning: "It made me sick at heart. I felt I wanted to give up public life & avoid a break in my health.... The strain is terrible — mental fatigue & physical combined, but depression as well." He went on to refer to Meighen's "Hitler tactics" to gain the Conservative Party leadership: "I have known nothing like it."

Meighen was elected leader by a unanimous vote on November 13, 1941, and a vacancy was made for him to return in a by-election on

February 9, 1942. When the result of that by-election vote was known, showing that Meighen had lost, King was tremendously relieved. King was convinced that the hand of God was at work: "I felt most grateful to Providence for what Canada had been spared of division and strife."

Spared the torment of having to face Meighen, King still had to convince the House that the plebiscite on conscription for overseas service was necessary. This he did in a speech delivered on February 25 titled "Keeping Faith With the People." He went straight to the crux of the matter: a plebiscite was necessary since the government had previously given a solemn pledge that there would not be conscription for overseas service. "There may be some who take the view that, in matters of government, in time of war, moral obligations count for nothing. May I say that, in my opinion, moral obligations, especially where they relate to a specific measure, a concrete matter related to the war on which the government of the country itself has given a pledge, are as binding as any obligation could possibly be."

King finished his address, stating, "Canada has taken a great pride in this war. Canada's war effort, I believe, is something that when the war is over and we get through with political controversy, the people of this country will be more proud of than any other thing in the history of this Dominion; because it has been, in Mr. Churchill's own words, a magnificent effort and all of us should seek to have it known as such."[4]

The House of Commons approved the holding of the plebiscite and the date decided for it was April 27.

King delivered a radio broadcast on the CBC on April 7, and reiterated his House of Commons speech. He did not directly appeal to the people of Quebec, who he knew could not be expected to give a majority in favour. Instead he appealed to all, in the conclusion of the broadcast: "I ask you, my fellow-countrymen — every one of you — to help give to our country complete freedom and strength for an utmost effort both in our own eyes, and in the eyes of the world. You can do this by voting YES on Monday next."

The country did vote, with the results being 65 percent for allowing the government to renege on its promise not to invoke conscription and 35 percent voting against the proposal. To the surprise of no one, only

28 percent of Quebeckers voted "Yes," while 72 percent voted "No." King was disappointed, as he was hoping that at least 35 percent of Quebeckers would vote in favour.

In Quebec opposition to the referendum was organized by a new political party, the *Bloc populaire canadien*, which, besides opposing conscription, aimed to defend provincial autonomy and the rights of French Canadians. Members included Montreal mayor Camillien Houde, the future Montreal mayor Jean Drapeau, and future prime minister Pierre Elliott Trudeau.

Although the plebiscite had released the government from its pledge not to introduce compulsory conscription for overseas service, legislation had to be introduced to repeal the clause in the Mobilization Act that restricted its provisions to Canada. In the cabinet meeting on April 28, King pressed strongly for a gradual approach with conscription, recommending that it initially be extended to take in the Western Hemisphere only.

Ralston was against that approach, which would require Parliament to pass every step and would hamper the government if quick action was necessary. In one of the many conversations King had with Ralston, the defence minister accused King of being too conciliatory, saying that King thought too much about the unity of Canada. King didn't disagree with Ralston's assessment — he was still conscious that the general election of 1917, which focused mainly on conscription, had resulted in the decimation of the Sir Wilfrid Laurier-led Liberal Party. So, during the upcoming debate in the House of Commons, King attempted to soften the legislation by pitching it with an ambiguous statement — a statement that has annoyed (and amused) generations of Canadians since that time. He said that his policy was, "Not necessarily conscription but conscription if necessary."

The source of the line was a *Toronto Star* editorial published on April 28, 1942, the day after the plebiscite. Headed "Men by Any Necessary Method," the editorial provided an analysis of the vote: "Not necessarily conscription but conscription if necessary — that is the significance of Canada's overwhelming 'Yes' vote on the plebiscite." The editorial continued with a naive comment: "Quebec's even more emphatic 'No' means simply that one of the nine provinces is out of step with the rest." King obviously knew that the results from Quebec meant more than that, and he was determined that conscription would not be necessary.

On June 12 Ralston submitted his resignation. Ralston agreed to stay on, however, after King gave him a letter stating that future stages of conscription would have House of Commons debates restricted to a maximum of two days. That solved the matter for the time being, but King retained the resignation letter for possible future use.

That crisis behind them, King and Ralston were further cheered by a piece of news they received in early June. A judicial enquiry had been conducted into the Hong Kong expedition, which had been a disaster. In the enquiry's report, Chief Justice Sir L.P. Duff's report vindicated the government.

While King and his cabinet were distracted somewhat by the political scene in Canada, Churchill was focused on laying the groundwork for the next phase of the war. He decided that another meeting with Roosevelt was necessary, to finalize the decision of the operations for 1942–43. The Americans were anxious that some plan should be decided upon at once that would enable the United States to engage the Germans in force, on land, and in the air. Churchill was worried that if that did not occur then they might change to "Japan First" strategy.

Churchill arrived in Washington on June 18. Over the next week, intense discussions were held with Roosevelt and his senior staff. The first matter dealt with was "tube alloys" [the atomic bomb]. Churchill urged that they should pool their information, work together on equal terms, and share the results. The Americans agreed, and plans were arranged for the establishment of headquarters for the project, which were to be in the United States.

While there was full agreement on the arrangements for the atomic bomb research, the matter of a second front in Europe was a different matter. Churchill gave his opinion that it was not feasible to launch Bolero, the first code-name for the major invasion of France, in 1942. He tried to placate the Americans by promising a modified "landing of six to eight divisions on the coast of northern France early in September."[5] Churchill was referring here to the landing at Dieppe, which will be covered in the next chapter.

Churchill was worried about the consequences of mounting a premature attack, and he went out of his way to point out all the details that needed to be considered. He asked if the American staff had a plan, and if so, he questioned if it covered the actual sites for the landings, and the landing-craft and shipping available. He knew that the Americans wanted immediate action — they felt it imperative to take some of the weight off Russia, which they were concerned might try to make a peace deal with Hitler. As an alternative, Churchill proposed an invasion of French North Africa, while continuing to plan Bolero. The Americans backed off the idea of creating a second front at that time, but the timing of the invasion continued to be a bone of contention between them and Britain.

King was telephoned by Roosevelt on June 23, and invited to a meeting of the Pacific Council that was to take place two days later. Before the Pacific Council sat, there was a meeting of the representatives of each of the Dominions, and also of India. King sat next to Churchill and recorded that Churchill looked "remarkably fresh, almost like a cherub, scarcely a line in his face, and completely rested." This was in spite of the unexpected and serious surrender of the Libyan fortress of Tobruk, to the forces of Rommel, just four days before.

Churchill gave his analysis of the war situation. He expressed optimism with the overall progress in the North African desert — despite the recent setback in Libya — and also stated that he felt sure that the Russians would be able to hold back the Germans, though he acknowledged that the fight would be a very bitter one. Speaking of Britain's situation, he explained the difficulty in attempting to obtain sufficient supplies and men to meet the demands in all theatres of the war. "He said it was like a man trying to cover himself with a blanket which was not large enough. When his right shoulder was cold and he pulled it over to cover it, the left became uncovered and cold.... Similarly when he hauled the blanket up to around his neck and chest, his feet became cold and exposed.... When he went to cover them up, his chest became exposed and he got pneumonia or something like that."

Churchill then moved to a discussion of the European front, and summarized the view he had given to the Americans. His words comforted King, who was still concerned with Roosevelt's simplistic view of the immense undertaking required to invade continental Europe. Churchill stated strongly that nothing would ever induce him to launch an attack on Europe unless he was sure that the Allies had sufficient strength and could be positively certain that they would win. He said that to go there without an adequate force would be to risk another Dunkirk. At that time he thought the most effective policy was to keep the German's off guard with commando raids, thereby making them believe that an attack was going to be made. This would ensure that as many men as possible were confined to Western Europe, and accordingly not available for the Russian theatre.

After the meeting King told Churchill that at the vote on the conscription issue his majority, which should be 180, might drop to 30 or thereabouts. When King returned to Ottawa, he had to again face the antagonism of a faction of the English-language press, which was supportive of "no-strings" conscription. He had to have a thick skin to handle the barbs of the press. In his diary entry for June 26, he gave an example of the ill-treatment he was receiving from the press, citing a piece in the *Ottawa Citizen*: "There is a picture of Roosevelt and Churchill sitting together. It was the one on the front veranda. I was standing immediately between the two. They have cut it off so as to show only the two and not the rest of the group. I think I will hold this as an illustration of the kind of 'fairness' that I have from a large section of the Canadian press."

King was not swayed from his position, and on July 23 he introduced the third reading of the Conscription Bill, speaking for nearly two hours. The final vote was 141 to 45 — a majority of 96. The result was much better than the gloomy prediction he had given to Churchill, but only two French-speaking Liberal members from Quebec voted for the bill.

In looking at this issue seventy years later, a comparison with the situation in the United States is warranted. That country was strongly isolationist prior to being attacked by Japan and the declaration of war by Germany and Italy. Both Quebec and the United States had severed relations with their respective mother countries in the late eighteenth century; Quebec by being conquered, and the United States by a declaration of independence.

The United States fully abandoned its isolationist position after Pearl Harbor, with even the prominent "America First" proponent Charles

Lindbergh changing his attitude and flying combat missions. The majority of Quebeckers, on the other hand, stuck to their attitude that this was a British war, and no concern of theirs. However, many Quebeckers voluntarily enlisted and they played a significant part in the Canadian forces in the war.

Despite their objections, King had managed to successfully pave the way for "conscription if necessary." The end of the conscription debate gave King a brief respite. But then he had to face a disaster to the Canadian Army in Britain.

16

DIEPPE

Although the Americans agreed that a major invasion of northern France would not be conducted in 1942, they still pressed for a significant action. Their attitude was that the war would not be won if the concentration was on defence. Regular communications between Churchill and Roosevelt on the subject resulted in their agreement that the first major action would be Operation Torch in North Africa later that year.

Churchill had the unpleasant duty of informing Stalin that there would be no second front in Europe in 1942. At the time the German army had achieved a breakthrough in the Caucasus and was threatening Russia's principal oil fields. Stalin reacted with an indignant and vitriolic response, and Churchill decided that he had to meet the Soviet leader face to face.

Churchill arrived in Moscow on August 12, 1942. Stalin explained the serious situation, and became angry when Churchill reiterated that a second front in northern Europe could not be undertaken in 1942. After a heated exchange, relations improved when Churchill spoke of the British bombing of German cities, and told Stalin that a second front would be established in North Africa. At the final meeting, three days later, Churchill explained to Stalin that in order to make the Germans more anxious regarding an attack from across the Channel, there would be a reconnaissance raid of some eight thousand men and fifty tanks.

"They will stay a night and a day, kill as many Germans as possible and take prisoners. They will then withdraw.... The object is to get information and to create the impression of an invasion."[1]

Churchill was referring to the Dieppe raid, although he exaggerated the number of troops and tanks to be involved.

Like Stalin, the Americans were critical of what they saw as the timidity of the British, though they did acknowledge that some actions were underway. One example was Churchill's creation of the Ministry of Economic Warfare, which he established with the objective of "Setting Europe Ablaze." Another example was the Combined Operations Command, created by Churchill in 1940 to conduct raids against the German occupying forces in northern Europe.

With the ongoing intent of taking pressure off Russia, Combined Operations was instructed to "press forward as opportunities arise." One opportunity did arise in February 1942 — to destroy the dry dock at Saint-Nazaire, in northwest France. This had been built to accommodate the liner *Normandie* before the war, and was the only dock that could be used by the German battleship *Tirpitz*, which was lying in Bergen, Norway. The operation was conducted on March 27, 1942, and was a spectacular success; the dry dock was destroyed and was not rebuilt until after the war.

This success whetted the appetite of the new head of Combined Operations: Lord Louis Mountbatten, a cousin of King George VI, and one of the most colourful characters in the war. He was much admired by Churchill for his audacity and daring; however, his penchant for self-promotion — above what many considered the level of his ability — attracted conflicting opinions from other politicians and the military, and later from historians.

So, Mountbatten and his team set about to stage a bigger and even more daring operation — the result was the raid on Dieppe. There were a number of official reasons for the Dieppe raid. The first was to bolster Russia — an attack would force Germany to keep troops in northern Europe, which meant that they would not be available for the Eastern Front. Then there was the need to placate the impatient Americans, by showing them that the British were serious about an invasion in 1943.

Finally, and this was presented as the official reason for the raid, such an attack would serve as a preparation for D-Day. Since no amphibious assault had been staged since Gallipoli in 1915, there was a need to develop some experience before the invasion was launched. Of particular importance was the need to gain the experience needed to capture a port large enough to be used for the transport of men, supplies, and vehicles, including tanks.

In April 1942 Mountbatten's group designed a plan for the raid, to which they gave the code name "Rutter." The official Canadian history covers the reason for a frontal attack on the town: "It was feared that an attempt to 'pinch out' a port by landings on its flanks might produce delays which would give the enemy time to demolish the harbour, whereas if the place could be seized by a blow into the centre the problem would be solved."[2]

The choice of troops for the operation was a "no-brainer." The Canadian Army had been inactive so far in the war, and when General Montgomery, who was the commander of South-East Command, which included the Canadian troops, approached the Canadian Army chief, General McNaughton, for a Canadian division to be the main part of the force, the response was positive, subject to the approval of the Canadian war cabinet.

Accordingly, McNaughton "cabled to the Chief of the General Staff in Ottawa, referring to the permission given in October 1941 to commit Canadian troops to 'minor' operations without special authority. This 'Most Secret' personal cable said in part, 'plans are now being made which involve operations of type indicated but on a scale which cannot properly be classified as 'minor,' and asked that McNaughton's authority be widened by deleting the word 'minor projects of a temporary nature.'"[3]

In Ottawa, King was involved in attempting to convince the cabinet, and especially Defence Minister Ralston, that a gradual approach to conscription for overseas service was necessary. The need for additional troops in Britain was not evident, but he recorded in his diary entry of May 1 that he was concerned that that state of affairs might not continue: "I am most concerned about the probable early conflicts that will take place about any immediate offensives that are about to come … which is likely to involve considerable loss of life on the part of our own men. However the wire that Ralston showed me last night indicates that something is afoot, larger than anything thus far attempted. To these matters I must get into retreat and have time for thought and direction to be taken."

The original plan for Operation Rutter was to include heavy air bombardment. However, at a meeting on June 5, Air Vice Marshal Leigh-Mallory stated that this would not be profitable, as this might just result in putting the Germans on the alert. He suggested that, alternatively, Boulogne could be bombed as a diversionary tactic. Agreement was made on this point, and later it was also decided to substitute commandos for paratroopers.

The training for the operation went ahead, and an exercise with the code name "Yukon" was held on June 11–12 on the Dorset coast, which resembled the Dieppe area. This went badly, with units landed miles from the proper beaches and the tank landing craft arriving over an hour late. Accordingly, the staging of another training exercise, "Yukon 2," was deemed necessary. It took place on June 22–23, and was considered a great improvement, although certain defects were evident, particularly on the naval side.

General Montgomery, who was responsible for planning involving the army, expressed confidence that the operation would succeed. His report included a post script: "The Canadians are 1st Class chaps; if anyone can pull it off, they will."[4]

On June 30 Churchill held a conference on the operation, with those present including Brooke, Mountbatten, and Captain John Hughes-Hallett, who was the Combined Operations chief staff officer. Churchill had concerns and he "asked Mountbatten whether he could 'guarantee success,' to which Mountbatten naturally replied that he could not." However, Hughes-Hallett, who had trained in disguise with the Canadian troops, assured Churchill that they would "fight like hell."[5]

While historical analyses of the decisions made in wartime necessarily concentrate on the military reasons behind the decisions, there is often a political motive to them as well. In the case of the raid on Dieppe, there was great pressure from the public and media to "do something" to assist the beleaguered Russian army. Also, Brooke and his fellow chiefs of staff had incurred Churchill's wrath because of their opposition to the Jupiter operation, which is detailed in the next chapter, and they were under pressure from Churchill to be more offensive-minded. Thus, when Brooke's opinion of the raid was requested, he had little option other than to express support. He declared that the Dieppe operation was indispensable, as it was necessary to launch a preliminary operation before the major French invasion. Based on the opinions expressed, Churchill gave his approval.

The enterprise was to be launched on July 3. However, the weather was not suitable and did not improve during the following week. A key element of the plan was secrecy, and, with many thousands involved, this could not be maintained, so the operation was cancelled.

Subsequently, a decision was made to relaunch the operation — the decision being made on the basis that the troops were already trained and could be taken straight to the ships, which would reduce the risk of the Germans detecting a large force in advance. The planners also thought that the Germans, who would undoubtedly have known of the original plan by that time, would not expect the Allies to plan an attack on the same target.

Montgomery left England on August 10 to take command of the British Eighth Army in North Africa. His replacement was the commanding officer of the First Canadian Corps, General Harry Crerar, while the actual army commander was the Canadian major-general John Hamilton Roberts. Along with a new commander, the operation also had a new name: Jubilee.

The operation was launched on the evening of August 18, 1942, with 250 small naval craft transporting almost six thousand men.[6] On the following morning, the operation would be augmented by eight hundred fighter airplanes and one hundred bombers. However, unbeknownst to the Allies, the Germans were on alert during the summer of 1942, although there is no evidence that Dieppe had been specifically targeted.

On the evening of August 18, the ships set sail. Soon, an unexpected encounter occurred: the ships were spotted by a German convoy making its way from Boulogne to Dieppe. A battle ensued, with the firing alerting the Germany troops on shore. A key element of the operation, surprise, was lost.

Further problems arose when the navy tried to land the troops. Some troops were put ashore at incorrect locations, and, thus, they were unable to carry out their objectives. Also, the forces defending the port of Dieppe itself were much heavier than had been expected, and the key objective of the raid, which was to take the town and destroy the port facilities, was not practical.

Tanks were supposed to be a major part of the attack but they had trouble proceeding on the pebble shore. This fact gave rise to criticism later, with people asking how this could not have been foreseen. Actually, it was — as is made clear in the official history: "To give the tanks traction on the beach and assist them in climbing the low end sections of the wall, a track-laying device had been invented by which the leading tank on each craft would lay a path of 'chespaling' in front of it." However, the conditions encountered precluded this being done and thus no ramps were built.[7]

Another serious problem was the breakdown of the radio connection between the invading forces and the officer in command, General Roberts. Faulty information was received, stating that the first wave at Dieppe was successful. That was not the case, but based on that report, the reserve troops were landed. When the seriousness of the situation finally became evident to those in command, a retreat was ordered, but the withdrawal of troops under heavy fire saw a further toll of boats and men.

The result was a disaster: of the 4,963 Canadian troops engaged, only 2,104 returned to England, and many of them were wounded. A total of 913 men were killed and 1,946 captured. Heavy losses were also recorded by the other forces involved, including 210 killed. The air support also suffered a heavy toll, with 106 aircraft lost, which compared to the Luftwaffe loss of 48.[8]

King wrote in his diary on August 19: "The raid on Dieppe had been carefully planned.... While Council was sitting, the first authentic word came of its extent, and probable extent of our losses. It was that casualties were heavy. Number of Canadians taken prisoners but also many killed and wounded. One felt inclined to question the wisdom of the raid unless it were part of the agreement reached when Churchill was with Stalin."

Canadian prisoners of war in German custody in Dieppe after the disastrous raid, August 19, 1942.

Churchill's official statement was given in the House of Commons on September 8, 1942. "The military credit for this most gallant affair goes to the Canadian troops, who formed five-sixths of the assaulting force.... The raid must be considered as a reconnaissance in force.... We had to get all the information necessary before launching operations on a much larger scale.... I, personally, regarded the Dieppe assault, to which I gave my sanction, as an indispensable preliminary, to full-scale operations."[9]

However, Churchill remained concerned with the operation. In a minute to his chief of staff, Major General Ismay, on December 21, 1942, he stated: "'Although for many reasons everyone was concerned to make this business look as good as possible, the time has now come when I must be informed more precisely about the military plans.' At first sight, he said, 'it would appear to a layman very much out of accord with the accepted principles of war to attack the strongly fortified town front without first securing the cliffs on either side, and to use our tanks in frontal assault off the beaches.' The Prime Minister wanted Ismay to ascertain the facts, after which he would decide whether to hold a more formal inquiry."[10]

Ismay's response included a detailed report from Mountbatten, which lay overall responsibility for the raid on Montgomery, although when it was conducted, "Monty" was in the Middle East.

While that satisfied Churchill at the time, when he came to comment on the operation in the third volume of his war memoirs he brought up the matter again. There he stated that there must have been two plans: one for Rutter and one for Jubilee. Churchill wanted to know who had authorized Jubilee, noting that, as stated, by that time Montgomery had left the scene.

Ismay, who was assisting Churchill with his memoirs, was not able to find documentary evidence, and surmised that for secrecy reasons nothing was put in writing. Ismay, however, wrote to Churchill: "I can now recall the fury of General Nye, then vice chief of the Imperial General Staff [in the absence of Brooke, who was accompanying Churchill in Cairo], who had no idea that the operation was on until reports started to flow in from the scene of the action."[11] Ismay went on to state that Churchill must have approved the action before leaving England two days before, as he cabled from Cairo using the code word for the Jubilee operation.

However, Brian Loring Villa, in his *Unauthorized Action: Mountbatten and the Dieppe Raid*, questions Ismay's statement: "The files he consulted contained another telegraphic exchange that occurred two days earlier than the cable he cited. Churchill's cable from Moscow on the 15th was not about Jubilee but rather about Rutter; he was answered by Ismay, who corrected him saying, in an unpardonable breach of security, that the name had been changed to Jubilee, and that it was now scheduled to take place on or about the 17th of August."[12]

Ismay went on to contact Mountbatten and Hughes-Hallett, but they could not help. So Churchill moved the December 21 minute to the appendix, and provided his own account of the operation, including the statement that it was Mountbatten who had revived the operation, without approval of the chiefs of staff or by the war cabinet defence committee.

Understandably, Mountbatten was alarmed at Churchill's re-draft and he provided a voluminous response to Churchill. Ismay backed Mountbatten up, on the basis that he had no recollection of the events at that time.

By that time Churchill had lost interest, and he accepted Mountbatten's account and deleted the December 1942 minutes from the appendix. As David Reynolds stated in his book *In Command of History*, "*The Hinge of Fate* therefore prints Mountbatten's self-serving answers, not Churchill's soul searching questions."[13]

Churchill (assisted by Mountbatten) wrote that the raid was "the most considerable enterprise of its kind which we had attempted against the Occupied French coastline. From available intelligence Dieppe was held by Germany low-category troops.... Our post-war knowledge of German records shows that they did not have any special warning about Dieppe through leakage." The extract in the book goes on to state that the division responsible for the defence of Dieppe had been reinforced during July and August, and was at full strength and on routine alert at the moment of the raid. Writing of the sacrifice of the Canadian troops and the value of the raid, Churchill stated: "The Canadian Army in Britain had long been eager and impatient for action, and the main part of the landing force was provided by them.... Although the utmost gallantry and devotion were shown ... the results were disappointing and our casualties were very heavy.... Looking back, the casualties of this memorable action may seem out of proportion to the results. It would be wrong to judge the episode solely by such a standard. Dieppe occupies a place of its own in the story of the war."

Churchill listed the benefits of the operation, which included the lesson of the need to build new types of craft and appliances for later use and the need for powerful support by heavy naval guns. In the short term, he felt that the raid served to make the Germans hold troops in the west and take the weight off Russia. He concluded: "Their sacrifice was not in vain."[14]

In addition to Mountbatten's "spin" on the project, Montgomery also wrote of the raid. In his autobiography, he stated that when he heard that the operation was to be re-mounted he wrote to General Paget, the commander-in-chief of the home forces, telling him of his anxiety and recommending that the raid on Dieppe should be cancelled "for all time." He stated that if it was considered desirable to raid the Continent, then the objective should not be Dieppe. "This advice was disregarded....

Without doubt the lessons learned there were an important contribution to the eventual landing in Normandy on June 6, 1944. But the price was heavy in the numbers of killed and made prisoner. I believe we could have got the information and experience we needed without losing so many magnificent Canadian soldiers."[15]

When Montgomery wrote his biography in the late 1950s, it had been accepted that the Germans did not anticipate a relaunch of the attack. Thus, since they were no more prepared than they would have been if the original raid had taken place, it is likely that Operation Rutter would have suffered the same fate as its successor, and Montgomery's reputation would have been adversely affected.

King wrote in his diary on September 13, 1944, during the Second Quebec Conference, three months after the D-Day invasion of Normandy: "Clearly the martyrdom of the men at Dieppe has helped to save Britain and the countries of Europe. Has made possible the quick invasion and the sweep that has since taken place."

If it is accepted that lessons were learned that would benefit the Allies in the future, then, conversely, it should also be noted that lessons were also learned by the Germans. In this regard the *Official History of the Canadian Army in the Second World War* provides pertinent information: "Six days after the Raid, the Commander of the German forces in the West, Field-Marshal von Rundstedt, issued a communication to his Armies: 'It must be the aim of our operations to destroy the enemy on the very day of his landing.... I have disposed my motorized Army Group Reserves in such a manner that, on most of the coastal front, one motorized formation at least will be able to intervene on the first day.'[16] Eleven months later Hitler stated the same view very specifically during a conference with Mussolini: '...at Dieppe ... the attack was broken up by the most advanced regiment.... We must break up similar attempts before the enemy can set foot on land.'"[17]

On September 29, 1942, Hitler delivered a three-hour oration to Rundstedt and others, and commented specifically on Dieppe as the meeting report stated: "The Führer describes the Dieppe operation as highly instructive for both sides ... it should never be assumed that the enemy will draw wrong conclusions ... so we too should avoid the mistake of thinking that the British have realized that even now they can do nothing against our coastal defence. The enemy will not give up the idea of forming a Second Front, for he knows that it is definitely his only remaining chance of achieving victory. And so I regard it as my task to begin immediately doing everything humanly possible to increase the defence of the coastal area."[18]

The decision to build the Atlantic Wall in northern France had been made in March 1942, as Hitler was convinced that was where the Allies would attempt a landing, and the Dieppe raid confirmed his resolve for that project.

The taking of a major port was the main military objective of the operation. However, it is tragically ironic that one of the most imaginative ideas of World War II, the so-called "Mulberry harbour," eliminated the need to take a port for the D-Day invasion.

Military and historical analysts with no personal involvement have been very candid in their views of the Dieppe raid. Brereton Greenhouse, for example, wrote on the raid for *The Canadian Encyclopedia*. After stating that it was a "major disaster," he accepted the standard opinion that, "The raid did provide valuable experience for subsequent amphibious assaults in North Africa, Italy and, most notably, Normandy."[19]

That opinion was supported by Ralph Allen in *Ordeal by Fire,* the fifth volume of the Canadian History series. "As for the much discussed 'lessons' of Dieppe, the politicians and generals made so much of them in the first aftermath of shock that many people felt they were simply trying to cover up a senseless blunder.... Dieppe was not a total waste. Dieppe was a powerful contributor to the artificial harbours of D-Day 1944; the decision to give the assault troops overwhelming fire support from air and sea; to the formation of a special permanent naval force highly trained in assault landings."[20]

A contradictory opinion was given by Pierre Berton. "At Dieppe the intelligence on both sides — Canadian and German — was execrable. The Canadians thought they would be facing a small force of second-rate troops. In fact, the force against them was far larger and tougher than they expected." Berton summarized the raid as a "tragic bungle" and he quotes a British historian, stating: "Why, to use a Canadian expression, did we have to learn it the hard way? ... All these 'valuable lessons' were lessons that Earl Mountbatten's planners could have figured out for themselves, without the sacrifice of 1,137 lives."[21]

This is supported by Brian Nolan, in his *King's War.* "If the Brest excursion [re-embarking in France after Dunkirk] had been militarily dumb, Dieppe was criminal. The latter day visitor to the town ... merely has to stand on the towering cliffs over-looking the stony beach to realize the futility of the assault."[22]

British historian Andrew Roberts devoted eighty-two pages in his *Eminent Churchillians* to outlining the incompetence of Mountbatten. He continued this theme when commenting on the Dieppe operation in his *Masters and Commanders.* After referring to Mountbatten's comment on the lessons learned, he wrote: "This is tripe, unless the lesson of not attacking a well-defended town without proper intelligence and a preliminary aerial and naval bombardment is a 'priceless secret,' rather than the kind of assumption a lance-corporal might have made."[23]

King viewed Dieppe for himself on August 17, 1946, during the Paris Peace Conference.

> The place itself where the Royal Regiment landed seemed to be of the most difficult for a landing it would be possible to find anywhere. One sees cliffs rising steeply out of the sea; then there was a narrow sort of valley which led into the town, and then on the other side a very high hill on top of which was a gun emplacement which was occupied at the time by German soldiers and guns. The gun emplacement commands a complete view of the beach and one man with the help of a gun, it seemed to me, could destroy men as rapidly as they would land. It was a steep ascent everywhere. What would have been done once the heights were gained, I don't understand, as it would have been as difficult again getting into town as getting up. I really felt as though the men who had planned that raid should have been cashiered. It did strike me as the most impossible of all places to attempt

to effect a landing. It was sending men to certain death without a ghost of a chance. Apparently it was thought they might effect a surprise landing in the dark. I was told today the ships of the navy were an hour late in arriving so that the men were exposed in the light when they landed. I felt a hatred of war greater than I have experienced at any time as the names of a fine lot of young Canadians were read out. Men who were killed and one thought of many others. It just made one indignant beyond words.

Leaving aside for a moment whether or not the raid should have been undertaken, there remains the question of why it went so terribly wrong? While mistakes were made in the execution of the plan, the major reason for the disaster was the acceptance of the flawed intelligence reports. The British grossly underestimated the strength of the German garrison, and also did not ascertain that the cliffs in the headlands contained gun nests, which, as King noted, made "easy pickings" of any invasion forces. Major Reginald Unwin, a Canadian intelligence officer, warned "that the absence of confirmed enemy defences in the area did not preclude the possibility of it being heavily defended." His warnings were ignored, and "when the final appreciation of Dieppe's defences was submitted for inclusion in the plan, Unwin refused to sign it."[24]

There were certainly good reasons for conducting an operation in northern France at this time, not all of them military ones. But even without the benefit of hindsight, the plan to take a major port with a frontal assault, unless it was certain that it was undefended, should have been rejected as an impractical and suicidal enterprise. It is not stretching the imagination to compare the raid to the "Charge of the Light Brigade" in the Crimean War. This was immortalized in the poem by Alfred, Lord Tennyson, who wrote, "Cannon to the right of them; Cannon to the left of them; Into the valley of Death rode the six hundred."

Pierre Berton wrote of the raids historical significance in the eyes of his countrymen: "How ironic it is that for Canadians the defining battle of the Great War was a glorious victory [Vimy], while its counterpart, twenty-five years later, was a bitter defeat [Dieppe]."[25]

Three involved in the raid were awarded the Victoria Cross. The last word is left to one of them, Captain Patrick Porteous, quoted in his obituary in the *Globe & Mail* of October 16, 2000. He echoed King's words, but in a more direct fashion: "The people who planned it should be shot."

CHURCHILL DISAPPOINTED WITH CANADA — TWICE!

A fter the slow start of the Phony War, with the United States and Japan now involved, the course of the Second World War began to proceed more rapidly. In the Pacific Japan's attack on Pearl Harbor and its defeat of Hong Kong and Singapore quickly made that theatre an active one. In Europe the German attack on Russia had launched a massive struggle between the two powers. In the West the raid on Dieppe, while seen as important, was soon eclipsed by other events.

Churchill continued to be wholeheartedly against a second front in northern France at that time, but he was in full agreement with the Americans that the Soviets should be given all possible help, to ensure that they stayed in the war. To that end, convoys to deliver armaments and supplies were sent to Russia. These convoys had to sail north of Scandinavia, and much was lost through German attacks. The attacks came from two airports in northern Norway, which were manned by ten thousand personnel, along with some seventy bombers and a hundred fighters. For the Allies, the cost of fighting the aerial attacks and the difficulty of dealing with the frigid, dangerous conditions made the effort barely justifiable.

In the spring of 1942, Churchill came up with a plan, with the code name "Jupiter," which he described as "the liberation of northern Norway."[1] Churchill, ever one for seeing the big picture but not one who always allowed for difficulties, proposed that an expedition be mounted to take possession of the airfields. As he wrote at the time: "If the going was good we could advance gradually southward, unrolling the Nazi map of Europe from the top. All that had to be done is to oust the enemy from the airfields and destroy their garrison."[2]

The Joint Planning staff did not view the operation so favourably, however. They responded, saying that Britain "'could not capture and hold the Northern Norway air bases,' because of the inability to provide adequate defence for the shipping that would have to be left in the fiords, and because, having captured the airfields, itself 'a hazardous operation,' the chances of being able to hold them throughout the winter were, 'so slight as to be unacceptable.'"[3]

Churchill was not put off by the response. and he brought it up again on June 8, 1942, with the chiefs of staff. The minutes of the meeting record that they also were "doubtful that Jupiter was practical," but they diplomatically stated that the plan was being "carefully studied."[4]

Frustrated by the lack of enthusiasm displayed by his advisors, Churchill chose, to use a football expression, an end run. On July 8 Churchill informed General Brooke, the chief of the Imperial General Staff, that the Canadian Army chief, General Andrew McNaughton, was to be entrusted with the preliminary study and planning of Jupiter and to be given every assistance by his staff.

Brooke's reaction, made with understandable sarcasm, was recorded in his diary of the next day: "It had been suggested ... that with his more flexible and fertile brain, McNaughton would find a way out when the Chiefs of Staff had failed. After lunch I sent for him to my office and informed him privately how matters stood, as I did not want him afterwards to imagine that we were suggesting that the Canadians should undertake an operation, which we considered impracticable."[5] McNaughton studied the papers, and appointed the well-respected Canadian officer Brigadier Guy Simonds to head the staff to undertake the detailed work.

In the meantime McNaughton was invited by Churchill to visit him at Chequers to discuss the plan. Churchill's comments should be read in the context of the cancellation of the first Dieppe operation, Rutter, and before a decision had been made to relaunch it as Jubilee.

Churchill later wrote that he still had hopes for Jupiter. With little or no progress made with its detailed planning, he thought that this operation would be a glorious opportunity for the Canadian Army, which had been inactive in Britain, awaiting the invader. He therefore had a long talk with General McNaughton, of whom he had a high opinion, and "whose influence with the Canadian Government was powerful."[6]

McNaughton was given the royal treatment, including lunch with such prominent personages as Churchill's scientific advisor, Lord Cherwell, Major-General Ismay, and the MP Duncan Sandys and his wife, Churchill's daughter, Diana. Churchill privately told the general his thoughts on a number of subjects, before turning to Jupiter.

McNaughton's diary gave his version of the conversation: "In referring to his difficulties with corporate advice from the three Services, Churchill said: 'Soldier, sailor and airman are each by themselves bold fellows but together they become filled with doubts and inhibitions.'" McNaughton wrote that the prime minister referred to the Russian convoy, which had to be continued, although there were heavy losses. Thus the necessity of Jupiter. Churchill thought that Canadian troops would be ideal for this assignment as "our people naturally knew about cold climates."[7]

McNaughton informed Churchill that he had begun organizing the staff. The general concluded his diary report, with an understatement: "It had been an interesting experience."[8]

The Jupiter review was completed, and submitted to the chiefs of staff on August 6. It concluded that Jupiter was impracticable. It took some time for the response from the chiefs of staff committee, but when it was provided in early September, it was, not surprisingly, highly complemen-tary: "It was 'one of the clearest and most ably worked out appreciations which they had ever had before them.'"[9]

Although Churchill had many disagreements with his chiefs of staff during the war, he never once overruled them. However, in this case he came very close. He didn't accept the Canadians' considered opinion either, and his next move caused King sleepless nights.

McNaughton was invited again to Chequers, and he arrived there on September 19. Churchill brought up a number of points in the Canadian review with which he disagreed. As he was getting nowhere with the general, Churchill pulled himself up short and looked quizzically at McNaughton over the top of his spectacles.

"'I sometimes envy Stalin,' he said. 'He could shoot those who disagreed with him and had already expended a great deal of ammunition for that purpose.'

"'Perhaps so,' said McNaughton with a straight face, but 'democracy had some advantages too. Masters, as well as servants, could give up office without being shot.'

"Churchill conceded that there was something in that."[10]

Churchill was still not dissuaded, and he referred to the Canadian report, which had mentioned the benefits of talks with Stalin. He agreed but he needed to send someone who would have access to the Soviet leader. It could not be a diplomat, as Stalin would not want to see him, but he would certainly meet with a prominent soldier, such as General McNaughton. "Yes, that was it. He would approach Mackenzie King for his consent to McNaughton's undertaking this important mission."[11]

McNaughton wrote in his diary that the "Prime Minister's tone was most friendly. I felt he was seeking to persuade — perhaps flatter — me into a course of action concerning Jupiter on which he had set his heart."[12]

McNaughton's response was that he would do anything to help win the war. Churchill assured him that his going to Moscow would involve no commitment for the use of Canadian troops in the operation.

McNaughton advised Ottawa of the request from Churchill. King's diary of September 21 outlined the difficult position he found himself in. He did not want to disappoint or even antagonize Churchill, but he knew that whatever decision was made, it was bound to be misunderstood. If opposed, it would be said that but for the opposition the plan would have succeeded. If accepted and the plan was a disaster it would be said that the government should have, with the knowledge of McNaughton's report, opposed it strenuously. King sent what he thought was a low-key message, softening the negative decision. However, it was not received by Churchill in that manner. Sir Alan Brooke recorded, after being summoned to Churchill's presence, that he "found the Prime Minister greatly depressed by a telegram from Mackenzie King, the Canadian Premier."[13]

Jupiter became one of the lost opportunities, as Churchill later recorded, but this was not the end of the friction that developed between him and King in late 1942. Reports came that the Germans were shackling Dieppe prisoners. Churchill was determined to retaliate, and King initially agreed with that action. However, the Canadian war committee discussed the matter on October 10, and were unanimous that they should not seek to compete with the Germans in their brutalities. The recommendation to Britain was to seek mediation of the protecting power, Switzerland, and the Red Cross to end what had taken place.

However, the instructions to shackle one hundred inmates at the Bowmanville, Ontario, prisoner of war camp had already been given, and the attempt to implement the requirement had resulted in a riot. The prisoners barricaded themselves in a mess hall, armed with sticks, iron bars, and other implements, to be used as weapons. Canadian soldiers were brought in, and, rather sportingly it seemed, they used just baseball bats to attempt to overcome the Germans. This even match did not achieve the desired result and a brawl ensued. Eventually, water hoses were used, and what became known as the "Battle of Bowmanville" was over.

Defence Minister Ralston had been in Britain, and he returned and reported to the war cabinet Churchill's response to the Canadians' decision: again Churchill was disappointed with Canada. However, with the intercession of the Swiss government, the matter of shackling was resolved.

18

PROGRESS AT LAST

While Churchill did not get his own way in an invasion of northern Norway, a more important action commenced in North Africa on October 23, 1942: Operation Lightfoot, or, as it was later referred to, the Battle of El Alamein.

Churchill wrote to King on October 28, informing him that, with information on the German resources that had been decrypted by the code-breakers at Bletchley Park, "the great battle for Egypt has opened well, although one cannot yet forecast its result. The enemy are short of ammunition and fuel.... Our forces are substantially superior."[1]

In early November success was assured. Churchill wrote: "It marked in fact the turning of the 'Hinge of Fate.' It may almost be said, 'Before Alamein we never had a victory. After Alamein we never had a defeat.'"[2]

This was followed by Operation Torch on November 8, with the Americans now joining the Allied forces in landings at Algiers, Oran, and Casablanca. Resistance to the landings came from the Vichy French forces, until the notorious Admiral Darlan ordered them to lay down their arms. Darlan realized that his future would be better with the Allies, and he became a turncoat. Almost at the same time, Hitler gave instructions for his troops to occupy the part of France governed by the Vichy French.

King, who, at Churchill's behest, had continued to recognize the Vichy government, in order to have a window into France, now had to make the decision to sever the relationship. King's under-secretary of state, Norman Robertson, came up with an inspired position. In view of the Vichy French action in opposing the Allied forces landing in North Africa, Canada took the view that they no longer represented the French people. Thus, Canada did not recognize the Vichy French as the legal government of France but just a German puppet government. While King was usually averse to making a quick decision, here he wanted to ensure that the Canadian position was announced before Vichy declared a state of war with Canada. It would not do to have a government of one of the founding nations of Canada declare war on the country; but once Vichy was no longer legitimate, the declaration would have no validity.

The government's statement was broadcast on November 8 on the CBC Radio network, and the following day King met with the French ambassador to present him with the formal statement.

Winston Churchill took the opportunity, when speaking at a luncheon hosted by the lord mayor of London at the Mansion House on November 10, to cover the Alamein success and the northwest Africa invasion: "I have never promised anything but blood, tears, toil and sweat. Now, however, we have a new experience. We have victory — a remarkable and definite victory. The bright gleam has caught the helmets of our soldiers and warmed and cheered all our hearts.... Now this is not the end. It is not even the beginning of the end. But it is, perhaps, the end of the beginning."

Churchill then turned to France and showed the consistency of his francophile feelings: "At this time our thoughts turn to France, groaning in bondage under the German heel. Many ask themselves the question: Is France finished? ... I declare to you my faith that France will rise again. While there are men like General de Gaulle and all those who follow him … my confidence in the future of France is sure."[3]

While Churchill applauded de Gaulle in his addresses, the general was, in fact, a thorn in the prime minister's side for almost the whole war. On one occasion Churchill ordered that de Gaulle not to be allowed to leave England to stir up trouble abroad. This resulted in a meeting, where de Gaulle complained that he was a prisoner and presumably would be sent to the enemy alien prison on the Isle of Man. Churchill responded: "No. You are very distinguished, and so would go to the Tower of London!"[4]

As well as making many speeches to select audiences, Churchill made it a priority to keep the public directly informed. On November 29, for example, he gave a broadcast that was transmitted around the world. He started by reminding the listeners that at the outbreak in 1939 they were alone. He then extended his description: "That wonderful association of States and races spread all over the globe called the British Empire — or British Commonwealth if you will; I will not quarrel about it — and above all, our small Island, stood in the gap alone in the deadly hour. Here we stood, firm though all was drifting; throughout the British Empire no one faltered."

This recognition of the contribution made by Canada and the other members of the Commonwealth was particularly welcomed by King, since he had noted before — in Churchill's Mansion House speech, for example — how the British prime minister often did not give such recognition in his speeches.

Churchill continued his radio address, exploring the much improved situation and the recent military successes. He told his listeners of his promise to Stalin when meeting in August 1942: "'When we have decisively defeated Rommel in Egypt, I will send you a telegram.' And he replied: 'When we make our counter-offensive here' (and he drew the arrow on the map), 'I will send you one.' Both messages have duly arrived, and both have been thankfully received."[5]

The optimism Churchill displayed in his radio address was also found in his private correspondence. On November 30 Churchill turned sixty-eight and King sent him greetings. He responded: "I send to you and all the people of Canada my warm thanks for your very kind message. The unity of purpose and the resolution for victory of our two countries remained unshaken during the dark days, and I am confident that together we shall share the final victory."[6]

Although he was not as noted for the impact of his speeches as was Churchill, King knew the importance of transmitting information about the war to the Canadian public, as well as, at times, to a wider audience. On December 2 he gave an address in New York, which was broadcast in Canada and other countries. The address was to the Pilgrim Society of the United States, an exclusive Anglo-American group that tried to foster close relations between the United States and Britain.

King began by speaking of the friendly relations between the citizens of the United States and those of the British Commonwealth. Then he took advantage of the opportunity to set out details of Canada's war effort: It had, King said, 385,000 volunteers in the three services. In raw materials, it was supplying 95 percent of the nickel and 40 percent of the aluminum used by the United Nations [the term invented for the Allies by Roosevelt and Churchill]; it had the largest small-arms plant on the North American continent: its automotive industry produced three hundred thousand military vehicles; its aircraft production had risen from forty a year to four hundred a month; in 1942, Russia was supplied with one hundred million dollars' worth of tanks and other war supplies; and its industrial war production in 1942 to be some 2.5 billion dollars.[7]

These figures are mind boggling. But one statistic, which King also quoted, is perhaps easier to comprehend: "We are supplying about 200 pounds of food per annum for every man, woman and child in the United Kingdom."

Following his address to the Pilgrim Society, King continued on to Washington, after accepting an invitation from Roosevelt to spend a weekend at the White House. It was a low-key affair. During their talks they spent time discussing the current situation in the war and intentions for the coming year. It was clear that the president valued King's opinions, and he used the prime minister as a sounding board for his ideas.

Roosevelt told King of the genesis of the term "United Nations." During Churchill's visit in December 1941, they had been discussing the appropriate name for the countries that were fighting for freedom. During the night it came to him, and before breakfast the following morning, he told King, Roosevelt had "got his man to take him on his chair to Winston's room and knocked at the door. Winston called out to come in but that he was taking a bath. [Roosevelt] said he walked out of the bath in a few minutes and had not a stitch on him. The President said: 'Winston' — pointing at him — 'I have it: the United Nations.' Churchill at once said that was the title to call them."

The conversation moved to their affection for Churchill, even though both agreed that he occasionally said some outrageous things: "I said it gave him a great internal kick to say certain of these things. We had a laugh over it.... The President said he did not know how he did it at all. He would sit up till 3, and get up looking as fresh as could be."

King then made mention of Churchill's Mansion House speech, indicating that there were parts of the speech that he found troublesome. In it, Churchill had stated, "I have not become the King's First Minister in order to preside over the liquidation of the British Empire" — a position that King did not like. Roosevelt stated that he had discussed this attitude with Churchill, who was negative on the matter of self-determination for British colonies. Certainly, this was a bone of contention when the Atlantic Charter was being drafted, with Churchill taking the stance that it should not apply to the British Empire. Churchill's mindset was in many ways decidedly Victorian, and he still saw the world from the standpoint of a British imperialist. The world had changed, however, and in spite of his feelings, he was powerless after the war, even when back as prime minister, to stop the natural erosion of the Empire.

Regardless of King's attitude towards Churchill's imperial mindset, he remained steadfast in his belief in the importance of Canada's British ties and of its responsibility to aid Britain in the fight against Germany and the other Axis powers. An important part of that contribution was the British Commonwealth Air Training Plan (BCATP) — a massive scheme that saw a number of schools set up in Canada for the training of air crews for the Royal Air Force, the Royal Australian Air Force, the Royal New Zealand Air Force, and the Royal Canadian Air Force. The third anniversary of the BCATP occurred on December 16, 1942, at which time Churchill wrote to King: "When I look back on the remorseless growth of the Air Forces of the United Nations and survey the shattering punishment we have already begun to inflict upon the enemy, I realize how much of our success is due to the great scheme which has been so energetically developed in Canada. Canadians in their thousands have answered the call of the air." After listing the many countries that had used the training facilities, he wrote of the very great effort that had been required. He finished: "Our thanks are due to the Government and people of Canada, and especially to the officers and men of the Royal Canadian Air Force, who by their wholehearted endeavours have established the plan on a sure foundation, and from it are now forging a potent instrument of victory."[8]

Churchill sent further kind words to King on December 17, when he wrote him to wish him well on his sixty-eighth birthday: "Please accept my warm greetings for your birthday and my best wishes for a victorious future. You have been a good friend and comrade in these tremendous times."[9]

The following day, the *Ottawa Journal*'s Grattan O'Leary stated that the prime minister's birthday was an occasion for good wishes. O'Leary was not content, however, to simply extend King a simple "Happy Birthday"; he continued with a highly incisive assessment of King. O'Leary mentioned King's "baffling qualities," which, he said, had allowed, "in an era of restless change, ... this sometimes unintelligible public man ... [to keep] unbroken place and power." He listed the many qualities that would be expected of a prime minister, few of which, he thought, King possessed. He then went over the attributes that King did possess: he was a great party leader; he had great political skill and masterly control over his colleagues; he had superb negotiating skills. O'Leary went on to state that King was full of contradictions, however. On the one hand, he was ruthless with opponents, and unforgiving of those who deserted him. One the other hand, according to O'Leary, "no man [was] more civilized socially or [paid] more attention to courtesy, ... which he often calls chivalry ... no politician of any time has turned corners more adroitly ... Other qualifications, some positive force, must be sought in him if we are to understand his long reign, his series of triumphs over formidable foes. It is a fascinating study."

King *was* full of contradictions, but as mentioned in the "Introduction," he took great care in ensuring that the public saw him as he wished them to see him. But there was the other side, hidden from all but a few.

One side of King that the public never saw was his romantic side. A lifelong bachelor, King was not viewed as a man who sought female company. Yet, the truth is, he did pay attention to women, and had several women companions throughout his life. His romantic side can be seen in King's involvement with one of the actresses who had been engaged to help sell another tranche of Victory Bonds during this period.

The financing of the war required that Victory Bonds be sold; to help promote their sale, notable figures from the entertainment industry were engaged. In 1944 stars such as Shirley Temple and Jack Benny would join the ranks of the entertainers who lent their glamour to help sell the bonds. In 1940 Madeleine Carroll, best known for playing opposite Robert Donat in *The 39 Steps*, gave her support to the sale of the third issue of the Victory Bonds.

King met her in October 1940 when she came to Ottawa to help with the bond sale that year, and immediately became very fond of her. Not above an innocent flirtation, he feigned having a broken heart when he received the news of her marriage to the actor Sterling Hayden. A few weeks later, a mutual friend brought a message from her in which she said that she wanted "to give me her love." King responded, quoting from the song "Daisy Bell," and telling her, "I'm half crazy all for the love of you." Needless to say, the public did not know of this innocent but very "un-King like" episode.

Decidedly more typical of his public persona was his suspicion of the intentions of the United States. The Permanent Joint Board of Defence, established at the Ogdensburg Conference in 1940, had considered creating a joint study of territory opened up by the Alaska Highway. King saw this as an attempt to control developments in Canada after the war, and to bring the country into the U.S. orbit. King set out his position in his diary of December 30. "I am strongly opposed to anything of that kind. I want to see Canada continue to be, in time, as our country certainly will, the greatest of nations in the British Commonwealth."

As 1942 came to a close, King had mixed feelings about the progress made during a further year in the bloodiest war mankind had experienced. Overall progress was evident, and even though the end of the war was in the distance, eventual success was confidently expected. The Dieppe raid had been a disaster; however, the Allies had learned from it, and the public had accepted that it had been worthwhile.

The beginning of 1943 saw the Allies making significant progress on all fronts. In North Africa the British Eighth Army was continuing to harass

Rommel's forces and pushing him westwards. In the Far East, Japan was on the defensive after American naval victories. But the major turn-around was in Russia — some three hundred thousand German forces, forbidden to retreat by Hitler, had been trapped at Stalingrad.

Churchill and Roosevelt met in Casablanca in January 1943 to discuss their combined strategy for the year. The major issue was the cross-Channel invasion, which they had agreed would occur in the spring of 1943. The British military had concluded, however, that it was unrealistic to work on that timetable — an inadequate number of American troops would be available in Britain at that point, and sufficient shipping wouldn't be available either. With an estimated forty-four German divisions stationed in France at the time, the Nazis would have easily been able to annihilate the invasion force that the Allies would have been able to deploy.

The Americans, and especially General Marshall, were not convinced by the British arguments, though, and fierce negotiations ensued. Finally, however, Roosevelt accepted Churchill's position. It was deemed essential, though, that once the North African fighting had concluded, an action should be undertaken against the "soft underbelly" of the European continent. It was eventually agreed that the target would be Sicily.

Another issue, which has been criticized by some since, was also decided during that meeting: the necessity of the unconditional surrender of Germany and Japan. Churchill and Roosevelt decided that there would be no peace conference, as had occurred to end World War I. The critics of the decision point out that, as a result, there was no incentive for the leaders of the defeated nations to give up the fight, since they would have known that they could expect no mercy from the victors. On the other hand, it would have been unconscionable for Hitler and his mass-murdering underlings to have been treated with other than full justice.

Churchill, back in London after the conference, received a telegram from King on February 17. King congratulated him on the Casablanca Conference and confirmed a previously advised intimation that Canada would be providing further financial assistance: "I have no doubt you will have been encouraged on your return to learn of our Government's intention, in furtherance of a total war effort, to ask Parliament to appropriate one billion dollars to provide funds for the production and transfer of war supplies for any of the United Nations, to be used in the joint and effective prosecution of the war.... You may be sure that no efforts will be spared to make Canada's contribution the most effective possible."[10]

Churchill responded on February 19 with thanks for the "further tremendous financial assistance... As soon as your Parliament's authority has been given, I shall hope to express publicly our recognition of these new measures. I know how much they owe to your own inspiration and leadership. Warmest regards to you, my old and trusted friend."[11]

On March 4 King's diary mentioned messages he'd sent to Roosevelt and Churchill, both of whom had experienced health problems after the conference, with Churchill having suffered pneumonia.

Churchill wrote to King on March 6: "I am deeply touched by your very generous message and I send to you and to all members of the Parliament of Canada my heartfelt thanks. I recall with gratitude the warmth of the reception which you all gave to me when I visited Canada in December 1941. In the darkest days Canada, under your leadership, remained confident and true. Now the days are brighter and when victory is won, you will be able to look back with just pride upon a record surpassed by none."[12]

On March 30 British Foreign Secretary Anthony Eden flew in to Ottawa after meeting with Roosevelt and American officials in Washington. He and King had lengthy talks, during which Eden told King that it was his opinion that, due to the submarine menace and the lack of buildup of troops in Britain, he did not think there would be an all-out invasion in 1943.

In early April Churchill wrote to King to ascertain his reaction to the suggestion of an Imperial Conference in London. King's immediate reaction was to point out the difficulty of his leaving Canada; but when Churchill advised that the purpose, besides showing the strength and union of the British Commonwealth and Empire, was to deal with negotiations that would take place at the time of the peace, and issues related to post-war organization, King gave his support.

The conference was set for some time in the future, though, and in the meantime, King needed to address more immediate concerns, such as the raising of additional funds to finance the war effort. The Fourth Victory Loan Campaign was launched in Toronto on April 19. King broadcast to the nation in support of it, and while his effort again demonstrated that he did not possess a Churchillian delivery, the content, which he wrote himself, was certainly comparable. He talked of the rise of Canada during the war to the position of a world power, and the major part played by the BCATP, mentioning Roosevelt's quotation that it had made Canada, "the Aerodrome of Democracy." After detailing the number of Canadian forces involved in the war and the scale of the production of the country's factories, King looked to the future. He spoke of the supreme hour for Canada which would come with the eventual "mighty effort to batter down the ramparts of Prussian power, and to slay the dragon of Nazi brutality in its native lair."[13]

Like its predecessors, the Victory Bond campaign would be a success. Alongside this financial success, the Allied campaign in North Africa continued to do well, and by early May, it had turned into a rout of the German and Italian forces, with some 250,000 prisoners taken. Churchill congratulated the commander of the forces. General Eisenhower responded: "Today your heart-warming telegram arrived, and I regret that I have no words to tell you how pleased I am. I can only say 'Thank You,' and assure you that this army will never stop pounding until Hitlerism is abolished from the earth."[14] General Alexander also advised Churchill on May 13: "Sir: It is my duty to report that the Tunisian campaign is over. All enemy resistance has ceased; we are masters of the North African shores."[15]

Although it was only a few months since the Casablanca Conference, Churchill was "conscious of serious divergences beneath the surface which, if not adjusted, would lead to grave difficulties and feeble action during the rest of the year. [He] was therefore resolved," he continued, "to have a conference on the highest possible level."[16]

Roosevelt agreed, and Churchill sailed to the United States arriving on May 11, going immediately to Washington. The conference, which Churchill named "Trident," commenced the next day.

BACK TO THE CONTINENT

The Trident Conference began on May 12, 1943. The main subject of discussion was what should come next after the invasion of Sicily. Churchill stated that the priority should be to invade the mainland of Italy and eliminate it as a combatant. However, Roosevelt was concerned that if that was done, there would be additional German forces available for other areas, including Russia. In the end the Allies decided to continue operations in the Mediterranean and in the Pacific, and build up forces and landing craft in Britain for a cross-Channel enterprise in the spring of 1944.

While King was not invited to the conference itself, he received an invitation from Churchill on May 12 to meet him in Washington. This was followed by a telegram from Roosevelt.

King arrived at the White House on May 18 and found Churchill lying in bed in a nightgown of black-and-white silk. Churchill informed him that he was very worried lest he might say anything in his speech to Congress that would be embarrassing in the existing political situation. He spoke of the African victory, and the way that the Germans surrendered, falling and crawling, whereas, an hour before, when they thought they could win, they were most savage and brutal.

King offered to read the speech in advance, and this offer was accepted. Afterwards King remarked to Leslie Rowan, Churchill's private secretary, that like Churchill's other speeches, the references were just to

British and U.S. forces. He told Rowan that Canadians would be most hurt if no specific reference was made to them.

The next day King accompanied Churchill to Congress. En route, King complimented him on the content of the speech, and Churchill remarked that he intended to speak to all as one big family. When they arrived, King was seated in the Executive box, where he was joined by the duke of Windsor.

Churchill reminded the members of Congress of having had the honour of addressing them seventeen months before, continuing that in the meantime "we have toiled and suffered and dared shoulder to shoulder against the cruel and mighty enemy." After describing the current situation and the work being conducted by both Britain and the United States, he did mention the Dominions, and pleased King with a personal acknowledgement: "It is my special duty to promote and preserve this intimacy and concert between all parts of the British Commonwealth and Empire, and especially with the great self-governing Dominions, like Canada, whose Prime Minister is with us at this moment, whose contribution is so massive and invaluable."

Churchill concluded by saying that while great progress had been made, "The enemy is still proud and powerful.... By singleness of purpose, by steadfastness of conduct, by tenacity and endurance, such as we have so far displayed — by these, and only by these, can we discharge our duty to the future of the world and to the destiny of man."[1]

After a luncheon, King went back to the White House with Churchill. "I told him I was very sure that what he had said to Congress would be most helpful. Thanked him for his personal reference. He spoke again about the term "Commonwealth and Empire." I stressed once more that the two were alternatives depending on where the emphasis was to have been placed."

At the White House, Churchill and King went in to see the president, who was sitting in his shirt sleeves in his office. Roosevelt told Churchill that he had heard the proceedings over the radio and was pleased with what Churchill had said. He also commented on the hearty applause that Congress gave to King, after Churchill recognized him.

The following day the Pacific War Council met, with Roosevelt and Churchill giving their understanding of the Pacific Theatre. After lunch

Roosevelt, Churchill, and King discussed their own issues. The president said he would like to have Canada as a member of the Pan-American Union. Churchill agreed, stating that Canada should be just as strong as any Western Hemisphere country. Equally, she should hold as strong a place as she could within the British Empire. He went further, stating that, so far as this continent was concerned, he would be glad to see Canada represent more and more the British position, in relation to the United States.

Churchill spoke of a matter which had been festering in his mind for some twenty years, as he later outlined in the first volume of his war memoirs, *The Gathering Storm*. He talked of the League of Nations, which had been the child of President Wilson, but which had received an almost mortal blow in 1920 when the United States refused to join. There he wrote that, because of the American position that "Europe must be left to stew in its own juice ... conditions were swiftly created by the victorious Allies which, in the name of peace, cleared the way for the renewal of war."[2]

King recorded that Churchill spoke passionately and strongly to Roosevelt: "I am saying this in the presence of Canada's Prime Minister, deliberately to you, Mr. President. I beg of you not to keep aloof from the European situation, once this war is over." Churchill thought that after the war there should be a Council of Europe, a Council of Asia, and a Council of the Americas. Over all, there will be a World Council, to which there would be a final appeal. "You, Mr. President, should be on all three councils. We should be perhaps on all three councils, though I should be glad to have Canada represent the British, as well as their own interests, on the council of the Americas."

Churchill was determined that the carnage and bloodshed being expended in the war would not be wasted by opening the door to another world conflict. Thus, as King recorded, he was shocked with Roosevelt's reaction. "The President indicated that he was not too sure how far America should go in being on a European council. This caused Churchill to say quite earnestly: 'You are needed there as much as ever in your own interest. We have had two wars into which you have been drawn, and which are costing America a lot. Neither of them originated here. They both originated in Europe, and they will arise there again unless some of these countries can be kept in proper control by the rest of the world.'"

Roosevelt reacted by stating that what was needed was a sort of moderator to look into situations and notify the World Council when action should be taken. To Churchill, this proposal seemed like a recipe for another impotent League of Nations, and his response clearly indicated his opposition: "It [is] not a moderator or a pacifier that is needed but … someone to take a very firm hand to make it impossible for them to do anything."

Churchill had made his point, but it was Roosevelt's successor who would be involved in establishing the role of the United States in European affairs, after the end of the war.

After some lighthearted banter Churchill continued his plea with the president to not let America become isolated from Europe. That he wanted to see the strongest friendly relations between the British Empire and the United States. That there could not be too much friendship between them.

Later Churchill and King had a private conversation. Churchill brought up again the intended meeting of Dominion prime ministers, stating that it was essential that King be present. He attempted to flatter King by calling him the outstanding imperialist today.

That evening there was a meeting of the joint staffs of Britain, Canada, and Australia, along with a representative from India. The Canadian delegation included Ralston and Stuart. Churchill presented the points he had made to the Congress, and outlined the next strategy: the invasion of a few islands in the Mediterranean, as a stepping stone to the European mainland.

At Churchill's conclusion, King, as the prime minister of the senior Dominion, expressed thanks and announced a change in the usage of the Canadian Army. The British Army chiefs had been frustrated in handling the Canadian Army as the Canadian government had ordered that they be kept together, in one unit. King now advised that, if it helped in winning the war, the army could be divided up.

The following day, May 21, King had a private conversation with Roosevelt. The president stated that he wished to have a talk with Stalin alone, as he was concerned that the Russian leader would see himself at a disadvantage in meeting with the two Western leaders, who were in close union. King responded that Churchill had seen Stalin himself and would thoroughly understand.

Maybe Churchill would have understood at that time, but later, at the Yalta Conference, his nose was decidedly out of joint when Roosevelt decided to take sides with Stalin, for his own ends.

The conference ended that day with King taking his leave of Churchill, who again emphasized King's major position in the Empire and the importance of his attending the Commonwealth Prime Minister's Conference.

The invasion of Sicily was set to begin on July 10, with the forces including the 26,000-strong First Canadian Division. Prior to the invasion, an incident arose that caused some conflict amongst the Allies. Certainly, looking back at it from today, some seventy years later, the issue may seem trite, especially in comparison to what was at stake in the invasion; however, it certainly did not appear so to the Canadian government at the time.

King, quite rightly, took great pride in the part being played by Canada in the war. Accordingly, he was highly sensitive to the criticisms expressed by the Canadian media on the lack of action involving the Canadian Army, and he was anxious that their participation in the invasion would be known to the Canadian people. As has been mentioned before, Churchill often neglected to mention the contributions made by Canada to the war effort; in the case of the invasion of Italy, however, it was the Americans who failed to acknowledge the support of Canada and its troops.

In anticipation of the success of the Allied forces, General Eisenhower's headquarters in Algiers drafted three documents to be issued at the appropriate time: an initial communiqué announcing the landing; a message to the French people; and a message to the Italian people. These were sent to London, Washington, and Ottawa. The text for each included the words, "Anglo-American Forces" and "Forces of the United States and Great Britain."[3]

King was highly indignant at the omission of the Canadian participation in the drafts. He initially instructed High Commissioner Vincent Massey in London to argue for a change in the wording; however, Massey's efforts were fruitless. So, the Canadian legation in Washington was contacted, in hopes that they would have more success in getting the desired change made. The ambassador was on leave, and so the second-in-command, Lester Pearson, became involved. Pearson recounted the developments in his autobiography.

Pearson immediately telephoned Robertson (the under-secretary of state for external affairs) and told him there was no use in his going to the State Department, since they would disclaim any responsibility, and that there was only one thing to do, and that was to see the president himself.

"The only way I could do that in a hurry was to get Mr. King to telephone Harry Hopkins or, even better, the President himself, and tell him that he wanted me to go to the White House at once and discuss a matter of urgent national importance with Mr. Roosevelt.... Within fifteen minutes (who said Mr. King cannot work quickly) I had a call from Hopkins to say the President would be glad to receive me at 9.40."

Pearson later sent a telegram to Ottawa. "I saw the President and Harry Hopkins at 9.40 tonight on the matters mentioned in your telegrams. I found them most friendly and sympathetic to the position which I took." After a discussion on the alternative phrases, the president "ended by accepting the view that a specific mention of Canada was preferable and said he would take steps to see that this was done."

Pearson was concerned that there might not be enough time for the changes to be made, but he "heaved a sigh of relief and satisfaction" on hearing a radio report: "We interrupt this program to make an announcement. 'British, American (pause), and Canadian troops have commenced landing operations in Sicily.'"

The official text read: "Anglo-American-Canadian forces, under command of General Eisenhower, began landing operations in Sicily early this morning. Landings were preceded by an air attack. Naval forces escorted the assault forces and bombarded the coast defences during the assault."

Two days later Pearson received a telegram from King. "I would not wish the occasion to pass without expressing my warm appreciation of your efforts of the past few days with regard to the announcement dealing with the participation of Canadian forces in the Combined Allied Offensive against Sicily. I am sure it was with deep pride that the Canadian people heard that our Forces, together with Forces from Britain and the United States, are engaged in this great action."[4]

On the day of the invasion, King broadcast to the nation: "The fighting men of Canada, on land, at sea, and in the air, are risking their lives to preserve everything that all of us hold dear. They are joined together, in the cause of freedom, in the service of their fellowmen, and by an abiding attachment to their homeland. All Canada will share the pride of their loved ones in their courage and their achievements."[5]

However, the matter of the initial non-recognition did not die down. On July 15 questions were raised in the Canadian House of Commons, and King decided to depart from his usual guarded practice and discuss the matter. His comments were covered in the *Toronto Star* of July 16.

The front page of the newspaper ran with the headline: "Invasion is Led By Canadians," but it also included a separate heading: "Couldn't Get Authority to Tell of Sicily — King," with a sub-heading: "Announcement Came Only After Appeal to Roosevelt." The editorial that day discussed King's irritation with Churchill: "Prime Minister King and Colonel Ralston are evidently puzzled, and somewhat nettled as well, by the initial failure of the British to mention for publication that Canadian troops formed part of the invasion force.... Mr. King does not often speak heatedly but he did yesterday. 'I am going to keep all the military secrets I can but as far as the Canadian forces are concerned I regard their services as on a par with those of the British and U.S. forces, not necessarily in numbers, but in quality, efficiency and valor, they are entitled to equality.'"

King's comments hit the British media, and on July 18, High Commissioner MacDonald went to see him with a telegram from Churchill. King did not like the tone of the message, and he told MacDonald that he was highly indignant at having to, once again, insist that Canada's contribution be recognized.

MacDonald suggested that King prepare a draft of what MacDonald should send to Churchill. King reacted by saying that Churchill should just read *Hansard*. But after MacDonald and Under-Secretary Robertson drafted a response, King agreed that it should be sent as if it had originated from him.

On July 20 Churchill was questioned in the House of Commons, and it was clear that he had completely missed the fact that there were three original draft communiqués. The general one referred to "Allied Forces," whereas the ones for Italy and France referred to "Anglo-American Forces." Churchill's lack of understanding of the reason for Canada's irritation was illustrated by his response to the question in the House: "The Canadian Prime Minister objected to [the use of] the term 'Allied Forces.' On seeing this draft the Canadian authorities asked that at the earliest possible date reference should be made that Canadian forces had taken part in the landing."

Although Churchill had missed the point, he thought he had better attempt to calm the waters. He spoke of the valiant and successful part played by the Canadian First Division: "Our hearts go out to the rest of the powerful Canadian Army in this country, who have for more than three years guarded the centre of the Empire from invasion." He finished with a statement that King would not have agreed with: "I may add that I have had a very agreeable interchange of telegrams with Mr. Mackenzie King on this matter, and the misunderstanding, for which nobody is to blame, can now be regarded as cleared away."[6]

Normally, King would have been assuaged by flattery, but this time his diary indicates his dissatisfaction with Churchill for not understanding the situation. However, with the war raging, King felt that it was better to conclude the matter, and so nothing more was said.

QUADRANT CONFERENCE

W hile the encounter over the recognition of Canadian troops tak- ing part in the invasion of Sicily was being resolved, a request came for a different type of contribution from Canada.

Churchill decided that another meeting with Roosevelt was nec- essary. This would be their third meeting in 1943, and it confirmed Churchill's need to have hands-on control of the war schedule, to ensure that the planning did not go off the rails. He was not prepared to have another Dardanelles disaster, which he attributed to his lack of authority.

The president agreed to the meeting, and suggested Quebec City as the venue. A request was made to the Canadian prime minister. King prepared a response, cordially approving the idea, but before sending it to Churchill, he discussed the ramifications with his under- secretary, Norman Robertson, and the British high commissioner, Malcolm MacDonald.

Again, the sensitivity of Canada's position was the focal point of King's concern. Robertson's contention was that if Roosevelt and Churchill met on Canadian soil, King would have to be with them, as an equal at the conference. King knew from the previous meetings between Roosevelt and Churchill that that was not their intention. Thus he was in a quan- dary — as he wrote in his diary: "To refuse, except on conditions, would be to occasion real disappointment on the part of both Churchill and the President, and resentment as well by Churchill. On the other hand, to suggest it myself, that I would have to have the position mentioned, was to raise a difficulty that might be insuperable."

MacDonald suggested that it would be embarrassing for King to raise the requirement that he be more than just the host to Churchill and Roosevelt; as an alternative, MacDonald, offered to bring it up with Churchill.

In the end King decided to simply send a friendly worded response, agreeing with the request, without reserve. However, MacDonald was to send a message to Churchill, covering the sensitive position of the Canadian prime minister.

King's diary of July 20, a day later, outlined his amended thinking; he admitted that even if he was not formally a part of the discussions, it would be acceptable: "My own feeling is that Churchill and Roosevelt being at Quebec, and myself acting as host, will be quite sufficient to make clear that all three are in conference together, and will not only satisfy but will please the Canadian feeling, and really be very helpful to me personally." He went on to look at the bigger picture. The conference would be "a memorable and marvellous event in Canadian history as well as in the history of the entire war. It would, too, I believe, greatly please French Canadians."

In Churchill's response to High Commissioner MacDonald, the prime minister nicely ensured that there would be no aftermath similar to the Sicily matter. King wrote: "Telegram was most satisfactory and made clear Churchill saw the need of conference appearing to be a British-American-Canadian conference. Malcolm and I laughed very heartily as we read Churchill's words "Anglo-American-Canadian." King's diary of July 23 went on to detail a further telegram to himself from Churchill: "Spoke of the pleasure he had in looking forward to seeing Canada in the summer time and to talks with myself." King then went on to consider the ramifications of the conference to Canada: "Indeed, I doubt if there will have been a comparable event in Canadian history. It will serve to link the whole past and present of Canada into the world history of today."

Churchill sailed on the *Queen Mary*, with his wife, Clementine, and daughter Mary. This gave him a much-needed period of relaxation. General Brooke recorded in his diary that Churchill managed to keep his fellow passengers amused with his "one liners," as when he admonished a steward who was filling tumblers of water before going round with the champagne. "Winston stopped him by saying: 'Stop pouring all that water out. It is too depressing a sight!'"[1]

Churchill arrived at Halifax, in the afternoon of August 9, and was transported straight to his special train. He recorded: "In spite of all precautions about secrecy, large crowds were assembled. As my wife and I sat in our saloon at the end of the train, the people gathered round and gave us welcome. Before we started I made them sing 'The Maple Leaf' and 'O Canada'"[2]

During the train journey to Quebec City, the Churchills were greeted by waves and cheers, and on their arrival, King met them and welcomed them to Canada. Then Churchill walked along to greet the spectators, who applauded enthusiastically.

The *Globe & Mail* of August 11 covered the arrival of the Churchills in Quebec City: "Prime Minister Churchill in a dramatic arrival late today [August 10] in the fortress city opened closely guarded discussions with Prime Minister King in what is accepted as being a prelude-to-victory Conference of the United Nations. Mr. Churchill is the guest of the Canadian Government."

After the obligatory photographs, the Churchills were shown their rooms in the Citadel, the Quebec residence of the governor general. King wrote that they seemed very pleased with the accommodation, and were filled with delight at the charm of the whole surroundings. Especially Mary, who said that all her life she had hoped to come to Canada and would never believe she would have had such a wonderful opportunity.

King's diary includes a separate memorandum detailing the long discussions between him and Churchill on the day of their arrival. Churchill stated he wanted to have an extended stay, maybe a month, and King suggested he visit Toronto and Montreal. Churchill also enquired about Kingsmere, which he had visited in 1929. He intimated that he would like to visit Niagara Falls, with King responding that if he went to Brock's monument, he would be visiting the place where "my grandfather lived, and he would see the stone carrying the words: 'The birthplace of responsible government in Canada.'"

King welcomes Winston, Clementine, and Mary Churchill to the Quadrant Conference, August 10, 1943.

Churchill gave King a general outline of the current situation in the war, which he said was in a fluid state and so necessitated this further meeting with the president. He expressed confidence with the situation in Italy, and said that they would not insist on unconditional surrender. However, he declared that the Italians would not get back their empire. With regard to Germany, he was optimistic: "We have got them beaten, but it may take some time."

King brought up the danger of a premature invasion of France. Churchill agreed with King, adding that they might have some difficulty convincing the Americans of the wisdom of waiting: "The trouble was the Americans did not realize how long it took to accomplish some things."

Although he did not mention the Sicily misunderstanding, King told Churchill of the need to have the Canadian people believe that the country had a voice in all matters pertaining to the war. He explained that he was facing pressure, not just from the opposition but also from his own party. Surprisingly, considering the recent testy incident, he wrote that Churchill was "very understanding in matters of this kind."

Churchill outlined his "understanding" in his war memoirs. "The President, while gladly accepting Canadian hospitality did not feel it possible that Canada should be a formal member of the Conference, as similar demands could be made by Brazil, and other American partners in the United Nations. We also had to think of the claims of Australia, and the other Dominions." However, Churchill continued: "This delicate question was solved and surmounted by the broadminded attitude of the Canadian Prime Minister and Government." Churchill included his own opinion that that he was also against having any third party: "I for my part was determined that we and the United States should have the conference to ourselves, in view of all the vital business we had in common."[3]

King, to his credit, did understand, and the two other leaders ensured that he was highly visible when the photographers were in evidence. Some years later he was questioned by Charles Wilson about his role at the Quebec Conferences, and he replied: "I was, as you recall, not so much a participant in any of the discussions as a sort of general host, whose task at the Citadel was similar to that of the General Manager of the Château Frontenac."[4]

Continuing the conversation with King, Churchill brought up a matter of increasing importance: "tube alloys," the name for the nuclear weapons project. Churchill thought that there should be a tripartite policy committee established between the United States, Britain, and Canada. He obtained King's agreement, and it was decided that the Canadian representative would be C.D. Howe. Canada's involvement was essential, as the country was the primary source of uranium and heavy water. A formal agreement was signed by Churchill and Roosevelt. The agreement declared: "First, that we will never use this agency against each other. Secondly, that we will not use it against third parties without each other's consent. Thirdly, that we will not either of us communicate any information about Tube Alloys to third parties except by mutual consent."

Although Canada was represented on the committee, it was not brought into the discussion that formulated the agreement. However, on August 19 Churchill presented King with a copy, stating: "I enclose, for your most secret information a copy of the Articles of Agreement governing collaboration between the authorities of the United States and the United Kingdom in the matter of Tube Alloys, signed by President Roosevelt and myself today."[5]

Churchill then met the Canadian cabinet in the Château Frontenac Hotel, and attended a meeting of the cabinet war committee. Not surprisingly, the term Anglo-American was again discussed. Churchill explained the problem with specifically mentioning Canada, when other countries were also involved. King brought up a pertinent matter relating to Canadian-American relations after the war. There would be times when it would be in Canada's interest to take a North American point of view, rather than a British one. Also, it would not do for the United States to think that "we of the British Empire were ganging up against them."

As well as discussing relations with the United States, King and Churchill also discussed relations with the Soviet Union. A message had been received from Stalin, containing congratulations upon the success in Sicily, and apologies for not answering previous communications — Stalin declaring that he had been away at the front with his armies. He also stated that he was in favour of a meeting with the president and Churchill.

Concerning Russia, Churchill was full of praise for their efforts but he criticized Stalin, calling him, "very ill-mannered and stubborn." While Churchill's predictions were usually accurate, regarding the future intentions of Stalin he was completely wrong: "Thought after the lives [Russia] had lost [Stalin] would not be anxious to spread Communism in other countries, but would [take] time to restoring [his] own country." Churchill's optimistic assessment was only a temporary one, though.

King wrote of Churchill's later thoughts: "Really a marvellous statement. [He stated that] '[Russia's] doctrines were certain to influence all parts of the world and that she might someday become a nation that would be powerful enough to more than control the rest of the world, unless, in the interval, some new system of world control was instituted which would prevent anything of the kind on the part of any country.'"

At the luncheon following the meeting, the guests included the recently famous wing commander Guy Gibson, who had led the "Dam Busters" raids, and had been awarded the Victoria Cross. Then it was on to the Quebec Legislative Buildings to meet Premier Godbout and the Quebec cabinet.

On the way King had suggested that Churchill say a few words in French at the meeting. This Churchill did, rather slowly and choosing his words carefully. King recorded that Churchill became quite emotional when he referred to Quebec and the historic significance of meeting there and making decisions that would see France restored and given a worthy place in the world. After they left Churchill said that he probably mixed up genders and verbs but he thought that the French language was a beautiful medium of expression.

King wrote in his diary that he expressed his admiration for Churchill's achievements: "I said to him when we were talking that I believed he was the one man who had saved the British Empire. He said no, if I had not been here someone else would have done it. I said I did not believe that was so. I could not think of any other man who could have done what he did at the time. It was so necessary." Churchill responded that he had been through a previous war and had long experience in government. "I said yes, it almost confirmed the old Presbyterian idea of pre-destination or pre-ordination; of his having been the man selected for this task. I truly believe that but for his bold stand and vision Britain would never have been able to meet the situation as she has."

The next day Churchill left for Hyde Park, the president's residence, with Mary. He asked King to keep an eye on Clementine, who was suffering from nervous exhaustion, and had decided not to accompany him. "He said: 'I wish you would go in and have lunch with her. She is very fond of you. Likes you very much, and she will appreciate having a chance to talk with you.' I told him it would be a pleasure to have any opportunity of conversation, but I would try to have her take all the rest possible."

On the way to Hyde Park, Churchill took a side trip to show Mary Niagara Falls. He was asked by reporters as to what he thought of them, and he replied: "I saw them before you were born. I first came here in 1900." To the question: "Do they look the same?" he replied: "Well the principle seems the same. The water still keeps falling over."[6]

King was delighted to "keep an eye" on Clementine, and he accepted her invitation for tea on August 12. They had a two-hour conversation, which King wrote was "very interesting." As he later recorded, he was pleased to learn "how much Churchill relied upon me, and spoke of how glad he was to be with me, and to share days together.... She told me many things about Winston. One thing was how his being out of office for a number of years and writing the life of Marlborough had had a real effect upon his character. He had discovered that Marlborough possessed great patience. That patience became the secret of his achievements."

Clementine went on to say that "Winston would ask her whether she thought he would ever be back in government again. That she had told him he might not. She then told me that when Neville Chamberlain took over and succeeded Baldwin, and did not invite him into his cabinet, she said that she did not think he would be in any future government." She also told King that if war had not come he would not have been taken into the cabinet.

On August 15 Churchill returned after his preliminary talks with Roosevelt. He and King chatted about the talks, and Churchill said that the president and Cordell Hull were determined not to use the word "recognition" regarding the Free French.

At the luncheon following, in which King and Churchill were joined by Clementine and Mary, King mentioned his decision not to drink alcohol during the war. He wrote in his diary: "Mrs. Churchill said that I looked remarkably well, and I replied that it was due in large part to having given up stimulants. Churchill said that he had not but he was feeling well. I said that of course everything depended on habits that a man had from youth. That were he to give up completely, it would probably kill him. I felt no embarrassment in the conversation."

King and Churchill continued their conversation of a few days before, with King repeating that Churchill was the only man who could have saved the day for Britain. Churchill agreed that it did look as though he was reserved for this purpose. He noted how fortunate it was that he was out of office for ten years, saying that it gave him time to study the situation. King brought up a special interest of his. He told Churchill that he thought there were forces beyond their understanding that were responsible for controlling and guiding in ways that we did not know. King did not record whether Churchill responded to his suggestion of supernatural influences, but did say, "He could not have been kinder or really in a more gentle mood. He seemed to like to talk just quietly and reflectively. He then asked me to come and see the map room. We went together. As we went through the sun room, he said, 'I love this room; I love this country.'"

Churchill also said that he would like to visit Churchill, Manitoba, named after his ancestor, John Churchill, the first duke of Marlborough. Sadly this did not occur.

On August 17 President Roosevelt arrived in Quebec City, and King met him at the train station. Roosevelt told him of his recent fishing holiday in Little Current, on Manitoulin Island in Ontario, and how much he enjoyed it.

The following day the Canadian government hosted a dinner at the Citadel. King spoke of the appreciation they had that Quebec City had been chosen for the conference. He continued: "In years gone by, the fate of nations had been decided here. The fate of the nations may well be decided for the future." King spoke of the meeting at Ogdensburg three years ago where the Permanent Joint Board of Defence had been established, stating that it was a beginning of the wider measure for defence between the Empire and the United States. After referring to a dream that Roosevelt had advised him of, regarding Quebec being an ideal place for an international conference, King continued: "I said I, too, had had my dreams, and one that I had cherished through life was that the British Empire and the U.S. might be drawn closer together, and that in some small way, immediate or remote, Canada might be an instrument toward that end and toward furthering the friendship between the two."

King, Roosevelt, and Churchill at the Quadrant Conference with, behind them, General "Hap" Arnold, Air Chief Marshal Charles Portal, General Sir Alan Brooke, Admiral Ernest King, Field Marshal Sir John Dill, General George C. Marshall, Admiral Sir Dudley Pound, and Admiral William Leahy, August 18, 1943.

Roosevelt said he was an undergraduate at Harvard when King was getting a Ph.D. degree there. They were soon to add the third member to this connection — on September 6, 1943, Winston Churchill received an honorary degree.

On August 19 the first plenary session of the conference was held. The major matter agreed upon was that Operation Overlord, the invasion of northern France, would take place on May 1, 1944. In his memoirs Churchill stated that as the invading forces would be predominately American, the commander should not be General Brooke, as had previously been agreed, but an American. Churchill wrote, "I informed General Brooke, who had my entire confidence, of this change, and of the reasons for it. He bore the disappointment with soldierly dignity."[7]

A much less formal King, Roosevelt, and Churchill enjoy a moment of jollity. This picture was taken on the same occasion as the previous photograph.

Churchill appeared to have missed the depth of the "crushing blow," as Brooke referred to it in his diary. "Not for one moment did he realize what this meant to me. He offered no sympathy, no regrets at having had to change his mind, and dealt with this matter as if it were one of minor importance."[8]

However, in spite of his deep disappointment, just eleven days later Brooke wrote in his diary: "I wonder whether any historian will ever be able to paint Winston in his true colours. It is a wonderful character, the most marvellous qualities and superhuman genius mixed with an astonishing lack of vision at times, and an impetuosity which, if not guided, must inevitably bring him into trouble again and again." Brooke ended his capsule summation of Churchill: "He is quite the most difficult man to work with that I have ever struck, but I would not have missed the chance of working with him for anything on earth."[9]

While the leaders were looking ahead to the invasion of the northern coast of France, they received very welcome news that the whole of Sicily was under Allied control. The operation had taken just thirty-eight days.

Discussions were acrimonious at times, with the matter of recognition of the Free French being one area of disagreement. Along with the heated exchanges, one incident occurred that in a strange fashion brought some levity into the proceedings. Louis Mountbatten, head of combined operations, received permission to demonstrate a new product called *Pykrete,* a mixture of sawdust, wood pulp, and ice, which he proposed be utilized to build artificial islands, for the use of fighter planes in the upcoming Normandy invasion. Mountbatten brought into the conference room a large block of ice and a large block of *Pykrete,* and announced that he was going to demonstrate their different defensive qualities. He took a revolver out of his pocket and fired into the ice, which just splintered. Then he shot into the *Pykrete,* and the bullet ricocheted off and buzzed around the legs of the assembled chiefs of staff. "When the shots were heard outside the room, one of the Staff officers who had left at the start of the meeting explained: 'Good Heavens, they've started shooting now!'"[10]

Churchill also described the scene in his memoirs, stating that the bullet ricocheted, narrowly missing Portal. After quoting the staff officer, he wrote: "But who in war will not have his laugh amid the skulls? — and here was one."[11]

It should be noted that despite the risks Mountbatten took, *Pykrete* was not utilized in the war. More conventional materials were used. While this reads as an amusing incident, there is no evidence that Churchill saw this as another evidence of the irresponsibility of Mountbatten, and that the recent decision to promote him to be the supreme commander of the newly formed Southeast Asia Command should be reconsidered.

While King was not part of the high level discussions, there were ample opportunities for him to be in evidence, and he took full advantage of them. On August 23 he drove with Churchill in a triumphal procession through the streets of Quebec through an enthusiastic crowd. King wrote: "As we looked at the people from the car, it was like a vast throng hailing a deliverer."

King went back to Ottawa for a few days, but returned to Quebec City on August 31 to listen to Churchill's broadcast from the Citadel. Churchill started by mentioning that it was President Roosevelt's suggestion that Quebec be used as the location for the meeting, and added, "No more fitting and splendid setting could have been chosen.... Here at the gateway of Canada, in mighty lands which have never known the totalitarian tyrannies of Hitler and Mussolini, the spirit of freedom has found a safe and abiding home." He followed by noting that he was in the heart of French Canada. He referred to the agony of France but declared, "We may be sure that France will rise again free, united and independent."

While Churchill was often amiss in not recognizing Canada's contribution in the war, when he was in the country he made sure that there could be no criticism in that regard. "I have also had the advantage of conferring with the Prime Minister of Canada, Mr. Mackenzie King, that experienced statesman who led the Dominion instantly and unitedly into the war, and of sitting on several occasions with his cabinet, and the British and Canadian Staffs have been over the whole ground of the war together." He also delivered a statement of clear recognition of Canada's role: "The contribution which Canada has made to the combined effort of the British Commonwealth and Empire in these tremendous times has deeply touched the heart of the Mother Country, and of all the members of our widespread family of States and races."

He proceeded to assure the people that Canada's army, which had, until recently, been inactive in Britain, except for the ill-fated Dieppe raid, had "played an indispensable part in guarding our British homeland from invasion. Now it is fighting with distinction in wider and ever-widening fields." He went on to talk of the success of the British Commonwealth Air Training Plan, the Canadian merchant navy guarding the "vital life-line" across the Atlantic Ocean, and the most important part played by the munitions industry. "Last, but not least, Canada has relieved Great Britain of what would otherwise have been a debt for these munitions of no less than $2,000,000,000. All this, of course, was dictated by no law. It came from no treaty or formal obligation. It sprang in perfect freedom from sentiment and tradition and a generous resolve to serve the future of mankind. I am glad to pay my tribute on behalf of the people of Great Britain to the great Dominion, and to pay it from Canadian soil."[12]

King was well-pleased with the broadcast and congratulated Churchill. King recorded in his diary Churchill's response: "'I wanted to say what I did, and I wanted to say you are the only man who could have brought Canada into the war unitedly.' I said something about this being too much and he replied: 'Not at all, not at all. I don't know how we could have done without you. Your services have meant everything.'"

Churchill told King that preparing the broadcast had taken about six hours in all. King responded: "I said to him one thing about your broadcasts is that they are all your own. He said: 'Yes, I have to do that myself. I have others yet, check what I have written but find I have to do it practically all myself.'" King commented to Churchill: "My trouble is to get started. He said: 'I suppose you have your way too.' I said the difficulty was to get the plough to move. Once started in the furrow, it was easy going. He said: 'That was it exactly.'"

The Churchills were leaving Quebec on August 31, and the last formal engagement was a meeting of the Canadian war cabinet. King told him "it had been a privilege to all Canada to have him here, and to feel that it had been possible for him to enjoy a little change and freedom here. I expressed the hope that he would return refreshed by the change. That the visit had served a useful purpose.... Churchill made a fitting acknowledgement of what I had said, speaking quite deeply of the hospitality extended by Canada, thanking us all very warmly."

Churchill also covered this final meeting: "I attended a meeting of the Canadian Cabinet and told them all they did not know about the Conference and the war. I had the honour to be sworn a Privy Councillor [*sic*] of the Dominion Cabinet. This complement was paid me at the instance of my old friend of forty years' standing and trusted colleague, Mr. Mackenzie King."[13]

King saw the Churchills off at the train station, calling for three cheers from the crowd. Churchill responded: "God Bless You All."

THE BIG THREE MEET

Churchill arrived at the White House on September 1, 1943. He had decided to prolong his stay in North America in view of the developments in the Italian theatre. Talks with the Italians were proceeding well, and on that day the surrender terms proposed by the Allies were accepted. The landings by Allied forces, including the First Canadian Division, on the mainland of Italy were to occur on September 3, and Churchill wished to discuss strategy.

Another reason for Churchill choosing to prolong his stay — one of personal importance — was in order to accept an honorary degree from Harvard University. As well as being heard by the important audience at Harvard, his acceptance speech was also broadcast. While not one of his longest, it was one of his most important and effective. The major theme paralleled the subject of his emotional pleadings to President Roosevelt during the Trident Conference: the importance of the United States in world affairs, and the consequent dangers should it revert back to isolationism after the end of the war.

He started by talking of the two world wars, which Churchill told his audience, had "involved the entire life and manhood of the United States in a deadly struggle." Addressing those in his audience who had wished to keep America free of foreign entanglements, he said: "There was no use saying: 'We don't want it, we won't have it; our forebears left Europe to avoid those quarrels; we have founded a new world which has no contact with the old' — there was no use in that. The long arm reaches out remorselessly and every one's existence, environment, and outlook, undergo a swift and irresistible change."

He continued to press the point that the people of the United States could not revert to the pre-war isolationism, as their responsibilities were growing, whereas the world itself was contracting: "Even elderly parliamentarians like myself are forced to acquire a high degree of mobility.... We have now reached a point in the journey where there can be no pause. We must go on; it must be world anarchy or world order."[1]

King listened to the speech, and realized its significance. He wrote to Churchill: "Deeply moved by the greatest of all your utterances. So glad it was delivered at Harvard. It will ring down through the centuries as ever-present inspiration to English-speaking peoples from these tremendous times, to cherish their common heritage and to realize its highest possibilities in the service of mankind."

The following day King received a message from Churchill: "Thank you so much for your charming letter." And then on subject of the Canadian Army success in Italy, he added: "Many congratulations on the Canadian advance."

On September 10 King gave a broadcast on the CBC, entitled "Four Years of War." He spoke of the dire situation of the year before, but turning to recent events, his outlook was more optimistic: "Today the world picture has changed. The Axis dream of world domination has been transformed into a nightmare of defeat and destruction. On every battlefront around the globe, the United Nations have seized and kept the initiative.... The very heart of Germany has, day and night, been pounded from the air on a scale which, even a year ago, would have seemed incredible. Great cities have been reduced to smouldering ruins."

He moved on to Canada's contribution: "In fighting on land, Hong Kong and Dieppe showed the world what every Canadian knew in his heart, that Canadian soldiers of today have all the courage and all the spirit their fathers displayed in the fields of France and Flanders."

On the Italian campaign, he said that he had sent a message of congratulations to the troops at the conclusion of the Sicilian fighting, and quoted a future chief of the general staff, General Guy Simonds's reply.

Winston and Clementine with Nova Scotia Premier A.S. MacMillan aboard
HMS Renown *in Halifax before it departed for England on September 15, 1943.*

"On behalf of all ranks of the First Canadian Division, I thank you for your inspiring message. We shall continue in our duty reinforced by your words of encouragement.... We have taken the measure of our enemies, and though there may be bitter fighting ahead, with its inevitable losses, we shall not look back until those enemies are finally defeated."[2]

Churchill gave a detailed report to the British House of Commons on September 21 on the talks in Quebec City and Washington. He mentioned the progress in Italy, including the overthrow of Mussolini and the negotiations that had led the Badoglio government to switch to the Allied side. While the speech was upbeat, Churchill did express a matter of concern: "The speeches of the German leaders, from Hitler downwards, contain mysterious allusions to new methods and new weapons which will presently be tried against us. It would, of course, be natural for the enemy to spread such rumours in order to encourage his own people, but there is probably more in it than that."[3]

Churchill and Roosevelt had discussed the atomic bomb at the Quebec Conference, and they were concerned that the German technology might be sufficiently advanced that they could produce and use the bomb in the war. Fortunately, this concern did not materialize. But the Germans were advanced in rocket technology, and they were shortly to launch the V1 rocket, followed by the V2.

In spite of the progress that had been made in the war, Churchill, like King, was subject to criticism in the media. In the course of his speech, he compared his situation with "a sailor who jumped into a dock to rescue a small boy from drowning. About a week later this sailor was accosted by a woman, who asked, 'Are you the man who picked my son out of the dock the other night?' The sailor replied modestly, 'That is true, Ma'am.' 'Ah,' said the woman, 'you are the man I am looking for. Where is his cap?'"[4]

After the disruption of the Quebec Conference, King was able to return to his regular duties and deal with domestic issues. However, on September 27, personal tragedy came to him, with the news that his nephew Lyon, the son of his only brother, had been declared missing after his ship was torpedoed in the Atlantic. He was a medical doctor, and King wrote, "What I felt most deeply was the loss to the country at this time, and in the years to come, of one, whom I believed, would have been one of the great surgeons and members of the medical profession. He had given some eleven years of his life to preparing wholly for the work of surgery." A short while later, he wrote: "Received a cable signed by Winston and Clementine Churchill, expressing sympathy in Lyon's loss. I was sure some word would come from him. It was pleasant having [it] come from both."

Despite his loss King was able to focus — for a while anyway — on the home front. Churchill, however, was not able to deal with domestic issues as he was on the move again. A meeting of the foreign ministers of the three major Allied powers had been held in Moscow in October, in anticipation of a meeting of Roosevelt, Churchill, and Stalin that was to be held in Tehran, Iran.

On November 28 the conference commenced. Things got off to a rocky start when Churchill found out that an hour beforehand Stalin and Roosevelt had met alone. He was upset at being excluded, but decided to let the matter drop so that important issues could be addressed. The main issue to be covered at the conference was the future army campaigns. Churchill wanted to continue to stress the Italian theatre, whereas Stalin wanted all emphasis to be given to a cross-Channel invasion, which had been agreed upon for May 1944. Roosevelt had another item on his agenda: he proposed an Allied advance from Italy northeast to the Danube. This proposal was very much opposed by Stalin, no doubt because this would adversely affect his long-term plan to control all of eastern and central Europe.

Churchill later wrote: "I realized at Tehran for the first time what a small nation we are. There I sat with the great Russian bear on one side of me, with paws outstretched, and on the other side, the great American buffalo, and between the two sat the poor little English donkey, who was the only one of the three who knew the right way home."[5]

Despite their disagreements about strategy, Churchill did make one comment that received Stalin's wholehearted approval. On the matter of the use of deception to confuse the Germans as to where the D-Day landings would occur, Churchill said: "Truth is so precious that she should always be attended by a bodyguard of lies."[6]

The conference concluded with agreement on the cross-Channel invasion, with no further talk of the American and British forces advancing into eastern Europe. Russia was to continue to retain Polish lands, with Poland to be compensated at the expense of Germany.

Churchill flew back to Cairo, and he was clearly unwell. On December 14 he was diagnosed with pneumonia, although he continued to work, against his doctor's advice. King's diary of December 16 stated that he learned that day that Churchill had pneumonia and was seriously ill. He wrote: "I confess I instantly felt the weight of added responsibility, also a deepening concern about the future of the war."

The following day, at a press conference, King stated his great concern for Churchill and asked all to pray for his full recovery. He quoted his comments in his diary. "I then spoke of no man being needed more in the world of today than Churchill. I said he had the lion's strength. I believed that that strength, which meant everything to him in the past, would stand him in good stead at present."

Churchill's lion's strength did come through again. On December 18 there was much improvement, and his doctor recorded the next day: "The temperature remains normal and the signs of pneumonia are disappearing."[7]

As has been mentioned, King's admiration for Churchill at times bordered on hero worship, and when Churchill fell ill King displayed genuine alarm, but with Churchill now showing signs of recovery, King recorded in his diary his clinical and religious opinion that Churchill's illness was due to his less than abstemious life style. "Churchill, I greatly fear, may not last out the war — because of drink.... It is clear ... that already it has him 'down,' and however much he may recover, his strength & endurance will be greatly lessened for all time, and at the moment, he may suffer an attack which will take him off."

When King wrote the above, it was after reading the Bible, and he comes across as more tolerant and generous three days later. On December 22 he received a cable from Churchill, who was still in Cairo, thanking him for a telegram on his illness. "I may, however, be advised to take a few weeks rest as a half-timer at some sunny place up here before returning to the fogs and flu of London. This further manifestation by you of our long friendship gives me great pleasure. Give my best of wishes to all your colleagues. Very hard days lie ahead of all of us, and I am glad to think that we shall meet in the spring."

King recorded being relieved and touched by this warm expression: "It gave me much happiness to have this direct word from Churchill, first because of the assurance it brought of his recovery, and secondly, in what it expresses of genuine friendship. I confess the reference it contains to very hard times ahead is what I, myself, have all along been anticipating. The mention of it from him adds greatly to my concern."

Both Churchill and King were anticipating horrendous losses when the cross-Channel invasion was attempted in 1944. The Germans knew that it would be coming, and while they did not know the exact location, the concrete wall they had constructed all across northern France would be a formidable barrier to be overcome.

PLANNING FOR D-DAY

New Year's Day, 1944, saw King in a reflective mood, as he wrote in his diary: "Rested part of the time on the sofa looking at the painting of my dear mother. Thought over events of the past year and the year to come.... Prayed for purity, strength and uprightness in all things in the New Year, as the bells rang out 1943 and rang in 1944. As they were ringing I prayed most earnestly for peace for the world in the New Year."

Winston Churchill was still recuperating from his pneumonia attack in Marrakesh. In a New Year's message, he spoke of the year ahead as "this year of decision." He laid emphasis on the formidable tasks of war and the problems of the peace that would follow, but he also expressed a glowing confidence, which was shared by millions throughout the Allied countries.[1]

Churchill's confidence was well-founded. Russian forces continued to advance, and on January 4, Churchill telegraphed Stalin, congratulating him on his troops crossing the 1939 Russo-Polish frontier. The air assault was devastating German cities, with half of Berlin in ruins, and the bombers continued their task of destroying the Germans' capacity to wage war. Although the Allied army was meeting heavy resistance in Italy, a new strategy that had been heavily promoted by Churchill, an amphibious landing at Anzio, behind the German lines, showed promise. This took place in late January. After meeting little initial resistance, the Allied forces did eventually face strong German opposition; however, by May the Allies had won the territory.

Although convalescing Churchill took the opportunity, while in French territory, of attempting to improve relations with General de Gaulle. An invitation was sent on January 1 to the general, inviting him to dine and sleep in Churchill's villa two days later. The general, always highly sensitive to anything that he felt showed less than full respect to France, thought the notice was too short, and declined, citing prior engagements. However, after making his point, de Gaulle arrived in Marrakesh on January 12 for lunch. Churchill decided to speak in French to add a lighter touch. Mr. Narn, the British consul, recorded afterwards: "I heard Mr. Churchill say to Mr. Duff Cooper, in English, in a very audible whisper, 'I'm doing well, aren't I? Now that the General speaks English so well he understands my French perfectly.' Then everyone, General de Gaulle setting the example, burst out laughing."[2]

Churchill left Marrakesh on January 12. His arrival in England was not announced. Harold Nicholson wrote in his diary of January 18: "I was idly glancing at my Order Paper when I saw (*saw* is the word) a gasp of astonishment pass over the faces of the Labour Party opposite. Suddenly they jumped to their feet and started shouting, waving their papers in the air. We also jumped up and the whole House broke into cheer after cheer while Winston, very pink, rather shy, beamed with mischief, crept along the front bench and flung himself into his accustomed seat. He was flushed with pleasure and emotion, and hardly had he sat down when two large tears began to trickle down his cheeks."[3]

The front page of the *Globe & Mail* of January 19 ran the headline: "Churchill, Back Home. Goes Direct from Train to House of Commons." According to the text of the article, "A bomb through the roof could not have created greater surprise than his sudden emergence from the shadows behind the Speaker's chair. Cheers thundered spontaneously and members sprang to their feet."

This reception, led by the Labour opposition, illustrates the position Churchill had established for himself in Parliament. There was relief that their leader had returned. They admired him. They respected him. Most of all they needed him.

While Churchill received a warm reception from all of the parties on his return to Parliament after his stay in North Africa, and while he had managed to charm de Gaulle (after the latter's initial feeling of offence was overcome), he was soon to be the object of King's anger, when the British again caused King to take offence on behalf of his beloved Canada.

The occasion, which left King dumfounded, took place on January 24, when the British ambassador to the United States, Lord Halifax, spoke in Toronto to the Toronto Board of Trade. The *Globe & Mail* stated that the audience was the largest ever held by the Board, overflowing from the Royal York Hotel banquet hall to adjoining rooms. At the commencement a telegram was read from Prime Minister King expressing regrets at being unable to be present.

Reporting on the speech, the *Globe* ran with a headline, "Halifax Seeks United Commonwealth Policy." Halifax was reported as stating that the British Commonwealth of Nations — and not Britain alone — must be the fourth power to stand with Russia, China, and the United States in the determination of future policies. He went on to state that the Statute of Westminster was a declaration of independence but also of interdependence.

Premier George Drew of Ontario gave the vote of thanks after the speech and described the ambassador's remarks as a truly outstanding statement that might well mark the turning point in Empire policies.

Vincent Massey wrote in his diary: "Edward Halifax has made a speech in Toronto on Empire relationships which I am sure will cause trouble. Although what he said was pretty moderate and to my way of thinking pretty sound. Whether it should have been said when it was and by him is another matter.... My Prime Minister reacted to the speech with what may be fairly described as paranoiac fury."[4]

Massey did not exaggerate. King was livid and he concluded that Halifax's comments were "a conspiracy on the part of the Imperialists to win their own victory in the middle of the war." Overly suspicious by nature, King decided that "Halifax's work was all part of a plan which has been worked out with Churchill to take advantage of the war to try and bring about this development of centralization, of making policies in London, etc. As Englishmen of course, they seek to recover for Britain and the U.K. and the Empire the prestige which they are losing as a nation."

While not being as impetuous as his grandfather, William Lyon Mackenzie, who had been nicknamed the "Firebrand," King could be just as determined. In this case King was insistent that this dangerous new policy of the British government — as he saw it — be contested. He telephoned the Canadian ambassador to the United States, Leighton McCarthy, who stated that he had not seen the speech beforehand. A meeting was held in London, too; there, Vincent Massey was told by the Dominions secretary, Bobbety Cranborne, that he had not seen the speech before it was delivered. It was decided that the governor general, the earl of Athlone, would be brought into the discussion; he advised King that he would inform King George.

King slowly calmed down and was comforted on February 1 when Churchill stated in the House of Commons that Halifax's speech was without the authority of the British government. Halifax expressed his regrets on February 8, through Lester Pearson, stating that he was very sorry he had embarrassed King. That was the end of the matter. But centralization was to come up again in the upcoming meeting of the Dominion prime ministers.

Firmly settled back in England, and with the tempest over the Halifax speech behind him, Churchill decided that it was time for a major speech on the war situation. This was given in the House of Commons on February 22. The title was "Preparation, Effort, Resolve."

He began by saying there was no guarantee that the war in Europe would end in 1944. While there were very positive developments, including the steady move westwards by the Russian army, and the success of the bombing raids, the strength of the German army was still formidable.

After giving impressive statistics on the war effort, he warned that the Germans were preparing to launch a new, large-scale assault on Britain from the French shore, either by pilotless aircraft or rockets, or both. He offered hope, however, by announcing that forces were being assembled for the upcoming Allied invasion across the English Channel. While it might seem as if, in sharing this information, he was giving away a secret, in fact, the Germans were well-aware that an invasion would be coming; they did not know, however, exactly where, or when, it would take place.

Churchill then moved on to a matter that would increase in importance as the war progressed: the future of Poland. Churchill said that he had reminded Stalin that Great Britain had declared war on Nazi Germany to fulfil its guarantee to Poland, and that it had never weakened its resolve to maintain its promise to defend the Polish people, even in the period when it was alone. Thus, the fate of the Polish nation was crucial to Britain. Churchill announced that he heard, with great pleasure, Stalin's declaration that he, too, was resolved upon the creation and maintenance of a strong, integral, independent Poland as one of the leading powers in Europe. Churchill said that Stalin had repeated these declarations in public, and that he was convinced that this represented the policy of the Soviet Union. It is difficult to accept that Churchill fully believed the words of Stalin. In any event, the Soviet dictator's true intentions would soon become abundantly clear.

Churchill concluded his speech by referring to the "greatest joint operations between two Allies that have ever been planned in history." As usual he ended with an uplifting phrase: "Victory may be not so far away, and will certainly not be denied us in the end."[5]

It comes as no surprise that when King read the content of the speech, he was again upset that Churchill took all the credit for Britain and ignored the Dominions. King's annoyance soon evaporated, however, after he received a great honour. This came in the form of a telegram from Churchill, stating that during the upcoming meeting of Dominion prime ministers, King was invited to address a gathering of both Houses of Parliament, and if he wished he, Churchill, would preside.

King was thrilled. He told British high commissioner, Malcolm MacDonald, that at such moments in his life his thoughts naturally turned back to his father and mother, and that he was sure it would have given them great happiness to see him in Westminster.

Prior to the conference, the British House of Commons debated the subject of Empire unity, and Churchill spoke on the subject on April 21. The title of his speech was the "Spirit of the Empire." While he did focus on the Empire, he extended the discussion to include the concept of a "commonwealth." Another major topic was the need for close relations with the United States, and the importance of being part of a "Supreme Council" for the maintenance of world peace.

After describing the existing situation, he went on to the main topic of his speech: "How to gain greater results from Britain's already close ties with the United States?" He presented two ideas, which he would bring up at the upcoming meeting of Dominion prime ministers: the creation of a "Committee of Imperial Defence of the British Empire," which could be extended to include the co-ordination of maritime, economic, and financial affairs; and the formalization of the meetings of the prime ministers, so that they were scheduled on a regular basis — every year, or even more often.[6]

King was unaware of Churchill's comments when he arrived in London on April 27, but he would soon have the opportunity of addressing them.

The day after his arrival, King went to 10 Downing Street, where, he wrote, "Mr. Churchill came along the corridor to meet me. Put out his hand and we shook hands and walked together down a long hallway, he holding my hand all the way.... [He] said: 'We are in a much better position than we were at the time you and I danced the can-can,' referring to the evening at Chequers after one of his broadcasts in September 1941."

King noted in his diary his concern at Churchill's appearance: "He is very soft and flabby. He is much more stooped in walking.... As he talked I came increasingly impressed with his great weariness.... I became convinced that his real spring has gone.... I feel that a great strain at any time might suddenly carry him off.... I should indeed be surprised if he is spared to preside at a peace conference. It gives me a feeling of deep sadness, compassion and concern."

Churchill talked confidentially of the upcoming invasion, as he thought King had a right to the information in view of the large number of Canadians who would be involved. Churchill stated: "It was desirable to have the enemy kept anxious and uncertain. When the time comes, he said, we shall get the beachhead and fight them from there. It may be we shall get the beachhead without any trouble or much loss, but there may be much loss in securing it. Once secured, we shall have very hard fighting."

The conference itself was not to start for three days, and this gave King the opportunity of meeting friends and working on his big speech. During his travels around the capital, he saw the widespread destruction, including the area around St. Paul's Cathedral.

On May 1 Churchill opened the conference by extending a most hearty and cordial welcome. He talked of the meeting being undoubtedly one of the most important events that had taken place since the outbreak of the war. He ventured that he did not expect that they would reach complete solutions for all of the problems that confronted the British Empire and vexed mankind, "But," he said, "it should be our duty to seek and to find where divergences, or potential divergences exist, and to see how they can be adjusted while they are still small."[7]

Despite his grand words, Churchill did not really consider this meeting of great importance. Its lack of importance — in his eyes — is indicated by the fact that he could find no room for even a small mention of it in his six-volume history of the war, *The Second World War.*

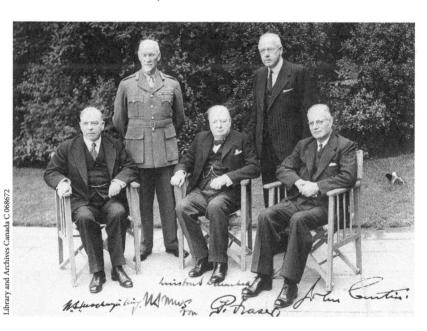

King, General Smuts of South Africa, Churchill, Peter Fraser of New Zealand, and John Curtin of Australia at the Commonwealth Prime Ministers' Conference, May 1, 1944.

That evening there was a state dinner for the prime ministers at Buckingham Palace. King recorded having a very pleasant talk with Princess Elizabeth. He wrote that he found her very natural, not in the least shy, and very happy and graceful. He also spoke with Queen Elizabeth, whom he said spoke most emphatically about her love for Canada and the people, and what Canada had done in the war. She spoke to him again of the visit she and King George had made to Canada in 1939, repeating that it was the happiest time in their lives and that it had done a lot for them. King was touched when she said that they all had great confidence in him.

The prime minister also met with King George, who talked of the duke of Gloucester. According to King, "He then turned and, in a pathetic sort of way, said to me: 'He is the only brother I have.' At the time, I hardly grasped the fact that it was one way of referring to Edward as no longer one who could be recognized as a brother." Then, talking of the king's speech impediment, King wrote, "The King has mastered his difficulty in speaking very well. On only two occasions did I see him pause for a word."

The conference reconvened the next day and continued until May 5, with the discussions interspersed with attendance at British cabinet meetings. Churchill, as expected, brought up the matter of annual prime ministers' conferences and the importance of closer ties within the Empire and Commonwealth. King countered, saying that annual meetings were not practical, especially as there would be a general election in Canada in 1945. He also made clear that a common policy could be reached without any centralization in London. King was pleased to be supported in his statement by General Smuts of South Africa.

Alan Lascelles, King George's private secretary, wrote in his diary of May 5: "Mackenzie King has not said much yet, but his brief speeches show a commendable appreciation of past achievements and present difficulties; he paid a generous, and deserved, tribute to Winston's wisdom in refusing to be induced by USA to launch a European venture in 1942 or 1943."[8]

King had blocked Churchill's efforts to centralize the Commonwealth, but in his diary he expressed his agreement with Churchill's comments at the conclusion of the conference. Churchill stated that the real aim of the British foreign policy was to see that the world never again became involved in war. Thus, it felt that there was the need for a formation of some kind of international organization, with force behind it, which would ensure a durable peace. That unless such could be accomplished, he did not know what would happen to the world.

On Saturday, May 6, King was invited to Chequers for the weekend. At dinner he sat next to Clementine Churchill. King noted that, as normal, Churchill took over the table discussions. One of the main topics was the Soviets; by this time Churchill's prior opinion of the intentions of Stalin had been shaken, and he now feared that Russia might attempt to take control of a large part of Europe. On a more pleasant topic, Churchill spoke eloquently of the British Empire, praising how all parts had risen up during the war. He asked how this could be accounted for. King responded that it was the British sense of freedom and justice.

In spite of the lack of acknowledgement in Churchill's speeches of the contribution of Canada in the war, and of Churchill's attempts to bind the Dominions under the mother country, King's personal opinion had not changed. He referred in his diary to the sense of wonder he felt at being "the guest of honour of Churchill, whose fame today is greater than that of any other living man, and [of the distinction King felt] to be on intimate, friendly terms with him.... All this on the eve of the greatest battle in the history of the world. Also being invited to address members of the Houses of Parliament.... The mystery and solemnity of it all overwhelms me — at times, seems to quite overpower me. It all lies completely beyond my comprehension."

The following day the Dominion leaders met again at 10 Downing Street. The main topic was the future world organization that Churchill envisioned. King was the first of the Dominion prime ministers to speak. He stated that Canada had accepted the leadership of Churchill and Roosevelt during the war. After the war Canada wished to have her own right of representation. King wrote in his diary that Churchill said that some parts of his (King's) statement ran counter to his views. King, however, received the backing of Smuts, who spoke of the danger of anyone speaking with a single voice for the Empire and Commonwealth.

King referred to this disagreement with Churchill as being the hardest battle of the conference. "The truth is he speaks of Communism, etc.

being a religion to some people; the British Empire and Commonwealth is a religion to him."

Not surprisingly King found the morning's discussion very tiring. But he managed to have a brief rest before he headed to the Houses of Parliament for one of the most important functions of his life.

Churchill escorted him into the robing room of the House of Lords and, as King recorded, he opened the proceedings with a few exceptionally well-chosen and extremely kind remarks. "He went all out with his reference to myself and my part in the war, saying that no other man … could have brought Canada so unitedly in the war. Also spoke of my 25 years of leadership of the party and 18 years as P.M. of Canada. Referred to the magnificence of Canada's war effort, and to maintaining the fraternal association of the U.S. and the British Commonwealth and Empire."

King stated that when he received the invitation, he found himself at a loss for words because of the high honour. He referred directly to Churchill: "Your friendship and mine over many years of peace, and our close companionship throughout the years of war … afford me a support I greatly welcome in addressing this distinguished assembly."

King began his speech, which is included in his book *Canada and the Fight For Freedom,* with the visit of the king and queen in 1939, and the example they had shown in the war, which had deepened the meaning and significance of Canada's allegiance to the Crown. After acknowledging the heroic endurance of the British people in the dark days of the war, he then focused on Canada, saying it was timely to mention the part played by Canada.

He spoke of the significance of the fact that Canada had entered the war of its own free will and not as the result of any formal obligation. He emphasized that Canada's participation was not primarily a response to a call of blood or race, but, rather, it was the outcome of Canadians' "deepest political instinct — a love of freedom and a sense of justice."

King went on to give specific details of Canada's war effort, starting with the fact that from a population of eleven and a half million, "three-quarters of a million of our finest young men are serving in the armed forces." He followed with information on the British Commonwealth Air Training Plan, stating that the one hundred thousandth airman had just completed his training. He further stated that Canadian contributions to Britain, of ships, machines, weapons, and other supplies, had amounted to nine hundred million pounds, or four billion Canadian dollars, with half being an outright gift.

After speaking of the strength and unity of the British Commonwealth, he talked of the prime object of the Canadian policy, which was to work for the maintenance of a fraternal association of the British and American people. He declared that when "peace comes, it is our highest hope that the people of the British Commonwealth and the United States will continue to march at each other's side, united more closely than ever. But we equally hope that they will march in a larger company, in which all nations united today in defence of freedom, will remain united in the service of mankind."

King closed with a reference to the fateful hour of the upcoming invasion, and then the duty to "fashion a new world order in which social

King addresses the combined Houses of Parliament in Westminster. Sitting behind him are Churchill and Deputy Prime Minister Clement Attlee, May 11, 1944.

security and human welfare will become a part of the inheritance of mankind.... It is for us to make of our association of free British nations a model of what we hope the whole world will someday become."[9]

The lord chancellor moved a vote of thanks. Then Churchill "called for the ayes and nays, and the entire room responded with ayes.... Churchill began to walk with me down the aisle.... On the way he said to me that the speech was very good, very good indeed."

The front page of the *Toronto Star* the next day included extracts from British newspapers on the speech:

The *Manchester Guardian:* "Mr. King spoke as the representative of a North American people mindful of its ties with the United States and of its key position in bridging the ocean gap between the United States and Britain."

The *Daily Mail:* "The Canadian Prime Minister re-affirmed the principles which animate the countries of the British Commonwealth and their hopes for the future. He comes armed not only with words but with a record of deeds to pay service to these ideals."

The *Daily Mirror:* "Mr. King warned against changing the form of the Commonwealth and concluded that the Dominion prime ministers had decided that contact with Whitehall did not need tightening. They are going to carry on with the loose knit family arrangement that has worked up to now."

The *London Star:* "The Canadian premier has proved himself one of the outstanding statesmen of the Empire. Under his political generalship … Canada gave every man and bullet she could spare in the perilous days when the British Commonwealth of Nations fought alone."

The *Times* described the speech as "a far-reaching estimate of a statesman thinking of the British Commonwealth and the world in worldwide terms." It added that among the free peoples of the world, "none has done more than Canada to define the purposes of the United Nations or the principles of the unity of the Commonwealth."

King noted a little incident of that day, concerning his long-time personal valet, Nicol: "I was much touched by Nicol's appreciation of a ticket being secured for him today. His eyes filled with tears.... He said to me he thought it was the greatest event of my life, and in a simple quiet way, linked his own with it, having been with me so long."

The following day King went with Churchill and other prime ministers for a tour of the assembled troops on the south coast, and to watch army demonstrations. They dined with General Eisenhower, the commander of the invasion forces. Eisenhower remarked to King that it seemed funny he had to cross the ocean to meet so close a neighbour. "On leaving the door of the train as he was saying good-night, Eisenhower turned back and said: 'I will invite you all to Paris....' After Eisenhower left, Churchill said: 'Isn't he a fine fellow? Are we [not] fortunate in having such a man?' I personally was very favourably impressed in Eisenhower. He is a fine manly type. Has a strong powerful hand."

The meeting of Commonwealth prime ministers concluded on May 15, with the delegates attempting to prepare a final communiqué. King, ever the one to read into phrases something that the originator had not intended, not surprisingly had problems with the original draft. He insisted that the line, "We were all agreed on plans for the future of the war with Germany and Japan," be omitted, as the Canadian cabinet had not agreed, and he was but one member of the cabinet. He also disagreed with the use of the word "policy," and insisted it be replaced with "policies," because he felt there could be no such thing as a common policy, as each Dominion made its own. In the end the declaration just reaffirmed the determination of the countries of the Commonwealth to continue with their allies all needful exertions to achieve victory and an enduring peace.

King's diary recounted: "When I was through, I said to myself, I have fought my last battle at this conference ... and ... held my ground throughout."

On May 17 King visited the Canadian Army. He was given a guard of honour and a demonstration from some of the twenty thousand troops, which would soon be taking part in the invasion. The following day he drove to Montgomery's headquarters for lunch. The general forewarned him that when the invasion came there would be great slaughter for the first few weeks.

Having done his duty overseas, King was anxious to return to Canada. He met with Churchill on May 19, and Churchill suggested that he stay until D-Day: "It will be something to be here for." However,

Churchill stated that they did not know the date, "It all depend[s] on wind, tide and the like" King decided to decline the invitation and leave.

Before going King, who laid great emphasis on extending courtesies, wrote to Clementine Churchill. King clearly appreciated the warmth of the Churchills' hospitality and the closeness of the relationship: "My last word before leaving London must be one of deepest gratitude and thanks to Winston and yourself, and indeed to all of the family. I shall have to leave you to imagine what this visit to London has meant to me — quite the greatest event of my life.... My many associations with Winston and yourself have been so full of meaning and so precious that you have both become, if I may say so, almost a part of my life ... may God continue to protect, to guide and to bless you both."[10] It is interesting to note that despite the closeness he felt for them, and after all the many occasions during which they had met over the years, he still referred to her as, "Dear Mrs. Churchill" and he signed himself as "W.L. Mackenzie King."

King arrived in Ottawa on May 21, and the next day he returned to the House of Commons. He had expected recognition of his efforts from his own party, but what he received exceeded all his expectations. The *Toronto Star* reported this as the zenith of his long career. "He received an ovation from all groups, such as seldom has been extended any Canadian prime minister or political leader. Rising when Mr. King entered the Chamber, the entire House cheered whole-heartedly as the prime minister walked to his seat. The cheering, applause, and desk-thumping from all parts of the Chamber continued as Mr. King, obviously moved, stood waiting for the outburst of approbation to subside."

Maybe unexpectedly, when considering the attitude of opposing politicians in the current century, the *Star* continued with its report on the other party leaders, starting with the leader of the Conservatives, the official opposition party, Gordon Graydon, who "crossed the floor, warmly shook his hand, mentioned the open-hearted welcome King had received from the people of Britain and said: 'We are glad to have you safely back.'"

M.J. Coldwell, the CCF leader, was even more complimentary: "We feel, as I think all the House feels, regardless of political affiliations, that the prime minister on his recent trip acted with distinction to himself and honour to his country."

King spoke of the conference and that there would be the greatest conflict of arms that had ever taken place in the history of the world, although this last phase would be long and hard. He concluded that he was never more proud to be a Canadian, and never more proud to be a citizen of the British Commonwealth.

However, there were also reasons for Canada not to be proud at that time. A blot on Canada's and King's wartime record remains its treatment of Canadians of Japanese descent. In February 1942 Parliament amended the War Measures Act, updating it to include, among other measures, provision for the internment of the 23,000 Canadians of Japanese descent living in the country at the time, even though 14,000 of them had been born in Canada. King had put forward this amendment after the Japanese attack on Pearl Harbor, although there was no evidence that the Japanese in Canada posed any threat. Despite his earlier actions against the Japanese, King was incensed to learn, on his return from England in May 1944, that a bill to amend the Elections Act had been passed that took away the right to vote from Japanese who were Canadian citizens. He criticized the cabinet for enacting this legislation while he was away, and after consulting with the government leader in the Senate, he had the decision reversed.

Churchill was heavily involved with the planning for the invasion of northern France, and he advised King George that he intended to witness the bombardment from one of the cruiser squadrons. "His Majesty immediately said that he would like to come too. He had not been under fire, except in air raids, since the Battle of Jutland, and eagerly welcomed the prospect of renewing the experiences of his youth."

Sir Alan Lascelles wrote in his diary on May 31: "I persuaded the King, without much difficulty, that it would be wrong from many points of view, for either him or Winston, to carry out their 'Overlord jaunt.'"

Churchill was relieved at the king's decision, in view of the danger, but, Lascelles continued, "it soon became clear that Winston had no intention of applying this wise decision to himself.... Winston knows perfectly well that he oughtn't to do this but when he gets these puckish notions, he is just like a naughty child."

While messages were going back and forth between the king and Churchill, Lascelles felt the need to write: "But let nothing I may say of Winston's minor failures ever seem to imply an apostasy from my firm faith that he is the greatest war leader we have ever had (not forgetting John Churchill or Chatham), an orator of a quality that has seldom been equalled, and one to whom we owe a debt we cannot even estimate, let alone repay, for his superb courage in 1940."[11]

Common sense prevailed, and on June 3 Churchill wrote to King George: "Since Your Majesty does me the honour to be so much concerned about my personal safety on this occasion, I must defer to your Majesty's wishes, and indeed commands."[12]

Lascelles commented: "It is quite a nice letter. Anyhow, we have bested him, which not many people have succeeded in doing in the last four years!"[13]

The weather was the crucial factor for the timing of the invasion. This had been unfavourable, but the forecasters predicted a window of acceptable weather for June 6, and Eisenhower gave the decision to launch the invasion.

King was wakened at 4:30 in the morning to be advised of the news, and he broadcast to the nation at 8:00 a.m. He announced that the Allied invasion of Europe had begun and that Canadian troops were among the invading armies. He also said that Canadians would be proud to know that the Royal Canadian Navy and the Royal Canadian Air Force were also involved. He referred to the invasion as a decisive phase in the war against Germany. However, he warned that casualties could be high, and Canadians must remain patient.

The text of the D-Day communiqué from General Eisenhower was consistent with the draft statement of the Sicily invasion, in referring only to "British and American" troops. After another strong Canadian objection, the actual announcement was revised to refer to "American, British and Canadian" troops. However, Churchill, true to his prior practice, in advising the British House of Commons of the invasion, referred to "Anglo-American Allies," making no reference to Canada or any of the other Allies. Later in the day, possibly after he had been advised of the irritation this produced, he gave a further statement, this time referring to "Allied Troops," though he added, "I will not give lists of all the different nationalities they represent."[14]

So, with D-Day, to paraphrase Churchill: a further "climacteric" had occurred.

23

FRANCE REVENGED

D-Day, or Operation Overlord, saw the largest seaborne invasion in history. A fleet of 5,000 ships, including 110 from the Royal Canadian Navy, transported 160,000 soldiers, with 1,100 airplanes bombarding the defences.

Of the five beaches stormed, Canada was allocated Juno beach. It landed 14,000 soldiers there and established a beachhead within two hours.

Casualties on D-Day were expected to be high. The previous evening Churchill told Clementine, "'Do you realize that by the time you wake up in the morning, twenty thousand men might have been killed?' The actual number was thankfully less tragic — 4,570, which included 2,500 Americans, 1,641 Britons and 359 Canadians."[1]

Dieppe had taught the Allies at least one thing: a port could not be taken intact, to be used to transport troops, armaments, and supplies. The answer was the Mulberry, an artificial harbour that was towed across the Channel in sections and assembled off the coast. This innovative scheme had been supported by Churchill, and was brought to reality. Actually, two Mulberries were constructed, but the one utilized by the Americans was destroyed in a storm on June 19, 1944. The British one saw heavy use for eight months, with the transportation of two and a half million troops and five hundred thousand vehicles.

Although Churchill had promised King George that he would not accompany the invasion force on D-Day, he did go over four days later.

He was met by General Montgomery, five miles inland, in a place, some three miles from the front, that had been heavily bombed the night before. Churchill enquired of the possibility of "an incursion of German armour breaking up our luncheon." Montgomery said he "did not think that they would come." However, "he did in fact move two days later, though not till he and his staff had had another dose."[2]

Although the invasion had initially gone well, progress in northern France slowed down soon after. Germany was not going to go down without inflicting more death and destruction, and although it did not impede the Allied effort, the German resistance brought more misery to the people of London and the south of England. On June 13, 1944, the first pilotless aircraft, the "Flying Bomb," or V1, was launched against London. This was the German retaliation for the bombing of its cities, and a further three thousand were launched within the next five weeks. The last V1 attack took place in October 1944, prior to the site being overrun by Allied Forces. However, the more advanced V2 could be launched from mobile sites, and the Germans continued using them to attack England until March 1945. Casualties in the south of England, mainly London, totalled 8,908 killed, with an additional 24,448, seriously injured.

While Churchill was heavily involved in all aspects of the war, King took no direct part in the proceedings. Surprisingly, King's diary at this time makes little reference to the Canadian forces, which were heavily involved in the invasion of France. However, on July 6 he does comment on the hard fighting they were involved in near Caen. As a result of the losses that Canada incurred, it became clear that reinforcements would soon be needed, and with inadequate reserves a serious problem loomed. It would be a problem that tested King's leadership.

That crisis was still a little ways away, however. In the meantime, while issues arising from the war naturally occupied most of King's time, the summer of 1944 also saw other important events, unrelated to the war. August 7 was a milestone in King's life. It marked the twenty-fifth anniversary of his election as leader of the Liberal Party. In the House of Commons that day, he was given a great ovation, as well as messages of congratulations from the opposition leaders. That evening a dinner was given in his honour at the Château Laurier Hotel, with some one thousand guests.

Churchill had not forgotten that historic day and a highlight of the day for King was a telegram from Churchill. To say that Churchill had a way with words is an understatement.

> I learn that you are today celebrating the Silver Jubilee of your assumption of the leadership of your Party. In the whole history of free Parliamentary institutions few if any can claim to have led a Party of the State so long and so pre-eminently. Throughout these twenty-five years you and I have watched Canada advance along the road of liberty and progress with admiration and pride. Yet never, perhaps, has this country held Canada in higher esteem than in these last few years of bitter conflict, during which, under your inspired guidance as Prime Minister, she has played so splendid a part in the now imminent overthrow of the powers of evil. It is a peculiar pleasure therefore to offer you at this time my warmest congratulations and if I may add my sincere good wishes for a prosperous future.[3]

Of course, such celebrations were but brief interludes, and the war soon intruded again. King now found himself planning for another conference. While King was in London, Churchill had enquired about the possibility of utilizing the Quebec facilities again for another meeting with Roosevelt. The purpose was to harmonize the plans and projects underway, including actions against Japan, which would be redoubled after Germany was defeated. King agreed, and on August 12 the formal request came, to which King happily and readily approved. This gave him another opportunity to obtain first-hand information. Another benefit, as he stated in his diary, was the publicity, which would be of great help at the time of the next general election, to be held after the war was over.

September 1944 saw the steady progress of the Allied armies in France. Of special satisfaction was the capture of Dieppe on September 1.

General Montgomery had thoughtfully assigned the assault on the city to the Second Canadian Infantry Division. However, the Germans evacuated the city the day before the assault was to commence. The reception given to the Canadian soldiers was emotional and overwhelming. They formally marched through the city on September 3. That date was another milestone — it was also the fifth anniversary of the start of the war.

(Following the war, the town of Dieppe created a small park at the western end of the esplanade. Standing in the centre of the "Square du Canada" is a monument inscribed [English translation], "On the 19th of August 1942, on the beaches of Dieppe, our Canadian cousins marked

The entry of the Second Canadian Infantry Division to liberate Dieppe, September 3, 1944.

with their blood the road to our final liberation foretelling thus their victorious return on the 1st of September 1944.")

A further indication that the war was moving into its final stages occurred in Ottawa on September 8. Princess Juliana of the Netherlands, who had been in Ottawa for four years, was returning home with her three daughters. One of them, Margriet, had been born in Canada, at which time the birth room had been declared international territory, in order to allow her to have Dutch nationality, and so be in the line of succession. As a sign of gratitude to Canada for accommodating them, Princess Juliana sent one hundred thousand tulip bulbs to Ottawa in 1945, and further bulbs have been gifted in succeeding years.

Churchill was in ill health when he boarded the *Queen Mary* in Scotland on September 5 for the journey to Halifax. He was obliged to take malaria pills, which upset his constitution, and he was in a bad temper for the whole voyage. However, as Malcolm MacDonald wrote to Lord Halifax: "Then he set foot on Canadian earth and was given a wild sing song reception from Canadian crowds. All the harm that the sulphur drugs had done disappeared, and all the good that they had done remained. He was at once in his most friendly and glorious form and remained so throughout the Conference."[4]

MacDonald's comments were confirmed by the *Globe & Mail*, which reported that Churchill led the crowd in singing "Land of Hope and Glory," "The Maple Leaf Forever," "O Canada," and "God Save the King."

On September 11 King was in the Quebec City railway station to welcome President and Mrs. Roosevelt. He was shocked by Roosevelt's sickly appearance, evidence of the heart problems that would result in his death in just seven months' time. Almost at the same time, the Churchills arrived. The president drove to the Citadel with the governor general, and King accompanied Churchill. King wrote in his diary that Churchill remarked that although the military authorities thought that the war would be over in 1944, he disagreed. He also told King that he had visited the Canadian troops in Normandy and that he had been to the front as far as the firing line. He thought they were fighting exceedingly well, and he told King that he regretted the losses they had suffered. Churchill repeated that it was really wonderful what Canada was doing in the war, and spoke particularly of the latest financial assistance given to Britain.

At luncheon that day, King noted that Churchill said quite frankly he was sure if Britain had not fought as she did at the start, while others were getting under way, that America would have had to fight for her existence. If Hitler had got into Britain and some Quisling government had given them possession of the British navy, along with what they had of the French fleet, nothing would have saved this continent. The president stated that he agreed, as they could not have got ready in time.

King noted in his diary that he brought up another matter — one that would gather momentum during the next few months. He asked if it had been decided which of the Allies — the Russians or one of the Western powers — would enter Berlin first. There was a lack of response, but eventually Churchill stated that they had to get to Vienna, before the Russians.

The Octagon Conference was convened on September 13. Compared to the Quebec Conference of the previous year, this conference boasted almost unanimous agreement. The only disagreement was over Churchill's request that the Royal Navy be more heavily involved in the fighting against Japan. The American navy chief, Admiral King, not the most tactful of men, pointedly dismissed the offer.

As at the Quadrant Conference, King was not included in the formal talks, but he was there for the photograph sessions, and dog lover that he was, he enjoyed the company of Roosevelt's Scottish terrier, Fala.

The following day Churchill addressed the Canadian war committee and told the ministers and chiefs of staff that on behalf of Britain he was happy to thank Canada for what it had done in the war. Malcolm MacDonald, wrote to the colonial minister, Lord Cranborne, of the meeting:

> Between you and me, his attitude with the Canadians is far better now than it was up to eighteen months ago.... This makes them feel that he regards them as real comrades. They used to admire him enormously, but from a distance and with a certain sense that they were naughty children whom the headmaster saw occasionally, with

Governor General Lord Athlone, Roosevelt (showing his deteriorated health), Churchill, and King at the Octagon Conference in Quebec City, September 12, 1944.

no particular pleasure. They now admire him at least as much as they ever did, not only as a great but forbidding leader, but also as a friend and good companion.... At the end of the meeting, he made a very sincere and moving speech to Mr. Mackenzie King and his colleagues about Canada's war effort and the position of greatly enhanced importance which this has given the Dominion in world

Churchill with Premier Maurice Duplessis leaves the Quebec Legislature, September 14, 1944.

affairs. Mackenzie King replied with some equally sincere and moving words about Canada's admiration and affection for Winston. It was a good show.[5]

As he did in 1943, Churchill went with King to visit the Quebec government, although the premier was now Maurice Duplessis, who was to continue in office, in an autocratic manner, for the next fifteen years. On the way back to the Citadel, as King recorded, they talked on elections. Churchill stated that after the war they would have to hold an election, and he was confident that he would be successful. King suggested that he should not continue for too long, and he should concentrate on documenting his record.

On September 16 Roosevelt and Churchill were awarded honorary degrees by McGill University. When lunching with the two of them, King

Churchill with King and Canadian Cabinet ministers, including C.G. Power and C.D. Howe, during the Octagon Conference, September 14, 1944.

took the opportunity of giving his opinion on the world organization after the war. The structure of what would be called the United Nations was being debated at that time at Dumbarton Oaks, in Washington D.C., by representatives of the United States, Britain, the Soviet Union, and China. As he had stated in the past, King agreed with the four great powers being the main authority at the outset, but he made the point that it would have to be made clear that this was only for the transitional period. He stated that if the smaller nations were not given a say, after that time there would be strong objections.

Both Roosevelt and Churchill agreed. Churchill stated that at the moment the problem was Stalin, who wanted the right to veto anything to do with disputes in which she was involved.

As the conference was winding down, Churchill gave King a gift of models of the Mulberry harbours. King, was deeply touched and thanked him in writing:

Dear Winston:

No remembrance could have begun to express in like manner the intimacy of the friendship and the completeness of the confidence you have accorded me throughout these years of war as do the silver models, so beautiful in themselves, and which symbolize, so perfectly, the secret of the success of the invasion.

To have received this gift from your own hand, here at the Citadel, where so many of the plans have been worked out ... lends to your gift a preciousness quite beyond words. I can only thank you for what it means to me, and will ever mean, but this I do with all my heart.

May God continue to guide, and guard and strengthen you in the service you are rendering the cause of freedom in this war...

Your devoted friend, Mackenzie[6]

The Churchills were to leave on September 17, and King dined with them that evening. "When Mrs. Churchill came into the room, she said, 'This is our last night here. It is a very special occasion. We must have some little celebration before we start. Mr. King, will you join us in a glass of champagne?' I said, 'All right, Mrs. Churchill, if you say so, I will, but it is only because you ask it and because of the occasion."

King continued in his diary:

> The dinner was really a very enjoyable one. Churchill
> sat and talked like he was the father of a family. I have
> seldom seen him more placid [and] quiet and in a thor-
> oughly contented mood.... He spoke particularly of
> Canada's part in the war, of how exceptional in every
> way it was. He raised his glass to me and reached across
> the table to touch mine, and then was quite eloquent
> on the relief from bondage, regaining full freedom, etc.
> It was really quite a little ceremony, all related to close
> friendship which we had enjoyed. I recalled it was forty-
> four years since we had first met. He placed his empha-
> sis not on the meeting in Canada, but on the meeting
> later when I went to England to get legislation through
> the British Parliament.

It came time to leave: "Finally, when he was about to arise, I lifted my glass, looked across at him and said 'God bless, guide and guard you.' His eyes filled with tears, he rose and when he came across to my side of the table he put my arm in his and spoke about the years we have had together; how faithful a friend I had been; of the little dance we had together at Chequers. I told him if spared we would yet have another in the days of Victory."

The Octagon Conference was a great success. The war was winding down. King was well-satisfied. However, he was soon to face the greatest challenge in his parliamentary career.

24

CONSCRIPTION IS NECESSARY

When Churchill returned to Britain, he was faced with the news that the Dumbarton Oaks Conference had not resulted in agreement on the structure of the United Nations. He considered it imperative that the organization be properly established, and this required the Soviet Union as a full participant. There were, however, contentious issues involving Russia, including the Soviets's participation in the war against Japan, and the future of the countries that were being cleared of German forces.

In keeping with his policy that personal contact was the best way to deal with difficult issues, Churchill telegraphed Stalin to request a meeting in Moscow. The Soviet leader responded in the affirmative on September 30, 1944. President Roosevelt could not join them, as he was occupied with a presidential election, but he was to be represented by the U.S. ambassador to the Soviet Union, Averell Harriman.

Churchill was anxious to obtain Stalin's commitment that the Soviet government would not interfere in the internal political affairs of other countries. However, he had to accept the reality that Russian troops were occupying some of the countries in and abutting the Balkans. He proposed to Stalin that their two countries should agree on a temporary measure, acknowledging their respective interests in these countries. This was effected in a very unusual document. Churchill wrote out on a half-sheet of paper a percentage agreement, which accorded Britain the major interest in Greece, and Russia the major interest in Romania and Bulgaria, with both countries sharing Yugoslavia and Hungary. It would soon be clear that Stalin had no intention of relinquishing control of any of the eastern European countries after the war. However, he did keep to the agreement regarding Greece.

One country that was not part of the percentage agreement was Poland. Britain had gone to war for that country, and Churchill felt its future was not negotiable — full democracy had to be granted to it after the war. This would be a major subject of discussion at the next "Big Three" conference.

King was on the sideline in top-level matters, although he followed the progress of the Allied advances. This, of course, included the activities of the Canadian Army, which distinguished itself in the fighting, and captured the port of Calais on September 30. Although the progress of the Allied forces was very encouraging, and ultimate victory was certain, the German army was continuing to provide stiff opposition. While the Canadian Army chief of the general staff was still assuring the cabinet that they had adequate troops, newspaper reports from the front stated the opposite.

On September 19 the *Globe & Mail* included a report headed: "Untrained Troops Hazard at Front." This came from Major Conn Smythe, the owner of Maple Leaf Gardens and the Toronto Maple Leafs hockey team. He had been wounded while on active service and spoke with the newspaper from his hospital bed in Toronto. The following day the newspaper's editorial was headed: "Major Smythe's Grave Charge."

Smythe's contention was supported by other officers, and the *Globe & Mail* kept up the pressure for conscription of the fully trained army on home duty in Canada. The editorial of October 21 concluded: "The fact that the Government wants votes in Quebec is no answer to the need for trained reinforcements." The newspaper was even more direct eleven days later: "Canada waits for the Cabinet to do its duty. Dare it forget that manoeuvring for votes in Quebec is political knavery when limbs and lives of Canadians are being placed in jeopardy."

King was sensitive to the strong opinions on the issue; as usual, he was trying to weigh his options. The argument for conscription was bolstered by a report he received from James Ralston, who had just returned from Europe, where he had gone to see the situation for himself. On October 18 Ralston returned and gave a report to King. He had forewarned the prime minister that he would be bringing unpalatable news.

King wrote down Ralston's opening words: "Mr. King, I want to speak of the question of reinforcements, which is a serious one." He stated that the fighting had been more intense than had been anticipated and that this had resulted in the reserves being inadequate. He also noted that some men had been away for five years, and in active conflict too long, and would have to be allowed to come home. Regarding morale, he said the men resented the standing army in Canada doing nothing, while they were so short of reinforcements.

King brought his expertise as a negotiator to play, providing answers to all of Ralston's concerns. He spoke of the expected early termination of the war, and the effect that bringing in conscription at this stage would have on the fortunes of the Liberal Party at the post-war election. His trump card was to remind Ralston of the situation in World War I — the damaging effect on the Liberal Party of conscription being imposed.

The meeting concluded with no agreement. The next day the war committee considered the matter. Ralston gave his report, and King wrote: "I waited some little time and then said quite quietly that the question that had been raised was the most serious one that had come before the Cabinet since Confederation. That we could not weigh it too carefully. That I hoped the Cabinet would realize exactly what was involved; that it meant the calling of [Parliament]. A bitter debate in Parliament, and then almost certainly taking the issue from [Parliament] to the people."

That evening King decided that the answer was to convince the National Reserve Mobilization Act (NRMA) men, who had been conscripted just for Canadian defence, to volunteer for overseas service.

King also thought of another avenue, which he discussed with the British high commissioner, Malcolm MacDonald. King's suggestion was that in view of all Canada had done, the problem should be referred to Churchill, asking him to have "matters arranged so that the situation could be met without any question of conscription being raised at this time."

MacDonald contacted Colonial Minister Cranborne, to advise that an important message would be coming from the Canadian prime minister. The message was sent on October 22 marked "TOP SECRET AND PERSONAL," and King outlined his problem in a lengthy and dramatic appeal: "I am faced with the most critical situation which has arisen since Canada's entry into the war. It is beset with possible consequences so dangerous to the remainder of Canada's war effort in Europe and Asia, to the future of Canada, to future relations with the Commonwealth, and to all Government war activities and policies, including those being considered with respect to organization for maintenance of world peace, that I feel I should inform you of the situation, and inquire of you whether in your opinion conditions as they are in Europe, at the moment, or as they are likely to become at any time before the conclusion of the war, render the step that is being proposed."

King went on to state that General Stuart, the chief of staff of the Canadian Army, had previously assured him that they had adequate troops, but Stuart had now reported that "for a series of military reasons beyond my control, I must admit that reinforcements have been inadequate as to numbers in respect to the infantry arm.... I recommend, therefore, if the numbers required cannot be found from General Service personnel in Canada, that the terms of service of NRMA personnel be extended to include overseas service in any theatre."

King outlined the effect of taking this course of action: "Any recommendation involving conscription for service overseas would necessitate the reassembling of Parliament, which has been adjourned till January 31, 1945, the most acrimonious discussion in the House of Commons, the adoption of closure as the only means, without endless discussion, of obtaining the vote of confidence which would have to be sought, the possible defeat of the Government, and most certainly a dissolution of Parliament itself to be followed by a general election extending over two months, this length of time being required by our Election Act so as to permit of obtaining the votes of the Armed Forces in different parts of the world."

King pulled no punches, stating that if conscription for overseas service became an issue, "I can see no escape from the bitterest controversy

Canada has ever known in her Parliament or in the country. How perilous such controversy might become at any moment and how far-reaching in its consequences in relation to all further war and post-war plans, and for Canadian unity for years to come, I would not venture to predict."

After outlining the dire consequences, King attempted to put the onus on Churchill to consider whether it would be advisable "[to take] the risks involved in raising a conscription issue in Canada at this stage of the war."

After clearly putting the ball in Churchill's court, King attempted to state the reverse, but did not succeed:

> In no way do I desire to shift any responsibility upon you for a decision. I am quite prepared, as it is my duty, to become responsible for any decision the Canadian Government may take in relation to any matter of policy in so far as it relates exclusively to the Canadian forces. I recognize, however, that in this matter I have a special responsibility to bring to the attention of yourself what is involved in the decision to be reached and wherein it cannot fail to have far reaching effects upon the immediate and prospective efforts of all the United Nations and in particular those of the United Kingdom. I also recognize that once these have been brought to your attention the British Government not less than our own could not escape responsibility if all aspects of the situation were not fully thought out by both Governments.

King finished with a plea: "This I believe is the first and only occasion since the beginning of the war that I have felt it imperative to ascertain your views before deciding on a matter of policy which is primarily one for the Government of Canada to decide. As, however, the present situation is one which is anything but exclusively Canadian in its bearing, I know you will appreciate why I feel it to be of the utmost importance to ascertain your views, in so far as you may wish to express them, before a final decision is reached."[1]

Pending a response from Churchill, the matter was presented to the twenty-three members of the cabinet on October 24. Ralston began, giving his report and recommendation. After he had finished, King wrote of their reaction: "The men who had not heard anything before looked intensely surprised, amazed and concerned." King followed Ralston. He stated that the defence minister quite rightly had given the military point of view, and his duty was "to raise points of national significance, which would have to be considered in connection with the question in all its bearings."

King's diary recorded his concern at the serious result of conscription being imposed, including his "fear that civil strife could not be avoided" and his feeling that "any attempt to enforce conscription now would be certain to lead to bloodshed in many parts of the country." He even quoted Governor General Lord Durham a century before, who referred to Quebec in Canada as "two nations warring in the bosom of a single state."

The prime minister did not hold anything back in finishing his oration, making a clear reference to party political considerations. As ministers of the Crown, he stated, they had an obligation, but if conscription was imposed, the Liberal Party would be completely destroyed and the country would be governed by the CCF.

King had hoped that his lengthy appeal to Churchill would result in the British prime minister finding the troops to cover the Canadian shortage. However, this expectation was dashed when the response was received. He entered the gist of Churchill's response in his diary: "I greatly surprised that Churchill had not indicated his desire to meet the situation; merely indicated he was concerned about the difficulties, the seriousness of which he appreciated but that the British [government] and himself would be everlastingly grateful for the help that Canada had given them in the war." Churchill was saying that this was a Canadian problem and he would not become involved.

Matters soon became worse. Ralston was talking of resigning, and King, thinking that other ministers would follow, dissuaded him. Meanwhile the government was under intense criticism from the English-language press to bring in conscription. But King was not finished with his exploration of alternatives, and he turned to a Canadian hero, the former head of the Canadian Army in Britain and a man who was well-respected in Quebec: General Andrew McNaughton.

King met with McNaughton on October 31 at Laurier House. He knew that McNaughton was not in favour of conscription, and he asked him if he would become the minister of defence. He also asked him if he thought he would be able to persuade enough of the standing army in Canada to volunteer for overseas service. Of the 130,000 in the army, King argued, surely the required 15,000 would answer the call, he thought. McNaughton answered in the affirmative to both questions.

Two days later the cabinet met, and King showed his ruthless side. King referred to a letter of resignation that Ralston had given him two years ago, which had never been withdrawn. King turned to Ralston and said he would now accept it. He stated he could not continue on the present basis. King referred to the close relationship that he and Ralston had had, but in times of war, he said, tough decisions had to be made. Ralston responded that he would formally resign.

In looking at this scenario, one wonders why King, normally highly sensitive to people's feelings, decided that he had to dispense with Ralston's services in such a dramatic fashion. Whatever the reason, one is forced to agree with journalist Bruce Hutchinson's characterization of the incident: "[King engaged in the] cold-blooded destruction of J.L. Ralston, the selfless defence minister."[2]

On November 2 McNaughton was sworn in as the minister of defence, and he started a recruiting campaign. No other resignations were submitted to King, but some ministers wanted a deadline of November 30 for McNaughton's efforts, stating that if it did not prove successful then conscription would have to be imposed.

McNaughton did not achieve the objective and King had no option other than to acknowledge defeat. He now had to decide how to proceed. He knew what this issue had done to his hero Sir Wilfrid Laurier. It seemed likely that he might lose the next election, and as he was also almost seventy years of age, it also seemed likely that he would not be able to lead the Liberals to another victory should they be defeated in the next election. He had advised the Liberal caucus that bringing in conscription would have serious repercussion for the country and for the party. The logical action would have been to hand the challenge over to someone else, and retire to his beloved Kingsmere.

Remarkably, now that the fight against conscription was over, King found himself feeling rejuvenated, with a new lease of life. He decided that he would continue, though there was now only one option. Conscription for overseas service had to be imposed.

In his diary he recorded the evolution of his plan: "Instantly there came to my mind the statement I had made to Parliament in June 1942, as to the action the Government would necessarily take, if we were agreed that the time had come when conscription was necessary."

His negotiating skills and conciliatory powers would be taxed to the maximum, but he knew what he had to do. First a meeting of the Liberal Party caucus was held to explain the current situation. This was followed by a meeting with the government ministers, and a separate one with the Quebec ministers.

The next day the draft order-in-council was prepared, in time for a further meeting of the Liberal caucus. This document called for a "partial conscription," as it just authorized the drafting of 16,000 NRMA men for overseas service. At the meeting King pleaded that they stay united for the sake of the country. One who did resign was from Quebec, the air defence minister, Chubby Power.

The cabinet passed the order-in-council, and King proceeded to telephone people who could help explain the government's about-face. These included newsmen at the *Montreal Star,* the *Toronto Star,* and the *Winnipeg Free Press.* He also spoke with the provincial Liberal leader in Quebec, Adélard Godbout, and the Catholic cardinal, Jean-Marie-Roderique Villeneuve.

The vote was held on December 7. The result was positive, 143 to 70. King declared that he "was really amazed when the vote was counted.... It took me some little time after to realize that I had 2/3 of the House with me. I had been expecting 30 of a majority.... The result was really a miracle." When he "rose to thank the House for the confidence it expressed in the Government's undertaking to maintain a vigorous war policy, [he] was given a tremendous ovation." He wrote, "Never before have I received such applause from the House of Commons."

Particularly gratifying to King was the fact that not one of the five French-Canadian members of the cabinet resigned. However, thirty-two Liberal backbenchers from Quebec voted against the bill.

The key to King's victory was the support of his Quebec lieutenant, Louis St. Laurent. The justice minister spoke briefly but effectively in the debate, stating that he had a job to do in the war, and it was not yet finished. He was not concerned with a backlash from his supporters as he intended to leave politics at the end of the war.

The *Toronto Star,* which had consistently supported King and his government during the war, ran a triumphal headline on its December 8 issue: "House Vote Greatest Triumph for King." This was not how the *Globe & Mail,* which had been consistently critical, saw it: "King Sustained 143 to 70." That newspaper's leading article noted that instead of doing the "simple, straightforward thing," which would have been to conscript all the draftees, the order-in-council just stipulated that the 16,000 NRMA men would be sent overseas. According to the paper, this would have a serious effect on the morale of the men in the firing line.

In his biography of King, published in 1953, Bruce Hutchinson portrayed St. Laurent as accepting conscription because he lacked the courage to stand up to King. St. Laurent, who was prime minister at the time Hutchinson's book was published, strongly objected to this statement, and Hutchinson was advised to speak to a general, whose name was to be withheld from publication. He did so, and the general told him that in a meeting of the Armed Forces Council held on November 22, the members had agreed to resign if conscription was not brought in. Hutchinson reported this "great scoop" in *Maclean's* magazine but it was received by the public with "a great yawn. Elizabeth, and the dawning second Elizabethan Age were the only interesting news at the time."[3]

While there is no reason to doubt St. Laurent's sincerity, in Richard S. Malone's *A World in Flames, 1944–1945,* the author disputes this contention, which he said did not agree with the memories of most of the senior generals.[4]

The conscription crisis — a major episode in both King's life and the life of his country — did nothing to enhance his public standing. However, whether or not one agrees with his actions, it must be admitted that he showed enormous strength in resisting the pressure from the public and the media, and sticking to his conviction that conscription should be brought in only when it was absolutely necessary to keep the country together.

In the middle of the very contentious debate that was underway in Parliament, King did not forget Churchill's birthday. On November 29 he recorded in his diary: "I sent a message to Churchill on his 70th birthday anniversary in the following words: 'You know, I am sure, all the wishes that I send to you. May this new year of your life see their fulfilment in abundant measure.'"

King's diary also showed that he was still disappointed in Churchill for not helping him in the political crisis underway: "A very different message from the one which had been drafted. I had the strongest of reasons for not saying more, and the best of reasons for making the message as cordial as I did. It will be interesting to see his reply. I shall be surprised if he does not take the opportunity of the message to say something that will let me see that he is really interested in what I am doing."

Churchill did send him a message on December 9, regarding the vote in Parliament, and all was forgiven. "Without venturing to enter in any way into Canadian politics, I feel I may now say what relief and pleasure it has given me to find you still so effectively at the helm."

King was elated as he recorded: "This is a fine message. Churchill has the marvellous gift of expression, using the right word at the right place. It is a comforting message. A fine word to receive from the Prime Minister of Great Britain."

After the vote King went back to domestic matters and supporting the Allied war effort. However, when a request came from Britain for Canada to take an additional ten thousand more German prisoners of war, in addition to the thirty-six thousand they already had incarcerated, it was refused.

On December 17 King celebrated his seventieth birthday. Personal messages of congratulations were received from the king and queen, Chiang Kai-shek, Roosevelt, de Gaulle, Stalin, and many other world leaders. From Churchill: "Birthday greetings came; less expressive than other wires but I can understand that with his preoccupations what they are, it is a marvel he gets off anything on his own. I sent a message back on this matter."

After the ceremonies on the silver anniversary of his leadership of the Liberal Party, he asked his senior cabinet ministers to "see that this birthday be allowed to pass without a further expression of the generosity of my colleagues." But this was not to be. King received a silver framed picture of the governor general, Churchill, Roosevelt, and himself at the Quebec Conference. He was also much surprised, especially in view of the pressure from the English-language media in the conscription crisis, to be honoured with a life membership in the parliamentary press gallery. This was presented at a banquet in the Château Laurier Hotel. As reported in the *Ottawa Journal,* the ninety-seven members of the gallery who attended were reminded of the prime minister's prior life as a newspaperman, with the chairman of the proceedings stating: "And look where he is now!" The speaker continued, saying, "This is an occasion which speaks for itself. It is a birthday party for a man we all know and love." Then all ceremony was dropped: "While the gathering sang 'Happy Birthday, dear Willie, happy birthday to you,' a big cake topped by seven candles, a token of Mr. King's seventy years, was paraded into the hall."

While some may have thought that the familiarity displayed by the journalists would have been resented by the very private prime minister, this was not the case. In fact he revelled in it, stating in his diary that he thought of the occasion "and all it represented as the crowning event of my years in public life, and recognition which to me in some ways meant more than any other which I had received in the course of my public life."

Such celebrations were, of course, only brief interludes in what remained an extremely difficult period. In Europe the tide had turned against the Germans, and while the Allies were still engaged in a brutal war with Germany, they were already starting to plan for what would happen once hostilities ceased. The future that Churchill had discussed with Stalin was becoming more and more of a reality. The question now became: What would replace the vacuum? In France the Allies were in firm control, and the leader-in-waiting, de Gaulle, had widespread support. However, in Greece, Communist elements were attempting to seize power by force. In a speech to the House of Commons on December 8,

Churchill described the chaotic situation, and stated: "Democracy is no harlot to be picked up in the street by a man with a tommy gun."[5]

King supported Churchill's effort as he recorded in his diary: "In regard to Greece, I feel that Churchill has been right in realizing that Democratic rule does not mean rule only by mobs, and that there is a right time to settle the question between monarchy and the republic." However, King went on to warn that others might misconstrue Churchill's motives, since he was known to be a monarchist. "He needs to be upheld at this time rather than denounced."

While King was supportive of Churchill's efforts, he did point out the criticisms that had been expressed. Churchill covered the correspondence in his war memoirs. "Mr. Mackenzie King in Canada also felt the unfavourable reactions to our Greek policy which had been so volubly expressed in the United States. He revealed his embarrassment in several telegrams." This led to Churchill responding on December 15: "In the House I have done my best to clarify our position. To our mind the essential point is that, having obtained the written assent of all parties … the Greek Prime Minister invited British troops to enter Greece to keep order and safeguard our supplies. We accepted this invitation, and must still do our best to carry it out."

In addition to this letter, Churchill also wrote that he sent King further information including the verbal approval of Stalin to British troops entering Greece and liberating Athens: "In deference to these facts, arguments and appeals, Mr. Mackenzie King refrained from any public reflection on our action."[6]

Churchill had become increasingly concerned with the situation in Greece, and as was his nature, he "took the bull by the horns." The courage of Churchill throughout his life has been recognized. Now he showed not only courage, but determination, with no thought of his own safety and creature comforts.

He stated in his war memoirs that on Christmas Eve he was at Chequers and ready to celebrate Christmas. There was a Christmas tree, courtesy of President Roosevelt, and a family and children's party was underway. However, he came to the conclusion that he had to fly to Athens to see the situation first-hand and attempt to effect a favourable solution. Thus he "spoilt Mr. Eden's Christmas by the proposal, which he immediately accepted, that he should come too."[7]

In the biography of her mother, Mary Soames wrote that when Winston told Clementine, her reaction was to break down in a flood of tears. "It was so rare for Clementine to give way; she was accustomed to sudden changes of plan, and had, in these last years especially, developed a strict sense of priorities. Somehow this sudden departure of Winston laid her low; but not for long."[8]

On Boxing Day Churchill and Eden arrived in Athens, together with Field Marshal Alexander. They met with Archbishop Damaskinos, whom Churchill decided should be the person to take over the position of regent. The archbishop was an imposing figure, and prior to his entering the Orthodox Church had been a champion wrestler. During the German occupation, in view of his efforts for his people, he had been threatened with being shot. He responded with an often quoted comment: "According to the traditions of the Greek Orthodox Church, our prelates are hanged, not shot. Please respect our traditions!"[9]

A meeting with the participants in the civil war was arranged and, much to the surprise of many, the Communists attended. Churchill emphasized that he was not trying to interfere but attempting to "make this effort to rescue Greece from a miserable fate and raise her to a point of great fame and repute."[10]

Churchill sent a telegram to Clementine, "towards whom [he] felt penitent because of [his] desertion on Christmas Eve." He was able to tell her that they had a fruitful day. "We have now left them together, as it was a Greek show. It may break up at any moment. We shall have to wait for a day or two if necessary to see. At least we have done our best."[11]

The conference unanimously agreed to appoint the archbishop as regent, and later the king of Greece, then in exile, was persuaded to confirm the appointment. Churchill concluded this chapter: "Thus ended the six weeks' struggle for Athens, and as it ultimately proved, for the freedom of Greece from Communist subjugation."[12]

The United States had been the source of the sternest criticism; they saw Churchill as an imperialist, empire building and interfering in the internal affairs of the country. Churchill remarked in his war memoirs that once the free world had the facts of the Communist movement in Greece and elsewhere they would be astonished at the vehement attacks to which the British government, and in particular himself, had been subject. "The State Department, in the charge of Mr. Stettinius [secretary of state], issued a markedly critical announcement, which they in turn were to regret, or at least reverse, in after years."[13]

Stalin could have supported the Communists in Greece, but, in one of the few occasions when he kept his word on a matter which was against his interests, he kept to the agreement he had made with Churchill in October 1944.

Churchill's courageous action in meeting the Greek turmoil head-on was one of his greatest achievements. However, he was unable to protect every country. Poland was to be fully occupied by the Soviet army in late December. Churchill had spoken about its future in the House of Commons on December 15. He repeated his remarks of February 22, 1944, after the Tehran Conference, stating that "the fate of the Polish nation holds a prime place in the thoughts and policies of His Majesty's Government and of the British Parliament." He repeated his commitment: "We have never weakened in any way in our resolve that Poland shall be restored and stand erect as a sovereign, independent nation, free to model her social institutions, or any other institutions, in any way her people choose."[14]

This would not occur. Britain declared war to attempt to save Poland from one invader, only to see it dominated by another invader.

25

THE END AND THE BEGINNING

A s 1945 began, it was clear that Germany would soon be defeated. But the big challenge for the Western leaders was how to win the peace that would follow.

A meeting of the Big Three was arranged. Churchill then received a request from de Gaulle claiming that France should also participate. This request was refused. As Churchill pointed out in a letter to Eden: "France contributes a very small fighting stake to the pool at present. It is not French blood that is being shed to any extent in any quarter of the globe.... Canada had more right to be considered the 'Fourth Power.'"[1]

On February 3 Churchill arrived at Yalta in the Soviet Crimea. The first session was on the treatment of Germany. The Russians emphasized reparations and the dismantling of her munitions industries. Churchill recalled the disappointing experience after World War I, stating that "if you wanted a horse to pull your wagon you had to feed it first."[2] This matter was referred to the foreign ministers, and after their recommendation, it was agreed that Germany and Berlin would be split into four zones. It was also agreed that German reparations would partly take the form of forced labour.

As described earlier Churchill had pleaded with Roosevelt "not to keep aloof from the European situation once the war is over." Thus, he was dismayed when the president "made a momentous statement. He had said that the United States would take all reasonable steps to preserve peace, but not at the expense of keeping a large army in Europe, three thousand miles away from home. The American occupation would therefore be limited to two years." This alarmed Churchill. "Formidable questions rose in my mind. If the Americans left Europe, Britain would have to occupy single-handed the entire western portion of Germany. Such a task was far beyond our strength."[3]

But that problem was for the future. The major issues to be discussed at the conference were the future of the United Nations, the question of the Soviets entering the war against Japan, and what all knew would be the most contentious matter: Poland.

Stalin agreed to participate in the United Nations. He also agreed to join in the war against Japan, within ninety days after the defeat of Germany.

The next item up for discussion was Poland: the catalyst for Britain's declaration of war on Germany. In London the Polish government-in-exile had been recognized by the British. However, after the Russians had overrun the country, they established the Polish Committee of National Liberation in Lublin.

Churchill wrote that of the eight plenary meetings of the conference, Poland was discussed at no fewer than seven, with the interchange by the three leaders amounting to nearly eighteen thousand words. In the final volume of his *Memoirs of the Second World War,* he devoted a whole chapter of twenty-three pages to "The Soviet Promise," in view of the criticisms that he had received on the agreement.[4]

The major matter was the establishment of a provisional government prior to free elections. Naturally, Churchill favoured the London group and Stalin the Lublin group. The Soviet leader took a firm line. He stated that the Lublin group consisted of men who were fighting the Germans and had the backing of the majority of the Polish people; the London group, he stated, had not attempted to return to Poland and join in the fight.

The talks between the three leaders were getting nowhere. However, the three foreign secretaries met and Molotov (the Russian minister) produced fresh proposals that were nearer to the Western leaders' position. Although Churchill was suspicious of the intentions of the Soviets, he made a statement on February 23 in support of Stalin — a statement that he was to regret soon afterwards. "Poor Neville Chamberlain," Churchill said, "believed he could trust Hitler. He was wrong, but I don't think I'm wrong about Stalin."[5]

But Churchill was completely wrong about Stalin. It seems impossible to believe that this experienced politician could have been so naive about the Soviet dictator. The purges conducted by Stalin were well-known, as was his practice of inflicting the ultimate penalty on anyone of whom there was the slightest suspicion of disloyalty. However, Churchill was convinced that, with the personal relationship that had been built up during the war, Stalin would keep his word, as he had done in not interfering in the Greek turmoil.

If Churchill was naive in trusting Stalin, the comments Roosevelt made to his cabinet after he returned to Washington are staggering. Indeed, it is difficult to accept that he actually believed his own assessment of the

Churchill with General H.D.G. Crerar, commander of the First Canadian Army; Field Marshal Sir Alan Brooke; Lieutenant-General Guy Simonds (First Canadian Corps); and Field Marshal Bernard Montgomery, overlooking the Rhine River, March 4, 1945.

man: "Stalin has something else in his being besides this revolutionist, bolshevist thing. Perhaps it is to do with his early training for the priesthood. I think that something entered into his nature of the way in which a Christian gentleman should behave."[6]

Churchill and Roosevelt have been criticized for such statements and, of course, for the Polish Agreement at Yalta, but with that country occupied by Russian troops, they were in fact powerless. Short of starting a third world war, which was obviously unacceptable, there was nothing they could do to prevent Russia from seizing control of Poland.

King, as the prime minister of a middle power, had the luxury of not being involved in the major matters confronting the three Allied leaders. His priority in early 1945 was to prepare his party for the upcoming election, which would take place after the European war was over. He knew that he had his work cut out, as a Gallup Poll in the summer of 1944 had given the Liberals only a slim lead over the Conservatives, and that was prior to the humiliation of the conscription issue. However, he was confident of his well-honed skill at convincing the Canadian people that he was their best choice. They would give their opinion on the federal election, to be held on June 11.

One of his "marketing" methods was to show his close relationship with the prime minister of Britain and the president of the United States. So, when a trip to Washington was planned for him to be briefed by Roosevelt on the Yalta Conference, he ensured that the members of the press were informed.

On arriving at the White House on March 9, King was shocked at Roosevelt's appearance. "The visit has left the impression on me that the President has distinctly failed.... He has lost a certain merriment, looks older and wearier, but he has a certain firmness which might carry him along for some time."

In spite of Roosevelt's health, the two talked for almost three hours. "The President gave me a pretty full account of what happened at the Crimea Conference. Spoke of Churchill doing 80% of the talking. Said Stalin had quite a sense of humour. That once when Churchill was making a long speech, Stalin put up his hand to the side of his face, turned to the President and winked one of his eyes as much as to say: there he is talking again."

King as usual had to bring up the matter of recognition of the smaller Allies, including Canada. He wanted to ensure that their contribution was recognized in relation to the upcoming expected announcement of the unconditional surrender of Germany. Roosevelt agreed and stated he would communicate with Churchill on the matter.

On March 30 Churchill wrote to King on the dismantling of the Air Training Scheme. He sent his warmest congratulations to the Canadian government, and the Royal Canadian Air Force, on the successful accomplishment of an imaginative task, most faithfully carried out. "This master plan has done much to speed us along the road to victory. In Canada alone, trained air crews, of which more than half were Canadian, have been turned out at an average rate of 25,000 a year over the last five years. Moreover, the quality of the training has been outstanding, and has shown itself triumphantly in the superiority which we have gained over the enemy in every type of air combat."[7]

With the war virtually won, Churchill was concerned that the Allied forces under the direction of General Eisenhower were not giving priority to occupying as much German land as possible, and, thus, denying it to the advancing Russian troops. Correspondence between the prime minister and the general included Churchill's letter of April 2, 1945, when he took issue with Eisenhower's comment of a few days before that "Berlin has lost its former strategic importance." Churchill gave his view clearly: "I deem it highly important that we should shake hands with the Russians as far east as possible."[8]

Churchill was dealing with the political ramifications, whereas Eisenhower was solely concerned with the military aspect. A race to Berlin would cost thousands of American lives and those forces might be needed to fight the Japanese. Roosevelt was rapidly declining in health and so Eisenhower enquired of General Marshall if he should take heed of Churchill. However, Eisenhower was not given instructions to change his strategy.

In Churchill's correspondence with Eisenhower, as presented in the final volume of his history of World War II, it is clear that Churchill was convinced that Berlin could have been taken by the American-led forces.

However, Churchill also sent a message on April 19, 1945, to Anthony Eden, in Washington at the time: "It would seem that the Western Allies are not immediately in a position to force their way into Berlin. The Russians have two and a half million troops on the section of the front opposite that city."[9]

When the final volume of Churchill's war memoirs was published, Churchill was prime minister and Eisenhower was the newly elected president. This fact may help to explain the reason behind the presentation of these opposing (or diplomatically balanced) comments.

On March 26 Churchill suffered a personal loss with the death of David Lloyd George. Then an even more traumatic blow, two weeks later, with the death of Franklin Roosevelt. Their close relationship had overcome the many disagreements between their respective military staffs, which had resulted in a unified direction in the conduct of the war. Now, with victory in sight, Roosevelt was gone.

A personal recollection was provided by Churchill's secretary, Elizabeth Nel. "We had the news about midnight, and some minutes later I was hurried into the study for dictation. Mr. Churchill was sitting crumpled up in his chair, his face white. When he dictated he was gentle as a lamb, but his voice sounded quite dead."[10]

Churchill spoke in the House of Commons on April 17 of the "sense of loss which the British Commonwealth and Empire and the cause of the Allied Nations have sustained." He mentioned the nine meetings which he had had with Roosevelt during the war and the assistance through the Lend-Lease program, "which will stand forth as the most unselfish and unsordid financial act of any country in all history." He closed: "It remains only to say that in Franklin Roosevelt there died the greatest American friend we have ever known and the greatest champion of freedom who has ever brought help and comfort from the new world to the old."[11]

Churchill had planned to fly to Washington to attend the funeral, but he sent a message of regrets to the new president, Harry Truman, citing the necessity of his remaining in London in view of his parliamentary duties. This was, rightly, much criticized later. He concurred in his memoirs, not for his lack of sensitivity and respect in not attending the funeral,

Churchill enters St. Paul's Cathedral for the memorial service for President Roosevelt, April 17, 1945.

but for the fact that he missed the opportunity of conversing with Truman, and ensuring that both countries would continue on the same path as before. "In the after-light I regret that I did not adopt the new President's suggestion. I had never met him, and I feel that there were many points on which personal talks would have been of the greatest value."[12]

King did attend the funeral. He noted in his diary two days later: "Read Churchill's speech and the account of the Abbey service to President Roosevelt. I can imagine what a terrible blow this is to Churchill. I can see from his speech he had not been able to speak as he usually does. I received a wire from him yesterday, or the day before, thanking me for my wire to him and mentioning wherein I would realize what the loss meant."

With the end of the German war in sight, the focus went towards winning the peace. The whole free world was looking for this to be achieved through the United Nations. While this bore a resemblance to the anaemic League of Nations, there was a notable difference — the United States was a member.

The first conference was to begin on April 25 in San Francisco, with representatives from some fifty countries. The main objective was the drafting of a charter. Canada was represented by an impressive body of experienced politicians and officials, led by King. Churchill did not attend, and the British delegation was led by Foreign Minister Anthony Eden.

At the outset King made a significant contribution, with a motion, which was accepted, that the original plan to just use the English language for working purposes be expanded to also use the French language.

While the conference was underway, much was happening in Europe. Mussolini was killed by partisans on April 28, and two days later Hitler committed suicide. On May 8 Churchill gave a "world broadcast":

> Grand Admiral Doenitz, the designated head of the German State, signed the act of unconditional surrender.... The German war is therefore at an end. After years of intense preparation, Germany hurled herself on Poland at the beginning of September 1939; and in pursuance of our guarantee to Poland, and in agreement with the French Republic, Great Britain, the British Empire and the Commonwealth of Nations, declared war upon this foul aggression.... We may allow ourselves a brief period of rejoicing: but let us not forget for a moment the toil and efforts that lie ahead. Japan, with all her treachery and greed, remains unsubdued.... Advance Britannia. Long live the cause of freedom. God save the King.[13]

Churchill also spoke from the balcony of the Ministry of Health building in Whitehall. "This is your victory! It is the victory of the cause of freedom in every land. In all our long history we have never seen a greater day than this. Everyone, man or woman, has done their best. Everyone has tried. Neither the long years, nor the dangers, nor the fierce attacks of the enemy, have in any way weakened the independent resolve of the British nation. God bless you all."[14]

Anthony Eden, in San Francisco, sent Churchill a telegram: "All my thoughts are with you on this day, which is so essentially your day. It is you who have led, uplifted and inspired us through the worst days. Without you this day could not have been."[15]

King broadcast from San Francisco on May 8. He spoke of the victory over the evil forces of Germany. While Churchill talked of the joy in the achievement, the sensitive King thought of the sacrifices that had been made. "Our rejoicing, however, would fail to give expression of our true feelings if our first thoughts were not of those who have given their lives for that victory." He cautioned that no pause in the endeavours would be made until Japan had been "completely defeated and his inflated and insane ambitions forever crushed."

After speaking of the war, King moved to the future. The United Nations Conference would result in a charter that would "be a mighty instrument for world security... In that way the sacrifices which had been made by those who fought for freedom will have secured victory and peace."[16]

Later that day King wrote, "A wonderful message came from Churchill on Canada's contribution to victory. I have read nothing to equal it. I am sure Churchill had in mind not only feelings of gratitude, which he entertains, but, in this way, lending a hand in the present campaign."

The editorial of the *Toronto Star* on May 9 stated: "The record of achievements should cause thrills for generations. An agricultural nation with less than twelve million population, Canada contributed almost a million men and women volunteers for battle service in the air, on land and sea. It is estimated that in proportion to her population the Dominion contributed more fighting airmen than any nation in the war."

On May 10 King recorded speaking with Smuts of South Africa, who told him that King George was anxious to honour Churchill with the Order of the Garter, but wished this to be acceptable to Smuts and King. King responded that this was purely a United Kingdom matter, but he thought that nothing was too good for Churchill, although he already has the highest honour that a nation could pay, and the confidence they have shown in him.

Churchill gave another world broadcast on May 13. In recounting the five years since he had been commissioned to form a national government, he spoke of the history of the British nation and the British Empire in standing up against tyrants. This included a favourite expression of his: "It is only from the past that one can judge the future."

He specifically mentioned the Canadian forces, which, with the British, "had one-third as many men as the Americans in the invasion of Europe in 1944." Near the end of his address, he gave a warning that the honourable purposes for which the war was fought must not be brushed aside or overlooked. Thus the need to ensure that the United Nations organization did not become "a shield for the strong and a mockery for the weak. It is the victors who must search their hearts in their glowing hours, and be worthy by their nobility of the immense forces that they wield."[17]

The following day King wrote in his diary of discussing Churchill's warning with the U.S. secretary of state, Edward Stettinius. A problem was evident in the makeup of the Security Council, with the United States naturally requiring more powers than, for instance, Canada. "I said it was very essential to get into the charter itself something that would be reassuring to the smaller powers, when approval of the charter was being worked out. I said Mr. Churchill must have had a real reason for saying what he had yesterday."

King emphasized to Stettinius that it had been very difficult for him and the rest of the Canadian delegation to concede the veto of the five "Great Powers" (the United States, Britain, Russia, China, and France). Thus, he stressed the need of protection for the smaller powers. King proposed that if there were eleven countries on the Security Council, where there was a case involving another country, that country would become represented on the Council to make its case. The efforts to accord the smaller powers greater status and protection achieved some success, as will be recounted later.

King returned to Canada on May 14 to campaign. His first stop was Vancouver; from there he proceeded east, making speeches across the country. One stop was in his own constituency of Prince Albert, Saskatchewan. While there, he "received a nice telegram from Churchill.... 'I cannot forget how much we owe to Canada and to you, yourself, for the victory which has been vouchsafed to us. My very best wishes for all that lies before us.'"

Three days later King wrote, "Churchill has resigned.... I imagine Churchill would give a good deal to have his election as far along the way and as near the day of victory as ours." The date set for the British election was July 5.

Churchill gave the first of four election broadcasts on June 4. While the first part was friendly towards the Labour and Liberal ministers who served with him in the government, the main part was a vitriolic attack on the Labour Party. This speech is now remembered for one callous word that Churchill used in his attack. "No Socialist Government," Churchill declared, "conducting the entire life and industry of the country could afford to allow free, sharp, or violently-worded expressions of public discontent. They would have to fall back on some sort of Gestapo."[18]

A headline on the front page of the June 5 issue of the *Toronto Star* stated, "Churchill's Speech Starts U.K. Election Fireworks." The report included excerpts from British newspapers. According to the Socialist *Daily Herald,* "It is a human tragedy that Winston Churchill honoured as an individual of all parties should so readily lend himself to these cheap electioneering tricks." The Liberal *News Chronicle* stated, "The noble eloquence of the Prime Minister's finest hours was sadly missing."

While Churchill could have been excused if the remarks had been given off the cuff in the heat of the moment, the speech was a carefully crafted one. He was extremely upset with Attlee and the other Labour Party members of the wartime cabinet for instigating the election call, as he thought they should have continued the partnership until after Japan had been defeated. He had shown Clementine the script and "she begged Winston to delete the odious and invidious reference to the Gestapo. But he would not heed her."[19]

The following three broadcasts were more sober in content, but they were still centred on attacking Socialism. Gone were the stirring phrases that had uplifted the spirits of the people during the war. Instead, the tone was uniformly negative. While he rightly did not try to delude the listeners by making unrealistic promises, he should have delivered a message of optimism.

King campaigned vigorously, under the slogan "A New Social Order," and was confident of victory on June 11. He was helped by the Conservative leader, John Bracken, who emphasized the reluctance of the Liberal government to introduce conscription during the war. King understood, however, that the electorate were not concerned with the past; they were already looking towards the future. New social measures were to be an important feature of his platform. One such measure was the family allowance, or the "baby bonus" as it was popularly called. The government had introduced legislation in 1944 to provide for it, and King took "a great deal of satisfaction [that] the wording of the clause [which included] the words 'minimum of human well-being' [were] from [his book] *Industry and Humanity.*" In Quebec it was appreciated that King had tried to avoid bringing in conscription, only doing so reluctantly when it was absolutely necessary, and even then only imposing partial conscription. Thus, he held the support of the French Canadians.

The Canadian electorate did not disappoint King, with the Liberals taking 118 of the 245 seats, the Progressive Conservatives, 66, the CCF, 28, with others accounting for 33. While the Liberals had lost 59 seats from the landslide 1940 election, and now had a minority government, King was well-pleased. Surprisingly, the Liberals won the largest share of the military vote: 118,537. The CCF were a close second, with 109,679, while the Progressive Conservatives were a distant third, with 87,530.

One disappointment was that King was narrowly defeated in his own riding of Prince Albert. Two months later he returned to Parliament in a by-election, in the riding of Glengarry, Ontario.

The two main Toronto newspapers offered sharply differing perspectives in their reporting of the election. The *Globe & Mail* offered a bland headline: "King Government Returned," with commentary basically confined to the fact that there was now a minority government. In contrast the *Toronto Star's* headline was, "Victory For Unity, King Says." The accompanying article included highly positive comments: "The result of yesterday's election stamps Premier King as the outstanding Canadian statesman. By the time he has finished his current term he will have headed the nation for a longer term than Sir John A. Macdonald, his closest rival in term of years."

Churchill sent King a message of congratulation on June 23. "Although, at times, to British eyes, things got rather mixed, I was, however, confident that Canada would stand by you as the pilot who weathered the storm. You and I being in the last lap of public life can afford to be very bold in defence of the main cause for which we fought."

With the general election out of the way, King returned to San Francisco for the final days of the United Nations conference. A decision had been reached that the Security Council would have the five permanent veto-wielding members and ten elected non-permanent members, each of which would be elected to two-year terms. King was satisfied that this gave the smaller nations an adequate voice.

The ceremony of the charter confirmation was held on June 26, with King and St. Laurent signing on behalf of Canada. The occasion was the first meeting between King and Truman, and the Canadian prime minister was very impressed.

After the British election on July 5, but before the votes were counted, Churchill had to direct his attention to the Big Three meeting at Potsdam. He arrived in Berlin on July 15 and went on a tour of the city, which was in ruins. "Then we entered the Chancellery, and for quite a long time walked through the shattered galleries and halls. Our Russian guides then took us to Hitler's air-raid shelter. I went down to the bottom and saw the room in which he and his mistress had committed suicide, and when we came up again they showed us the place where his body had been burned."[20]

This was Churchill's first meeting with President Truman, and they established an immediate rapport. Churchill explained that Great Britain had spent more than half of her foreign investments during the war, and now had an external debt of three billion pounds. Truman expressed sympathy and "declared that the United States owed Great Britain an immense debt for having held the fort at the beginning. 'If you had gone down like France,' he said, 'we might be fighting the Germans on the American coast at the present time. This justifies us in regarding these matters as above the purely financial plane.'"[21]

A major item on the agenda was the timing of the Soviet declaration of war on Japan. However, this became just an academic matter when world-changing news arrived on July 16. The Americans had successfully tested the atomic bomb. Thus, rather than having to invade Japan, where they were likely to meet suicidal defenders, there was a course available that would surely end the conflict.

While President Truman and his advisors were contemplating the use of the bomb against Japan, other matters came before the three leaders. Once again Poland was the main item, and now Stalin was going back on his agreement on the frontiers of that country, which he had agreed to at Yalta.

Truman advised Stalin on July 24 of the existence and successful testing of the atomic bomb. Churchill wrote that he was some five yards away, and closely watched for the effect on Stalin. "I can see it all as if it were yesterday. He seemed to be delighted. A new bomb! Of extraordinary power! Probably decisive on the whole Japanese war! What a bit of luck! This was my impression at the moment, and I was sure that he had no idea of the significance of what he was being told."[22]

While Churchill stated he was certain that Stalin had no prior knowledge of the existence of the bomb, he was wrong, and he should have known he was wrong. David Reynolds referred to this passage, which Churchill had dictated in May 1951: "He clung to it in defiance of the evidence piling up in public from 1950 about the way Klaus Fuchs and other Soviet agents had betrayed the Manhattan Project to Moscow." Reynolds continued, "He will not countenance the thought he (Stalin) was play acting. This would have undermined his most cherished belief, or illusion — both in 1945 and in his memoirs — that the Soviet dictator was, at heart, a man who could be trusted."[23]

The Potsdam Conference was a major disappointment for Churchill. As he wrote near the end of his war memoirs: "A formidable body of questions on which there was disagreement was in consequence piled upon the shelves. I intended, if I was returned by the electorate, to come to grips with the Soviet Government on this catalogue of decisions."[24]

However, he was fully aware that he and President Truman had no power to force Stalin to adhere to their proposals, unless they were prepared to back them up with force. Even if they had wished to take that step, they knew that the war-weary British and American people would not support them.

Churchill returned to England on July 25. That evening he went to bed confident of victory in the election. "However, just before dawn, I woke suddenly with a sharp stab of almost physical pain. A hitherto subconscious conviction that we were beaten broke forth and dominated my mind."[25] His subconscious was right. Not only was the Conservative Party defeated, it was a landslide victory for the Labour Party. They obtained 393 seats, while the Conservatives won only 197, with the minor parties getting 50.

King had expected that Churchill would win, and he expressed his sorrow for Churchill's loss, which he blamed on the campaign managers, Beaverbrook and Bracken. His stated sorrow and assignment of blame is contradicted, however, by his diary comments in which he stated, somewhat illogically, that Churchill was the cause of his own ruin. "I think he has made a mistake in running again.... His ambition has over-reached itself and he has fallen from a terrible height. It will be an awful blow to him." In commenting further on the subject, the innate priggishness of King came to the fore: "[It is the] kind of blow that stimulants do not help to recover from. I doubt very much if the mass of the people care for the ostentatious display of cigars, drinking, etc., which was inseparable from one side of Churchill's nature."

King felt that this would likely be the end for Churchill, and he was concerned that the latter would age very rapidly, adding that he would not be surprised if "a certain bitterness developed."

Actually, Churchill took the high road in a statement after the election results were known. "It only remains for me to express to the British people, for whom I have acted in these perilous years, my profound gratitude for the unflinching, unswerving support which they have given me during my task, and for the many expressions of kindness which they have shown towards their servant."[26]

King sent a telegram of condolences, which Churchill acknowledged.

In his diary of July 27 King noted that "Japan intended to decline the ultimatum sent to her ... and to fight it out to the bitter end." King was well aware that this would result in using the atomic bomb on Japan and understood the implications of this weapon for the future of the world: "I feel that we are approaching a moment of terror for mankind, for it seems that under the stress of war men have at last not only found but created the Frankenstein, which conceivably could destroy the human race."

On August 6 the first atomic bomb was dropped on Hiroshima.

With no agreement to surrender being received, a second bomb was dropped on Nagasaki on August 9. The next day Japan offered to surrender. Agreement was reached on August 14.

World War II was now over — at last!

On August 15 Churchill spoke of the surrender of Japan. "Once again the British Commonwealth and Empire emerges safe, undiminished and united from a mortal struggle. Monstrous tyrannies which menaced our life have been beaten to the ground in ruin, and a brighter radiance illumines the Imperial Crown than any which our annals record."[27]

King made a broadcast on the CBC on August 14, and on the following day there was a march past of military on Parliament Hill. After the governor general left, "as the crowd kept expecting something more I said a few words of thanks to the people of Canada for all they had done in the war and particularly the armed services. Spoke of the dark epoch having closed and a new era opening up and expressed the hope for better and happier days for all."

With the end of the war Canada counted its cost. Out of a total population of eleven million, there were 2.5 million men between eighteen and forty-five years of age. Of these 40 percent had voluntarily enlisted; 47,000 of these were killed and 58,000 were wounded. The total cost in dollar terms was $18 billion, of which $10.5 billion was added to the national debt. Canada also gave Britain a gift of $1 billion in early 1942, which was almost double the pre-war budget. By the end of the war, Britain had received almost $3.5 billion in gifts and more in loans from Canada, much of which was used to purchase Canadian munitions and goods. In addition, Canada also provided a $1.2 billion loan in 1946, at a very low rate of interest.

The population of the United States was some twelve times that of Canada at the end of the war, but "Canadian gifts were equal to more than a quarter of the aid coming to Britain from the United States under Lend-Lease. In other words, the Canadian contribution per head of population had been more than three times as great."[28]

26

PEACE BUT THE BEAR GROWLS

On August 23, 1941, Churchill had told King that he had no plans to seek re-election after the end of the war, "I have no ambition beyond getting us through this mess. There is nothing that anyone could give me or that I could wish for."

With his shattering defeat in the election, the logical step for this seventy-year-old would have been to put his feet up and write his history of the war, which would make him financially comfortable. Clementine encouraged him in that regard, stating of the election result: "It may well be a blessing in disguise." Winston responded: "At the moment it seems quite effectively disguised."[1]

To another, like suggestion, when an acquaintance encouraged him to tour Britain, "so that thousands of his own countrymen, who had never seen him, could have a chance to honour him," he growled: "I refuse to be exhibited like a prize bull, whose chief attraction is its past prowess.'"[2]

King also had contemplated retirement after the war was over. In his case, however, the victory at the polls was an encouragement to stay on, in spite of his complaining of overwhelming fatigue.

Both had spent a lifetime in politics at a high level. Both loved political power, or what R.A. Butler, quoting Bismarck, called in the title of his autobiography, *The Art of the Possible*. And neither thought their potential successors could do the job to the standard which they could.

These were undoubtedly major factors in their decision to continue. But as King recorded in his diary, there was also a sense of duty. The war might have been over, but picking up the pieces required leaders of proven experience.

Although Churchill was now out of office, he had not taken a back seat on international matters. On August 16 he spoke in the House of Commons. He referred to the atomic bomb, which had brought peace, then added, "but men alone can keep the peace, and henceforward they will keep it under penalties which threaten the survival, not only of civilization but of humanity itself."

He was critical of the result of the Potsdam Conference, and in particular the expanded frontiers of Poland, which resulted in the expulsion of large numbers of Germans. He also warned of the dominance of the Soviet Union in eastern Europe, using a phrase that he was to repeat seven months later to a larger audience: "Tragedy on a prodigious scale is unfolding itself behind the iron curtain which at the moment divides Europe in twain."[3]

His comments were not well-received by a populace still in the euphoria of peace.

Churchill's concerns about the intentions and actions of the Soviet Union were confirmed in September, with what has become known as the "Gouzenko Affair."

The twenty-six-year-old Igor Gouzenko worked in the cyber department of the Soviet Embassy in Ottawa. When he was informed that he had been recalled to Moscow, he and his wife decided that life in Canada was much better than in Russia, and that they would not go back. But in order to stay, they would need to defect and have Canada accept them. So, Gouzenko decided that he had to offer something that would ensure that he would be welcomed with open arms. The something was secret information about the Soviet spy system in Canada. Accordingly, he stole documents of particular interest. But the story did not play out according to Gouzenko's plan.

He went to the offices of the *Ottawa Journal* to offer them this "scoop of a lifetime," but the city editor rejected the gift and told him to go to the Royal Canadian Mounted Police. They told him to come back in the morning.

Naturally, Gouzenko was in a high state of anxiety, as he knew that when he did not report for work his former colleagues would act quickly. The next morning he frantically visited various government departments, including the Ministry of Justice, to endeavour to show them the files that he had stolen, but no one was prepared to listen to his story. The consensus at the time was that the Russians were friends and no one wanted to upset that relationship. However, when the information came to the Prime Minister's Office, the matter had to be addressed.

King's diary contains a separate section dealing with this affair. This gives the details of the information that Gouzenko provided, which showed that "Russia had her spies and secret service people in Canada and in the U.S. and was practising a species of espionage ... evidence to prove that instead of being friends, the Russians were really enemies."

King's whole political career had been developed on the basis of keeping things equable. When matters had to be confronted, he did so in a calculated fashion. This was evident with the conscription crisis, where he methodically went through a series of manoeuvres to attempt to calm conflicting attitudes. In this case, he did not have time to carefully establish a plan. So he decided to use another of his tricks of political leadership. He had learned that at times the real secret of leadership was to ensure that something was prevented rather than that something was accomplished. So he decided to do nothing. He expressed in his diary the belief that the Canadians had to be extremely careful not to act in a manner that could be viewed by the Russians as unfriendly. He wrote that Gouzenko might be a crank.

Later that day King was given an update, which included a statement from Gouzenko that without Canadian support he was going back to his flat where his only action would be to commit suicide. King responded in a surprisingly cold manner, which showed that he was only concerned at not upsetting Canadian-Russian relations. "I suggested that a Secret Service man in plain clothes watch the premises. If suicide took place let the city police take charge and this man to follow in and secure what was there in the way of documents, but on no account for us to take the initiative."

With no help given by the government, the Gouzenkos, still in possession of the incriminating documents, took refuge in a neighbour's apartment. That was a wise move, as that same evening, four men from the Russian Embassy broke into the Gouzenko's apartment. The police arrived, and after an angry scene, the four men withdrew.

Fortunately, someone arrived on the scene who knew what to do. The Winnipeg-born Sir William Stephenson — famously known as "the Man Called Intrepid" — had recently been knighted in the British Honours list, and happened to be in Ottawa. He had been the head of British Security Coordination in New York during the war, and had also established Camp X in Whitby, Ontario, a spy training school. Stephenson recommended that the Royal Canadian Mounted Police take the Gouzenkos into protective custody. This was done.

Gouzenko was interviewed and his disclosures, backed by the documents he had stolen, confirmed that espionage on a large scale was being conducted in Canada. Soviet agents were inside various government departments, and in the office of the British High Commission.

One document that Gouzenko handed over was a telegram dated July 9, 1945, which stated: "Alek handed over to us a platinum with 162 micrograms of uranium 233 in the form of acid, contained in a thin lamina."[4] The identity of "Alek" was soon ascertained. He was Dr. Alan Nunn May, a British physicist working in nuclear fission in the Montreal laboratories of the Canadian National Research Council. This office was involved in the Manhattan project, which developed the atomic bomb.

As mentioned in the previous chapter, Churchill clung to the contention, even as late in 1951, while writing the final volume of his war memoirs, that he was certain that Stalin had no knowledge of the existence of the atomic bomb prior to being told of it by President Truman at Potsdam. This was not the case. Nunn May not only kept the Russian Embassy in Ottawa informed of progress in the development, but he also told them of the successful testing of the bomb on July 16, 1945. King, in his diary of September 10, wrote that "Gouzenko had said that on the day the atomic bomb was first used there was tremendous excitement at the Embassy."

The British high commissioner and the United States ambassador were advised of the Gouzenko documents. This resulted in the British Secret Service sending two men to Ottawa, and the Americans sending an FBI representative. Cloak and dagger activities were not King's cup of tea, and his diary confirms the effect of the affair. "I feel very strongly as though I should drop out of public life at once."

On September 23 King met with Stephenson and the British and American officials, but decided that he had to talk directly with Truman and Attlee.

The first stop was the White House on September 30. President Truman was already aware that something major had occurred in Ottawa, but now he was given the full story, which included the existence of Soviet agents in the United States. At the conclusion of the talk, King recorded that Truman said, "Whatever action should be taken, it should be at the highest level — between Attlee, himself and me. It was not desirable to have precipitate action. Everything should be most carefully explored."

King then travelled to Britain, sailing on the *Queen Mary*, arriving on October 7. He was told that Truman had sent a telegram, through the British ambassador in Washington, to the Foreign Office, that the president was anxious that "Primrose" (another name for Nunn May) should not be arrested unless it was obviously necessary for security reasons. (Nunn May was not arrested until March 1946. He was eventually sentenced to ten years hard labour, although he was released after six and a half years.)

King met Attlee at Chequers on the day of his arrival. In his diary he recorded that he found "young Attlee [he was 62] quite attractive, highly intelligent and well-informed." He told King that he had expected a stalemate at the recent election and was surprised at the result; but not as surprised as Churchill.

They discussed the Gouzenko revelations, and Attlee stated that the time had come for a showdown with the Russians. Attlee informed King that he had told Churchill that he thought that the Soviets should have been told of the development of the atomic bomb and that this view was held by Roosevelt, but Churchill was adamantly opposed.

King spent the next few days meeting with members of the British cabinet. Foreign Secretary Ernest Bevin advised him that Churchill was a great statesman, above any party. This led to King noting the fine relationships that existed between men in public life in Britain, as compared to the bitterness that prevailed in Canadian politics. He had obviously forgotten Churchill's Gestapo reference.

One startling opinion was expressed by Lord Addison, the Dominions secretary, who stated that the present situation was as bad, if not worse, than before Hitler declared war.

On October 23 King lunched at Buckingham Palace with King George, Queen Elizabeth, and the two princesses. They talked of the change of the government, with the king stating that Attlee was a difficult man to talk to. After King George said that it was a pity that Hitler had not been shot, Princess Elizabeth said she would have been prepared to shoot him.

On October 26 King lunched with Churchill at his new London home at Hyde Park Gate. "When the front door was opened Winston came along from the front of the hall to the steps to meet me. He could not have given me a warmer, or more friendly greeting.... Mrs. Churchill was waiting and came forward. She also greeted me in the warmest way, saying, 'Dear Mr. King, how glad we are to have you with us again.'"

During the war King was abstemious but not now. "Glasses of sherry were passed around and we all had a little talk together. A little wine was served, also some vodka and port. The vodka had been brought from Russia. Mrs. Churchill told the waiter not to use it but to throw it out. She said brandy was a better substitute."

King wrote, "Churchill did most of the talking in an exceedingly nice way. He has a marvellous mind, ranges from one subject to another with perfect ease and adequate expression." Churchill spoke of the election and that it had been the greatest surprise to him and quite a blow. King continued, noting that Churchill "feared things were going to be pretty serious in England as a consequence of the policy of destroying the rich to equalize incomes of all. That he himself would have been prepared to take three quarters of the income of wealthy men, but he would have left them enough to have an incentive to work."

After Churchill spoke of his concerns about Russia, King decided to tell him of the Gouzenko affair. "I said to him, 'Would you think it disloyalty to the Government if I were to tell you of a situation which I had come over about, which was one that concerned us all?' It was not a party matter but something that I felt he ought to know about. I would be glad to have his view on it." Churchill responded that he would keep the information in strict confidence. After King had informed him of the happenings in Ottawa, "he said, 'This is most interesting and most important.' It did not, however, seem to take him by surprise. He said that you must remember that with the Communists, Communism is a religion … they were realists to the extreme."

The conversation moved to a matter that Churchill had nurtured throughout the war, and he considered just as important in the post-war era: British-American relations, and the importance of Canada's continuing role as the linchpin. He emphasized to King that he should do all he could to keep the two together. Churchill told King that President Truman had invited him to give a course on European conditions at the University of Missouri, and he had mentioned a large honorarium. Churchill said he did not wish any honorarium but he might go and deliver one lecture on the conditions of the world. He added that this might give him a chance to talk with Truman on British-American relations.

King suggested that it was perhaps just as well he lost the election and no longer had the burden of office, which might affect his health. Churchill responded that his health was all right but added that there was a certain relief. He said that he intended to take his part as leader of the opposition, but then made a comment that would have been music to Eden's ears, if he thought that Churchill was being honest. He told King that "he had given up any thought of ever again being in Office."

"When I was leaving he said to me, in reference to the elections, other men are children in the leadership of the party as compared to yourself…. He used the expression that he hoped that God would bless me. No words could have been kinder than his as we parted. It was the sweetest side of his nature throughout — a really beautiful side. One cannot help loving him when that side of his nature is to the fore."

A few days later, King received a gift from Churchill. "Five volumes of his speeches, beautifully bound, in blue morocco leather. He had written in each one and in one he had placed the inscription: 'A Long Struggle — A Still Longer Friendship.'"

When King got back to his hotel, he telephoned Mrs. Churchill to say goodbye. "She said that Winston had been much touched by the very beautiful letter I had sent him. She spoke very appreciatively of it. I spoke of the great pleasure the lunch had been and what it meant to me to see them again. I also sent my love to Winston."

Churchill may have been out of office but as he had told King, he was still determined to give his opinion on major issues. On October 27 President Truman had referred to the atomic bomb, and he urged world co-operation as a means of outlawing atomic destruction. Churchill spoke on the subject in the House of Commons on November 7. He expressed approval of Truman's statement that "the United States must abandon old fashioned isolation." This was the policy on which Churchill had failed to convince Roosevelt. Churchill repeated his contention: "Such a declaration in 1919 would have led to a real Treaty of Peace and a real armed League of Nations. Such a declaration at any time between the two wars, would have prevented the second."[5]

Some of the themes of Churchill's talk were picked up by the leaders of Britain, the United States, and Canada when they met shortly after in Washington to discuss the immense responsibility shared by them regarding the atomic bomb. Churchill wished success to Attlee "in his highly important visit to Washington. We should not abandon our special relationship with the United States and Canada about the atomic bomb," Churchill told him, "and we should aid the United States to guard this weapon as a sacred trust for the maintenance of peace."[6]

King sailed from Southampton, arriving in New York on November 9, and was in Washington the next day. After a state dinner and the laying of wreaths at the Tomb of the Unknown Soldier in Arlington National Cemetery, the discussion on the atomic bomb took place. At the conclusion a joint declaration was formulated. This proposed that a commission be set up under the auspices of the United Nations to prepare recommendations to entirely eliminate the use of atomic energy for destructive purposes, and to promote its peaceful use. On January 24, 1946, the General Assembly of the United Nations adopted as its first official decision: a resolution related to the problems of atomic energy.

Although Churchill no longer had the responsibilities of office, he was fully occupied. While the British people had given him "the boot," the former occupied countries of Europe showed their appreciation. In mid-November he was in Brussels, and the British ambassador to

Belgium, a man with the resplendent name of Sir Hughe Knatchbull-Hugessen, later recalled: "I have never seen such excitement and enthusiasm. Presents of all kinds began to pour in to the Embassy ... people stretched out their hands to touch him ... remarks in the street included one from an old lady, who had placed her camp-stool at a street corner — 'Now I have seen Mr. Churchill, I can die' ... people broke through the police cordon ... one girl leapt onto the running board, threw her arms around his neck and kissed him fervently."[7]

On November 28 Churchill addressed a meeting of the Conservative Central Council. He began by saying: "You give a generous welcome to one who has led you through one of the greatest political defeats in the history of the Tory Party. It may perhaps be that you give me some indulgence for leading you in some other matters which have not turned out so badly."

He proceeded to give the reasons why he had decided to continue as the head of the party. "I am sure you will all realize that I hold the Leadership you have conferred upon me, not from any motives of personal ambition — for what could I possibly want? — but only because of the strong convictions which I hold about the future of our country, and my desire to serve you as long as you may think me of any use, or I feel that I have anything worthy of your acceptance to give."[8]

A few weeks later, on December 15, Churchill wrote to the duke of Windsor in a similar vein: "The difficulties of leading the opposition are very great, and I increasingly wonder whether the game is worth the candle. It is only from a sense of duty, and not leaving my friends in the lurch, that I continue to persevere."[9]

When King was reviewing the past year, in his diary of New Year's Day, 1946, he ignored the many difficult periods and was upbeat: "I shall always feel that 1945 was the best year of my life. I hope and pray that the New Year may, in an equally significant way, afford opportunities for service in the world as great, if not greater, than those of 1945. It will have, I believe, so far as my own life is concerned, real national and international significance."

27

THE COLD WAR STARTS IN OTTAWA AND HEATS UP IN FULTON

Churchill had been invited by President Truman to speak at Westminster College in Fulton, Missouri. On February 28 King received a telephone call from Miami. Churchill, who was staying there, wished to speak with him. "It was very pleasant to hear Churchill's voice. He started by saying, 'How are you my friend?'" King recorded that Churchill asked if he could come down to see him in Miami, as he wished to talk to him about the speech he was to deliver. King, however, responded that the espionage matter had reached an acute stage and he had to remain in Ottawa.

The acute stage had been precipitated by the well-known U.S. broadcaster and columnist Drew Pearson reporting the Soviet espionage activity. It appears that William Stephenson had leaked the information to him, as he thought the three governments were not acting quickly enough.

This forced King and the other governments to act. A press release was issued on February 15. This stated that two justices of the Supreme Court of Canada had been appointed to act as royal commissioners to hear evidence and to present a report that would be made public. The sensational announcement that Soviet spies had been uncovered in Canada and elsewhere made headlines around the world, and many look on this as the start of the Cold War.

On March 1 Churchill telephoned King. "He said he had learned there was a private line between Washington and Ottawa and that he, if

I agreed, would read over it what he purposed saying. He said he was going to speak on an agreement between the British Commonwealth and the U.S. on defence along lines of our permanent joint board of defence." King recalled his speech on the Ogdensburg Agreement. He reread it, and "was amazed how very apposite it was and how very helpful it would be to him." King thought it would "really ... be an anticipation in large part of what [Churchill] had to say." Continuing on, King wrote: "He probably has not seen it and will be surprised when he does. I am sure he will be grateful for it. I sent copies to Miami and also to Washington."

The following day King telephoned Lester Pearson in Washington. He was concerned with the security of the telephone, if Churchill read his speech over the line, and he asked Pearson to go over Churchill's manuscript.

The next day, March 3, King telephoned Churchill. "He was most appreciative of my having rung him up and was glad I had suggested Pearson going over the material with him. I told him that Pearson thought it was excellent. Pearson had assured me that such was the case, particularly with the first part. He felt that Churchill was using pretty strong language in the second half, but that, so far as we were concerned, our end was protected, and that he of course was speaking for himself."

Churchill invited King to come to New York before he left. "Clemmie would be there, also Mrs. Oliver [his daughter Sarah] and Randolph ... I thanked him warmly and told him I would certainly accept the invitation if at all possible."

On March 5, after Westminster College had conferred honorary degrees on Churchill and Truman, came time for the address, which became known as the "Iron Curtain Speech." Churchill actually referred to it as "The Sinews of Peace," denoting the strength in collective security that was necessary to protect the free world. He started with comments on the pre-war inaction, and came to the present with the United Nations Organisation (UNO) and the need for this to be "a force for action and not merely a frothing of words." He continued with his proposal for UNO to be equipped with an "international armed force."

On the subject of the atomic bomb, he restated his belief that while it was in its infancy it must be entrusted only to the United States, Britain, and Canada. "It would be criminal madness to cast it adrift in this still agitated and un-united world." After talking of the dangers if Communist and Fascist states had the atomic knowledge, he moved to a topic that would result in widespread criticism in the United States. "A special relationship [exists] between the British Commonwealth and Empire and the United States.... The United States has already a Permanent Defence Agreement with the Government of Canada, which is so devotedly attached to the British Commonwealth and Empire." He extended this proposal further than all but a few Americans would accept: "Eventually there may come — I feel eventually there will come — the principle of common citizenship, but that we may be content to leave to destiny, whose outstretched arm many of us can already clearly see."

Churchill pulled no punches when proceeding to the situation with the Soviets. "From Stettin in the Baltic to Trieste in the Adriatic, an iron curtain has descended across the Continent.... The Russian-dominated Polish Government has been encouraged to make enormous and wrongful inroads into Germany, and mass expulsions of millions of Germans on a scale grievous and undreamed of are now taking place.... The safety of the world requires a new unity in Europe.... Twice in our lifetime we have seen the United States, against their wishes and their traditions ... drawn by irresistible forces to these wars in time to secure the victory of the good cause, but only after frightful slaughter and devastation had occurred."

He called for the Western democracies to stand together, for, he said, if they do not, "catastrophe may overwhelm all. Last time I saw it all coming and cried aloud to my own fellow-countrymen and to the world, but no one paid any attention. Up to the year 1933, or even 1935, Germany might have been saved from the awful fate which has overtaken her and we might all have been spared the miseries Hitler let loose upon mankind.... We must surely not let that happen again. This can only be achieved by reaching now, in 1946, a good understanding on all points with Russia under the general authority of the United Nations Organization ... supported by the whole strength of the English-speaking world and all its connections."[1]

Truman had read the speech beforehand and "thought it admirable and would do nothing but good, though it would make a stir."[2]

King listened to the radio broadcast. "Churchill was in every way at his best. He sounded fresh and vigorous and less hesitant in speaking than I have ever heard him before. His introduction was very clever — full of wit and humour. He led into his subject in an admirable manner. It was the most courageous speech I have ever listened to, considering what we know of Russia's behaviour in Europe and in Asia since the war, and what has been disclosed here in Ottawa." King took some of the credit: "Churchill's address today was all built around the Ogdensburg agreement, which was essentially and wholly something worked out by myself."

After Churchill had finished, King telephoned the college. "He and the President were together. He was obviously both relieved and greatly pleased that I had rung up. I told him what I thought about his speech, being all circumstances considered, the most courageous made by any man, at any time, having regard to what he had said, etc. He thanked me very warmly, said it was so kind to let him know.... He said of course he had been careful to say that he had been speaking only for himself but he did not think that he had said anything which would embarrass Attlee."

Churchill proceeded to pay King a compliment, no doubt to show Truman the close, long-standing relationship between them: "I have followed your career over so many years and have been impressed so deeply with it, with your political wisdom and sound judgement that I value very deeply your approval of what I have said."

Truman came on the line. "I congratulated him on receiving a degree and on his speech. I also told him how glad I was to hear his voice again. He spoke of it being nice to hear my voice and asked, 'Was that not a fine speech, a great speech, given by Mr. Churchill?' I told him the whole proceedings were intensely interesting and that I felt we must all work very closely together ... to see that our position was made secure. That I felt what Churchill had said was most opportune and needed saying very much at this time."

Churchill and Truman only had a brief time to bask in the euphoria of the occasion. Rarely if ever had one speech resulted in such an avalanche of opinions. The American press generally was highly critical, with one being particularly vehement. The *Chicago Sun,* which just a week before had signed a contract to publish Churchill's *Secret Session*

Speeches (a book of five wartime speeches Churchill delivered in secret sessions of Parliament), declared that Churchill's objective "is world domination, through arms, by the United States and the British Empire."

Churchill wrote to the *Sun* publisher, Marshall Field, on its leading article: "As the views expressed here are the stock Communist output, I feel it might be an embarrassment to you, if your publications were in any way connected with me."[3]

It is interesting to compare the editorials of the two major Toronto-based newspapers on the speech. The *Toronto Star* of March 6 started by complimenting Churchill on his "mastery of English, which makes him one of the most impressive speakers of our time." But then it gave its opinion on the content of the speech: "But in its advocacy of a close military alliance of Britain and the United States against Russia it cannot be described as a contribution to the Big Three entente." It noted that Churchill did not mention the recent happenings in Canada [the Gouzenko Affair] but it asked the question: If Russia had the secret [the atomic bomb], would "her suspicious Allies have endeavoured to obtain it by undercover means? The answer may explain, although, it does not excuse, the tactics of the Soviets in Canada — a Soviet as suspicious of her Allies as her Allies are of her."

The *Globe & Mail* took a day to digest the speech and its reaction, published on May 7, was very different. It offered the opinion that this was perhaps Churchill's finest speech. "His is the gift to reveal their problems to the people in all their wretched ugliness, without casting the people down.... What he did was face the American people and the whole English-speaking world with the realities out of which peace must be wrought. Realism and candour were the means by which Winston Churchill rallied the Allied people to victory. Russia, Mother Church of an ideology ... directly in conflict with democracy .. is astraddle the world [—] not seeking war but 'the fruits of war.'" It quoted from Churchill's speech. "Through that world Communist fifth columns are at work in complete unity and absolute obedience to the directions they receive from the Communist centre." Then it offered a response to the criticisms in the United States of so-called British imperialism. "He did not propose an exclusive alliance of English-speaking nations. Only that they should make common cause, jointly sharing the burdens of a common effort within the precincts of the United Nations, openly pledged to the fulfillment of the Charter principles."

Stalin, not surprisingly, vented his anger by calling Churchill a "warmonger." But the most significant of the negative opinions was clearly registered by ninety-three Labour MPs in Britain, who signed a motion of censure against Churchill. One was the future prime minister James Callaghan. It was not long before those short-sighted politicians would regret their action.

Churchill was surprised but unfazed at the outpourings of hostility against his proposals. While he was no longer prime minister, he was still a world figure. With Roosevelt gone and Stalin steadily showing himself to be a ruthless, expansionist dictator, Churchill was for many the face of the victory over Hitler. Whereas for some idealists the Fulton speech was an affront to their idea of a peaceful existence, for realists, Churchill offered the voice of sanity, setting out the necessary actions to ensure peace.

Three days after the speech, on March 8, Churchill spoke to the General Assembly of Virginia. His sense of humour was undiminished as he said: "I hope I shall acquit myself to your satisfaction but the responsibility for what happens is yours. Do you not think you are running some risk in inviting me to give you my faithful counsel on this occasion? You have not asked to see beforehand what I am going to say. I might easily blurt out a lot of things which people know in their hearts are true, but are a bit shy of saying in public, and this might cause a commotion and get you all into trouble."[4]

Churchill, however, took a safe route in this address, recalling the history of Virginia before moving to his favourite subject, the need for the English-speaking peoples to work together for peace and their common ideals.

On March 15 Churchill spoke at a reception given by the mayor of New York, at the Waldorf Astoria Hotel. The under-secretary of state, Dean Acheson, was to have attended as the representative of the U.S. government, but was dissuaded by the president.

Churchill's first words showed that the criticisms he had received had not persuaded him to change his tune: "When I spoke at Fulton ten days ago, I felt it was necessary for someone in an unofficial position to speak in arresting terms about the present plight of the world. I do not wish to withdraw or modify a single word.... I do not believe that the rulers of Russia wish for war at the present time. I am sure that if we stand together, calmly and resolutely, in defence of those ideals and principles embodied in the Charter of the United Nations, we shall find ourselves sustained by the overwhelming assent of the peoples of the world."[5]

With the espionage matter still requiring close attention, King did not feel able to accept Churchill's invitation and attend the reception in person. Also he was concerned that spending the night with the Churchills at the Waldorf would, in the light of existing controversy, be certain to be greatly misconstrued. Nevertheless, King listened to the speech on the radio and, as usual, was most impressed and wrote that it was most courageous, as always.

King telephoned Churchill on his last evening in New York, and was told that if matters did not turn out well, it could not be said that he had not at least sounded a warning in time. If all turned out well, it could do no harm.

On March 25 Randolph Churchill came to Laurier House for luncheon. He told King that Byrnes (the U.S. secretary of state) and Admiral Leahy (the U.S. chief of staff) had read his father's speech before he delivered it at Fulton, and had fully approved it. The president had also read it on the way and seemed to be for it. But once it became apparent there was going to be controversy, they did not try to back it in any way

Though King felt unable to support Churchill at the time, he still felt it important to continue the assistance that Canada had offered to Britain during the war. The spring session of the Canadian Parliament included another remarkable level of financial assistance to the mother country. Britain was still reeling from the after effects of the war. An appeal was made to the United States and Canada for financial help. This was granted with loans of $3.75 billion from the United States and $1.25 billion from Canada, at a nominal interest rate of 2 percent. Canada would, of course, have to borrow this money herself at a much higher interest

King witnesses the signing of the loan of $1.25 billion to the United Kingdom. Left to right: W.C. Clark, R.B. Bryce, Sir Wilfred Eady, Norman A. Robertson, unknown, the Right Honourable Malcolm MacDonald, and Gordon Monro, March 6, 1946.

rate. On a per capita basis the Canadian loan was four times greater than the U.S. loan.

The timing of the new loan coincided with the arrival of a new governor general in Ottawa on April 12. Former Field Marshal, and now Lord, Alexander of Tunis had been appointed by Churchill the previous summer, during the Potsdam Conference. As recounted in a biography of Alexander: "'I know that Brookie wants you to succeed him as CIGS,' said Churchill, 'but Canada is a much more important post, and I hope you will accept it.'"[6]

Alexander dined with King on April 15 and told him that Churchill was a lovable fellow but could be an extremely difficult man at times. He had pressed Alexander to attack in North Africa, and Alexander had sent a communication in which he said that to make a premature attack would, he felt, spell disaster. Churchill finally accepted what he said, and from that time on, had been a strong supporter of him in every way. King wrote that they both agreed that he was a marvellous person and stood for qualities which had helped to save the world. King added that he had told Alexander that but for Churchill the war would have been lost.

Alexander had dined with King five months beforehand on November 6, 1945, and told King George's private secretary, Alan Lascelles, that he thought him "a charming old gentlemen." Lascelles responded with a cricket expression. "Maybe, I said, but don't forget for one moment that he is a spin bowler, whose ball breaks both ways."[7]

A meeting of Commonwealth prime ministers was arranged for late April. Previously, the always suspicious King had advised Attlee that he could not see the point of a conference while the British government was preoccupied with major issues, such as Indian independence, but he relented. Rather than flying over, which would have saved a considerable amount of time, he took the opportunity for a relaxing sea voyage on the *Queen Mary*, leaving New York on May 13. Among his interesting fellow passengers were Lord and Lady Halifax. They had tea together and talked of Churchill's Fulton speech. King noted their conversation in his diary: "Halifax bears out the statement that both the President and Secretary Byrnes saw Winston's address before it was delivered and approved it."

28

MACKENZIE KING BREAKS RECORD, CHURCHILL LAYS PATH FOR EUROPE

L osing the British election and making controversial speeches in the United States did not affect the feelings for Churchill in the liberated countries of Western Europe. On May 9, 1946, Holland welcomed him. He had been invited by Queen Wilhelmina to address the States-General of the Netherlands in the Hague. Before his speech he was presented by the queen with 613 letters, which his ancestor John Churchill, the first duke of Marlborough, had written during the ten years when he was leader of the Grand Alliance, which defeated the armies of King Louis XIV of France.

Churchill's address focused on a recurring theme: the need for American participation in world affairs. "If the United States had taken an active part in the League of Nations ... in order to prevent the rearmament of Germany," Churchill declared, "there [would have been] no reason for serious bloodshed." He finished with a call, which he was to emphasize later in the year: There is a need for "a United States of Europe ... which will unify this continent in a manner never known since the fall of the Roman Empire."[1]

On May19 King arrived in Britain for a Commonwealth Conference, which resulted in no significant decisions. Again he met privately with Churchill, who had invited him to Hyde Park Gate for dinner. "Spoke very nicely to me over the phone.... Said he was most anxious for a good talk.... He said he was glad to be back in England." And then an understatement: "Did not speak too enthusiastically about the effect of the trip in America."

King dined with Churchill on May 22, and "enjoyed himself immensely." In a letter to his friend in Ottawa, Joan Patteson, he wrote, "I had dinner with Winston.… There is no doubt about the feeling of affection and close friendship which Churchill has for me. Our talk together was one of the most memorable I have had with him."

Churchill spoke of the Fulton speech, and repeated what others had said: Truman had read the narrative on the train, and it had been given to the press before it was delivered. Then he turned to the Empire/Commonwealth, and of the important position it still held. He asked King to give it support, saying, "a word or two from you, spoken individually or publicly, will go very far."

The depth of intimacy between the two is illustrated by their discussion of the use of the atomic bomb, which King thought the most interesting part of the evening. According to King, Churchill was anguished by the decision but felt it was the right one:

> The way Churchill put it when discussing it with me was he expected that he would have to account to God as he had to his own conscience for the decision made, which involved killing women and children and in such numbers. That God would ask him why he had done this and that he would reply he had seen the terrors of war. He knew something of what the Japanese method of warfare was like. That there were thousands of lives — fine American soldiers — all of which would likely be destroyed or tortured. War might go on for another year or two with cities destroyed and numbers so much greater than could possibly be foreseen, and with a breaking down of civilization, bit by bit. He had had to decide what in the end would be best for mankind and felt that he, regardless of what the consequences might be, had done what is right. He said something to the equivalent of welcoming a chance to be judged in the light of omnipotent knowledge.

While the order to utilize the bomb was not given by Churchill, he did not absolve himself from responsibility for the decision. In the final volume of his war memoirs, Churchill stated: "British consent in principle to the use of the weapon had been given on July 4 before the test had taken place. The final decision now lay in the main with President Truman, who had the weapon; but I never doubted what it would be, nor have I ever doubted since that he was right."[2]

The use of the atomic bomb has been debated at length over the years, with many claiming that its use was unnecessary, as Japan was close to surrender. That was clearly not the case. The effects were devastating for Japan, of course, but weighed against the Allied lives that would have been lost in a conventional invasion, the decision was justifiable. It must be stated, too, that once the shocking and horrendous effects of the use of the atomic bomb became clear, it also became clear that it was too dangerous a weapon to consider using, except in the most extreme of circumstances. As a result, it has never been used again in a conflict.

With Churchill talking of his future meeting with the Almighty, King thought it an opportune time to ask him about his personal beliefs. In his youth Churchill had declared himself an unbeliever, but some have claimed that in his latter years, it would be more accurate to refer to him as an optimistic agnostic. This opinion is supported by his response to King: "He said he did not know [if there was an afterlife] — could not say whether that would be so. That he felt one might lie down — he used some expression which sounded to me like a black velvet pillow, and that would be all. On the other hand, he felt there was reason to believe that life would go on. But he said of one thing he was perfectly certain; that the order of the world was a moral order. That this was a universe governed by moral laws of justice and right."

The conversation then moved on to a discussion of Russia and Stalin. "We spoke about Stalin," King wrote. "He [Churchill] said he would trust him further than any other Russian leader. He felt Stalin's word could be relied upon.... He asked me if he had not told me about his agreement with Stalin to let Stalin look after Romania, etc. while he would be busy getting peace restored in Greece. This involved killing of large numbers of Communists in Greece. Stalin knew that. It went on for a month. Never once said a word. He held to the undertaking he had given."

These comments illustrate a paradox in Churchill's utterances. To the rest of the free world, Soviet Communism and Josef Stalin were the same. As Hitler had been in Germany so Stalin was in Russia: a dictatorship in all but name. Stalin had kept his word on Greece, but on Poland, the country for which Britain and Canada had gone to war, Stalin had refused to live up to his promise to Churchill. Instead, he had installed a government of his choice in Warsaw, and it ruled there without the approval of the population.

The two then moved on to a discussion of the future, with Churchill's comments paralleling his predictions in the 1930s. He saw a terrible war, which could mean the end of civilization. But he said that it could still be prevented.

King thanked Churchill for the great pleasure of the evening and for "having given … so much of his confidence." Churchill replied that King was the one to be thanked.

On May 24 King was in Buckingham Palace for luncheon with the king and queen. King George liked to have intimate conversations with King. "He told me he found it very difficult to have anyone to talk to. He missed Churchill very much. Attlee, when he came to the Palace, never talked at all. In fact, he said, speaking humorously and quite confidentially, he referred to him as 'Clem the Clam' because he said nothing."

King was back at Buckingham Palace on May 30 for a formal dinner for the delegates to the conference. Churchill also attended and spoke with King, commenting sadly on the disappearing of the British Empire. King wrote that he told Churchill that he was wrong, as he was for self-government and this would work out in the case of India. King suggested to Churchill that he should get out of party politics and should devote himself to world affairs. Churchill's response was that he was going to stay in and fight to the end.

He was true to his word, and on June 5 Churchill was back in the House of Commons, speaking in a debate on foreign affairs. He repeated his earlier warnings of the dangers from the Soviets, who he said had been able to do themselves so much harm, and chill so many friendships in the English-speaking world, because of "the Communist spy system, the exposure of which is at present confined to Canada. It has made a deep mark on transatlantic opinion. These revelations, by no means complete, have stirred the whole Dominion of Canada." He repeated what he had said to King about Communism being a religion. And commented that "the Canadian Government and its Prime Minister, Mr. Mackenzie King, have only done their duty with courage and justice in exposing what has been brought up in the Dominion of Canada."[3]

King also received mention in the June 4 edition of the *Evening Standard,* which included an article entitled "A Great Statesman." This article stated that the British people had a very welcome visitor in their midst, "Mr. Mackenzie King," and pointed out that on June 8, Victory Day, "his period in office as Prime Minister of Canada will exceed by one day Sir John A. Macdonald's record term of 19 years. The match-less experience of this great Imperial figure, who has served King and Country through five reigns, entitles him to speak with authority upon every issue of international and Commonwealth affairs. But as the acknowledged leader of the mightiest Dominion in the British Empire his voice carries even greater weight."

In surpassing Macdonald, King not only became the longest serving Canadian prime minister, but the longest serving prime minister in the history of the Commonwealth, with the exception of Sir Robert Walpole, who served in the Parliament of Britain in the eighteenth century. While Walpole did not hold the official title of prime minister, he performed the duties of that post, which he held for almost twenty-one years. However, King was to surpass even his record before handing in the seals of office.

On the occasion of the anniversary, King received a telegram of con-gratulations from the Liberal Party of Canada, which declared: "We feel it is largely due to your effort and direction that our country has suc-ceeded through a common effort both in peacetime and in war in build-ing up an ever growing and true spirit of nationhood of which every Canadian citizen can be justly proud."

To celebrate the occasion, Prime Minister Attlee held a dinner at 10 Downing Street on June 7, with a distinguished gathering, including the delegates at the conference, and Winston Churchill. Attlee spoke of

King's long record, beginning with his term serving as deputy minister of labour. King recorded his thoughts on the evening: "When I came up to reply, I found it quite easy to speak though I was a little tired.... After the dinner, I received no end of congratulations from those present. Churchill said that what I had said was just right; that I could do more here than anyone else. He spoke of Canada amazing him once again in what we had done on many matters."

The following day was the occasion of the Victory Day parade and celebrations. King was thrilled to be driven in one of the royal coaches, past cheering crowds, estimated at two million, from Downing Street to the saluting base. All Allied countries were represented, except for Russia, Yugoslavia, and Poland. King's thoughts naturally "came to the multitudes that had been slain. Churchill spoke to me of that himself."

It had been an exhausting time for the seventy-one-year-old King, and he felt considerable relief when he boarded the *Queen Mary* at Southampton on June 10 for the five-day voyage home.

On June 23 Anthony Eden visited Ottawa as a member of an Empire Parliamentary Association delegation. Eden told King that he thought Churchill had gone too far at Fulton in his criticism of Stalin, and he had cabled him before his New York speech telling him not to say anything further on those lines. Then, on a more personal matter, Eden mentioned that on his return from the United States Churchill had talked of retiring, but then, much to Eden's frustration, changed his mind.

King told Eden that he had encouraged Churchill to retire, as had Smuts. He continued that both he and Smuts had agreed that Churchill was not as strong as he had been, and thought it would be wiser for him to take the larger role of heading the party but not leading it in the House. Both thought it would be even better if he were to quit party politics together. It is interesting to note that despite their comments, there is no evidence in his diary that King thought that he, being the same age as Churchill, should retire. Smuts, who was four years older than Churchill, seems to have had no intention of stepping down at that time either.

Upon his return from Britain, King was able to attend to domestic matters — and some personal matters. One such matter involved making a decision about a new cook for Laurier House. One was judged "perfectly competent." However, she was a "Pole of Russian extraction." In the light of the espionage matter, King wrote, he felt he could not hire her, since it "would not do in Canada!"

At the same time as King was struggling with this decision, he met with Igor Gouzenko. King told him that he had done a great service, and told him that he wanted him to know that he "appreciated his manliness." King asked Gouzenko his opinion of what would be the result if he (King) were to see Stalin. Gouzenko responded that he would be greeted in a friendly manner, but that Stalin would deny that he knew anything about what had happened in Ottawa, and he would assure King that this did not represent his government's attitude to Canada. In the long run, though, nothing would change.

Barely had King had time to deal with a few issues at home when he was required to return to Britain — for the Paris Peace Conference. World War I was formally concluded when Germany accepted the terms of the Treaty of Versailles. No such agreement was needed in the case of World War II, since Germany had, eventually, surrendered unconditionally. However, the Allies did need to negotiate the resolution of a number of matters, especially those dealing with the level and division of compensation to be imposed on Germany and Italy.

The Paris Peace Conference was scheduled to begin on July 29, and this required King, with assorted ministers and civil servants, to again cross the Atlantic. One person who would not be at the conference was Churchill. King wrote of this while at sea: "I am sure he must feel keenly the decision of the [government] not to have him present at the Peace Conference and more keenly the fact that he lost the election [that] robbed him of all this. Politics is indeed tyrannical and brutal in some of its twists and turns."

King found the long, drawn-out discussions at the conference very tiresome, and the many functions he was obliged to attend, tedious. But he took advantage of his stay in Europe to visit the battlefields of Normandy. There he was uplifted by the spontaneous, very sincere, and very hearty welcome given by the people everywhere. He received addresses of welcome from the various mayors, who spoke in terms of profound gratitude to Canada for the liberation. He received many flower bouquets, saw cottages with banners, *"Honneur aux Canadiens,"* and he was greeted by crowds cheering, *"Vive le Canada."* He was especially touched by the little groups of children who had learned by heart the Canadian national anthem.

One obligation was stressful to King. He had to give a major speech at Dieppe, and he was conscious "that so far as Canada is concerned, an effective speech at Dieppe will mean more in the eyes of our people than a month's effort at the Conference. I must do my utmost to make it worthy of the occasion. God knows, as I dictate, I feel more deeply than ever what an appalling curse the war mind is."

On August 19 King attended a service at the war cemetery. There was a ceremony in the council chamber, where he was given the freedom of the city. With that day being the fourth anniversary of the raid, King spoke of the landing, and he gave the official verdict that it had been a real contribution to the eventual defeat of the invaders. However, he confessed in his diary his personal feeling that it had been a terrible thing

King lays a wreath on a grave of Canadian soldiers in Dieppe, August 8, 1946.

to send men into that area to discharge a mission that could only end in death to large numbers.

With the joy of encounters with grateful people, there were further sober and reflective incidents. He visited one of the Canadian cemeteries, and wrote that it touched him deeply to read "Unknown Soldier" on some graves. "I found it quite impossible to give any expression to my feelings. Indeed, I felt silence was the only language in such a place."

Another incident was described by King as "one of the saddest moments which I have known." This occurred when he was visiting the graves of the twenty-three Canadian prisoners of war murdered by the German SS. The commander, Kurt Meyer, was charged and sentenced to death, though his sentence was commuted, and he spent ten years in prison. King wrote: "Our young men from the Winnipeg Rifles, for the most part, had been murdered there. What a terrible thing! How appalling the cruelty of war!"

Following his tour of Normandy, King returned to Paris, but not to the conference. Instead, he took a flight to Berlin the following day. On August 21 King was given a tour of the city. "It was all very familiar but an appalling sight. Tiergarden [*sic*], one waste of land. Beautiful buildings demolished beyond recognition. The whole centre of the city all but totally destroyed.... After covering a part of the city and seeing particularly the Reichstag, which Göring had set on fire, and other well-known buildings, we were taken to the Chancellery buildings."

What King found most interesting of all was being taken down to the bunker that Hitler had had constructed during the war as a place of final refuge. He went down flights of stone stairs to a series of rooms that Hitler and his mistress, Eva Braun, had lived in. King also visited the Chancellery, including the room where he had been received by Hitler. The scenes he witnessed caused King to reminisce on the level of degradation to which Hitler and his colleagues had sunk.

The following day King was driven to Nuremburg, where the trials of the Nazi leaders were underway. He was particularly interested in one of the prisoners, Von Ribbentrop, whom he had met in London in May 1937, when he was the confident, indeed somewhat arrogant, German ambassador to Britain. But now, King wrote, he "looked a mere shadow of himself. An old, weary looking man." Later, waiting to be executed, Von Ribbentrop wrote about how his life would have changed if he had stayed in Ottawa in 1914.

King returned to the Paris Conference, but decided that he could leave the long, drawn-out proceedings to subordinates.

King arrived in Halifax on August 31. Soon after returning to Ottawa, he decided to relinquish his position of secretary of state for external affairs, which he had held in conjunction with the office of prime minister. Although Louis St. Laurent had stated that he wished to return to his law practice, he agreed to assume the position on a temporary basis. King also decided to bring Lester Pearson back from Washington, to become under-secretary of state for external affairs. King had a high opinion of the abilities of both men. The decision to promote them to senior posts in foreign affairs was an inspired one, as their positions there provided them with essential training for the office of prime minister, which they both attained.

While King was busy with domestic affairs, Churchill was, in spite of not being in office, continuing his role as the major statesman of the Western Allies. On September 19, at Zurich University, he gave one of the most important and far-reaching speeches of his life. It was also, unusual for him, one of the shortest speeches of his life.

He opened with a recitation of the achievements in Europe over the centuries. He then came to the actions of the Teutonic nations, which, he said, had put the world in its present plight. To this problem, Churchill proposed a remedy. "[We must] re-create the European Family.... We must build a United States of Europe.... There is no reason why a regional organization of Europe should in any way conflict with the world organization of the United Nations.... We British have our own Commonwealth of Nations. These do not weaken, on the contrary they strengthen, the world organization."

Then followed what was, even with the benefit of hindsight, one of the most startling exhortations of his life. "I am now going to say something that will astonish you. The first step in the re-creation of the European family must be a partnership between France and Germany. In that way only can France recover the moral leadership of Europe. There can be no revival of Europe without a spiritually great France and a spiritually great Germany."[4]

France had been invaded by Germany in 1870, 1914, and 1940, and to expect the politicians and the public to welcome being a partner with a country that had done it so much damage was widely considered outrageous. However, Churchill was right, once again. In the end others concurred with his proposals, and eventually the Council of Europe and the North Atlantic Treaty Organization were created.

There were other beneficial repercussions. "On 12 June 1947, in introducing his Plan, at a News Conference, General Marshall had declared that it was Churchill's call for a United Europe, in his Zurich speech in September 1946, that had influenced his belief that the European States could work out their own economic recovery, with financial help from the United States."[5]

A NEW WORLD ORDER: STANDING UP TO THE REDS

While Churchill was continuing with his efforts for a United States of Europe, the United Nations held the opening session of its General Assembly on October 23, 1946, in New York City. King attended, as did President Truman, and the Soviet foreign minister, Molotov.

The president clearly set out the change in American foreign policy, which was now fully in line with the one that Churchill had argued for to his predecessor. After World War I, the United States had refused to join the League of Nations, and its seat was empty at the first meeting of the League Assembly. "This time," President Truman said, "the United States is not only a member; it is the host to the United Nations."

And then followed the comment that was music in Churchill's ears: "This meeting of the Assembly symbolises the abandonment by the United States of a policy of isolation."

Truman extended the principles of the Atlantic Charter by emphasizing the desire for everlasting peace. This he said, would be based on four essential freedoms — the freedom of speech, religion, from want and from fear. [1]

Five days later King met Truman at the White House and told him that he strongly approved of what he had said, which mirrored the Canadian view.

On December 17 King was very pleased to receive a package from Churchill. It contained one of the souvenir medallions which he had

had struck off for his colleagues in the coalition government. It was accompanied by a letter mentioning those to whom he was presenting a medallion, and making King one of the inner circle that had helped to "preserve the world's freedom." He added a significant qualifier to this message: "For a time."

King received a further gift the following day. A painting by Gouzenko, with a note thanking King and the Canadian people for taking him into the country. King's overactive brain saw a cause for trouble in the gift, speculating that if the press found out, they could surmise that there had been a relationship between King and Gouzenko from the beginning. King's reaction could be considered an example of paranoia, but one of the reasons he had managed to stay in power so long was his ability to shield himself from criticism.

A much more weighty matter came before him later in December. A year before, Prime Minister Attlee had announced that a national convention would be elected in Newfoundland to make recommendations on alternative forms of government for the island. King had previously given his support to Newfoundland joining the Canadian federation, if that was what the people decided.

The last day of the year brought a significant step, which symbolized Canada's status as an independent nation. Previously, Canadian passport holders were designated as British subjects, but on that day came the announcement of the first passport designating its holder as a Canadian citizen. The first person to receive a Canadian passport — Passport No. 1 — was King.

King saw his being accorded the honour of receiving Passport No. 1 as an indication of the appreciation for his contribution to the country felt by those in government. However, the treatment he received from another segment of society, namely the fourth estate, left him with mixed feelings. An example of this treatment occurred on February 14, 1947, when he read a review in the *Ottawa Evening Journal* of an article by Canadian journalist Bruce Hutchinson, previously published in *The American Mercury* magazine. It was entitled "Explaining Mr. King." Hutchinson contrasted the prime minister with Roosevelt, whom he described as "the Great Guy," and Churchill as "John Bull."

He described King as a leader of mediocrity, which he had consciously cultivated. But in spite of that, Hutchinson wrote, King had some mysterious, indefinable power.

The *Ottawa Evening Journal* did not agree: "There is nothing mysterious about Mr. King. He is partly the architect of his own fortunes.... In an era when most Canadians of talent were concentrating on making money Mr. King was concentrating on politics. Public life became his mistress. Others might make politics a part-time job, he would make it his career. He would get to know how to manage men and parties and study the history and philosophy of government, know all about its arts, its problems and compromises. In the end it would all be a matter of the man with the better mouse trap."

In his diary King gave his own opinion of these attempts to define him. He decried what would later be called charisma, a characteristic that he did not have, and did not wish to have. He called it "exhibitionism," which he stated he loathed; he thought he had something better: "political astuteness." This, he stated, "has the further factor of belief in what is right as the course most likely to of itself defend itself."

Bruce Hutchinson found King a fascinating subject, and he pursued his writings about him in a biography, which won the Governor General's award in 1952, entitled *The Incredible Canadian*. Two days later Hutchinson wrote an additional article in *The American Mercury*. King thought that, on the whole, Hutchinson was trying to be kindly, but King took strong exception to a number of Hutchinson's comments, such as his description of King as a "throat cutter," based on the incident involving the resignation of Ralston. King also thought that Hutchinson's claim that King was not popular was ridiculous, in view of his election successes. Hutchinson further said that King's parliamentary colleagues were in awe of him, while King, reacting in his diary, stated that no prime minister had friendlier colleagues.

If Hutchinson's portrayal of King raised some annoyance in the latter, another incident — this time involving a tribute — was to infuriate King.

On the Canadian side of the Niagara Falls Bridge there were to be placed two bells, with the larger to be labelled "Churchill" in raised letters, and the other, "Roosevelt." The base was to bear the inscription: "To

God's glory and in grateful memory of our nation's leaders, Winston Churchill and Franklin Delano Roosevelt."[2]

When King heard of these plans, he was, quite rightly, incensed. He blamed the Ontario Conservative premier, George Drew, and sundry others, for excluding him. Later it was ascertained that an Ontario Liberal MPP had written the inscription, with no ulterior motive, but he later agreed that it was not appropriate. Eventually, the matter was cleared up by having the names of Churchill and Roosevelt removed. King was placated.

The creation of such public monuments and the writing of political autopsies in the press were a clear signal that — in the eyes of others at least — King's tenure was coming to an end. King's strong sense of duty directed him to continue to give service to his country, but in the end his declining health and the pressure of the position forced him to face the inevitable. In early 1947 he began the process of finding a successor. He wished to stay on at least until June of that year when he would have completed twenty-eight years as leader of the Liberal Party, and also twenty years as prime minister. He was also aware that there was another record of longevity. Sir Robert Walpole had been the longest serving British first/prime minister, and if King continued in office until April 14, 1948, he would surpass him.

King's choice to succeed him was the external affairs minister, Louis St. Laurent. However, St. Laurent had lost heavily in the stock market some years before, and wished to return to his law practice to improve his finances. King had been helped financially when he assumed the leadership of the Liberal Party in 1919, and friends came forward to offer similar assistance to St. Laurent. To King's immense relief St. Laurent agreed to stand for the leadership.

King's ability to pick and nurture people of ability has been previously mentioned. One in that category was Lester Pearson. After diplomatic posts in London during the war, in Washington during and after the war, and in Ottawa as deputy minister of external affairs, he received a very attractive offer to become the president of the Rockefeller Foundation in the United States. King no doubt recalled the entreaty he had received from Sir Wilfrid Laurier, some forty years before, and he urged Pearson to turn this down and remain in Ottawa. Pearson did turn the offer down, and he succeeded St. Laurent as minister of external affairs, and later as prime minister.

While King was contemplating retirement, Churchill remained fully occupied as opposition leader in the House of Commons, where he was attacking the government's handling of the economy, which was in crisis mode. But as his future chancellor of the exchequer, Rab Butler, wrote, "the constructive part of his mind always dwelt more naturally on the international scene than on bread and butter issues."[3]

The international scene was dominated by the question of Indian independence, a cause that Churchill opposed, but which he also knew he was unlikely to defeat. However, he was not to lose the cause he had espoused in his Zurich speech of September 19, 1946. A provisional British "United Europe Committee" was formed, with Churchill serving as chairman of the board. It was comprised of twenty-two members, from all political parties. On May 14 he spoke at a meeting in the Royal Albert Hall in London. He continued his previous utterances on the need for a partnership between Germany and France, while acknowledging that this required an act of faith from France.

A major, non-political event in Britain was soon to bring the two prime ministers together again: the wedding of Princess Elizabeth and Prince Philip, which was scheduled to take place on November 20, 1947.

King was, of course, invited to the wedding. Before he set off across the Atlantic, however, a significant offer came from King George. The king wished to confer on him the Order of Merit. The Order, a personal honour from the monarch, is limited to twenty-four recipients at any time. King was thrilled and noted that current members included Churchill and Smuts. He wrote in his diary: "It will be a remarkable rounding out of the circle which links the reward placed on Mackenzie's head by the Crown, with the highest award from the Crown to his grandson, who has been carrying on his work."

While King would have been expected to promptly respond with an expression of appreciation, he spent the next two days balancing off his previous stand against taking on titles, before concluding that it would be churlish and ungracious to decline.

After arriving in London on November 7, King proceeded to Brussels to receive an honorary university degree. Also at the ceremony were the Belgian prime minister and the queen of Belgium, who thanked him for the part played by Canada in the war. Then King went on to Amsterdam for a similar investiture.

After returning to London, King met with Princess Elizabeth and gave her wedding gifts from the people of Canada. These included a wild mink coat, and a silver cup, 227 years old. The Princess thanked him and told King of the most extraordinary gift she had received. It came from Trinidad. A lunatic asylum was needed on the island and the money raised by the people for her wedding gift was used for that purpose.

Churchill telephoned King on November 18. After exchanging greetings and arranging to meet, King spoke of the Order of Merit. "I told him that getting into the same class as Smuts and himself was getting up in the world. He said something about being so pleased. How merited it was. He said they call it the Old Man Order. He said we both qualify for that."

On November 18 King attended a formal dinner at Buckingham Palace for selected guests at the wedding. He remarked in his diary that "Winston was looking much older, and just a bit tottering or doddering." On the other hand, Clementine, in writing to a friend at the time, referred to "Mackenzie King as unchanging as a Chinese image."[4]

A sad occasion the next day was a memorial service in St. Paul's Cathedral for the well-respected former U.S. ambassador to Britain John G. Winant, who had committed suicide. Again King commented in his diary on Churchill's health, noting that he had difficulty raising himself from his seat.

In Westminster Abbey for the wedding, King had mixed feelings: "Enjoyed looking at the people.... Listened to the music, enjoyed seeing choir boys in their crimson robes.... The King and Queen looked very fine. So did the bride and groom.... Churchill seemed to be much impressed with the beauty of the service as everyone indeed must have been who loves pageantry and colour." But King's puritanical attitude surfaced: "There was a series of lovely tableaux but one felt that all this pomp was a demonstration of power and ceremonial — something that is really helping to foment the unrest of the day, and that in the nature of things would not last long. It will someday be swept away in a great class struggle." On November 25 King went to lunch at the home of Sir John and Lady Anderson. He had been Churchill's chancellor of the exchequer in the last two years of the war. Also in the party were Winston and Clementine Churchill, Smuts, and Harold Macmillan. King said that Churchill looked wonderfully well —much better than the previous two occasions. As usual Churchill dominated the conversation with a view that he believed that Britain was in the same position as when Hitler threatened to go in to the Ruhr. This was an overly pessimistic assessment, as this time the United States was no longer isolated. However, there was no formal organization in Europe to stand as a bulwark to the Soviet ambitions.

After the luncheon Churchill, King, and Smuts, the three senior statesmen of the Commonwealth, talked together. King wrote: "It must have been in the minds of the others, as it was in my mind, that we might never be together again or, beyond the next day or two, see each other again. It was pleasant to feel a deep friendly atmosphere." Winston told them that the first volume of his war memoirs, which included the ten years prior to the war, was complete and would be published in 1948, and he promised to send the volumes to King, as they came out.

The writing of his World War II memoirs was a mammoth undertaking, and Churchill followed his usual manner of production: "I write a book the way they built the Canadian Pacific Railway. First I lay the track from coast to coast, and then I put in all the stations."[5] The first volume included as the moral of the work: "In War: Resolution, In Defeat: Defiance, In Victory: Magnanimity, In Peace: Good Will."

King's pre-war diary entries detailing his encounters with Churchill present a very mixed assessment of the man. Now there was no doubt as to his feeling. "I confess that as I looked at him at the table, I felt that perhaps in more respects than one, he was the greatest man of our times. Not by any means the greatest in any one field but rather in a combination of fields — in the aggregate. I felt that his great knowledge of history, which gave him a great outlook, would cause him to speak with authority, causing other men to realize how little their knowledge and vision really was. The form with which he expressed his views was what gave him his great influence."

King's interest in spiritualism had taken a back seat during World War II, but on this trip to London he had two sittings with a medium, to establish contact with the departed. He recorded the details of these sittings in his diary. He was visited by Wilfrid Laurier, Franklin Roosevelt, and a living person, Winston Churchill. He wrote in his diary that during the luncheon, he quietly told Churchill of the sittings, and that he had certain messages from Roosevelt, which he would send to him.

Like many Canadians who learned of the spiritualist side of King after his death, Churchill must have been surprised by King's revelation. However, if we accept King's diary as accurate, Churchill did not consider it abnormal: "He was quite reverent in his attitude. Seemed to think it quite natural that I should have brought up the subject with him. I recalled how he had said, in the presence of Eisenhower, that he believed man was an angel struggling to be free. His whole reference to this side of things was of a character which led me to feel that it was a subject he would welcome talking over."

Back at his hotel, King sent the record of his sittings to Churchill. Later in the day, King noted, "Churchill sent back the material I had sent him with a most significant note." It would have been of great interest to have seen what Churchill had written; however, this episode showed the degree of intimacy that had been developed, and also the trust King had that Churchill would not divulge his "secret life."

King sailed back to Canada the following day, November 26. Back in Ottawa he felt a "new zeal and strength for politics," but on reflection he went back to his earlier decision that he should step down. He certainly was not being pushed by his cabinet colleagues, as evidenced by his diary record of the comments of Ian Mackenzie, government House leader, upon King's seventy-third birthday, on December 17. "Mackenzie then rose and said that the entire cabinet wished to extend to me warmest birthday greetings. Referred to the regard and affection which they had for me. Hoped I would continue in public life for years to come." However, they did anticipate his retirement at some time, as they gave him a marble desk set, which they thought he would find of use when writing his memoirs.

THE END OF AN ERA

E arly in 1948 Churchill's "Iron Curtain" speech of two years before was shown to be a mild prediction of the intentions of the Soviets. He referred to that speech in an address in the House of Commons on January 23. "It had a mixed reception and quite a few Members of this House put their names to a Motion condemning me for having made it; but what I said at Fulton in the presence of the President of the United States has been outpaced and over passed by the movement of events and of American opinion." He referred to the Soviet leaders, who "have it in their power to loose on the world horrors and devastations, compared with which we have gone through would be just a prelude ... the best chance of avoiding war is, in accord with the other Western democracies, to bring matters to a head with the Soviet Government."[1]

While King was fearful of the Cold War in Europe, he was concerned with personal and domestic matters. It had been decided that the Liberal Party would hold a convention in August to select a new leader. King had not deviated from his opinion that St. Laurent was not only the ideal candidate, but the only candidate who could adequately replace him. However, there was a potential problem. King wrote, "I shall never forget Sir Wilfrid having said to me he did not believe another French Canadian would ever be P.M. of Canada, because of his being in the minority of race and religion." King disagreed with that comment, but he knew it had to be addressed.

The opportunity to state his position on the matter of suitability of can didates came at a Liberal Party caucus meeting on January 28. "I said I had noticed Mr. St. Laurent, who was sitting right beside me, had said that he would be prepared to consider running providing it would not raise any question of race or religion. I said for Heaven's sake, let nobody raise ques tion of either race or religion at this time, in connection with leadership Surely we had reached the stage in our citizenship where we could base our rights on everything as Canadian citizens, and leave aside all references to any governing possibility outside of that — leave other matters unsaid."

A lighter moment in January was the arrival in Ottawa of the Toronto born, "America's Sweetheart," Mary Pickford. She was repre senting UNESCO, and functions included a luncheon at the Château Laurier and a dinner at the Elgin Theatre. King spoke at the luncheon and extended a warm welcome to her, and said that he did not intend to let the American ambassador, who was present, get ahead of him by claiming her as an American.

In the afternoon Mary Pickford went to Laurier House for tea. As King had shown with the actress Madeleine Carroll, during the war, he enjoyed the company of glamorous women. With Mary Pickford he was more than happy to encourage a degree of familiarity, which he denied his political colleagues. "We had been referring to names and how one was addressed. She had been referring to me as His Ex. I told her to drop that It belonged to the Governor General, and besides I would much rather be addressed in any other way." The title Chief was also dismissed. "She helped me out by saying her name was Mary. I said: 'Well my friends call me Rex.' So on going into the dinner tonight she addressed me as Rex."

Relations between the Western democracies and the Soviet Union con tinued to deteriorate. Poland was now firmly in the grip of Moscow. Also Czechoslovakia, the country that had been at the centre of the Munich Agreement in 1938, became another satellite, after a coup d'état, in February

On April 21 Churchill gave a speech in the Royal Albert Hall in London. He spoke of the shock at the fate of Czechoslovakia, which, he said, had no sooner been freed "from the tyranny of Hitler's Gauleiters then, like Poland, they were dragged down into subjugation by the Soviet Quislings."[2] Further deterioration resulted after the Soviets brought in the

Berlin blockade, with the West reacting with the Berlin airlift. Concern in the United States was clearly demonstrated by the reinstitution of the draft. On May 7 Churchill spoke at the Congress of Europe, in the Hague. He reiterated his previous statements on the need for unity between the democratic countries. In that regard he welcomed the delegation from Germany, and stressed the need to "restore the economic life of Germany, and revive the ancient fame of the German race, without thereby exposing their neighbours and ourselves to any rebuilding or reassertion of their military power, of which we still bear the scars."

As he had done in the dark days of World War II, Churchill finished his speech on an optimistic note. He stated that if all free countries pull together, "we shall move into a happier sunlit age when all the little children who are now growing up in this tormented world may find themselves not the victors nor the vanquished in the fleeting triumphs of one country over another in the bloody turmoil of destructive war, but the heirs of all the treasurers of the past and the masters of all the science, the abundance and the glories of the future."[3]

King, while fully supportive of the position of the United States and Britain, was careful to ensure Canada should not, at that time, become directly embroiled in the Cold War. This was partly due to his health, which was of increasing concern, and partly due to his natural reticence, which was further extenuated by his "lame duck" status as a prime minister soon to leave office. But he was also very concerned that direct participation might again bring another "conscription crisis."

As previously stated, King wanted to break Walpole's record as prime minister. This occurred on April 21, and King received a flood of congratulatory messages on the occasion. The winding down of a unique political career, especially of someone who had defied analysis, did not stop journalists from attempting to interpret the prime minister to their readers. On May 21 the *Ottawa Citizen* used an occasion of two days before to publish an article headed "The Other Mr. King," which describes a different prime minister:

> Mr. Mackenzie King smiling broadly from under an elaborate Indian head-dress, with which he had just

been adorned by Chief Poking Fire of Caughnawaga, appeared highly photogenic on the front page of the *Evening Citizen* yesterday. The Prime Minister in no way suggested the "Hermit of Kingsmere," which many glad-handing politicians like to call him. On the contrary, he radiated good fellowship and friendliness and looked a good companion for a lively social occasion. That was the other "Mr. King," the man whom few know with real intimacy. He had to suppress that side of himself because he held so many important offices for so long and took his heavy responsibilities so seriously.

The article went on to talk of the iron will and self-discipline that it was necessary for King to display. It stated that he was not naturally aloof but he could not be "Hail-fellow, well-met to one and sundry," in view of his public duties. "So he pushed the other half of himself into the limbo of the might-have-been and that was that."

A conference of Dominion prime ministers was announced, to be held in the autumn. This brought a rather unusual reaction from Louis St. Laurent. He suggested that, after the convention, King should stay on as prime minister and attend the conference and also a United Nations one in Paris. This would give St. Laurent, if elected leader, the time to tour the country. This arrangement would also have the benefit of allowing King, if contentious matters were brought up, to say that as a new leader was soon to take over, he could not be expected to make a commitment. King would have preferred to fully hand power over after the convention, but he did agree.

King had had a full physical examination in February 1948, and his doctor had cautioned him that he had to lose weight. A concern for some years had been his heart. While it was no worse, he was told that if he did experience exceptional pressure it could be serious. Thus his doctor was supportive of his decision to step down.

Across the Atlantic Ocean, another overweight politician had no intention of reducing his work load. After the Hague speech of May 7, Churchill spoke at an open-air meeting in Amsterdam on May 9; at a dinner in the Royal Palace in Oslo on May 12; on receiving a doctorate from the University of Oslo, also on May 12; in Oslo city Hall on May 13; and on that same day, he addressed the Norwegian Parliament. To a young man, that would have been a tremendous strain; to a normal seventy-three-year-old, it would have been impossible. But Winston Churchill was no normal seventy-three-year-old.

King's final appearance in the House of Commons as prime minister was on June 30, the last day of the parliamentary session. The next day the press gave prominence to the significance of the event. The *Ottawa Citizen's* front page ran a Karsh photograph of him, with the headline, "Mr. King says Farewell to the Commons." It added: "It was an historic occasion and in many ways the end of an era."

On July 6 King received a copy of *The Gathering Storm*, with a note: "My dear Mackenzie King: Herewith my first volume of our war! With all good wishes — Yours ever — W." King recorded his feelings on receipt: "This is a very precious possession. I have sent him today a cable of acknowledgement."

A final, very pleasant duty remained. In Newfoundland the vote in a referendum resulted in a narrow victory for Confederation. The result was announced in London on July 30, 1948, and the front page of the *Globe & Mail* newspaper the following day included King's statement: "The Union of Newfoundland and Canada, two North American democracies in the British Commonwealth of Nations, will add strength to both. Together as partners we may look forward to the future with more confidence than if we had remained separate political communities." The newspaper also stated with the 320,000 Newfoundlanders, the population of Canada would increase to 12,920,000.

King wrote in his diary: "I could not help but realize that this act rounds out the Dominion and its ten Provinces, bringing to completion the work that had been begun by the Fathers of Confederation so many years ago. It was gratifying that it was possible for me to make this decision and to welcome the Newfoundland electors while still ... Prime Minister of the Country."

The Liberal Party Convention opened on August 5. King was given a great reception when he addressed the delegates, after twenty-nine years as party leader. King was officially neutral in the choice of his successor but all knew that he was fully committed to Louis St. Laurent. When the voting was announced, he was well-pleased, as St. Laurent recorded 843 votes; James Gardiner received 323, and Chubby Power, from Quebec, who had resigned from King's cabinet in 1944 over the conscription decision, 56. Victory on the first ballot.

The Third General Assembly of the United Nations began in Paris on September 21. King had agreed to attend this on St. Laurent's behalf, along with a Commonwealth Conference in London. He was not feeling well and decided that when he arrived in London he would consult a heart specialist. However, he did address the Assembly on September 28, and was obliged to attend some functions.

One occasion gave King great pleasure. The French foreign minister asked if he would accept France's highest honour, the Order of the Legion of Honour. King responded that he was deeply touched and hoped they would not consider him ungrateful if he declined it, noting that he had declined similar honours in the past. So, in substitution, he was given a printed copy of Virgil, inscribed: "Presented to Mr. Mackenzie King, Prime Minister of Canada, a great friend of France, in testimony of our affectionate gratitude." It was signed by the prime minister and foreign minister. King responded that he would treasure it as long as he lived.

King arrived in London on October 6. It was arranged that Churchill's doctor would examine him in his hotel room on October 8. Wilson had concerns especially with King's heart. Accordingly, later that day, King was examined by a specialist, Sir John Parkinson. After various tests, the two doctors diagnosed that although there was no immediate danger to his life there would be if he did not take to his bed for some time. Medications were prescribed and two nurses hired. As a result, King was not able to attend the Commonwealth Conference.

During the next three weeks King welcomed a steady stream of well wishers. They included Prime Minister Attlee, Foreign Minister Bevin Indian Prime Minister Nehru, and Lord Privy Seal Lord Addison. King George VI also came, by way of a side entrance into the hotel.

On October 29 Winston Churchill arrived at the hotel. "'Well Mackenzie, my dear friend, I am sorry to see you here. You were greatly missed at the Conference. We all wished you were there.' I remarked how exceedingly well he was looking and how pleased I was to see that.... He called out once or twice: 'I have brought you my book,' and then went back into the other room and autographed it himself. He said I have already given you the American edition. This is a copy of the English edition."

The conversation naturally turned to memories of the war. In response to King's question as to Canada failing him at any time Churchill responded: "'You have never failed. You were always helpful. There was nothing that you did not do that could be done.' He spoke two or three times of the tremendous help Canada had given in the Air Training Plan and in the air.... He also spoke of my having been helpful at the beginning of the war when the question was whether the British Fleet should be moved to the U.S.... He said the Americans were very different at that time. That I had been helpful in getting the true position understood."

Churchill asked when King intended to retire, and said, "You have had a great career. You have built a bridge between the United States and the United Kingdom. As he was leaving I referred to his great service to the World and to Freedom, and said God Bless You.... He came to my bedside and his eyes filled up with tears. He shook my hands very warmly and affectionately. As he went out of the door I could see that he was restraining feelings of emotion. We could not have had a pleasanter talk together."

In *The Prime Ministers*, Bruce Hutchinson referred to the last meeting. "Churchill as he rose to leave was surprised by the patient's last request. In this final moment of parting Britain's old warrior did not hesitate. Churchill leaned over the bed and kissed King's cheek."[4]

EPILOGUE

T he two elderly statesmen were not to meet again. Their future relationship was confined to Churchill sending King the next volume
of his World War II memoirs, occasional telegrams, and best wishes
through British politicians visiting Ottawa. One of these was Anthony
Eden, the shadow foreign secretary, who, on January 23, 1949, "brought
greetings from Churchill." King noted Eden's assessment of Churchill:
"He is 'mellowing' but [Eden] wishes he would give up leadership."

Their final communication of substance was on March 31, 1949. King
wrote in his diary of listening on the radio to Churchill speaking at the
Massachusetts Institute of Technology: "It was a magnificent address,
splendidly proportioned, beautifully expressed, well-delivered.... I was
deeply moved at places, especially his reference to the humanities, the spir-
itual side of life and its importance, the hereafter as well as the here, related.
I thought he reached heights not attained to before, & a very just estimate
all through, etc. It was the full flowering of his life's experiences & thought,
a sort of valedictory to this continent, a reference to Lloyd George & Bevin,
which was a tribute to friends who had meant much to him."

King sent Churchill a telegram of congratulations: "My Dear Friend:
Your address tonight reached the summit of all to which you have aspired
in your great messages to the human family. It will touch the heart of the
world and influence its course. I wish I might have been at your side, as
was my privilege so often in the years of war. You will recall our exchange

of greetings after the Fulton speech. Again, from my home at Laurier House, I send warmest congratulations to you. All our hours together have been much in my thoughts tonight. Please give my affectionate remembrances to Mrs. Churchill and Mary. My every good wish to you all. Mackenzie King."[1]

On April 4 he received a reply: "Thank you so much, my dear friend — all good wishes from us both — Winston."

Churchill continued his active political life with his main attention given to the matter of European unity. His was a vital contribution to the formation of the North Atlantic Treaty Organization (NATO) in April 1949, and the Council of Europe in May 1949.

Both had health issues, with King's heart problems and various other ailments resulting in a steady decline. Churchill suffered a stroke in August 1949 but his strong constitution resulted in his recovery.

King's diary shows his continued quest for salvation: "Knelt and prayed earnestly for God's guidance and complete consecration of my life to His service for the remainder of my days." Churchill who, surprisingly for a self-proclaimed non-believer, brought God into many of his discourses, commented on November 30, 1949: "I am ready to meet my Maker. Whether my Maker is prepared for the great ordeal of meeting me is another matter."[2]

Churchill was back as prime minister in 1951. He had committed to only staying in office for one year but hung on, with the reason being his quest for peace. This seemed unreachable, with the Cold War in effect. However, the death of Stalin in early 1953 gave rise to optimism for dialogue with the Soviets, but this was rebuffed by President Eisenhower.

For his eightieth birthday, he was presented with a book written by various hands, including Clement Attlee and Anthony Eden. At the time Eden was furious with Churchill for continuing to stay in office after repeatedly promising to step down. However, he made a fine contribution, finishing by saying, "He expressed the instinctive conviction of the British people that they could not be beaten, and he gave them the leadership that made victory possible. That is why, despite the wide range of his achievements, he could never be greater than in 1940, because it was our finest hour and his."[3]

Eden did receive his due when Churchill at last gave in to the realities of age and health, and resigned in April 1955

Although King had flashes of regret in resigning as prime minister, he stuck to his retirement plan, and did not run in the April 1949 general election. He was delighted that the now St. Laurent-led Liberal Party won decisively, although his egotism thought there should have been more acknowledgement of his part in handing over a strong organization.

In spite of his medical problems and sleepless nights, King did not fit the image of a declining, lonely bachelor, living in a "Miss Havisham" haze. Now that he was no longer prime minister, there was no reason not to accept recognition from grateful nations. In the last year of his life, the Italian government offered to place, at their expense, a villa for his occupancy during the winter months; Prince Bernhard of the Netherlands presented him with his country's highest honour; the Belgium ambassador invested him in the Insignia of the Grand Cross of the Order of Leopold; from Luxembourg came the Grand Cross of the Oaken Crown. The French foreign minister, M. Schuman, presented him with the Legion of Honour, Grand Cross, at a formal dinner in the French Embassy in Ottawa.

While King had concerns in projecting an image of self-aggrandizement, Churchill had no such inhibitions. He was awarded thirty-seven orders, decorations, and medals; of these, eleven came from countries other than the United Kingdom. He was also offered the Freedom of the City of Toronto by Mayor Nathan Phillips in 1958. Ill health resulted in his response: "My wife and I are most honoured by your offer of the Freedom of your famous city. We are happy to accept it, but I fear that I cannot foresee at the present, an opportunity of coming to Toronto to receive it."[4]

Other pleasing matters for King were the decision to turn the King homestead, in Kitchener, Ontario, into an historic site, and the formal opening of Mackenzie House in Toronto. He was also gladdened by the announcement that a new bridge over the Rideau Canal in Ottawa was to be named after him.

While in his diary King complained of loneliness, he was visited by many past acquaintances, including the duke of Windsor, Prime

The last photograph taken of Mackenzie King on July 18, 1950. He died four days later.

Minister Nehru and Lord Moran. King was confined to Laurier House for the winter of 1949–50. In the spring he was able to move back into the countryside. Here at his beloved Kingsmere he died on July 22, 1950.

When Churchill visited Ottawa as prime minister in 1952, he spoke at a state banquet in the Château Laurier. He referred to meeting King in the early years of the century, and noted: "I made a lifelong friendship with him and I shared my grief with all Canada, and indeed the free world, at his death after so many years of faithful and skilful service to the great causes which we uphold today."[5]

King, with his belief in extrasensory matters, would have been intrigued, if he had still been alive and known of a strange and accurate prediction. Churchill's principal private secretary, Sir John Colville, recalled: "I think it was in 1953. I went up to his bedroom one morning to talk about something, and he was shaving. He said to me, 'Today is the 24th of January.' I said yes, and he said, 'It's the day my father died.' I said something suitable, and he went on, 'It's the day I shall die, too.'"[6] Churchill fulfilled his prediction, dying on January 24, 1965, seventy years to the day after his father's death.

The funerals of both were major and moving events. Churchill lay in state in Westminster Hall for three days with more than three hundred thousand people, who had waited patiently for hours in bitter weather, filing past. The funeral itself saw the greatest outpouring of respect and affection that Britain had accorded a person, other than royalty. In the congregation in St. Paul's Cathedral, there were six monarchs, five presidents, fifteen prime ministers, and 110 nations represented. Messages of condolence came from divergent sources such as Chairman Kosygin of Russia and Pope Paul VI. Churchill's old nemesis, President de Gaulle, wrote to Queen Elizabeth of World War II: "In the great drama he was the greatest of all."[7]

In Toronto's *Telegram* there was this tribute: "He marches today in the glittering procession of history. He marches erect, strong and determined. Probably no man in history has come closer to the attainment of immortality than this great commoner."

Clementine Churchill bore the strain of the funeral with calm and fortitude. Her daughter, Mary Soames, wrote: "We were very tired when we got back to No. 28 (Hyde Park Gate). It had been a long, long day.... Then my mother got up to go to bed, and I busied myself switching out the lamps. As she reached the door she paused, and turning round said, 'You know, Mary, it wasn't a funeral — it was a Triumph.'"[8]

Just inside the west entrance of Westminster Abbey, near the grave of the Unknown Warrior, is a green marble memorial stone. It was placed there on September 15, 1965, the twenty-fifth anniversary of the Battle of Britain, and unveiled by Queen Elizabeth four days later. The inscription reads simply: "Remember Winston Churchill."

King was also given a state funeral. His body lay in the Parliament Buildings in an open casket. The *Toronto Star* reported that the "mile long procession wound and circled the Hill." British Pathé News com pared the ceremony in Ottawa to that given five years before for Franklin Roosevelt in Washington.

The newsman and author Bruce Hutchinson, who knew King well gave an insightful report in the final words of his biography.

> The crowds in Parliament Hill filed past his bier and watched his last procession in a peculiar silence. They did not weep, for they had never loved the man. They were respectful, they glimpsed King's greatness even if they had seen in life only his self-made caricature, but they were puzzled because King reflected them, as in a true glass, and the Canadian people did not understand themselves. In the crowd a little boy asked his mother who the dead man was. She tried to tell the child that King had been the Prime Minister, that he had made Canada a better place for all little boys. And suddenly she turned away in tears unable to answer her son or explain her own feelings. The mystery of King and Canada remained, unanswerable.[9]

After the ceremony in Ottawa, King's body was taken by train accompanied by Prime Minister Louis St. Laurent and his cabinet col leagues, from Ottawa to Toronto. There the body was placed on a gun carriage and the procession marched up University Avenue, on the way to Mount Pleasant Cemetery, where there was a simple ceremony Members of the Armed Forces lined the route and the *Toronto Star* esti mated the "vast throng" at five hundred thousand. However, that same newspaper reported that the attitude of the mourners was similar to that described by Hutchinson. They offered a "silent tribute." The procession was, "without pomp but with homage in its simplicity."

Tributes came from all over the world, with British Prime Minister Clement Attlee calling him a great statesman. President Truman said that with King, "freedom loving peoples and democratic institutions found an unwavering champion." The *Toronto Star's* July 24 headline was, "Canada Mourns Loss of Her Greatest Son," and commented that the "death of Mackenzie King brings to a close a career which probably will not be equalled."

While people tend to exaggerate the qualities of the recently deceased, it is difficult to think that a hard-nosed politician such as C.D. Howe would give other than his honest opinion. As the *Toronto Star* reported, "His colleagues were given the widest possible latitude in conducting the responsibilities of their offices, although he was quick to point out the pitfalls inherent in any new programme. I never found it difficult to follow his leadership."

Winston Churchill's message, reported in the *Toronto Star*, read: "I deeply regret the loss of this great statesman whose friendship I enjoyed for so many years and whose services to Canada and the British Empire will long be remembered."

Winston Churchill to this day has remained a person of fascination. He was his own biographer for a crucial period of his life, by way of his books on the First and Second World Wars. Almost fifty years after his death, a dozen or so books are published every year on aspects of his life. Not all books have been positive, as there have been the inevitable books by revisionist historians.

Statues of Churchill can be found all around the world. Interestingly, the first statue of him was unveiled in 1943, at Albert E. Peacock Collegiate, in Moose Jaw, Saskatchewan. Others in Canada are in Toronto, Edmonton, and Halifax. There is also a bust of him in Quebec City.

In 1968 Richard Langworth founded the International Churchill Society in the United States. This later became the Churchill Centre (*www.winstonchurchill.org*), with the name adopting the British spelling, as a sign of respect to the nationality of their hero. The centre produces a high-class glossy magazine, *Finest Hour,* four times a year. The allied organization in Canada is the International Churchill Society Canada (*www.winstonchurchillcanada.ca*). Also in Canada are affiliated societies in Ottawa, Vancouver, and Victoria, and independent societies in Calgary and Edmonton. Another society, with a dual mandate, is the Toronto-based Churchill Society for the Advancement of Parliamentary Democracy.

Churchill's life and achievements have been analysed at depth. His chief of staff in World War II, Major-General, and later Lord, Ismay wrote in his memoirs, "It struck me as odd that he failed to realize that the upsurge of the national spirit was largely his own creation. The great qualities of the British race had seemed dormant until he aroused them. The people then saw themselves as he portrayed them. They put their trust in him. They were ready to do anything that he asked, make any sacrifice that he demanded, and follow wherever he led."[10]

Eisenhower wrote of Churchill: "Greatness in a man was to achieve pre-eminence in some broad field of human thought or endeavour and then to discharge one's duties in such a way as 'to have left a marked and favourable imprint upon the future.' The qualities were 'vision, integrity, courage, understanding, the power of articulation and profundity of character. Winston," he continued, "came nearer to fulfilling the requirements of greatness in any individual than I have met in my lifetime. I have known finer and greater characters, wiser philosophers, more understanding personalities, but no greater man."[11]

King has been the subject of only a modest number of biographies. Only two statues have been erected of him. One is on Parliament Hill in Ottawa. The other depicts him as a school boy in front of his old high school in Kitchener, Ontario.

Both men have sites where the public has the opportunity to becoming better acquainted with them and their achievements. For Churchill there is his place of birth, Blenheim Palace, and his home, Chartwell. Also the Churchill Museum and Cabinet War Rooms in London. For King there is his childhood home, Woodside, and his homes, Laurier House and Kingsmere — all three being National Historic Sites.

Churchill was, of course, a world figure with a heroic image. William Manchester referred to him as "The Last Lion."[12] King was not a world statesman, and the careful way that he developed his public image, with a lack of charisma, made him unattractive to potential biographers, or to publishers.

King became the subject of ridicule when his diaries became public. The CBC, in its 1967 program, *Century, In celebration of Canada's Centennial*, included this comment on King by novelist Edward McCourt: "The ultra-conventional little horse trader, who in our more despondent moments we equate with the national character, was at times, perhaps during certain phases of the moon, a non-conformist beyond the wildest imaginings of the most nihilistic, pot smoking, pad dweller amongst us."[13]

Since that time there has been a more balanced perspective. King could not compete in the imagination of the public with the warlike image of Churchill. But he led Canada from being a respectful junior member of the Imperial family, into a mature independent nation, while still retaining an affection and admiration for the mother country. It was inevitable that Canada would move closer to her southern neighbour, but that did not diminish the desire to retain the ties of old, and take pride in its place as the senior Dominion in the British Commonwealth of Nations. Although an unwarlike man, King took the country united into the Second World War, and led the transition from war to peace

In her biography of King's mother, *Mrs. King*, Charlotte Gray wrote: "Immediately after his death, William Lyon Mackenzie King was mourned as the man who created modern Canada. Since then, he has been dismissed as a pudgy waffler, disparaged for his mediocrity and ridiculed for his strange fantasy life. Most recently, his political stock has risen with dizzying speed, as his skill in papering over the fractures within Canadian society is recognized. 'Canada's most successful and most misunderstood Prime Minister,' is the verdict of historian Michael Bliss. [According to him,] 'Isabel Mackenzie King was the only person who ever came close to understanding him.'"[14]

Professor J.L. Granatstein wrote in 1977: "By supreme skill and judgement, he shaped a mighty war effort that kept Canadians together (as much as could be expected) and gave them incredible prosperity and power. For his achievements from 1940 to 1948, he should be honoured across the land.... King always had a difficult row to hoe, a divided, fractious country to govern. But govern it he did and he did it well. In the longer perspective, history will surely be more kind and Mackenzie King will rank with Macdonald and Laurier as the greatest of Canadian prime ministers."[15]

During the lifetime of these two products of the Victorian age the world evolved into a global village. On the world stage, Winston Churchill still towers as the great leader in the cause of freedom. In Canada the orchestrator of the successful development of the country during the turbulent first half of the twentieth century has been recognized as Mackenzie King.

In a BBC nationwide poll conducted in 2002, the greatest Briton of all time was judged to be Winston Leonard Spencer Churchill. In 1997 *Maclean's* magazine queried twenty-six academics, historians, and political scientists regarding their opinion of the twenty (at that time) Canadian prime ministers. The greatest prime minister was judged to be William Lyon Mackenzie King.

ACKNOWLEDGEMENTS

The first prompting to contemplate writing a book on these two men came from Professor David Dilks, while in Toronto in 2005 to promote his book *The Great Dominion: Winston Churchill in Canada, 1900–1954*. He stated that a book should be written on them, but it had to be written by a Canadian.

I considered the idea, as I had just submitted an article on Churchill and King for the Churchill Centre's *Finest Hour* magazine, which was published in its Spring 2006 issue. This was accorded its Journal Award (now entitled The Somervell Award, after Churchill's English teacher at Harrow) for 2006. But as I was informed by a sceptical publisher, "There's a lot more to writing a book, than writing an article!" However, as no one else was stepping forward, I decided to take up Professor Dilks's challenge.

The main person responsible for my having the nerve and audacity to take on this task was the founder of the International Churchill Society, now the Churchill Centre, and editor of *Finest Hour*, Richard Langworth. He encouraged my early writings and published my articles in the journal. Two of these, the one on King and Churchill, and "When Mice Roared: The Thirty Minute Invasion of St. Pierre and Miquelon" (covered in Chapter 14, in a different format), were included on the list of the "Hundred Best *Finest Hour* Articles in the Last Forty Years" in 2008. The publication of these articles, and the status accorded them, with inclusion in a list of learned professors and prominent personages, helped the self-confidence of a former career banker.

At the advice of a prominent Churchillian and friend, Professor Peter Russell, I approached my former Member of Parliament, Patrick Boyer, of Blue Butterfly Books, and he gave me a commitment. When Blue Butterfly amalgamated with Dundurn Press, I received the same commitment from Kirk Howard and Michael Carroll. I thank them for their confidence. I am also grateful to the staff at Dundurn for their professionalism and assistance.

I realized that an *unknown* writer needed to show credibility. Thus, I was delighted that former prime minister John Turner agreed to provide the foreword. It was a special day in my life to meet with him, armed with a tape recorder, and listen to his recollections. A highlight was Mr. Turner's telling me of his part in the first sub-four minute mile, while he was a member of the Oxford University track team. Unfortunately, this could not be included in the book. My gratitude to John Turner is immense.

I am also indebted to Professor Russell for providing his views on the King-Byng affair, which had resurfaced in late 2008, when Prime Minister Harper asked the governor general to prorogue Parliament. I also owe a debt of thanks to the friends who read parts of the narrative and offered helpful advice. In this regard Anne Anderson was especially helpful. Former chairman of the Churchill Centre John Plumpton provided invaluable assistance by reading the whole of the manuscript, challenging some comments, and correcting some embarrassing typographical errors.

A special thanks is given to my editor, Dominic Farrell, who corrected mangled sentences, put my early English language into modern usage, and offset my serious inadequacy in word processing.

All the photographs are from Library and Archives Canada, and the assistance of the staff, especially Jill Delaney, who provided access to the material, is much appreciated. What was especially gratifying was the discovery of additional photographs by Yousuf Karsh of Churchill and King, apparently not published before, taken at the same time as the "Roaring Lion" one on December 30, 1941.

Acknowledgements

Last, and certainly not least, to my wife, Fran, to whom this book is dedicated, for her patience in tolerating my solitary years of two finger typing in the basement of our home, surrounded by mounds of books.

Of course, the main acknowledgement is to two extraordinary men — Winston Churchill and Mackenzie King.

CHRONOLOGY OF CHURCHILL AND KING TO JULY 1950

1874   Churchill born November 30; King born December 17.

1891   King enrolls at the University of Toronto.

1893   Churchill enrolls in the Royal Military College, Sandhurst.

1896   Churchill posted to India.

1897   King attends Harvard, until 1900.

1898   Churchill participates in the Battle of Omdurman; King ends affair with Mathilde Grossert.

1899   Churchill escapes from a Boer prisoner of war camp in South Africa.

1900   King appointed deputy minister of labour — mediates strikes; Churchill elected to Parliament; first meeting of Churchill and King, in Ottawa.

1904   Churchill crosses the floor in House of Commons; moves from the Conservatives to the Liberals.

1905   Churchill appointed under-secretary of state for the colonies.

1906   Second meeting of Churchill and King, in London.

1907   King has leading role in drafting the Industrial Disputes Act.

1908   Churchill appointed president of the Board of Trade; marries Clementine (September 12).

1908   King elected MP; visits London re immigration problem and meets Churchill.

1909   King appointed Canada's first minister of labour.

1910   Churchill appointed home secretary.

1911   King loses his seat in the general election; Churchill appointed first lord of the Admiralty.

1914   World War I begins; King accepts position with the Rockefeller Foundation.

1915   Dardanelles disaster; Churchill resigns from the cabinet and rejoins the army.

1916   Churchill leaves the army and resumes his political career.

1917   Churchill appointed minister of munitions.

1918   World War I ends.

1919   King elected leader of the Liberal Party; Churchill appointed secretary of state for war and air.

1921   Liberals win election. King now prime minister; Churchill appointed colonial secretary.

1922   Chanak crisis; Churchill loses seat in general election.

1923   Imperial Conference; King asserts Canada's right to establish own foreign policy.

1924   Churchill rejoins Conservative Party; re-elected to Parliament and appointed chancellor of the exchequer.

1925   King loses seats in general election; continues to lead a minority government.

1926   General strike in Britain in May, which lasts for ten days; Churchill publishes *British Gazette*; King asks the governor general to dissolve Parliament and call an election; Byng refuses; Conservatives form government but defeated after three days; general election and King back as prime minister with a minority government; Imperial Conference (October) where King discusses Byng matter with Churchill.

1927   Churchill meets Mussolini — impressed.

1928   King meets Mussolini — impressed.

1929   Churchill and Conservatives defeated in general election; Churchill on holiday in Canada and United States; Churchill visits Kingsmere in August and is shown around Parliament by King; stock market crash — Churchill suffers major losses but King unaffected.

1930	General election in Canada; King and Liberals lose to Bennett and Conservatives; a blessing in disguise in view of the Great Depression.
1931	Churchill strongly opposes policy of Dominion status for India; forced to resign as shadow chancellor; wilderness years commence; King's policy results in the Statute of Westminster, establishing Canada's independence.
1932	Churchill visits Canada and lunches with King; speaks in Toronto at Maple Leaf Gardens.
1934	King given tour of Chartwell by Churchill.
1935	King and Liberals returned to power with a majority government.
1936	Churchill supports King Edward VIII in the abdication crisis; continues to warn of German rearmament; at a dinner Churchill speaks to King of the upcoming danger from Germany.
1937	King meets Hitler — impressed.
1938	Munich crisis. Churchill opposes Chamberlain; King supports Chamberlain.
1939	Germany invades Czechoslovakia in May; royal tour of Canada in May; Britain declares war on September 3, and Canada on September 10; Canadian troops in Britain (December).
1940	On May 10 Churchill becomes prime minister; Dunkirk; the Battle of Britain and the Blitz; King the linchpin between Britain and United States.
1941	Lend-Lease Act passed by Congress (March); Germany invades Russia (June); Atlantic Charter (August); King visits Churchill in London (August); Pearl Harbor (December); United States in the war; conference in Washington with Roosevelt and Churchill; King joins in talks.
1942	Conscription for overseas service approved by referendum in Canada; Dieppe raid (August); Canada declares war on Vichy France (November).
1943	Casablanca Conference (January); Trident Conference (May); Sicily invasion (July); Quadrant Conference in Quebec City (August); Tehran Conference (November).

1944   Dominion Prime Ministers' Conference in London (April-May); King addresses the British Parliament; D-Day (June); Dieppe liberated (September); Second Quebec (Octagon) Conference (September); Conscription crisis (November) and partial conscription (December); seventieth birthday of both (November–December); Churchill flies to Greece to solve crisis there (December).

1945   King attends Roosevelt's presidential inauguration (January); Yalta Conference (February); Roosevelt dies (April) —King attends funeral, Churchill does not; VE Day (May); King and Liberals re-elected (June); Potsdam Conference (July); Churchill and Conservatives lose election (July); Japan surrenders (August); Gouzenko affair (September); King, Truman and Attlee meet in Washington re atomic bomb (November).

1946   Churchill gives "Iron Curtain" speech (March); Churchill speaks in Zurich (September) on Western European unity.

1947   Royal wedding (November); King tells Churchill of his interest in spiritualism.

1948   King becomes the longest serving British/Commonwealth prime minister (April); King resigns as leader of the Liberal Party (August); King confined to bed in London with heart problems and visited by Churchill (their last meeting, October 29); King resigns as prime minister (November).

1949   Churchill suffers a stroke (August).

1950   King dies at Kingsmere (July 22).

NOTES

All photographs in this book are from the collection at Library and Archives Canada: *www.collectionscanada.gc.ca*. With the diary of William Lyon Mackenzie King being a major reference source, where King is quoted with no attribution this will be from the *Diary*.

Foreword

1. Winston S. Churchill, *The Unrelenting Struggle*, vol. 2 of *The War Speeches of Winston Churchill* (London: Cassell, 1942), 345.
2. John G. Diefenbaker, *One Canada: The Years of Achievement, 1956 to 1962*, vol. 2 of *Memoirs* (Toronto: Macmillan, 1976), 191.
3. John G. Diefenbaker, *One Canada: The Crusading Years, 1895 to 1956*, vol. 1 of *Memoirs* (Toronto: Macmillan, 1975), 196.
4. *Ibid.*, 199–200.
5. Lester B. Pearson, *Mike — The Memoirs of the Rt. Hon. Lester B. Pearson*, vol. 1 (Toronto: University of Toronto Press, 1972), 234.
6. *Ibid.*, 235.
7. *Ibid.*, 197.

Introduction

1. J.W. Pickersgill, *The Mackenzie King Record*, vol. 1 (Toronto: University of Toronto Press, 1960), 10.
2. Winston S. Churchill, *Churchill by Himself*, ed. Richard M. Langworth (New York: Public Affairs, 2008), 25.

3.   Martin Gilbert, *Never Despair: 1945–1965*, vol. 8 of *Winston S. Churchill* (Toronto: Stoddart, 1988), 835.

4.   David Dilks, *The Great Dominion: Winston Churchill in Canada, 1900–1954* (Toronto: Thomas Allen, 2005), xii.

5.   John Colville, *Footprints in Time: Memories* (London: Collins, 1976), 131.

6.   Winston S. Churchill, *The End of the Beginning*, vol. 3 of *The War Speeches of Winston Churchill* (Toronto: McClelland & Stewart, 1943), 176.

7.   Bruce Hutchinson, *The Incredible Canadian* (Toronto: Longmans, Green and Company, 1964), 4.

8.   Henry S. Ferns and Bernard Ostry, *The Age of Mackenzie King* (Toronto: William Heinemann, 1955), 279.

Chapter 1: The Early Years

1.   Winston S. Churchill, *The River War: An Account of the Reconquest of the Sudan* (London: Eyre and Spottiswoode, 1949), 21.

2.   Winston S. Churchill, *Marlborough: His Life and Times* (London: Harrap & Co., 1933), 29.

3.   R. MacGregor Dawson, *William Lyon Mackenzie King: A Political Biography* (Toronto: University of Toronto Press, 1958), 13.

4.   Peter de Mendelssohn, *The Age of Churchill: Heritage and Adventure, 1974–1911* (London: Thames and Hudson, 1961), 352.

5.   C.P. Stacey, *A Very Double Life* (Toronto: Macmillan, 1976), 55.

Chapter 2: The Edwardian Decade: 1900–1910

1.   Winston S. Churchill, *My Early Life: A Roving Commission* (London: Thornton Butterworth, 1930), 357.

2.   Lord Moran [Charles Wilson], *Churchill Taken from the Diaries of Lord Moran* (Boston: Houghton Mifflin, 1966), 20.

3.   Dawson, *William Lyon Mackenzie King*, 147

4.   Hutchinson, *The Incredible Canadian*, 278.

5.   Evelyn Wrench, *Churchill by His Contemporaries*, ed. Charles Eade (London: Hutchinson, 1954), 289.

6.   *Ibid.*, 289.

7.   Dawson, *William Lyon Mackenzie King*, 154.

8.   *Ibid.*, 160.

9.   *Ibid.*, 161.

10. *Ibid.*, 162.

11. *Ibid.*, 165.

Chapter 3: Mixed Fortunes: 1911–1921

1. Martin Gilbert, *Churchill: A Life* (London: William Heinemann, 1991), 291.
2. William Manchester, *Winston Spencer Churchill, Visions of Glory, 1874–1932*, vol. 1 of *The Last Lion* (Toronto: Little, Brown and Company, 1983), 564.
3. Gilbert, *Churchill: A Life*, 321.
4. Frank Owen, *Tempestuous Journey: Lloyd George, His Life and Times* (London: Hutchinson, 1954), 411–12.
5. Dawson, *William Lyon Mackenzie King*, 232.
6. *Ibid.*, 243.
7. Ferns and Ostry, *The Age of Mackenzie King*, 238.

Chapter 4: Chanak

1. Winston S. Churchill to William Lyon Mackenzie King, September 15, 1922, Prime Minister to Prime Minister, William Lyon Mackenzie King Papers, Library and Archives Canada.
2. King to Churchill, September 17, 1922, Prime Minister to Prime Minister, King Papers.
3. King to Churchill, September 18, 1922, Prime Minister to Prime Minister, King Papers.
4. Dawson, *William Lyon Mackenzie King*, 411.
5. *Ibid.*, 414.
6. Winston S. Churchill, *The World Crisis: The Aftermath, 1918–1928* (New York: Charles Scribner's Sons, 1929), 455.
7. Winston S. Churchill, *The Gathering Storm*, vol. 1 of *The Second World War* (Boston: Houghton Mifflin, 1948), 20–21.

Chapter 5: The Decline of the Empire and the Birth of the Commonwealth

1. Laurier L. LaPierre, *Sir Wilfrid Laurier and the Romance of Canada* (Toronto: Stoddart, 1996), 257.
2. William Lyon Mackenzie King, *The Message of the Carillon* (Toronto: Macmillan, 1927), 110.
3. Dawson, *William Lyon Mackenzie King*, 477.
4. *Ibid.*, 480.
5. H. Blair Neatby, *William Lyon Mackenzie King*, vol. 2 (Toronto: University of Toronto Press, 1963), 201–02.

6. Martin Gilbert, *The Exchequer Years: 1922–1929*, vol. 11 of *The Churchill Documents* (Hillsdale, MI: Hillsdale College Press, 2009), 240.
7. *Ibid.*, 650–51.
8. *Ibid.*, 311.
9. *Ibid.*, 739–40.
10. Neatby, 181.

Chapter 6: Opposition and the Rumblings of War

1. King, *The Message of the Carillion*, 14, 22.
2. Gilbert, *The Exchequer Years*, 916.
3. *Ibid.*, 916.
4. Martin Gilbert, *The Wilderness Years: 1929–1935*, vol. 12 of *The Churchill Documents* (Hillsdale, MI: Hillsdale College Press, 2009), 22.
5. *Ibid.*, 43–44.
6. *Ibid.*, 42.
7. *Ibid.*, 49–50.
8. Dilks, *The Great Dominion*, 62–66.
9. Winston S. Churchill and Clementine Churchill, *Speaking for Themselves: The Personal Letters of Winston and Clementine Churchill*, ed. Mary Soames (Toronto: Stoddart, 1998), 338.
10. Dilks, *The Great Dominion*, 97.
11. *Ibid.*, 101.
12. Maple Leaf Sports and Entertainment, *Maple Leaf Gardens: Memories and Dreams, 1931–1999* (Toronto: MLG, 1999), 199.

Chapter 7: The Coming of War

1. Winston S. Churchill, *Arms and the Covenant: Speeches on Foreign Affairs and National Defence* (London: G. Harrap & Co., 1938), 38–45.
2. *Ibid.*, 125.
3. Martin Gilbert, *The Prophet of Truth, 1922–1939*, vol. 5 of *Winston S. Churchill* (London: Heinemann, 1976), 666.
4. Winston S. Churchill, *Step by Step: Speeches* (London: Odhams Press Ltd. 1949), 25–26.
5. Churchill, *Arms and the Covenant*, 378.
6. Churchill, *Step by Step*, 71.
7. Pearson, *Mike*, vol.1, 126.
8. Martin Gilbert, *In Search of Churchill* (London: HarperCollins, 1994), 273.
9. Winston S. Churchill, *Great Contemporaries* (London: Thornton Butterworth

1937), 268.
10. Philip Guedalla, *Mr. Churchill: A Portrait* (London: Hodder and Stoughton, 1950), 271–72.
11. Churchill, *Churchill by Himself*, 576.
12. Churchill, *Arms and the Covenant*, 465.
13. Churchill, *The Gathering Storm*, 290.
14. Winston S. Churchill, *Blood, Sweat and Tears* (Toronto: McClelland & Stewart, 1941), 65–80.
15. Gilbert, *In Search of Churchill*, 110.
16. Martin Gilbert, *The Coming of War: 1936–1939*, vol. 13 of *The Churchill Documents* (Hillsdale, MI: Hillsdale College Press, 2009), 1473.
17. *Ibid.*, 1475.
18. Windsor, Elizabeth (Queen). "Royal Visits to Canada," CBC.ca, *www.cbc.ca/news/interactive/royalvisits/52.html.*
19. King, *Canada at Britain's Side*, 1–4.
20. *Ibid.*, 7–9.

Chapter 8: At War

1. Winston S. Churchill, *Churchill Speaks: Winston S. Churchill in Peace and War: Collected Speeches, 1897–1963*, ed. Robert Rhodes James (New York: Barnes & Noble, 1998), 695.
2. F.J. Hatch and Norman Hillmer, "British Commonwealth Air Training Plan," in *The Canadian Encyclopedia* (Toronto: McClelland & Stewart, 2000), 306.
3. Churchill, *Churchill Speaks*, 694–96.
4. King, *Canada at Britain's Side*, 39.
5. Martin Gilbert, *At the Admiralty: September 1939–May 1940*, vol. 1 of *The Churchill War Papers* (New York: W.W. Norton & Company, 1993), 520.
6. Churchill, *Churchill Speaks*, 698–700.
7. Gilbert, *At the Admiralty*, 698.
8. *Ibid.*, 922.
9. Churchill, *Churchill by Himself*, 532–33.
10. *Ibid.*, 536.
11. Churchill, *My Early Life*, 125.
12. Churchill, *The Gathering Storm*, 658.
13. *Ibid.*, 659.
14. *Ibid.*, 660.
15. Harold Macmillan, *The Blast of War, 1939–1945*, vol. 2 of *Memoirs* (London: Macmillan, 1967), 74.

16. Henry Channon, *Chips: The Diaries of Sir Henry Channon*, ed. Robert Rhodes James (London: Weidenfeld and Nicolson, 1967), 246.

17. Churchill, *Step by Step*, 323.

18. Gilbert, *In Search of Churchill*, 106.

19. Churchill, *The Gathering Storm*, 662.

20. Earl of Birkenhead, *Halifax: The Life of Lord Halifax* (London: Hamish Hamilton, 1965), 453–55.

21. Churchill, *The Gathering Storm*, 667.

Chapter 9: Fighting for Their Lives

1. Andrew Roberts, *Eminent Churchillians* (New York: Simon & Schuster, 1994), 203.

2. Churchill, *Churchill Speaks*, 705.

3. Harold Nicolson, *Diaries and Letters, 1939–1945*, ed. Nigel Nicholson (London: Collins, 1967), 85.

4. Channon, *Chips*, 252.

5. Churchill, *Churchill Speaks*, 706–08.

6. Martin Gilbert, *Finest Hour: 1939–1941*, vol. 6 of *Winston S. Churchill* (London: Heinemann, 1984), 358.

7. C.P. Stacey, *Mackenzie King and the Atlantic Triangle* (Toronto: Macmillan, 1976), 53.

8. John Toland, *Adolf Hitler*, vol. 1 (New York: Doubleday & Company, 1976), 703.

9. Ibid., 703–05.

10. Churchill, *Churchill Speaks*, 709–13.

11. Pickersgill, *The Mackenzie King Record*, vol. 1, 121–22.

12. Ibid., 122–23.

13. King, *Canada at Britain's Side*, 117–18.

14. Jon Meacham, *Franklin and Winston: An Intimate Portrait of an Epic Friendship* (New York: Random House, 2004), 60.

15. Winston S. Churchill, *Their Finest Hour*, vol. 2 of *The Second World War* (Boston: Houghton Mifflin, 1949), 132–33.

16. Ibid., 183.

17. Pickersgill, *The Mackenzie King Record*, vol. 1, 123–24.

18. Churchill, *Their Finest Hour*, 213.

19. Churchill, *Churchill Speaks*, 714–20.

20. Churchill, *Their Finest Hour*, 225–26.

21. Ibid., 231.

22. Churchill, *Churchill Speaks*, 721–22.

23. Channon, *Chips*, 260.
24. François Kersaudy, *Churchill and De Gaulle* (New York: Atheneum, 1983), 85.

Chapter 10: The Tiger and Her Cubs

1. Meacham, *Franklin and Winston*, 55.
2. *Ibid.*, 74.
3. William L. Shirer, *The Rise And Fall of the Third Reich: A History of Nazi Germany* (New York: Simon and Schuster, 1960), 3.
4. John Colville, *The Fringes of Power: Downing Street Diaries, 1939–1955* (London: Hodder and Stoughton, 1985), 200.
5. Joseph P. Lash, *Roosevelt and Churchill: The Partnership That Saved the West* (New York: W.W. Norton & Company, 1976), 213.
6. J.L. Granatstein and Desmond Morton, *Canada and the Two World Wars* (Toronto: Key Porter Books, 2003), 190.
7. *Ibid.*, 190.
8. Churchill, *Churchill Speaks*, 727–28.
9. King, *Canada at Britain's Side*, 146–47.
10. Churchill, *Churchill Speaks*, 730–31.
11. Pickersgill, *The Mackenzie King Record*, vol. 1, 143.
12. King, *Canada at Britain's Side*, 176.
13. Anthony Cave Brown, *"C": The Secret Life of Sir Stewart Menzies, Spymaster to Winston Churchill* (New York: Macmillan, 1987), 302–03.
14. Churchill, *Their Finest Hour*, 671.
15. Gilbert, *Churchill: A Life*, 654.
16. Churchill, *Blood, Sweat and Tears*, 463–68.
17. Kersaudy, *Churchill and De Gaulle*, 110.
18. Churchill, *The Unrelenting Struggle*, 1–4.
19. Gilbert, *Finest Hour*, 902.
20. Colville, *The Fringes of Power*, 292.
21. Churchill, *Their Finest Hour*, 558.
22. Lash, *Roosevelt and Churchill*, 263.
23. *Ibid.*, 263.
24. *Ibid.*, 265.
25. Churchill, *The Unrelenting Struggle*, 28.
26. Ian Kershaw, *Fateful Choices: Ten Decisions That Changed the World, 1940–1941* (New York: Penguin Books, 2008), 231.
27. King, *Canada at Britain's Side*, 196–200.
28. Churchill, *Blood, Sweat and Tears*, 368.

Chapter 11: The Eagle Flaps Its Wings

1. Winston S. Churchill, *The Grand Alliance*, vol. 3 of *The Second World War* (Boston: Houghton Mifflin, 1950), 23.
2. Gilbert, *Finest Hour*, 988.
3. Moran, *Churchill: Taken from the Diaries of Lord Moran*, 6.
4. Richard Holmes, *In The Footsteps of Churchill: A Study in Character* (New York: Basic Books, 2005), 230.
5. King, *Canada at Britain's Side*, 209–10.
6. Churchill, *Churchill Speaks*, 741.
7. King, *Canada at Britain's Side*, 213–18.
8. Churchill, *The Grand Alliance*, 739–40.
9. Churchill, *The Unrelenting Struggle*, 79.
10. *Ibid.*, 285–86.
11. King, *Canada at Britain's Side*, 227–28.
12. Government of Canada, "Canada Treaty Information," *www. treaty-accord gc.ca/index.aspx.*
13. Hutchinson, *The Incredible Canadian*, 289.
14. Granatstein and Morton, *Canada and the Two World Wars*, 192.
15. Churchill, *Churchill Speaks*, 748–52.
16. Vincent Massey, *What's Past Is Prologue: The Memoirs of the Right Honourable Vincent Massey, C.H.* (Toronto: Macmillan, 1963), 313–14.
17. King, *Canada at Britain's Side*, 272.
18. *Ibid.*, 273–78.
19. Churchill, *The Unrelenting Struggle*, 147–48.
20. King, *Canada at Britain's Side*, 307–08.
21. Churchill, *The Unrelenting Struggle*, 176–80.
22. *Ibid.*, 176–80.
23. Colville, *The Fringes of Power*, 404.
24. H.V. Morton, *Atlantic Meeting: An Account of Mr. Churchill's Voyage in H.M.S. Prince of Wales, in August 1941 with President Roosevelt Which Resulted in the Atlantic Charter* (Toronto: Reginald Saunders, 1943), 3.
25. *Ibid.*, 33–34.

Chapter 12: Mr. King Goes to London

1. Churchill, *The Grand Alliance*, 379.
2. Churchill, *Churchill Speaks*, 765–66.
3. William Lyon Mackenzie King, *Canada and the Fight for Freedom* (Toronto Macmillan, 1944), 12.
4. Massey, *What's Past Is Prologue*, 316.

5. *Ibid.*, 316.

6. Churchill, *The Unrelenting Struggle*, 239–41.

7. Pickersgill, *The Mackenzie King Record*, vol. 1, 254.

Chapter 13: So We Had Won After All!

1. Franklin Delano Roosevelt, "Presidential Library and Museum," *www.fdrlibrary.marist.edu.*

2. Shirer, *The Rise and Fall of the Third Reich*, 882.

3. Churchill, *Churchill Speaks*, 772.

4. Churchill, *The Grand Alliance*, 599.

5. *Ibid.*, 604–05.

6. Lash, *Roosevelt and Churchill*, 488.

7. Churchill, *The Grand Alliance*, 606.

8. *Ibid.*, 594.

9. *Ibid.*, 609.

10. Churchill, *Churchill Speaks*, 774–75.

11. Churchill, *The Grand Alliance*, 610–11.

12. Roosevelt, "Library and Museum."

13. Shirer, *The Rise and Fall of the Third Reich*, 897–900.

14. Meacham, *Franklin and Winston*, 135.

15. David Bercuson and Holger Herwig, *One Christmas in Washington* (New York: Overlook Press, 2005), 124.

16. *Ibid.*, 140.

17. *Ibid.*, 155.

18. Churchill, *The Grand Alliance*, 669–70.

19. Andrew Roberts, *Masters and Commanders: The Military Geniuses Who Led the West to Victory in WW2* (Toronto: Penguin Books, 2009), 449.

20. Holmes, *In the Footsteps of Churchill*, 230.

21. Churchill, *Churchill Speaks*, 780–85.

22. Churchill, *The Grand Alliance*, 663.

23. Moran, *Churchill: Taken from the Diaries of Lord Moran*, 17–18.

24. Churchill, *Churchill Speaks*, 786–90.

25. Bercuson and Herwig, *One Christmas in Washington*, 201.

26. Yousuf Karsh, "The Portraits That Changed My Life," *Finest Hour: The Journal of Winston Churchill* (Washington, DC), no. 94 (Spring 1997): 12–14.

27. Diefenbaker, *One Canada*, vol. 1, 202.

28. Winston S. Churchill, *Thoughts and Adventures* (London: Thornton Butterworth, 1932), 225.

29. Churchill, *The Grand Alliance*, 681.

Chapter 14: The Thirty-Minute Invasion

1. Churchill, *The Grand Alliance*, 666.
2. Charles De Gaulle, *The Call to Honour*, vol. 1 of *War Memoirs of Charles de Gaulle* (New York: Viking Press, 1955), 215.
3. Le Grand Colombier, "Saint-Pierre et Miquelon," *www.grandcolombier.com*.
4. Pearson, *Mike*, vol. 1, 200.
5. Le Grand Colombier, "Saint-Pierre et Miquelon."
6. Kersaudy, *Churchill and De Gaulle*, 174.
7. Churchill, *Churchill Speaks*, 788.
8. Harry Hopkins, *The White House Papers of Harry Hopkins: An Intimate Portrait*, vol. 1, ed. Robert E. Sherwood (London: Eyre and Spottiswoode, 1948), 460.
9. Kersaudy, *Churchill and De Gaulle*, 177.
10. Dilks, *The Great Dominion*, 220–21.
11. Cordell Hull, *Memoirs*, vol. 2 (New York: Macmillan, 1948), 1134.
12. Richard Doody, "'Over by Christmas,' The Liberation of Saint Pierre and Miquelon," World at War, *www.worldatwar.net article/miquelon/index.html*.
13. *Ibid*.
14. Kersaudy, *Churchill and De Gaulle*, 176–77.
15. De Gaulle, *The Call to Honour*, 216–17.
16. Kersaudy, *Churchill and De Gaulle*, 177.
17. De Gaulle, *The Call to Honour*, 217.
18. Winston S. Churchill, *Irrepressible Churchill: A Treasury of Winston Churchill's Wit*, ed. Kay Halle (New York and Cleveland: World, 1966), 213.

Chapter 15: Truly a World War

1. King, *Canada and the Fight for Freedom*, 42–90.
2. Churchill, *The End of the Beginning*, 18–41.
3. Charles Ritchie, *The Siren Years: A Canadian Diplomat Abroad, 1937–1945* (Toronto: Macmillan, 1974), 133.
4. King, *Canada and the Fight for Freedom*, 91–101.
5. Winston S. Churchill, *The Hinge of Fate*, vol. 4 of *The Second World War* (Boston: Houghton Mifflin, 1950), 381.

Chapter 16: Dieppe

1. Martin Gilbert, *Road to Victory: 1941–1945*, vol. 7 of *Winston S. Churchill* (Toronto: Stoddart, 1986), 198.

2. C.P. Stacey, *Six Years of War: The Army in Canada, Britain and the Pacific,* Vol. 1 of the *Official History of the Canadian Army in the Second World War* (Ottawa: Queen's Printer, 1966), 326–27.

3. *Ibid.*, 332–33.

4. *Ibid.*, 335.

5. *Ibid.*, 337.

6. Brian Loring Villa, *Unauthorized Action: Mountbatten and the Dieppe Raid* (Toronto: Oxford University Press, 1994), 7.

7. Stacey, *Six Years of War*, 379.

8. Villa, *Unauthorized Action*, 24.

9. Churchill, *The End of the Beginning*, 205–06.

10. David Reynolds, *In Command of History: Churchill Fighting and Writing the Second World War* (London: Allen Lane, 2004), 345.

11. *Ibid.*, 346.

12. Villa, *Unauthorized Action*, 31.

13. Reynolds, *In Command of History*, 345–48.

14. Churchill, *The Hinge of Fate*, 509–11.

15. Viscount Montgomery, *The Memoirs of Field-Marshal Montgomery* (London: Collins, 1958), 76–77.

16. Stacey, *Six Years of War*, 405.

17. *Ibid.*, 405.

18. *Ibid.*, 405–06.

19. Brereton Greenhous, "Dieppe Raid," in *The Canadian Encyclopedia* (Toronto: McClelland & Stewart), 661.

20. Ralph Allen, *Ordeal by Fire, Canada, 1910–1945*, vol. 5 of *Canadian History* (Toronto: Doubleday, 1961), 406.

21. Pierre Berton, *Marching as to War: Canada's Turbulent Years, 1899–1953* (Toronto: Anchor Canada, 2002), 371–87.

22. Brian Nolan, *King's War: Mackenzie King and the Politics of War, 1939–1945* (Toronto: Random House, 1988), 115.

23. Roberts, *Masters and Commanders*, 273.

24. Terence Robertson, *The Shame and the Glory: Dieppe* (Toronto: McClelland & Stewart, 1962), 174.

25. Berton, *Marching as to War*, 371.

Chapter 17: Churchill Disappointed with Canada — Twice!

1. Churchill, *The Hinge of Fate*, 323.

2. *Ibid.*, 348–49.

3. Gilbert, *Road to Victory*, 116.

4. *Ibid.*, 116.

5. Arthur Bryant, *The Turn of the Tide: A Study Based on the Diaries and Autobiographical Notes of Field Marshal The Viscount Alanbrooke* (London: Collins, 1957), 420.

6. Churchill, *The Hinge of Fate*, 436.

7. John Swettenham, *McNaughton*, vol. 2 (Toronto: Ryerson Press, 1969), 241–42.

8. *Ibid.*, 242.

9. *Ibid.*, 250.

10. *Ibid.*, 255–56.

11. *Ibid.*, 256.

12. *Ibid.*, 257.

13. Bryant, *The Turn of the Tide*, 502.

Chapter 18: Progress at Last

1. Churchill, *The Hinge of Fate*, 595.

2. *Ibid.*, 603.

3. Churchill, *The End of the Beginning*, 265–68.

4. Kersaudy, *Churchill and De Gaulle*, 267.

5. Churchill, *The End of the Beginning*, 295–300.

6. *Ibid.*, 304.

7. King, *Canada and the Fight for Freedom*, 221–26.

8. Churchill, *The End of the Beginning*, 318–19.

9. *Ibid.*, 319.

10. Dilks, Papers.

11. *Ibid.*

12. Winston S. Churchill, *Onwards to Victory*, vol. 4 of *The War Speeches of Winston Churchill* (Toronto: McClelland & Stewart, 1944), 72.

13. King, *Canada and the Fight for Freedom*, 245–58.

14. Churchill, *The Hinge of Fate*, 778.

15. *Ibid.*, 780.

16. *Ibid.*, 783.

Chapter 19: Back to the Continent

1. Churchill, *Onwards to Victory*, 119–33.

2. Churchill, *The Gathering Storm*, 13–14.

3. Pearson, *Mike*, vol. 1, 241.

4. *Ibid.*, 242–43.

5. House of Commons, Debates, July 12, 1943, 4723.
6. Churchill, *Onwards to Victory*, 214.

Chapter 20: Quadrant Conference

1. Bryant, *The Turn of the Tide*, 693.
2. Winston S. Churchill, *Closing the Ring*, vol. 5 of *The Second World War* (Boston: Houghton Mifflin, 1951), 80.
3. *Ibid.*, 66–67.
4. Moran, *Churchill: Taken from the Diaries of Lord Moran*, 117.
5. Dilks, Papers.
6. Churchill, *Closing the Ring*, 81–82.
7. *Ibid.*, 85.
8. Bryant, *The Turn of the Tide*, 707.
9. *Ibid.*, 723.
10. Roberts, *Masters and Commanders*, 405.
11. Churchill, *Closing the Ring*, 91.
12. Churchill, *Onwards to Victory*, 224–25.
13. Churchill, *Closing the Ring*, 119. In fact, Churchill had been appointed to this position in December 1941.

Chapter 21: The Big Three Meet

1. Harvard University, *The Ceremonies in Honour of the Right Honourable Winston Spencer Churchill, Being the Proceedings of an Academic Meeting Held in Sanders Theater and of an Assemblage in the Harvard Yard of the Military and Naval Forces of the United States in Training at the University* (Cambridge: Harvard, 1943), 10–17.
2. King, *Canada and the Fight for Freedom*, 266–74.
3. Churchill, *Onwards to Victory*, 246–47.
4. *Ibid.*, 259.
5. Churchill, *Churchill by Himself*, 283.
6. Churchill, *Closing the Ring*, 383.
7. Moran, *Churchill: Taken from the Diaries of Lord Moran*, 165.

Chapter 22: Planning for D-Day

1. Winston S. Churchill, *The Dawn of Liberation*, vol. 5 of *The War Speeches of Winston Churchill* (Toronto: McClelland & Stewart, 1945), v.
2. Churchill, *Closing the Ring*, 453.

3. Nicolson, *Diaries and Letters*, 344–45.
4. Massey, *What's Past Is Prologue*, 393.
5. Churchill, *The Dawn of Liberation*, 6–28.
6. *Ibid.*, 87–97.
7. *Ibid.*, 98–99.
8. Alan Lascelles, *King's Counsellor: Abdication and War, the Diaries of Sir Alan Lascelles* (London: Weidenfeld and Nicolson, 2006), 217.
9. King, *Canada and the Fight for Freedom*, 310–26.
10. King, Papers.
11. Lascelles, *King's Counsellor*, 226–28.
12. Churchill, *Closing the Ring*, 623.
13. Lascelles, *King's Counsellor*, 229.
14. Churchill, *The Dawn of Liberation*, 136–37.

Chapter 23: France Revenged

1. Roberts, *Masters and Commanders*, 487.
2. Winston S. Churchill, *Triumph and Tragedy*, vol. 6 of *The Second World War* (Boston: Houghton Mifflin, 1953), 12.
3. Churchill, *The Dawn of Liberation*, 269.
4. Dilks, *The Great Dominion*, 354.
5. *Ibid.*, 348.
6. *Ibid.*, 346–47.

Chapter 24: Conscription Is Necessary

1. King, Papers.
2. Bruce Hutchinson, *The Unfinished Country: To Canada with Love and Some Misgivings* (Toronto: Douglas & McIntyre, 1985), 236.
3. Bruce Hutchinson, *The Far Side of the Street* (Toronto: Macmillan, 1976), 227–29.
4. Richard S. Malone, *A World in Flames, 1944–1945*, vol. 2 of *A Portrait of War* (Toronto: Collins, 1984), 289.
5. Churchill, *The Dawn of Liberation*, 354.
6. Churchill, *Triumph and Tragedy*, 305.
7. *Ibid.*, 311–12.
8. Mary Soames, *Clementine Churchill, the Biography of a Marriage* (Boston: Houghton Mifflin, 1979), 478–79.
9. Wikipedia, "Archbishop Damaskinos of Athens."
10. Churchill, *Triumph and Tragedy*, 317.

1. *Ibid.*, 317–18.
2. *Ibid.*, 325.
3. *Ibid.*, 292.
4. Churchill, *The Dawn of Liberation*, 384.

Chapter 25: The End and the Beginning

.. Gilbert, *Road to Victory*, 1155.
2. Churchill, *Triumph and Tragedy*, 353.
3. *Ibid.*, 353.
4. *Ibid.*, 365–87.
5. Churchill, *Churchill by Himself*, 374.
6. Conrad Black, *Franklin Delano Roosevelt: Champion of Freedom* (New York: Public Affairs, 2003), 1080.
7. Winston S. Churchill, *Victory*, vol. 6 of *The War Speeches of Winston Churchill* (Toronto: McClelland & Stewart, 1946), 121.
8. Churchill, *Triumph and Tragedy*, 467.
9. *Ibid.*, 515.
0. Elizabeth Nel, *Mr. Churchill's Secretary* (London: Hodder and Stoughton, 1960), 173.
1. Churchill, *Victory*, 134–38.
2. Churchill, *Triumph and Tragedy*, 479.
3. Churchill, *Victory*, 163–65.
4. *Ibid.*, 167.
5. Gilbert, *Road to Victory*, 1350–51.
6. William Lyon Mackenzie King, "VE-Day: Mackenzie King Addresses the Nation," CBC Digital Archives, *www.cbc.ca/archives/categories/war-conflict/second-world-war/victory-the-end-of-the-war-in-europe/mackenzie-king-addresses-the-nation.html*.
7. Churchill, *Victory*, 171–79.
8. *Ibid.*, 241–45.
9. Soames, *Clementine Churchill*, 504.
20. Churchill, *Triumph and Tragedy*, 630–31.
21. *Ibid.*, 632.
22. *Ibid.*, 670.
23. Reynolds, *In Command of History*, 485–86.
24. Churchill, *Triumph and Tragedy*, 672.
25. *Ibid.*, 674.
26. *Ibid.*, 676.
27. Churchill, *Victory*, 291.

28. Dilks, *The Great Dominion*, 236.

Chapter 26: Peace but the Bear Growls

1. Martin Gilbert, *Never Despair*, vol. 8 of *Winston S. Churchill* (Toronto Stoddart, 1988), 108.
2. Virginia Cowles, *Winston Churchill: The Era and the Man* (London: Cassell 1948), 356.
3. Churchill, *Churchill Speaks*, 873–74.
4. H. Montgomery Hyde, *The Quiet Canadian: The Secret Service Story of Sir William Stephenson* (London: Hamish Hamilton, 1962), 233.
5. Winston S. Churchill, *The Sinews of Peace: Post-War Speeches* (London Cassell, 1948), 29.
6. *Ibid.*, 27–36.
7. Gilbert, *Never Despair*, 170.
8. Churchill, *The Sinews of Peace*, 45.
9. Gilbert, *Never Despair*, 174.

Chapter 27: The Cold War Starts in Ottawa and Heats Up in Fulton

1. Churchill, *The Sinews of Peace*, 93–105.
2. Gilbert, *Never Despair*, 197.
3. *Ibid.*, 204.
4. Churchill, *The Sinews of Peace*, 107.
5. *Ibid.*, 115–20.
6. Nigel Nicolson, *Alex: The Life of Field Marshal Earl Alexander of Tunis* (London: Weidenfeld and Nicolson, 1973), 283.
7. Lascelles, *King's Counsellor*, 365.

Chapter 28: Mackenzie King Breaks Record,
Churchill Lays Path for Europe

1. Churchill, *The Sinews of Peace*, 128–34.
2. Churchill, *Triumph and Tragedy*, 639.
3. *Ibid.*, 198–202.
4. Gilbert, *Never Despair*, 266.
5. *Ibid.*, 337.

Chapter 29: A New World Order: Standing Up to the Reds

1. Harry S. Truman, "Address in New York City to the Opening Session of the United Nations," *www.trumanlibrary.org/calendar/viewpapers.phppid=914.*
2. J.W. Pickersgill and D.F. Forster, *The Mackenzie King Record,* vol. 4 (Toronto: University of Toronto Press, 1970), 36–37.
3. Lord Butler, *The Art of the Possible: The Memoirs of Lord Butler* (London: Hamish Hamilton, 1971), 133.
4. Soames, *Clementine Churchill,* 533.
5. Winston S. Churchill, *The Definitive Wit of Winston Churchill,* ed. Richard M. Langworth (New York: Public Affairs, 2009), 82.

Chapter 30: The End of an Era

1. Winston S. Churchill, *Europe Unite: Speeches, 1947–1948* (London: Cassell, 1950), 235–37.
2. *Ibid.,* 294–95.
3. *Ibid.,* 313–17.
4. Bruce Hutchinson, *Mr. Prime Minister 1867–1964* (Toronto: Longmans Canada), 283.

Epilogue

1. King, Papers.
2. Churchill, *Churchill by Himself,* 463.
3. James Marchant, ed., *Winston Spencer Churchill: Servant of Crown and Commonwealth: A Tribute by Various Hands* (London: Cassell, 1954), 172.
4. Nathan Phillips, *Mayor of All the People* (Toronto: McClelland & Stewart, 1967), 179–80.
5. Winston S. Churchill, *Stemming the Tide: Speeches, 1951 and 1952* (Boston: Houghton Mifflin, 1954), 215.
6. John Colville, "Churchill's England," *Finest Hour* 41 (Autumn 1983), 7.
7. Kersaudy, *Churchill and De Gaulle,* 428.
8. Soames, *Clementine Churchill,* 659.
9. Hutchinson, *The Incredible Canadian,* 450.
10. Lord Ismay, *The Memoirs of Lord Ismay* (London: Heinemann, 1960), 155.
11. Holmes, *In the Footsteps of Churchill,* 295.
12. William Manchester, *Winston Spencer Churchill, Alone, 1932–1940,* vol. 2 of *The Last Lion* (Boston: Little Brown, 1988).
13. Frank J. Willis, Joseph Schull, and the Canadian Broadcasting Corporation,

Century: A Recording of a Special 90-minute CBC Radio Production Broadcast, January 1, 1967, in Celebration of Canada's Centennial (Toronto: CBC Publications, 1967).

14. Charlotte Gray, *Mrs. King: The Life and Times of Isabel Mackenzie King* (Toronto: Penguin Canada, 2008), 430.

15. Granatstein, *Mackenzie King*, 193–94.

BIBLIOGRAPHY

Allen, Ralph. *Ordeal by Fire, Canada, 1910-1945*. Vol. 5, *Canadian History*. Toronto: Doubleday, 1961.

Archbishop Damaskinos of Athens." *http://en.wikipedia.org/wiki/Archbishop_ Damaskinos_of_Athens*. Wikipedia (accessed on August 16, 2011).

Bercuson, David, and Holger Herwig. *One Christmas in Washington*. New York: Overlook Press, 2005.

Berton, Pierre. *Marching as to War: Canada's Turbulent Years, 1899-1953*. Toronto: Anchor Canada, 2002.

Birkenhead, Frederick Edwin (Earl). *Halifax: The Life of Lord Halifax*. London: Hamish Hamilton, 1965.

Black, Conrad. *Franklin Delano Roosevelt: Champion of Freedom*. New York: Public Affairs, 2003.

Brown, Anthony Cave. *"C": The Secret Life of Sir Stewart Menzies, Spymaster to Winston Churchill*. New York: Macmillan, 1987.

Bryant, Arthur. *The Turn of the Tide: A Study Based on the Diaries and Autobiographical Notes of Field Marshal The Viscount Alanbrooke*. London: Collins, 1957.

Butler, Richard Austen (Lord). *The Art of the Possible: The Memoirs of Lord Butler*. London: Hamish Hamilton, 1971.

Canada. House of Commons. *Debates*, July 12, 1943.

Canada Treaty Information." Government of Canada. *www.treaty-accord.gc.ca/ index.aspx* (accessed on November 15, 2011).

Channon, Henry. *Chips: The Diaries of Sir Henry Channon*. Edited by Robert Rhodes James. London: Weidenfeld and Nicolson, 1967.

Churchill, Winston S. *Arms and the Covenant: Speeches on Foreign Affairs and*

National Defence. London: George G. Harrap & Co., 1938.

_____. *Blood, Sweat, and Tears*. Toronto: McClelland & Stewart, 1941.

_____. *Churchill by Himself*. Edited by Richard M. Langworth. New York: Public Affairs, 2008.

_____. *Churchill Speaks: Winston S. Churchill in Peace and War: Collected Speeches 1897–1963*. Edited by Robert Rhodes James. New York: Barnes & Noble, 1998.

_____. *Closing the Ring*. Vol. 5, *The Second World War*. Boston: Houghton Mifflin, 1951.

_____. *The Dawn of Liberation*. Vol. 5, *The War Speeches of Winston Churchill*. Toronto: McClelland & Stewart, 1945.

_____. *The Definitive Wit of Winston Churchill*. Edited by Richard M. Langworth. New York: Public Affairs, 2009.

_____. *The End of the Beginning*. Vol. 3, *The War Speeches of Winston Churchill*. Toronto: McClelland & Stewart, 1943.

_____. *Europe Unite: Speeches, 1947–1948*. London: Cassell, 1950.

_____. *The Gathering Storm*. Vol. 1, *The Second World War*. Boston: Houghton Mifflin, 1948.

_____. *The Grand Alliance*. Vol. 3, *The Second World War*. Boston: Houghton Mifflin, 1950.

_____. *Great Contemporaries*. London: Thornton Butterworth, 1937.

_____. *The Hinge of Fate*. Vol. 4, *The Second World War*. Boston: Houghton Mifflin, 1950.

_____. *Irrepressible Churchill: A Treasury of Winston Churchill's Wit*. Edited by Kay Halle. Cleveland, OH & New York: World Publishing, 1966.

_____. *Marlborough: His Life and Times*. London: George G. Harrap & Co., 1933.

_____. *My Early Life: A Roving Commission*. London: Thornton Butterworth, 1930.

_____. *Onwards to Victory*. Vol. 4, *The War Speeches of Winston Churchill*. Toronto: McClelland & Stewart, 1944.

_____. *The River War: An Account of the Reconquest of the Sudan*. London: Eyre and Spottiswoode, 1949.

_____. *The Sinews of Peace: Post-War Speeches*. London: Cassell, 1948.

_____. *Stemming the Tide: Speeches, 1951 and 1952*. Boston: Houghton Mifflin, 1954.

_____. *Step by Step: Speeches, 1936–1939*. London: Odhams Press Ltd, 1949.

_____. *Their Finest Hour*. Vol. 2, *The Second World War*. Boston: Houghton Mifflin, 1949.

_____. *Thoughts and Adventures*. London: Thornton Butterworth, 1932.

_____. *Triumph and Tragedy*. Vol. 6, *The Second World War*. Boston: Houghton Mifflin, 1953.

____. *The Unrelenting Struggle.* Vol. 2, *The War Speeches of Winston Churchill.* London: Cassell, 1942.

____. *Victory.* Vol. 6, *The War Speeches of Winston Churchill.* Toronto: McClelland & Stewart, 1946.

____. *The World Crisis: The Aftermath, 1918–1928.* New York: Charles Scribner's Sons, 1929.

Churchill, Winston S., and Clementine Churchill. *Speaking for Themselves: The Personal Letters of Winston and Clementine Churchill.* Edited by Mary Soames. Toronto: Stoddart, 1998.

Colville, John. "Churchill's England." *Finest Hour* 41 (Autumn 1983): 6 –8.

____. *Footprints in Time: Memories.* London: Collins, 1976.

____. *The Fringes of Power: Downing Street Diaries, 1939–1955.* London: Hodder and Stoughton, 1985.

Cowles, Virginia. *Winston Churchill: The Era and the Man.* London: Cassell, 1948.

Dawson, R. MacGregor. *William Lyon Mackenzie King: A Political Biography.* Toronto: University of Toronto Press, 1958.

de Gaulle, Charles. *The Call To Honor.* Vol. 1, *War Memoirs of Charles de Gaulle.* New York: Viking Press, 1955.

de Mendelssohn, Peter. *The Age of Churchill: Heritage and Adventure, 1874–1911.* London: Thames and Hudson, 1961.

Diefenbaker, John G. *One Canada: The Crusading Years, 1895 to 1956.* Vol. 1, *Memoirs.* Toronto: Macmillan, 1975.

____. *One Canada: The Years of Achievement, 1956 to 1962.* Vol. 2, *Memoirs.* Toronto: Macmillan, 1976.

Dilks, David. *The Great Dominion: Winston Churchill in Canada, 1900–1954.* Toronto: Thomas Allen, 2005.

____. Papers. Trinity College, University of Toronto. Toronto.

Doody, Richard. "'Over by Christmas.' The Liberation of Saint Pierre and Miquelon." World at War. *www.worldatwar.net/article/miquelon/index.html* (accessed on September 15, 2011).

Eade, Charles, ed. *Churchill by His Contemporaries.* London: Hutchinson, 1954.

Ferns, Henry S., and Bernard Ostry. *The Age of Mackenzie King.* Toronto: William Heinemann, 1955.

Gilbert, Martin. *At the Admiralty: September 1939–May 1940.* Vol. 1, *The Churchill War Papers.* New York: W.W. Norton & Company, 1993.

____. *Churchill: A Life.* London: William Heinemann, 1991.

____. *The Coming of War: 1936–1939.* Vol. 13, *The Churchill Documents.* Hillsdale, MI: Hillsdale College Press, 2009.

____. *The Exchequer Years: 1922–1929.* Vol. 11, *The Churchill Documents.* Hillsdale, MI: Hillsdale College Press, 2009.

_____. *Finest Hour: 1939–1941.* Vol. 6, *Winston S. Churchill.* London: Heinemann 1984.

_____. *In Search of Churchill.* London: HarperCollins, 1994.

_____. *Never Despair: 1945–1965.* Vol. 8, *Winston S. Churchill.* Toronto: Stoddart, 1988.

_____. *Road to Victory: 1941–1945.* Vol. 7, *Winston S. Churchill.* Toronto: Stoddart, 1986.

_____. *The Wilderness Years: 1929–1935.* Vol. 12, *The Churchill Documents.* Hillsdale, MI: Hillsdale College Press, 2009.

_____. *Winston S. Churchill, 1922–1939.* Vol. 5, *Winston S. Churchill.* London: Heinemann, 1976.

Granatstein, J.L. *Mackenzie King: His Life and World.* Toronto: McGraw-Hill Ryerson, 1977.

Granatstein, J.L., and Desmond Morton. *Canada and the Two World Wars.* Toronto: Key Porter Books, 2003.

Gray, Charlotte. *Mrs. King: The Life and Times of Isabel Mackenzie King.* Toronto: Penguin Canada, 2008.

Greenhous, Brereton. "Dieppe Raid." In *The Canadian Encyclopedia.* Toronto: McClelland & Stewart, 2000.

Guedalla, Philip. *Mr. Churchill: A Portrait.* London: Hodder and Stoughton, 1950.

Harvard University. *The Ceremonies In Honour Of The Right Honourable Winston Spencer Churchill, Being the Proceedings of an Academic Meeting held in Sanders Theater and of an assemblage in the Harvard Yard of the Military and Naval Forces of the United States in Training at the University.* Cambridge, MA: Harvard University, 1943.

Hatch, F.J., and Norman Hillmer. "British Commonwealth Training Plan." In *The Canadian Encyclopedia.* Toronto: McClelland & Stewart, 2000.

Holmes, Richard. *In The Footsteps of Churchill: A Study in Character.* New York: Basic Books, 2005.

Hopkins, Harry. *The White House Papers of Harry Hopkins: An Intimate Portrait.* Vol. 1. Ed. Robert E. Sherwood. London: Eyre and Spottiswoode, 1948.

Hull, Cordell. *Memoirs.* 2 vols. New York: Macmillan, 1948.

Hutchinson, Bruce. *The Far Side of the Street.* Toronto: Macmillan, 1976.

_____. *The Incredible Canadian.* Toronto: Longmans, Green and Company, 1952.

_____. *Mr. Prime Minister, 1867–1964.* Toronto: Longmans Canada, 1964.

_____. *The Unfinished Country: To Canada with Love and Some Misgivings.* Toronto: Douglas & McIntyre, 1985.

Hyde, H. Montgomery. *The Quiet Canadian: The Secret Service Story of Sir William Stephenson.* London: Hamish Hamilton, 1962.

Ismay, Hastings Lionel (Lord). *The Memoirs of Lord Ismay.* London: Heinemann, 1960.

Karsh, Yousuf. "The Portraits That Changed My Life." *Finest Hour: The Journal of Winston Churchill* 94 (Spring 1997): 12–14.

Kersaudy, François. *Churchill and de Gaulle.* New York: Atheneum, 1983.

Kershaw, Ian. *Fateful Choices: Ten Decisions That Changed the World, 1940–1941.* New York: Penguin Books, 2008.

King, William Lyon Mackenzie. *Canada and the Fight for Freedom.* Toronto: Macmillan, 1944.

___. *Canada at Britain's Side.* Toronto: Macmillan, 1941.

___. *The Message of the Carillon.* Toronto: Macmillan, 1927.

___. William Lyon Mackenzie King Papers. Library and Archives Canada. Ottawa.

LaPierre, Laurier L. *Sir Wilfrid Laurier and the Romance of Canada.* Toronto: Stoddart, 1996.

Lascelles, Alan. *King's Counsellor: Abdication and War. The Diaries of Sir Alan Lascelles.* Edited by Duff Hart-Davis. London: Weidenfeld and Nicolson, 2006.

Lash, Joseph P. *Roosevelt and Churchill: The Partnership That Saved the West.* New York: W.W. Norton & Company, 1976.

Macmillan, Harold. *The Blast of War, 1939–1945.* Vol. 2, *Memoirs.* London: Macmillan, 1967.

Malone, Richard S. *A World in Flames, 1944–1945.* Vol. 2, *A Portrait of War.* Toronto: Collins, 1984.

Manchester, William. *Winston Spencer Churchill, Alone, 1932–1940.* Vol. 2, *The Last Lion.* Boston: Little Brown, 1988.

___. *Winston Spencer Churchill, Visions of Glory, 1874–1932.* Vol. 1, *The Last Lion.* Toronto: Little Brown and Company, 1983.

Maple Leafs Sports and Entertainment. *Maple Leaf Gardens: Memories and Dreams, 1931–1999.* Toronto: MLG, 1999.

Marchant, James, ed. *Winston Spencer Churchill: Servant of Crown and Commonwealth. A Tribute by Various Hands.* London: Cassell, 1954.

Massey, Vincent. *What's Past Is Prologue: The Memoirs of the Right Honourable Vincent Massey, C.H.* Toronto: Macmillan, 1963.

Meacham, Jon. *Franklin and Winston: An Intimate Portrait of an Epic Friendship.* New York: Random House, 2004.

Montgomery, Bernard Law (Viscount). *The Memoirs of Field-Marshal Montgomery.* London: Collins, 1958.

Moran, Charles Wilson (Lord). *Churchill: Taken From the Diaries of Lord Moran.* Boston: Houghton Mifflin, 1966.

Morton, H.V. *Atlantic Meeting: An Account Of Mr. Churchill's Voyage in H.M.S. Prince of Wales, in August 1941 with President Roosevelt Which Resulted in the Atlantic Charter.* Toronto: Reginald Saunders, 1943.

Neatby, H. Blair. *William Lyon Mackenzie King.* Vol. 2. Toronto: University of Toronto Press, 1963.

Nel, Elizabeth. *Mr. Churchill's Secretary.* London: Hodder and Stoughton, 1960.

Nicolson, Harold. *Diaries and Letters, 1939–1945.* Edited by Nigel Nicolson. London: Collins, 1967.

Nicolson, Nigel. *Alex, The Life of Field Marshal Earl Alexander of Tunis.* London: Weidenfeld and Nicolson, 1973.

Nolan, Brian. *King's War: Mackenzie King and the Politics of War, 1939–1945.* Toronto: Random House, 1988.

Owen, Frank. *Tempestuous Journey: Lloyd George, His Life and Times.* London: Hutchinson, 1954.

Pearson, Lester B. *Mike — The Memoirs of the Rt. Hon. Lester B. Pearson.* 2 vols. Toronto: University of Toronto Press, 1972–73.

Phillips, Nathan. *Mayor of All the People.* Toronto: McClelland & Stewart, 1967.

Pickersgill, J.W. *The Mackenzie King Record.* Vol. 1. Toronto: University of Toronto Press, 1960.

Pickersgill, J.W., and D.F. Forster. *The Mackenzie King Record.* Vol. 4. Toronto: University of Toronto Press, 1970.

Reynolds, David. *In Command of History: Churchill Fighting and Writing the Second World War.* London: Allen Lane, 2004.

Ritchie, Charles. *The Siren Years: A Canadian Diplomat Abroad, 1937–1945.* Toronto: Macmillan, 1974.

Roberts, Andrew. *Eminent Churchillians.* New York: Simon & Schuster, 1994.

_____. *Masters and Commanders: The Military Geniuses Who Led the West to Victory in WWII.* Toronto: Penguin Books, 2009.

Robertson, Terence. *The Shame and the Glory: Dieppe.* Toronto: McClelland & Stewart, 1962.

Roosevelt, Franklin Delano. Presidential Library and Museum. *www.fdrlibrary. marist.edu* (accessed on July 22, 2011).

"Saint-Pierre et Miquelon." Le Grand Colombier. *www.grandcolombier.com* (accessed on June 15, 2011).

Shirer, William L. *The Rise and Fall of the Third Reich: A History of Nazi Germany.* New York: Simon and Schuster, 1960.

Soames, Mary. *Clementine Churchill: The Biography of a Marriage.* Boston: Houghton Mifflin, 1979.

Stacey, C.P. *Mackenzie King and the Atlantic Triangle.* Toronto: Macmillan, 1976.

_____. *Six Years of War: The Army in Canada, Britain and the Pacific.* Vol. Official History of the Canadian Army in the Second World War. Ottawa: Queen's Printer, 1966.

_____. *A Very Double Life.* Toronto: Macmillan, 1976.

Swettenham, John. *McNaughton*. Vol. 2. Toronto: Ryerson Press, 1969.

Toland, John. *Adolf Hitler*. Vol. 1. New York: Doubleday & Company, 1976.

Truman, Harry S. "Address in New York City to the Opening Session of the United Nations General Assembly." Harry S. Truman Library and Museum. *http://trumanlibrary.org/calendar/viewpapers.php?pid=914* (accessed on September 13, 2011).

Villa, Brian Loring. *Unauthorized Action: Mountbatten and the Dieppe Raid*. Toronto: Oxford University Press, 1994.

Willis, Frank J., Joseph Schull, and Canadian Broadcasting Corporation. *Century: A Recording of a Special 90-Minute CBC Radio Production Broadcast, January 1, 1967, in Celebration of Canada's Centennial*. Toronto: CBC Publications, 1967.

Windsor, Elizabeth (Queen). "Royal Visits to Canada." CBC.ca. *www.cbc.ca/ news/interactive/royalvisits/52.html* (accessed on February 9, 2011).

INDEX